LEONARD-HAWES™
REAL ESTATE SCHOOL
A **Kaplan Professional** Company

We provide excellence in education.
But most of all,
we care about YOU!

YOUR Real Estate Career Starts Here!

Congratulations on your decision to pursue a career in real estate—it can be a wonderful experience with unlimited possibilities. The first step is to obtain your real estate license. Fortunately, you've come to the right place.

Leonard-Hawes Real Estate School is helping people get started in the real estate industry, with over 40 years combined experience. We provide newcomers with the instruction, training materials and education options they need to pass the real estate licensing exam and reap the rewards of a career in real estate. Leonard-Hawed is owned by Dearborn Publishing, the leading publisher of real estate training materials and by Kaplan Professional, a division of Kaplan, the well known test preparation company.

Through the years, we have answered thousands of questions about getting a Texas real estate license. If your specific question isn't answered here, give us a call. We will be happy to answer your questions personally.

Toll Free 1-877-332-2630

PRE-LICENSING

Every class you need to obtain your salesperson or broker's license!

Residential
and
Commercial Courses

20 different courses from which to choose!

POST LICENSING (CE)

We offer both MCE and SAE

Salesperson Annual Education Choose any class you have not taken in the past 3 years

Courses that will further your career: Negotiations, Lending & Closing, Marketing, Selling, Property Management, Investments, and more!

Loan Officer Classes

Look for our Lending & Closing class and attend the first 15 hours or the full 30 hours for the same low price!

Mortgage Broker CE

Look for our Lending & Closing class and attend the first 15 hours or the full 30 hours for the same low price!

Corporate Training

Specific corporate training needs and/or Broker Office Training available with or without official credit.

- CPA Continuing Education
- Tax Consultant Continuing Ed
- Business Building Career Seminars
- Live and Correspondence Courses

Call us today for information or a career consultation.

The Process to Obtain a Real Estate License

- Completion of 180 classroom hours for Salesperson licensure or 900 classroom hours for Broker licensure is required. Of these hours, 120 must be in core real estate courses (30 hours in Law of Agency, 30 hours in Law of Contracts, and 60 hours in Principles of Real Estate courses are required) and the remainder may be in related college courses.
- The applicant must have ALL education documents evaluated, which includes college transcripts, certificates from real estate schools and the $20 fee. This must be done BEFORE the salesperson or broker application is sent to TREC. The forms are available from TREC at 1-800-250-TREC or may be downloaded from the TREC website at *www.trec.state.tx.us.*
- Each college class approved by TREC usually contains three semester hours (45 classroom hours). Two college classes usually meet the related credit hours allowed. Examples: English Composition, Psychology, Speech, Accounting, Government, Law and some Business classes, etc.
- Salespersons only: During the time students are taking classes, they should be deciding upon a sponsoring broker. An applicant MUST have a sponsoring broker who will be responsible for that licensee's actions before they will be issued an active license to practice real esate.
- When education approval is received from TREC, the student may then send the completed salesperson or broker application form to TREC, along with the education approval, and the applicable fee. The Sales and Broker applications may now be submitted on the TREC website at *www.trec.state.tx.us.*
- When approval is given, TREC will issue and mail a Candidate Information Brochure with an approval code assigned only to THAT STUDENT. (This is literally the "Permission to Take the Exam".) The student must then call Sylvan Learning Center's toll free number on their approval letter to schedule the two-hour computerized exam. The Centers are usually open five days per week and sometimes a half-day on Saturday for testing. There is a fee each time a student takes the state exam.
- When the student passes the exam, the results are electronically send to TREC and an active license will be sent to the sponsoring broker upon submission of a Salesperson Sponsorship Form.

We are proud to be a part of your real estate career. Please let us know how we can help!

Questions and Answers

Q. How long will it take to get my real estate license?

It could take as little as two weeks to complete your education, depending upon your individual requirements and your scheduling preference. Students with acceptable college hours find it takes less than a month plus another 20-30 days for processing time and state examination time.

Q. I have a four-year college degree. Do I still need to take the Principles, Agency and Law of Contracts courses?

These 120 hours are required, but some of your college hours may satisfy the other hours of related education. They may also satisfy the hours required for a brokers license.

Q. How many times can I take the state exam?

There is no limit to the number of times you can take the state exam within six months. Our goal at Leonard-Hawes is to help you pass as quickly as possible — hopefully on your first attempt.

Q. What is the State Exam like?

The Salesperson Exam:
Part 1 - Theory - 1 hour 30 minutes
75 questions including 5 "pretest" and 6-9 math questions
Part 2 - Law - 30 minutes
25 questions including 2 "pretest"

The Broker Exam:
Part 1 - Theory - 2 hour 15 minutes
85 questions including 5 "pretest"
7-10 math questions
Part 2 - Law - 45 minutes
38 questions including 3 "pretest"

"Pretest" questions are placed throughout the exam. Answers to these questions are not scored, but used as a means of testing those questions for future use.

Q. With a real estate license is selling real estate my only option?

You have many options with a real estate license. Listing and selling residential, commercial real estate and time shares, leasing, property management, mortgage brokering and title work are a few of the opportunities. Consult The Real Estate License Act for information.

Dallas Central - 10500 Steppington #110

Monday - Thursday	8:30 AM - 4:55 PM	Friday - Sunday	8:00 AM - 6:30 PM	Saturday, Saturday, Sunday	8:00 AM - 6:30 PM
January 1 - 3**		January 4 - 6	Principles 1	January 5, 12, 13	Principles 2
January 7 - 10	Property Management	January 11 - 13	Principles 2		
January 14 - 17	Negotiations	January 18 - 20	Law of Agency	January 19, 26, 27	Law of Contracts
January 21 - 24	Principles 1	January 25 - 27	Law of Contracts		
January 28 - 31	Principles 2	February 1 - 3	Commercial Sales	February 2, 9, 10	Lending & Closing
February 4 - 7	Law of Agency	February 8 - 10	Lending & Closing		
February 11 - 14	Law of Contracts	February 15 - 17	Principles 1	February 23, March 2, 3	Law of Agency
February 18 - 21	Math	February 22 - 24	Principles 2		
February 25 - 28	Commercial Sales	March 1 - 3	Law of Agency	March 9, 16, 17	Modern Marketing
March 4 - 7	Principles 1	March 8 - 10	Law of Contracts		
March 11 - 14	Principles 2	March 15 - 17	Modern Marketing	March 23, April 6, 7	Principles 1
March 18 - 21	Law of Agency	March 22 - 24	Investments		
March 25 - 28	Law of Contracts	March 28 - 30**			
April 1 - 4	Negotiations	April 5 - 7	Principles 1		
April 8 - 11	Lending & Closing	April 12 - 14	Principles 2	April 20, 27, 28	Law of Contracts
April 15 - 18	Principles 1	April 19 - 21	Law of Agency		
April 22 - 25	Principles 2	April 26 - 28	Law of Contracts	May 4, 11, 12	Property Management
April 29 - May 2	Law of Agency	May 3 - 5	Commercial Sales		
May 6 - 9	Law of Contracts	May 10 - 12	Property Management	May 18, 25, 26	Principles 2
May 13 - 16	Modern Marketing	May 17 - 19	Principles 1		
May 20 - 23	Math	May 24 - 26	Principles 2	June 1, 8, 9	Law of Agency
May 28 - 31**		May 31 - June 2			
June 3 - 6	Principles 1	June 7 - 9	Law of Agency	June 15, 22, 23	Negotiations
June 10 - 13	Principles 2	June 14 - 16	Law of Contracts		
June 17 - 20	Law of Agency	June 21 - 23	Negotiations		
June 24 - 27	Law of Contracts	June 28 - 30	Commercial Sales	July 6, 13, 14	Principles 1
July 1 - 3**		July 5 - 7			
July 8 - 11	Lending & Closing	July 12 - 14	Principles 1		
July 15 - 18	Investments	July 19 - 21	Principles 2	July 27, August 3, 4	Law of Contracts
July 22 - 25	Principles 1	July 26 - 28	Law of Agency		
July 29 - August 1	Principles 2	August 2 - 4	Law of Contracts	August 10, 17, 18	Modern Marketing
August 5 - 8	Law of Agency	August 9 - 11	Lending & Closing		
August 12 - 15	Law of Contracts	August 16 - 18	Modern Marketing	August 24, 31, September 1	Principles 2
August 19 - 22	Negotiations	August 23 - 25	Principles 1		
August 26 - 29	Math	August 30 - September 1	Principles 2		
September 2 - 5**		September 6 - 8		September 7, 14, 15	Law of Agency
September 9 - 12	Principles 1	September 13 - 15	Law of Agency		
September 16 - 19	Principles 2	September 20 - 22	Law of Contracts		
September 23 - 26	Law of Agency	September 27 - 29	Brokerage	September 21, 28, 29	Brokerage
September 30 - October 3	Law of Contracts	October 4 - 6	Lending & Closing		
October 7 - 10	Commercial Sales	October 11 - 13	Principles 1	October 5, 12, 13	Principles 1
October 14 - 17	Modern Marketing	October 18 - 20	Principles 2		
October 21 - 24	Principles 1	October 25 - 27	Law of Agency		
October 28 - 31	Principles 2	November 1 - 3	Law of Contracts	October 26, November 2, 3	Law of Contracts
November 4 - 7	Law of Agency	November 8 - 10	Investments		
November 11 - 14	Law of Contracts	November 15 - 17	Math	November 9, 16, 17	Math
November 18 - 21	Property Management	November 22 - 24	Principles 1		
November 25 - 27**		November 29 - December 1			
December 2 - 5	Commercial Sales	December 6 - 8	Principles 2		
December 9 - 12	Principles 1	December 13 - 15	Law of Agency	December 7, 14, 15	Law of Agency
December 16 - 19	Principles 2	December 20 - 22	Law of Contracts		
December 23 - 26**		December 27 - 29	Property Management	December 21, 28, 29	Property Management

** Holiday Schedule

Dallas North - 13614 Midway Road

Monday - Thursday		8:30 AM - 4:55 PM
January 1 - 3**		
January 7 - 10	Law of Contracts	Lending & Closing
January 14 - 17	Principles 1	Brokerage
January 21 - 24	Principles 2	
January 28 - 31	Law of Agency	Property Mgmnt
February 4 - 7	Law of Contracts	Math
February 11 - 14	Principles 1	
February 18 - 21	Principles 2	Marketing
February 25 - 28	Law of Agency	Investments
March 4 - 7	Law of Contracts	
March 11 - 14	Principles 1	Lending & Closing
March 18 - 21	Principles 2	
March 25 - 28	Law of Agency	Selling Strategies
April 1 - 4	Law of Contracts	
April 8 - 11	Principles 1	Negotiations
April 15 - 18	Principles 2	
April 22 - 25	Law of Agency	Lending & Closing
April 29 - May 2	Law of Contracts	
May 6 - 9	Principles 1	Math
May 13 - 16	Principles 2	Selling Strategies
May 20 - 23	Law of Agency	
May 28 - 31**		Brokerage
June 3 - 6	Law of Contracts	
June 10 - 13	Principles 1	Negotiations
June 17 - 20	Principles 2	
June 24 - 27	Law of Agency	Investments
July 1 - 3**		Property Mgmnt
July 8 - 11	Law of Contracts	
July 15 - 18	Principles 1	Brokerage
July 22 - 25	Principles 2	
July 29 - August 1	Law of Agency	Selling
August 5 - 8	Law of Contracts	
August 12 - 15	Principles 1	
August 19 - 22	Principles 2	Lending & Closing
August 26 - 29	Law of Agency	Negotiations
September 2 - 5**		
September 9 - 12	Law of Contracts	
September 16 - 19	Principles 1	Property Mgmnt
September 23 - 26	Principles 2	
Sept. 30 - October 3	Law of Agency	Negotiations
October 7 - 10	Law of Contracts	
October 14 - 17	Principles 1	Investments
October 21 - 24	Principles 2	Marketing
October 28 - 31	Law of Agency	
November 4 - 7	Law of Contracts	Brokerage
November 11 - 14	Principles 1	
November 18 - 21	Principles 2	
November 25 - 27**		Investments
December 2 - 5	Law of Agency	Selling Strategies
December 9 - 12	Law of Contracts	
December 16 - 19	Principles 1	Math
December 23 - 26**		

Friday - Sunday		8:00 AM - 6:30 PM
January 4 - 6	Principles 2	Math
January 11 - 13	Law of Agency	Selling Strategies
January 18 - 20	Law of Contracts	
January 25 - 27	Principles 1	Marketing
February 1 - 3	Principles 2	
February 8 - 10	Law of Agency	Negotiations
February 15 - 17	Law of Contracts	
February 22 - 24	Principles 1	Lending & Closing
March 1 - 3	Principles 2	
March 8 - 10	Law of Agency	Brokerage
March 15 - 17	Law of Contracts	
March 22 - 24	Principles 1	Marketing
March 28 - 30**		
April 5 - 7	Principles 2	
April 12 - 14	Law of Agency	Math
April 19 - 21	Law of Contracts	
April 26 - 28	Principles 1	Marketing
May 3 - 5	Principles 2	
May 10 - 12	Law of Agency	Investments
May 17 - 19	Law of Contracts	
May 24 - 26	Principles 1	Lending & Closing
May 31 - June 2		Property Mgmnt
June 7 - 9	Principles 2	
June 14 - 16	Law of Agency	Math
June 21 - 23	Law of Contracts	Marketing
June 28 - 30	Principles 1	
July 5 - 7		Lending & Closing
July 12 - 14	Principles 2	
July 19 - 21	Law of Agency	Negotiations
July 26 - 28	Law of Contracts	
August 2 - 4	Principles 1	Investments
August 9 - 11	Principles 2	
August 16 - 18	Law of Agency	Marketing
August 23 - 25	Law of Contracts	Math
August 30 - Sept. 1	Principles 1	
September 6 - 8		Brokerage
September 13 - 15	Principles 2	
September 20 - 22	Law of Agency	Selling Strategies
September 27 - 29	Law of Contracts	
October 4 - 6	Principles 1	Property Mgmnt
October 11 - 13	Principles 2	
October 18 - 20	Law of Agency	Brokerage
October 25 - 27	Law of Contracts	
November 1 - 3	Principles 1	Math
November 8 - 10	Principles 2	
November 15 - 17	Law of Agency	Lending & Closing
November 22 - 24	Law of Contracts	
November 29 - Dec. 1		Marketing
December 6 - 8	Principles 1	
December 13 - 15	Principles 2	Brokerage
December 20 - 22	Law of Agency	Lending & Closing
December 27 - 29	Law of Contracts	

Evenings	6:15 PM - 10:05 PM
Jan 7-10 & 14-17	
	Principles 2 or Marketing
Jan 21-24 & 28-31	
	Law of Agency
February 4-7 & 11-14	
	Law of Contracts
February 18-21 & 25-28	
	Principles 1 or Math
March 4-7 & 11-14	
	Principles 2 or Marketing
March 18-21 & 25-28	
	Law of Agency
April 1-4 & 8-11	
	Law of Contracts
April 15-18 & 22-25	
	Principles 1 or Math
April 29-May 2 & May 6-9	
	Principles 2 or Marketing
May 13-16 & 20-23	
	Law of Agency
May 28-31 & June 3-6**	
	Contracts
June 10-13 & 17-20	
	Principles 1 or Math
June 24-27 & July 1-3, 5	
	Principles 2 or Marketing
July 8-11 & 15-18	
	Law of Agency
July 22-25 & 29-August 1	
	Contracts
August 5-8 & 12-15	
	Principles 1 or Math
August 19-22 & 26-29	
	Principles 2 or Marketing
September 3-6 & 9-12**	
	Law of Agency
September 16-19 & 23-26	
	Law of Contracts
Sept 30 - Oct 3 & 7-10	
	Principles 1 or Math
October 14-17 & 21-24	
	Principles 2 or Marketing
October 28-31 & Nov 4-7	
	Law of Agency
November 11-14 & 18-21	
	Law of Contracts
December 2-5 & 9-11	
	Principles 1 or Math

** Holiday Schedule

Fort Worth - 1701 River Run #10

Euless - 150 Westpark Way #120

Monday - Wednesday	8:00 AM - 6:30 PM
January 1 - 3**	
January 7 - 9	
January 14 - 16	
January 21 - 23	Principles 1
January 28 - 30	Principles 2
February 4 - 6	Law of Agency
February 11 - 13	Law of Contracts
February 18 - 20	Selling Strategies
February 25 - 27	Math
March 4 - 6	
March 11 - 13	
March 18 - 20	
March 25 - 27	
April 1 - 3	
April 8 - 10	
April 15 - 17	
April 22 - 24	Principles 1
April 29 - May 1	Principles 2
May 6 - 8	Law of Agency
May 13 - 15	Law of Contracts
May 20 - 22	Math
May 28 - 30**	Modern Marketing
June 3 - 5	
June 10 - 12	Principles 1
June 17 -19	Principles 2
June 24 - 26	Law of Agency
July 1 - 3**	Law of Contracts
July 8 - 10	Selling Strategies
July 15 - 17	Lending & Closing
July 22 - 24	
July 29 - 31	
August 5 - 7	
August 12 - 14	
August 19 - 21	
August 26 - 28	
September 3 - 5**	
September 9 - 11	
September 16 - 18	
September 23 - 25	
September 30 - October 2	
October 7 - 9	
October 14 - 16	Principles 1
October 21 - 23	Principles 2
October 28 - 30	Law of Agency
November 4 - 6	Law of Contracts
November 11 - 13	Math
November 18 - 20	Negotiations
November 25 - 27**	
December 2 -4	
December 9 - 11	
December 16 - 18	
December 23 - 26**	

Friday - Sunday	8:00 AM - 6:30 PM
January 4 - 6	
January 11 - 13	Lending & Closing
January 18 - 20	
January 25 - 27	
February 1 - 3	
February 8 - 10	
February 15 - 17	
February 22 - 24	
March 1 - 3	Principles 1
March 8 - 10	Principles 2
March 15 - 17	Law of Agency
March 22 - 24	Law of Contracts
March 28 - 30**	Modern Marketing
April 5 - 7	Lending & Closing
April 12 - 14	
April 19 - 21	
April 26 - 28	
May 3 - 5	
May 10 - 12	Commercial Sales
May 17 - 19	
May 24 - 26	
May 31 - June 2	
June 7 - 9	
June 14 - 16	
June 21 - 23	
June 28 - 30	
July 5 - 7	
July 12 - 14	
July 19 - 21	Investments
July 26 - 28	
August 2 - 4	
August 9 - 11	
August 16 - 18	
August 23 - 25	
August 30 - September 1	
September 6 - 8	
September 13 - 15	
September 20 - 22	
September 27 - 29	
October 4 - 6	
October 11 - 13	Modern Marketing
October 18 - 20	
October 25 - 27	
November 1 - 3	
November 8 - 10	
November 15 - 17	
November 22 - 24	
November 29 - December 1	
December 6 - 8	
December 13 - 15	Lending & Closing
December 20 - 22	
December 27 - 29	

Mon - Wed or Fri - Sun	8:00 AM - 6:30 PM
March 4 -6	Principles 1
March 8 - 10	Principles 2
March 11 - 13	Law of Agency
March 15 - 17	Law of Contracts
April 28 - May 1	Principles 1
May 3 - 5	Principles 2
May 6 - 8	Law of Agency
May 10 - 12	Law of Contracts
June 28 - 30	Principles 1
July 1 - 3**	Principles 2
July 5 - 7	Law of Agency
July 8 - 10	Law of Contracts
August 26 - 28	Principles 1
August 30 - September 1	Principles 2
September 3 - 5**	Law of Agency
September 6 - 8	Law of Contracts
October 14 - 16	Principles 1
October 18 - 20	Principles 2
October 21 - 24	Law of Agency
October 25 - 27	Law of Contracts
December 13 - 15	Principles 1
December 16 - 18	Principles 2
December 20 - 22	Law of Agency
December 27 - 29	Law of Contracts

** Holiday Schedule

Arlington - 2225 East Randol Mill Rd. #100

Monday - Thursday	8:30 AM - 4:55 PM		Friday - Sunday	8:00 AM - 6:30 PM		Saturday, Saturday, Sunday	8:00 AM - 6:30 PM
January 1 - 3**			January 4 - 6	Law of Agency		January 5, 12, 13	Law of Contracts
January 7 - 10	Principles 1		January 11 - 13	Law of Contracts			
January 14 - 17	Principles 2		January 18 - 20	Investments		January 19, 26, 27	Lending & Closing
January 21 - 24	Law of Agency		January 25 - 27	Lending & Closing			
January 28 - 31	Law of Contracts		February 1 - 3	Principles 1		February 2, 9, 10	Principles 2
February 4 - 7	Math		February 8 - 10	Principles 2			
February 11 - 14	Modern Marketing		February 15 - 17	Law of Agency		February 23, March 2, 3	Modern Marketing
February 18 - 21	Principles 1		February 22 - 24	Law of Contracts			
February 25 - 28	Principles 2		March 1 - 3	Modern Marketing		March 9, 16, 17	Principles 1
March 4 - 7	Law of Agency		March 8 - 10	Math			
March 11 - 14	Law of Contracts		March 15 - 17	Principles 1			
March 18 - 21	Negotiations		March 22 - 24	Principles 2		April 6, 13, 14	Law of Contracts
March 25 - 28	Property Management		March 28 - 30**				
April 1 - 4	Principles 1		April 5 - 7	Law of Agency			
April 8 - 11	Principles 2		April 12 - 14	Law of Contracts		April 20, 27, 28	Negotiations
April 15 - 18	Law of Agency		April 19 - 21	Property Management			
April 22 - 25	Law of Contracts		April 26 - 28	Negotiations		May 11, 18, 19	Law of Agency
April 29 - May 2	Lending & Closing		May 3 - 5	Principles 1			
May 6 - 9	Investments		May 10 - 12	Principles 2			
May 13 - 16	Principles 1		May 17 - 19	Law of Agency			
May 20 - 23	Principles 2		May 24 - 26	Law of Contracts		June 1, 8, 9	Lending & Closing
May 28 - 31**	Selling Strategies		May 31 - June 2	Investments			
June 3 - 6	Law of Agency		June 7 - 9	Lending & Closing		June 15, 22, 23	Principles 2
June 10 - 13	Law of Contracts		June 14 - 16	Principles 1			
June 17 - 20	Math		June 21 - 23	Principles 2		June 29, July 6, 7	Law of Contracts
June 24 - 27	Modern Marketing		June 28 - 30	Law of Agency			
July 1 - 3**	Principles 1		July 5 - 7	Law of Contracts			
July 8 - 11	Principles 2		July 12 - 14	Modern Marketing		July 20, 27, 28	Principles 1
July 15 - 18	Law of Agency		July 19 - 21	Math		August 3, 10, 11	Law of Agency
July 22 - 25	Law of Contracts		July 26 - 28	Principles 1			
July 29 - August 1	Property Management		August 2 - 4	Principles 2		August 17, 24, 25	Property Management
August 5 - 8	Negotiations		August 9 - 11	Law of Agency			
August 12 - 15	Principles 1		August 16 - 18	Law of Contracts			
August 19 - 22	Principles 2		August 23 - 25	Property Management			
August 26 - 29	Law of Agency		August 30 - September 1	Modern Marketing			
September 2 - 5**			September 6 - 8	Principles 1		September 7, 14, 15	Principles 2
September 9 - 12	Law of Contracts		September 13 - 15	Principles 2			
September 16 - 19	Lending & Closing		September 20 - 22	Law of Agency			
September 23 - 26	Investments		September 27 - 29	Law of Contracts		September 21, 28, 29	Law of Contracts
September 30 - October 3	Principles 1		October 4 - 6	Lending & Closing			
October 7 - 10	Principles 2		October 11 - 13	Math		October 5, 12, 13	Math
October 14 - 17	Law of Agency		October 18 - 20	Principles 1			
October 21 - 24	Law of Contracts		October 25 - 27	Principles 2			
October 28 - 31	Negotiations		November 1 - 3	Law of Agency		October 26, November 2, 3	Law of Agency
November 4 - 7	Lending & Closing		November 8 - 10	Law of Contracts			
November 11 - 14	Principles 1		November 15 - 17	Modern Marketing		November 9, 16, 17	Modern Marketing
November 18 - 21	Principles 2		November 22 - 24	Math			
November 25 - 27**			November 29 - December 1	Principles 1		November 23, 30, Dec 1	Principles 1
December 2 - 5	Law of Agency		December 6 - 8	Principles 2			
December 9 - 12	Law of Contracts		December 13 - 15	Law of Agency		December 14, 21, 22	Law of Contracts
December 16 - 19	Property Management		December 20 - 22	Law of Contracts			
December 23 - 26**			December 27 - 29	Modern Marketing			

** Holiday Schedule

Southlake

630 East Southlake Blvd.

Monday - Wednesday	8:00 AM - 6:30 PM
January 1 - 3**	
January 7 - 9	
January 14 - 16	Principles 1
January 21 - 23	Principles 2
January 28 - 30	Law of Agency
February 4 - 6	Law of Contracts
February 11 - 13	Negotiations
February 18 - 20	Lending & Closing
February 25 - 27	
March 4 - 6	
March 11 - 13	
March 18 - 20	Principles 1
March 25 - 27	Principles 2
April 1 - 3	Law of Agency
April 8 - 10	Law of Contracts
April 15 - 17	Math
April 22 - 24	Investments
April 29 - May 1	
May 6 - 8	
May 13 - 15	
May 20 - 22	
May 28 - 30**	
June 3 - 5	Principles 1
June 10 - 12	Principles 2
June 17 -19	Law of Agency
June 24 - 26	Law of Contracts
July 1 - 3**	Marketing
July 8 - 10	Math
July 15 - 17	
July 22 - 24	Principles 1
July 29 - 31	Principles 2
August 5 - 7	Law of Agency
August 12 - 14	Law of Contracts
August 19 - 21	Lending & Closing
August 26 - 28	Negotiations
September 3 - 5**	
September 9 - 11	Principles 1
September 16 - 18	Principles 2
September 23 - 25	Law of Agency
September 30 - October 2	Law of Contracts
October 7 - 9	Math
October 14 - 16	Marketing
October 21 - 23	
October 28 - 30	
November 4 - 6	Principles 1
November 11 - 13	Principles 2
November 18 - 20	Law of Agency
November 25 - 27**	
December 2 -4	Law of Contracts
December 9 - 11	Lending & Closing
December 16 - 18	Math
December 23 - 26**	

620 East Southlake Blvd.

Saturday - Sunday	8:30 AM - 4:55 PM
January 5, 6, 12, 13	Principles 1
January 19, 20, 26, 27	Principles 2
February 2, 3, 9, 10	Law of Agency
February 16, 17, 23, 24	Law of Contracts
Feb 23, 24, Mar 2, 3	Selling Strategies
March 9, 10, 16, 17	Lending & Closing
April 6, 7, 13, 14	Principles 1
April 20, 21, 27, 28	Principles 2
May 4, 5, 11, 12	Law of Agency
May 18, 19, 25, 26	Law of Contracts
June 1, 2, 8, 9	Negotiations
June 15, 16, 22, 23	Math
June 29, 30, July 6, 7	Principles 1
July 13, 14, 20, 21	Principles 2
July 27, 28, Aug 3, 4	Law of Agency
August 10, 11, 17, 18	Law of Contracts
September 7, 8, 14, 15	Principles 1
September 21, 22, 28, 29	Principles 2
October 5, 6, 12, 13	Law of Agency
October 19, 20, 26, 27	Law of Contracts
November 2, 3, 9, 10	Selling Strategies
November 16, 17, 23, 24	Math
December 7, 8, 14, 15	Principles 1
December 21, 22, 28, 29	Principles 2

Garland - 911 Main Street

Mon, Tues, Mon, Tues	8:30 AM - 4:55 PM
January 7, 8, 14, 15	Principles 1
January 21, 22, 28, 29	Principles 2
February 4, 5, 11, 12	Law of Agency
February 18, 19, 25, 26	Law of Contracts
March 4, 5, 11, 12	Lending & Closing
March 18, 19, 25, 26	Modern Marketing
April 1, 2, 8, 9	Principles 1
April 15, 16, 22, 23	Principles 2
April 29, 30, May 6, 7	Law of Agency
May 13, 14, 20, 21	Law of Contracts
May 28, 29, June 3, 4**	Math
June 10, 11, 17, 18	Negotiations
June 24, 25, July 1, 2	Principles 1
July 8, 9, 15, 16	Principles 2
July 22, 23, 29, 30	Law of Agency
August 5, 6, 12, 13	Law of Contracts
August 19, 20, 26, 27	Negotiations
September 9, 10, 16, 17	Lending & Closing
Sept 23, 24, 30, Oct 1	Principles 1
October 7, 8, 14, 15	Principles 2
October 21, 22, 28, 29	Law of Agency
November 4, 5, 11, 12	Law of Contracts
November 18, 19, 25, 26	Modern Marketing
December 2, 3, 9, 10	Math

** Holiday Schedule

LEONARD - HAWES
REAL ESTATE SCHOOL
A **Kaplan Professional** Company

2002 SCHEDULE

Houston Central - 5851 Southwest Freeway #615

Monday - Thursday	8:30 AM - 4:55 PM	Friday - Sunday	8:00 AM - 6:30 PM	Saturday, Saturday, Sunday	8:00 AM - 6:30 PM
January 1 - 3**		January 4 - 6	Principles 1	January 5, 12, 13	Principles 2
January 7 - 10	Property Management	January 11 - 13	Principles 2		
January 14 - 17	Negotiations	January 18 - 20	Law of Agency	January 19, 26, 27	Law of Contracts
January 21 - 24	Principles 1	January 25 - 27	Law of Contracts		
January 28 - 31	Principles 2	February 1 - 3	Commercial Sales	February 2, 9, 10	Lending & Closing
February 4 - 7	Law of Agency	February 8 - 10	Lending & Closing		
February 11 - 14	Law of Contracts	February 15 - 17	Principles 1	February 23, March 2, 3	Law of Agency
February 18 - 21	Math	February 22 - 24	Principles 2		
February 25 - 28	Commercial Sales	March 1 - 3	Law of Agency	March 9, 16, 17	Modern Marketing
March 4 - 7	Principles 1	March 8 - 10	Law of Contracts		
March 11 - 14	Principles 2	March 15 - 17	Modern Marketing	March 23, April 6, 7	Principles 1
March 18 - 21	Law of Agency	March 22 - 24	Investments		
March 25 - 28	Law of Contracts	March 28 - 30**			
April 1 - 4	Negotiations	April 5 - 7	Principles 1		
April 8 - 11	Lending & Closing	April 12 - 14	Principles 2	April 20, 27, 28	Law of Contracts
April 15 - 18	Principles 1	April 19 - 21	Law of Agency		
April 22 - 25	Principles 2	April 26 - 28	Law of Contracts	May 4, 11, 12	Property Management
April 29 - May 2	Law of Agency	May 3 - 5	Commercial Sales		
May 6 - 9	Law of Contracts	May 10 - 12	Property Management	May 18, 25, 26	Principles 2
May 13 - 16	Modern Marketing	May 17 - 19	Principles 1		
May 20 - 23	Math	May 24 - 26	Principles 2	June 1, 8, 9	Law of Agency
May 28 - 31**		May 31 - June 2			
June 3 - 6	Principles 1	June 7 - 9	Law of Agency	June 15, 22, 23	Negotiations
June 10 - 13	Principles 2	June 14 - 16	Law of Contracts		
June 17 - 20	Law of Agency	June 21 - 23	Negotiations		
June 24 - 27	Law of Contracts	June 28 - 30	Commercial Sales		
July 1 - 3**		July 5 - 7		July 6, 13, 14	Principles 1
July 8 - 11	Lending & Closing	July 12 - 14	Principles 1		
July 15 - 18	Investments	July 19 - 21	Principles 2		
July 22 - 25	Principles 1	July 26 - 28	Law of Agency	July 27, August 3, 4	Law of Contracts
July 29 - August 1	Principles 2	August 2 - 4	Law of Contracts	August 10, 17, 18	Modern Marketing
August 5 - 8	Law of Agency	August 9 - 11	Lending & Closing		
August 12 - 15	Law of Contracts	August 16 - 18	Modern Marketing		
August 19 - 22	Negotiations	August 23 - 25	Principles 1		
August 26 - 29	Math	August 30 - September 1	Principles 2	August 24, 31, Sept 1	Principles 2
September 2 - 5**		September 6 - 8		September 7, 14, 15	Law of Agency
September 9 - 12	Principles 1	September 13 - 15	Law of Agency		
September 16 - 19	Principles 2	September 20 - 22	Law of Contracts		
September 23 - 26	Law of Agency	September 27 - 29	Brokerage	September 21, 28, 29	Brokerage
September 30 - October 3	Law of Contracts	October 4 - 6	Lending & Closing		
October 7 - 10	Commercial Sales	October 11 - 13	Principles 1	October 5, 12, 13	Principles 1
October 14 - 17	Modern Marketing	October 18 - 20	Principles 2		
October 21 - 24	Principles 1	October 25 - 27	Law of Agency		
October 28 - 31	Principles 2	November 1 - 3	Law of Contracts	October 26, November 2, 3	Law of Contracts
November 4 - 7	Law of Agency	November 8 - 10	Investments		
November 11 - 14	Law of Contracts	November 15 - 17	Math	November 9, 16, 17	Math
November 18 - 21	Property Management	November 22 - 24	Principles 1		
November 25 - 27**		November 29 - December 1			
December 2 - 5	Commercial Sales	December 6 - 8	Principles 2		
December 9 - 12	Principles 1	December 13 - 15	Law of Agency	December 7, 14, 15	Law of Agency
December 16 - 19	Principles 2	December 20 - 22	Law of Contracts	December 21, 28, 29	Property Management
December 23 - 26**		December 27 - 29	Property Management		

** Holiday Schedule

Houston North - 110 Cypress Station #210

Monday - Thursday 8:30 AM - 4:55 PM		Friday - Sunday 8:00 AM - 6:30 PM		Saturday, Saturday, Sunday 8:00 AM - 6:30 PM	
January 1 - 3**		January 4 - 6	Law of Agency	January 5, 12, 13	Law of Contracts
January 7 - 10	Principles 1	January 11 - 13	Law of Contracts		
January 14 - 17	Principles 2	January 18 - 20	Investments	January 19, 26, 27	Lending & Closing
January 21 - 24	Law of Agency	January 25 - 27	Lending & Closing		
January 28 - 31	Law of Contracts	February 1 - 3	Principles 1	February 2, 9, 10	Principles 2
February 4 - 7	Math	February 8 - 10	Principles 2		
February 11 - 14	Modern Marketing	February 15 - 17	Law of Agency	February 23, March 2, 3	Modern Marketing
February 18 - 21	Principles 1	February 22 - 24	Law of Contracts		
February 25 - 28	Principles 2	March 1 - 3	Modern Marketing	March 9, 16, 17	Principles 1
March 4 - 7	Law of Agency	March 8 - 10	Math		
March 11 - 14	Law of Contracts	March 15 - 17	Principles 1		
March 18 - 21	Negotiations	March 22 - 24	Principles 2	April 6, 13, 14	Law of Contracts
March 25 - 28	Property Management	March 28 - 30**			
April 1 - 4	Principles 1	April 5 - 7	Law of Agency		
April 8 - 11	Principles 2	April 12 - 14	Law of Contracts	April 20, 27, 28	Negotiations
April 15 - 18	Law of Agency	April 19 - 21	Property Management		
April 22 - 25	Law of Contracts	April 26 - 28	Negotiations	May 11, 18, 19	Law of Agency
April 29 May 2	Lending & Closing	May 3 - 5	Principles 1		
May 6 - 9	Investments	May 10 - 12	Principles 2		
May 13 - 16	Principles 1	May 17 - 19	Law of Agency		
May 20 - 23	Principles 2	May 24 - 26	Law of Contracts	June 1, 8, 9	Lending & Closing
May 28 - 31**	Selling Strategies	May 31 - June 2	Investments		
June 3 - 6	Law of Agency	June 7 - 9	Lending & Closing	June 15, 22, 23	Principles 2
June 10 - 13	Law of Contracts	June 14 - 16	Principles 1		
June 17 - 20	Math	June 21 - 23	Principles 2	June 29, July 6, 7	Law of Contracts
June 24 - 27	Modern Marketing	June 28 - 30	Law of Agency		
July 1 - 3**	Principles 1	July 5 - 7	Law of Contracts		
July 8 - 11	Principles 2	July 12 - 14	Modern Marketing	July 20, 27, 28	Principles 1
July 15 - 18	Law of Agency	July 19 - 21	Math	August 3, 10, 11	Law of Agency
July 22 - 25	Law of Contracts	July 26 - 28	Principles 1		
July 29 - August 1	Property Management	August 2 - 4	Principles 2	August 17, 24, 25	Property Management
August 5 - 8	Negotiations	August 9 - 11	Law of Agency		
August 12 - 15	Principles 1	August 16 - 18	Law of Contracts		
August 19 - 22	Principles 2	August 23 - 25	Property Management		
August 26 - 29	Law of Agency	August 30 - September 1	Modern Marketing		
September 2 - 5**		September 6 - 8	Principles 1	September 7, 14, 15	Principles 2
September 9 - 12	Law of Contracts	September 13 - 15	Principles 2		
September 16 - 19	Lending & Closing	September 20 - 22	Law of Agency		
September 23 - 26	Investments	September 27 - 29	Law of Contracts	September 21, 28, 29	Law of Contracts
September 30 - October 3	Principles 1	October 4 - 6	Lending & Closing		
October 7 - 10	Principles 2	October 11 - 13	Math	October 5, 12, 13	Math
October 14 - 17	Law of Agency	October 18 - 20	Principles 1		
October 21 - 24	Law of Contracts	October 25 - 27	Principles 2		
October 28 - 31	Negotiations	November 1 - 3	Law of Agency	October 26, November 2, 3	Law of Agency
November 4 - 7	Lending & Closing	November 8 - 10	Law of Contracts		
November 11 - 14	Principles 1	November 15 - 17	Modern Marketing	November 9, 16, 17	Modern Marketing
November 18 - 21	Principles 2	November 22 - 24	Math		
November 25 - 27**		November 29 - December 1	Principles 1	November 23, 30, Dec 1	Principles 1
December 2 - 5	Law of Agency	December 6 - 8	Principles 2		
December 9 - 12	Law of Contracts	December 13 - 15	Law of Agency	December 14, 21, 22	Law of Contracts
December 16 - 19	Property Management	December 20 - 22	Law of Contracts		
December 23 - 26**		December 27 - 29	Modern Marketing		

** Holiday Schedule

2002 State Exam Prep Schedule
8:30 AM – 5:00 PM $139

Pre-Pay and save $10

LOCATION	DATE	LOCATION	DATE	LOCATION	DATE
DALLAS NORTH	Jan. 15 - 16	DALLAS CENTRAL	Jan. 12 - 13	ARLINGTON	Jan. 9 - 10
	Jan. 29 - 30				Jan. 26 - 27
DALLAS NORTH	Feb. 12 - 13	DALLAS CENTRAL	Feb. 16 - 17	ARLINGTON	Feb. 19 - 20
	Feb. 26 - 27				
DALLAS NORTH	Mar. 13 - 14	DALLAS CENTRAL	Mar. 16 - 17	ARLINGTON	Mar. 2 - 3
	Mar. 26 - 27				Mar. 18 - 19
DALLAS NORTH	Apr. 9 - 10	DALLAS CENTRAL	Apr. 13 - 14	ARLINGTON	Apr. 11 - 12
	Apr. 23 - 24				Apr. 27 - 28
DALLAS NORTH	May 7 - 8	DALLAS CENTRAL	May 11 - 12	ARLINGTON	May 8 - 9
	May 20 - 21				May 18 - 19
DALLAS NORTH	June 5 - 6	DALLAS CENTRAL	June 29 - 30	ARLINGTON	June 15 - 16
	June 17 - 18				June 25 - 26
DALLAS NORTH	July 2 - 3	DALLAS CENTRAL	July 13 - 14	ARLINGTON	July 13 - 14
	July 30 - 31				July 23 - 2 4
DALLAS NORTH	Aug. 13 - 14	DALLAS CENTRAL	Aug. 3 - 4	ARLINGTON	Aug. 10 - 11
	Aug. 27 - 28				Aug. 21 - 22
DALLAS NORTH	Sept. 10 - 11	DALLAS CENTRAL	Sept. 1 - 2	ARLINGTON	Sept. 14 - 15
	Sept. 24 - 25		Sept. 28 - 29		Sept. 26 - 27
DALLAS NORTH	Oct. 10 - 11	DALLAS CENTRAL	Oct. 26 - 27	ARLINGTON	Oct. 15 - 16
	Oct. 23 - 24				Oct. 19 - 20
DALLAS NORTH	Nov. 5 - 6	DALLAS CENTRAL	Nov. 16 - 17	ARLINGTON	Nov. 13 - 14
	Nov. 19 - 20				Nov. 30-Dec. 1
DALLAS NORTH	Dec. 3 - 4	DALLAS CENTRAL	Dec. 28 - 29	ARLINGTON	Dec. 19 - 20
	Dec. 17 - 18				
FORT WORTH	March 11 - 12	Houston CENTRAL	Jan. 9 - 10	Houston NORTH	Jan. 16 - 17
			Jan. 26 - 27		
FORT WORTH	Apr. 20 - 21	Houston CENTRAL	Feb. 12 - 13	Houston NORTH	Feb. 16 - 17
FORT WORTH	June 3 - 4	Houston CENTRAL	Mar. 2 - 3	Houston NORTH	Mar. 13 - 14
			Mar. 20 - 21		
FORT WORTH	Dec. 3 - 4	Houston CENTRAL	Apr. 6 - 7	Houston NORTH	Apr. 27 - 28
			Apr. 17 - 18		
		Houston CENTRAL	May 6 - 7	Houston NORTH	May 21 - 22
			May 25 - 26		
		Houston CENTRAL	June 11 - 12	Houston NORTH	June 22 - 23
		Houston CENTRAL	July 6 - 7	Houston NORTH	July 16 - 17
			July 23 - 2 4		
		Houston CENTRAL	Aug. 3 - 4	Houston NORTH	Aug. 24 - 25
			Aug. 14 - 15		
		Houston CENTRAL	Sept. 7 - 8	Houston NORTH	Sept. 16 - 17
			Sept. 24 - 25		
		Houston CENTRAL	Oct. 12 - 13	Houston NORTH	Oct. 19 - 20
			Oct. 23 - 24		
		Houston CENTRAL	Nov. 11 - 12	Houston NORTH	Nov. 19 - 20
			Nov. 23 - 24		
		Houston CENTRAL	Dec. 11 - 12	Houston NORTH	Dec. 21 - 22
			Dec. 21 - 22		

Excellence in Real Estate Education—We are here for you!

CORRESPONDENCE CORE COURSES

These textbook home-study courses are offered in conjunction with the Finance, Insurance, Real Estate and Law department of the

University of North Texas

How Does It Work

- Present valid state identification and complete the course within one year.
- Return the school policy and evaluation manual before testing.
- Computer based courses require the return of the key disk to the school before testing.
- Call toll free 1-877-332-2630 to schedule the multiple-choice, open book exam.
- Exams may be taken Monday - Friday, 10:00 to 3:00 at some of our locations or;
- We can mail your exam, at your cost, to a school-approved proctor of your choice.
- Score 70% or better on the open book exam and you've done it!

✪ **#0111 PRINCIPLES & PRACTICES I (30 hrs)**
Basics, ownership rights & interests, liens, brokerage, Fair Housing, taxes, license law.

✪ **#0112 PRINCIPLES & PRACTICES II (30 hrs)**
Contracts, finance, mortgage theory, title transfer, Fair Housing, appraisal, closing, leasing, property management, investment.

#0211 BASIC APPRAISAL (60 hrs)
Standard valuation approaches. All the steps to complete an appraisal. Combine with USPAP to meet educational requirements for a designation.

#0411 COMPREHENSIVE R. E. FINANCE (30 hrs)
Historical concepts, primary/secondary market, mortgage documents, underwriting, qualifying, property analysis, commercial loans, settlement.

#0524 STRATEGIC MARKETING PLAN (60 hrs)
Plan to succeed! A personalized marketing plan. Worksheets & checklists to organize and track you real estate performance and results.

#0611 UNDERSTANDING R. E. MATH (30 hrs)
Overcome "Mathephobia!" Interest, commissions, taxes, finance, appraisal, qualifying, closing + more.

#0711 REAL ESTATE BROKERAGE (30 hrs)
How to own, operate & manage a real estate office. "Business Blueprint," risk reduction, recruiting, training, advertising, & promotion!

#0723 LICENSED ASSISTANTS (30 hrs)
The indispensable assistant! Knowledge & training in this new trend-setting position helps the agent/assistant to better serve sellers & buyers.

#0811 OVERVIEW OF PROPERTY MANAGEMENT (30 hrs)
Owner's objectives, landlord policies, management plan, maintenance, emergency, and legal issues.

#0911 INTRODUCTORY INVESTMENT (30 hrs)
Principles of investments, tax laws, financing, ownership, feasibility studies and financial analysis.

#0912 TAXATION & INVESTMENTS (30 hrs)
Techniques, tax basis, depreciation, installment sales, 1031 exchanges, risk & effect of ownership.

#1021 RESIDENTIAL INSPECTIONS (30 hrs)
All you need to know about residential property inspections.

✪ **#1111 LAW OF AGENCY (30 hrs - required course)**
Understand all types of agency + Texas intermediary! Employment law and case studies.

✪ **#1200 LAW OF CONTRACTS (30 hrs - required course)**
Covers contract law and explains, in detail, the contract forms, addenda and case studies.

LIVE CORE COURSES

ALL COURSES ARE 30 HOURS

✪ **#0111—PRINCIPLES AND PRACTICES I***
★ Basics, ownership rights and interests, liens, brokerage, Fair Housing, taxes, license law.

✪ **#0112—PRINCIPLES AND PRACTICES II***
★ Contracts, finance, mortgage theory, title transfer Fair Housing, appraisal, closing, leasing, property management, investment.

✪ **#1111—LAW OF AGENCY***
★ Understand all types of agency + Texas intermediary! Employment law and case studies.

✪ **#1200—LAW OF CONTRACTS***
★ The course covers contract law and explains contract forms and addenda promulgated by TREC.

#0421—LENDING & CLOSING PROCEDURES
After a contract is signed, track the lending process and closing functions. People, Paperwork, and Process!

#0511—MODERN MARKETING
How to list, sell, advertise, overcome objections. Time management, telephone and closing techniques. Don't practice real estate without it!

#0512—THE ART OF NEGOTIATION
Learn to be a power negotiator! Be a winner in the games people play! Fun and informative!

★ **#0611—REAL ESTATE MATH***
Overcome "Mathephobia!" Interest, taxes, commissions, finance, appraisal, qualifying, closing + more.

★ **#0811—OVERVIEW OF PROPERTY MANAGEMENT**
Owner's objectives, landlord policies, management plan, maintenance, emergency, and legal issues.

★ **#0911—INTRODUCTORY INVESTMENT**
Principles of investments, tax laws, financing, ownership, feasibility studies and financial analysis.

* *Covers basic material on State Exam*

★ *Available in both Live and Correspondence Courses*

✪ *Meets TREC licensing requirements*

All courses can count for SAE or MCE credit

REGISTRATION FORM

Name_____ Social Security # _____

Address_____

City/State/ZIP _____

Home Phone_____Work Phone _____

Fax_____E-mail _____

❑ **CHECK: Make checks payable to Leonard-Hawes Real Estate School**

❑ **CREDIT CARD:** ❑ **VISA** ❑ **MasterCard** ❑ **AMEX** ❑ **Discover**

Credit Card #_____ Exp. Date _____

Signature _____

ATTENDANCE POLICY   DON'T BE LATE FOR CLASS!

The Texas Real Estate Commission sets stringent rules on attendance. You must attend all sessions or make up any time missed before you will be allowed to take the final exam for a course. Arrive 15 minutes before class is scheduled to begin.

Call Leonard-Hawes Real Estate School or the Texas Real Estate Commission at 800-250-8732 for further explanation.

COURSE	LOCATION	DATE	TIME
Principles of Real Estate I—#0111			
Principles of Real Estate II—#0112			
Law of Contracts—#1200			
Law of Agency—#1111			
Real Estate Math—#0611			
Real Estate Marketing—#0511			
Other:			
Other:			
Other:			

DESCRIPTION	PRICE	QUANTITY	TOTAL
30-Hour Live Courses (Pre-pay for individual classes and save $10 per course)	$129		
Two-Day Live Exam Prep Course (Pre-pay for individual classes and save $10 per course)	$139		
Special Four 30-Hour Live Courses	$459		
Special Six 30-Hour Live Courses	$689		
30-Hour Correspondence Courses	$139		
Four 30-Hour Correspondence Courses	$539		
Six 30-Hour Correspondence Courses	$809		
Add-On Exam Prep Course (Available with pre-paid packages only)	$99		
	Add $10 for Shipping (only applicable for correspondence courses)		
	TOTAL		

REFUNDS: Requests for refunds must be in writing. Refunds will be made on the basis of a "per class hour" charge plus a $25 cancellation fee.

TRANSFERS: You will be allowed to transfer from one course to another offering of the same course without charge providing the student notifies Leonard-Hawes at least 72 hours prior to the beginning of the course in which you were enrolled. Otherwise, a $25 transfer fee will be charged.

Texas Real Estate Agency

FOURTH EDITION

Donna K. Peeples
Minor Peeples

Dearborn™
Real Estate Education

This publication is designed to provide accurate and authoritative information in regard to the subject matter covered. It is sold with the understanding that the publisher is not engaged in rendering legal, accounting or other professional service. If legal advice or other expert assistance is required, the services of a competent professional person should be sought.

Vice President: Carol L. Luitjens
Associate Publisher: Diana Faulhaber
Senior Development Editor: Louise Benzer
Managing Editor: Ronald J. Liszkowski
Art and Design Manager: Lucy Jenkins
Cover Design: DePinto Studios

Published by Real Estate Education Company®
a Division of Dearborn Financial Publishing, Inc.®
a Kaplan Professional Company®
155 North Wacker Drive
Chicago, IL 60606-1719
(312) 836-4400
http://www.dearborn.com

Printed in the United States of America.

01 02 10 9 8 7 6 5

Library of Congress Cataloging-in-Publication Data

Peeples, Donna K.
    Texas real estate agency / Donna K. Peeples, Minor Peeples, III. — 4th ed.
        p.   cm.
    Includes index.
    ISBN 0-7931-3585-0
    1. Real estate business—Law and legislation—Texas.   2. Agency
(Law)—Texas.   I. Peeples, Minor.   II. Title.

KFT1482.R4 R45   2000
346.76404'37—dc21   99–087480

Table of Contents

About the Authors

Donna K. Peeples (Katy) is the co-owner of the Real Estate Institute of Corpus Christi. She is licensed as a real estate broker in Texas, holds a BBA in Finance, an MBA from Texas A&M University at Corpus Christi, and a PhD from Texas A&M University at College Station. Her real estate designations include the GRI, CRB, and the Texas Real Estate Teachers Association's (TRETA) CREI designation. Katy is an Adjunct Professor of Management at Texas A&M University at Corpus Christi and a frequent public speaker on topics relating to business and real estate. She serves as a subject matter expert for NAI and the Texas Real Estate Commission in the question-writing process for the Texas real estate exam. Katy is a coauthor of *Prepare for the Texas Real Estate Exam* with Dr. Johnnie Rosenauer and Dr. Minor Peeples III.

Minor Peeples III is cofounder, owner and principal instructor of the Real Estate Institute of Corpus Christi. Minor is a Texas real estate broker with extensive experience in the real estate business and serves as a content expert for NAI in reference to the Texas real estate examination. He is a coauthor of *Prepare for the Texas Real Estate Exam* with Dr. Johnnie Rosenauer and Dr. Katy Peeples. His educational background includes a BA in Economics from Texas A&M at College Station, an MBA from Texas A&M-Corpus Christi and a PhD from Texas A&M at College Station. In addition to his duties with the Real Estate Institute, Dr. Peeples offers consulting services to real estate brokerage companies and is a frequent speaker at professional real estate meetings throughout south Texas.

Acknowledgements

The authors and publisher wish to thank the following reviewers for their valuable contributions to this edition: Patricia Banta, Collin County Community College; Dave Garcia, The Academy of Real Estate; and Thomas E. Powell, Lee College.

Special thanks also to Philip Schoewe, HomeIndex Real Estate Company, for his detailed review of the material and his valuable suggestions.

In addition, the authors and publisher wish to thank those who have helped with previous editions, including James E. George, EdD, Professional Development Institute, University of North Texas (North Denton); Nanci Hawes, Nanci Hawes Real Estate School; Rick Knowles, Capital Real Estate Training; Randy McKechnie, RLM Consulting, Inc.; Joe C. Pickett, Academy of Real Estate (El Paso); John Wesley Tomblin, J. Wesley Tomblin & Associates (Austin); and Sue Williams, Real Estate Institute of Corpus Christi.

Preface

Knowledge of agency relationships is vital to a licensee's survival and ultimate success in the field of real estate. As clients and customers become more aware of their rights, real estate licensees are often expected to increase their level of service and are being held to higher standards of practice. In addition, agency law is an evolving law and the practitioner must keep abreast of its changing nature. Many issues, such as those involving intermediary brokerage, have yet to be interpreted by the courts. The explanations in this text are consistent with The Texas Real Estate Commission's interpretations, but as more case law develops these interpretations are subject to change.

This book is designed to help students seeking a real estate license and real estate practitioners understand relationships that are created in real estate transactions. Agency is a course of study that is required by The Real Estate License Act (TRELA) for all persons seeking a real estate license. This edition covers all of the topics required by the TRELA for a core course in *Law of Agency*.

This edition retains many of the examples from the previous edition and adds new examples and figures to help students understand some of the new agency laws that have been enacted. Cases, used as learning tools, are meant to bring the "real world" into the study of agency and to give the student the benefit of seeing how the courts interpret these issues.

Many references to The Real Estate License Act (TRELA) are included in the text to remind the reader that the law dictates much of our basic practice. Students who have a clear understanding of the basis of practice will usually have a clearer understanding of how and why certain practices exist.

While this text covers agency issues and may be used in Law of Agency core courses offered by colleges, universities, and proprietary level real estate schools, it is not intended to replace competent legal counsel. Each real estate transaction is unique, therefore, this text cannot be the source of law for any particular transaction. General direction that will guide a licensee's practice can be gained from study of the materials in this text; the licensee's sponsoring broker and legal counsel who is retained to give advice will decide specific practices.

CHAPTER 1

Agency Concepts

In recent years, few real estate topics have received more attention than that of agency. Even the use of the term can be confusing because we refer to brokers as *agents*, to salespeople as *agents* and to our brokerage offices as real estate *agencies*. Numerous court cases have demonstrated that the public, as well as brokers and sales licensees, are often unclear about the various roles that the broker may be playing and about the duties those different roles may impose on the broker. For example, a broker *may* be an agent, a sales licensee holding an active license is *always* an agent of the sponsoring broker, a principal may be a *client* or a *customer* and a broker may be working *with* one principal and *for* another. Confusing? Indeed. It will be helpful to remember that for a licensee to be an agent for a principal there must be a principal/client relationship.

It is critical today that real estate professionals be well grounded in the fundamentals of agency law in order to perform the duties expected of them. Brokers must have a good understanding of the principles so that they may train their sales and broker associates properly. Licensees associated with a broker must likewise be able to communicate the principles of agency information to prospective customers and clients—both buyers and sellers—so they will be able to make informed decisions about the relationship that should be established with the broker to best serve their interests. This chapter introduces you to some basic agency concepts that will help you understand the larger, more complex issues introduced in succeeding chapters.

This chapter addresses the following:

What Is Agency?
Roles People Play in Agency Relationships
Client or Customer?
Why Study Agency?
  Increased Litigation Against Licensees
  Confusion Regarding Whom the Licensee Represents
  Public Perceptions

Emotional Aspects
Complexity
Greater Consumer Expectations
Increased Use of More than One Broker
Greater Licensee Professionalism
State Agency Disclosure Laws
Required Topic of Study for Potential Licensees
The Real Estate License Act, The Texas Real Estate Commission and the Licensee

■ What Is Agency?

Agency, in its most basic form, occurs when one person, the agent, acts on behalf of another, the principal (client). This can be as simple as a neighbor's authorizing you to accept a postal package for him or her or as complex as a business transaction involving millions of dollars. Agency relationships are not unique to real estate; they are an essential part of many business arrangements and are controlled by the principles of business law. The laws governing agency are drawn from both *common law* and *statutory law*. Common law is law that has evolved by custom or by court decisions (case law), and is contrasted with statutory law, which is enacted by legislatures. You should know that such legislative law is often specifically intended to contradict and supersede the common law.

For centuries people have engaged others to represent them in all types of situations. They may grant others the authority to act on their behalf in a single activity, in a specified group of activities or in the ongoing operation of a business. Some agency relationships, like those in real estate, involve money and/or property and create a fiduciary relationship, in which one party is bound to act in the best interest of another. A fiduciary handles money or property for the client; therefore, special duties are created. (These special *fiduciary duties* are discussed in detail in a later chapter.) In any event, agents must at all times act in the best interest of the parties they represent. Today, a licensee must know what the priorities are—especially when a fiduciary relationship is coupled with an agency activity such as a real estate transaction.

■ Roles People Play in Agency Relationships

In this book we use many terms that describe the relationships that are created as a result of real estate transactions. The following list of terms will assist you to understand the roles real estate licensees play and the terminology used in this book and in the real estate industry. You will notice that the terms may overlap at times, and several terms may apply to a single participant in a transaction.

- **Licensee**—A person licensed by the Texas Real Estate Commission (TREC) to act as a broker or salesperson in a real estate transaction.

- **Agent**—(1) A broker who represents a seller, landlord, buyer or tenant. (2) Salespersons or broker licensees who represent the broker with whom they are associated.

- **Subagent**—A licensee *not associated with the client's broker* but who is representing the client through a cooperative agreement with the client's broker. Also called the *other broker.*

- **Broker Licensee**—An individual holding a broker's license issued by TREC. Brokers may act independently in conducting real estate transactions or may engage other broker or salesperson licensees to represent them in the conduct of their real estate business.

- **Salesperson Licensee**—An individual holding a salesperson's license issued by TREC—an agent of the sponsoring broker. Salesperson licensees may conduct business only through their sponsoring broker.

- **Broker Associate**—A broker associated with and conducting his or her business as an agent of another broker.

- **Sales Associate**—A salesperson licensee associated with and conducting business as an agent of his or her sponsoring broker.

- **Seller's Agent**—A broker representing the seller in a real estate transaction. Also referred to as a *Seller's Broker, Listing Broker* or *Listing Agent.*

- **Buyer's Agent**—A broker representing the buyer in a real estate transaction. Also referred to as a *Buyer's Broker, Selling Broker* or *Selling Agent.*

- **Intermediary**—A broker acting as an agent for both a buyer client and a seller client in the same transaction.

- **Landlord's Agent**—A broker representing a landlord in a real estate transaction.

- **Tenant's Agent**—A broker representing a tenant in a real estate transaction.

- **Client**—A person, sometimes called a *principal,* who engages services that include the professional advice and advocacy of another, called an *agent,* and whose interests are protected by the specific duties and loyalties of an agency relationship.

- **Customer**—A person who receives limited brokerage services without establishing an agency relationship. Specifically, advice, advocacy and fiduciary relationships are not included in customer services.

The agency relationships that the above individuals can enter into are discussed in detail in the following chapters. As you study the subject of agency it is important that you pay close attention to the relationships that are created and begin to understand how these relationships affect the way you will relate to the person or entity you are working with in your real estate transactions. You cannot be all things to all people.

■ Client or Customer?

It is important that a licensee have a clear understanding of the difference between a client and a customer. The extent of services that a licensee can offer are determined by the relationships established with individuals.

Clients are represented by licensees who are acting as agents. Customers represent themselves. A licensee works *for* a client, providing services that include advice, opinions, and advocacy while carrying out the instructions of the client. The licensee works *with* a customer, giving limited services such as touring available properties, discussing financing options and, per the seller's instructions, relaying information from the seller, for example, the condition of the property and acceptable price and terms. The licensee *does not* assist the customer in negotiations by offering advice or opinions regarding price or negotiation strategy, or in any way acting as an advocate of the customer.

■ Why Study Agency?

Increased Litigation Against Real Estate Licensees

There are many good reasons to study agency law, but a key explanation for increased interest in agency is increasing litigation in this area of real estate practice. A real estate lawsuit usually results from something other than agency issues, such as breach of contract, misrepresentation or a decision by one of the contracting parties to rescind a contract. After the majority of lawsuits are filed, however, the issue of who represented whom frequently becomes the focal point. Licensees may not have adequately discussed or disclosed whom they represent. Therefore, a lawyer seeking to set aside a transaction may search for an undisclosed, often unintended agency relationship. For example, a lawyer interviewing a buyer-client before filing a misrepresentation action might ask the buyer:

- "How were you treated by the licensee who represented you?"
- "Did you think that the licensee was your agent?"
- "Did you know that the licensee with whom you were working was really the legal agent of the seller?"
- "How do you feel about that now?"

An undisclosed or inadequately disclosed agency relationship could result in the licensee's representation of both parties without their permission to do so—a circumstance strictly prohibited by law. Such undisclosed relationships can be grounds for not paying a brokerage commission or may be used as a basis to rescind a purchase contract between a buyer and seller. Many potential problems, even lawsuits, may be avoided by adherence to timely agency disclosure requirements.

Confusion Regarding Whom the Licensee Represents

As implied in the introduction to this chapter, what at first may appear quite simple can be complex and confusing to the participants in a real estate transaction. In some transactions the buyers and sellers (and licensees as well) are not sure if a licensee is an agent for the seller, the buyer, both or neither. Why? Because it is the nature of a real estate licensee to be solicitous, friendly, and service driven. This behavior can be misconstrued as implying an agency relationship to a customer. In an effort to reduce the confusion regarding agency relationships, TREC has produced the "Information About Brokerage Services" form (voluntary in format, but mandatory in content), which provides consumers with information relating to the differences when a broker represents a seller or buyer or acts as an intermediary. This form, which is critical to the understanding of agency law in Texas, is presented in detail in a later chapter.

The question of whether an agency relationship in a real estate transaction has been created is a question of fact—that is, one a judge or jury might be called on to determine. The particular circumstances of each case must be examined to determine whether the agent represents the buyer, the seller or both. Because of the ease with which agency relationships may be created and in the absence of any required formalities or written agreements, a real estate licensee may be held to be an unwitting agent in a so-called *unintended* or *accidental agency*. William D. North, past executive vice president of the National Association of REALTORS® (NAR), stated, "It's often hard to tell which party the broker represents, and both the buyer and seller are apt to visualize the broker as their broker."

A jury might find that the conduct of both the licensee and the consumer demonstrated that the consumer authorized the licensee to act on his or her behalf and that the licensee did so, thus creating a principal-agent relationship. Such a finding has serious legal, economic and ethical consequences to a broker, salesperson, seller and buyer.

Public Perceptions

Perhaps you have noticed the way the media portray real estate licensees. The image is often one of greedy, fast-talking salespersons whose primary purpose is to line their pockets with commissions while showing little regard for buyers and sellers. Granted, some licensees richly deserve such an image; however, many more try their best to be honest, knowledgeable professionals who make every effort to conduct their business in an ethical manner. An understanding of agency law is the foundation for sound business practices that will guide real estate professionals in their daily activities and help in changing public perceptions about the real estate industry.

Emotional Aspects

Unlike the purchase or sale of many items, a real estate transaction is frequently charged with emotion. Buyers, hopeful of realizing a part of the "American dream" through homeownership, are also faced with the prospect of a fearfully large financial obligation. Sellers, perhaps eager to improve their lifestyle, are sometimes struck with the prospect of leaving behind years of memories attached to the home they are selling. As a result of these high emotions, a small issue may blossom into a major event between the parties. Licensees who fail to understand and accommodate these emotional aspects will frequently lose the trust and confidence of the principals and have a difficult time becoming successful in the real estate business. Understanding the roles that licensees play also helps the professional maintain a clear sense of purpose and direction during emotional periods that may occur with clients and customers.

Complexity

Buying a home is an investment decision as well as a practical consideration. Today, many consumers buy, sell and buy again. Each time increases the consumer's understanding of the importance of receiving sound, objective advice and opinions in addition to accurate factual information about the property under consideration. These repeat buyers and sellers recognize the distinction between advice and information, especially with so much money at stake. Many less experienced consumers, however, do not understand that as *customers* they are entitled to any accurate, relevant information the licensee might possess, but as *clients* they are additionally entitled to advice and opinions, such as suggested negotiating strategies in light of the other party's marketing position.

Greater Consumer Expectations

Buyers are seeking representation more frequently in today's market because they are beginning to understand the benefits of the agency relationship. Both the buyer and the seller increasingly have come to expect professionalism and competence from real estate licensees. After all, state licensing requirements demand a higher knowledge and competency level for brokers and salespersons than for the average person. A judicial trend is emerging, away from the tradition of *caveat emptor* (let the buyer beware) and toward greater consumer protection and professional accountability on the part of the real estate licensee. Frequently, real estate licensees are the most visible experts in the transaction, and both the buyer and seller tend to defer to the judgment and skill of the real estate professional. The seasoned real estate professional is acutely aware of his or her importance, and wisely knows when to defer to another professional a matter not within the licensee's area of responsibility or expertise.

Increased Use of More Than One Broker

A Federal Trade Commission study on national residential brokerage practices noted that 66 percent of the home sales studied involved two brokers or salespersons, and more than half involved the services of two brokerage firms. With two brokers participating in one transaction, it is not surprising that buyers and sellers sometimes question whom the participating brokers really represent. To some, it seems a natural division of labor that the listing broker *represents* the seller and the other broker *represents* the buyer. In practice, however, many buyers are surprised to learn that the salesperson they regard as "theirs" actually represents the seller. The surge in buyer brokerage is, no doubt, due in part to better information regarding the services available from brokers and more complete disclosure of agency relationships.

Greater Licensee Professionalism

In the past, the listing broker was hired primarily to find a buyer. Today, it is likely that another broker will find the buyer. Sellers look to listing brokers to protect their best financial interests in the form of professional advice and opinions as to the soundness of a buyer's offer. Buyers usually look to the licensees who introduce them to the property to provide the same service.

Many licensees now emphasize the variety and quality of services they offer rather than their salesmanship and matchmaking skills. Real estate licensees promote themselves as advisers, problem solvers and data interpreters rather than solely as information providers. Licensees are expected to be generally knowledgeable in such areas as taxation, law, mortgage planning, contract preparation, investment analysis, finance, appraisal and property management. The law and the industry itself are demanding higher standards of skill, care and due diligence from brokers in promoting clients' best interests, in furnishing required disclosures, in treating everyone honestly, in spotting potential problems and in recommending the use of experts when necessary.

State Agency Disclosure Laws

Nearly every state, including Texas, has passed legislation requiring real estate licensees to disclose whom they represent in each transaction. Some state laws permit simple oral disclosure; other laws mandate the use of specific disclosure forms. In all cases, the licensee faces the likelihood that the buyer or seller will want to know what the licensee's role will be. A licensee who is not comfortable discussing his or her role may find the prospective client or customer seeking a more competent real estate licensee.

Required Topic of Study for Potential Licensees

For some, the most compelling reason to study agency law is the educational requirement mandated by the Texas legislature in 1993. The law, as implemented by TREC, requires that all applicants for licensure show evidence that a minimum of 30 clock hours (2 semester hours) in "Law of Agency" has been completed from an acceptable source of study.

■ The Real Estate License Act, the Texas Real Estate Commission and the Licensee

To deal with the issues regarding agency relationships and other laws pertinent to real estate, the Texas legislature created The Real Estate License Act (TRELA) in 1949. TRELA is the law that establishes the duties of real estate licensees in their dealings with the public; it provides the legal framework within which each licensee operates. The law regarding agency relationships, as it pertains to real estate licensees, is carefully detailed in the act. Each person licensed in Texas is obligated to be familiar with the act and to conduct his or her real estate transactions in strict accordance with the act.

The Texas Real Estate Commission (TREC) was established by TRELA in 1949. TREC is responsible for the administration of TRELA. The TREC consists of nine members, six brokers and three public members who serve staggered terms of six years each. The governor, with approval of the senate, appoints three replacement members every two years. The commissioners may appoint an administrator and an assistant administrator who oversee the day-to-day operations of the commission. From a real estate licensee's perspective, some of the key functions of the TREC are:

- enforcing TRELA in a manner that protects the public,
- overseeing the licensing process and
- monitoring and controlling the educational activities of approved providers of real estate education

If the commission receives a complaint about the practice of a licensee who has violated TRELA, it may investigate the complaint and take the appropriate action, which could result in fines and/or suspension or revocation of the license. The wise practitioner never forgets that TREC is a consumer protection agency.

The commission is empowered though the Texas Administrative Code (TAC) to establish the rules and regulations necessary to enforce the provisions of TRELA. Typically, each legislative session results in new legislation that affects real estate practice. Following new legislation, the commission creates rules that allow the law to be interpreted and enforced. Throughout this text the authors will reference specific sections of TRELA as well as the "Rules of the Texas Real Estate Commission," as passed under the provisions of the TAC.

■ Summary

From the most basic residential real estate transaction to the most complex commercial contract, it is important to understand whom the licensee represents and what services can or cannot be provided in accordance with Texas law. There exists an increased interest in clarifying agency issues, precipitated by expanded professional liability suits against real estate licensees.

By developing a positive, and applied, awareness of agency relationships, the real estate professional, when acting as an agent, will be able to adapt to consumer demands for greater representation in today's real estate marketplace.

■ Key Points

- An agent is one who acts on behalf of another—the principal or client.
- The Real Estate License Act (TRELA) is the law that establishes the duties of real estate licensees in Texas. The Texas Real Estate Commission (TREC) administers TRELA empowered by the Texas Administrative Code (TAC).

- The real estate licensee may work *for* a client in a principal-agent relationship, or the licensee may work *with* a customer in a nonagency relationship. A client has a legal right to expect accurate information, advice and informed opinions and advocacy. A customer has a legal right to expect fair treatment, accurate information, referral to sources when advice or advocacy is demanded, and the seller's honest disclosure of the property's condition.

- An undisclosed, underdisclosed or accidental agency relationship may create an unauthorized representation of more than one party, and could result in a lawsuit for rescission, forfeiture of commission, money damages, loss of license or disciplinary action.

- The study of agency is important because of misunderstandings among the public and licensees regarding agency issues, the complexities of real estate transactions, the presence of more than one broker in transactions, the growing demand for buyer representation, state disclosure laws and the escalation of lawsuits involving real estate transactions.

■ Suggestions for Brokers

Develop a company agency disclosure policy that emphasizes awareness of the various agency situations salespersons will encounter in daily practice. Establish training programs within your firm that will allow your sales staff to become comfortable in understanding and disclosing whom they represent (or don't represent), consistent with your established company policy. The lack of a clear company agency policy may easily lead to unlawful actions by the associated licensees of the broker. (The TREC holds the broker responsible for the professional acts of all licensees associated with the broker.)

■ Suggestions for Associates

Understand agency relationships and how you are required to conduct your business activities within the scope of the law. Attend seminars and training programs to keep abreast of the changing laws and to keep informed of new developments within the industry. Above all, know and apply your broker's services as your broker has defined those services. Associates should take care not to contradict their company agency offerings, and comply carefully with company policy regarding agency matters.

■ Quiz

1. Agency is

   A. a real estate brokerage.
   B. the operation of a business.
   C. one person acting on behalf of another.
   D. one person giving advice to another person.

2. An agent works on behalf of

   A. the customer.
   B. the client.
   C. both the customer and client.
   D. neither the customer nor the client.

3. TRELA

   A. enforces the License Act.
   B. may appoint an administrator for the TREC.
   C. is the law that establishes the duties of real estate licensees.
   D. is the law established by the TREC.

4. The Texas Real Estate Commission

   A. does not hold the broker accountable for the actions of sponsored associates.
   B. holds the broker accountable for the professional actions of sponsored associates.
   C. holds the buyer or seller accountable for the acts of their real estate brokers and salespeople.
   D. holds the public accountable for the acts of real estate licensees.

5. A broker is representing Jim Smith, a buyer. In this transaction Mr. Smith is considered a

   A. customer.   C. fiduciary.
   B. client.   D. agent.

6. The person who engages an agent to represent his or her interests in a transaction is called the *principal,* or

   A. customer.   C. seller.
   B. buyer.   D. client.

7. A key distinction between the services that are given to clients versus customers is

   A. advice, opinions and advocacy are given to clients, not customers.
   B. more advice and opinion are offered to the customer.
   C. that customers get advice and opinions free, while clients must pay.
   D. clients must have a contract to receive services, while customers do not.

8. A licensee not associated with the listing broker who represents the seller through the listing broker is known as a

   A. buyer's agent.   C. dual agent.
   B. seller's agent.   D. subagent.

9. One of the best ways a broker might protect against agency problems is

   A. never to represent buyers.
   B. never to discuss agency issues with the parties.
   C. always to treat both parties as valued customers.
   D. to develop a clear, written office policy regarding agency isssues.

10. One of the key reasons to study agency today is

   A. to better represent customers.
   B. the increased litigation against agents.
   C. to be able to settle legal disputes between buyers and sellers.
   D. that commissions are greater to the agent when agency law is followed.

■ Discussion Questions

1. What types of services does the typical buyer expect of a licensee?

2. What types of services does the typical seller expect of a licensee?

3. What are some of the emotions that a buyer and seller may experience in a real estate transaction?

4. What are some of the reasons for the increased interest in agency?

5. What is the essential difference between a client and a customer?

CHAPTER 2

Basic Agency Relationships, Disclosure and Duties to the Client

In real estate transactions, a variety of agency relationships may be created. For this reason, agency relationships must be clearly defined and recognized so they don't become a source of confusion and misunderstanding to buyers, sellers, real estate salespersons, brokers, lawyers and judges. Preconceived notions about the right to representation and misapplied terminology often create roadblocks to greater understanding.

This chapter addresses the following:

Agency Defined
Classifications of Agency
Universal Agency
General Agency
Special Agency
The Flow of Authority
Fiduciary Duties and Responsibilities
Obedience
Loyalty
Disclosure
Confidentiality
Accounting
Reasonable Care and Diligence

■ Agency Defined

As we learned in the previous chapter, agency occurs *when one person, the agent, acts on behalf of another person, the principal or client.* The basic doctrines of agency are common to all businesses.

In real estate practice a licensee can be an agent for a broker; a broker also can be an agent for the buyer or seller, or both. Because of the many opportunities for confusion, it is necessary to understand the general classifications of agency to determine the scope of authority to act for the client.

It is worth noting here that real estate brokers or licensee associates should not be referred to as *agents* until an actual agency relationship has been established. After an agency relationship has been established with the broker, the broker is referred to as the *agent of the client* and the licensee associates are referred to as *agents of the broker.*

■ Classifications of Agency

Agency is typically classified into three categories: *universal, general* and *special.* Each has its own unique set of duties, responsibilities and liabilities for both the principal and the agent. It is important for licensees to understand the scope of each type of agency so that they can understand and comply with the duties and obligations that are expected to be carried out in the course of conducting business.

Universal Agency

Universal agency gives a very broad and general scope of power to the agent to act for the principal. With this type of agency the agent is empowered to conduct every type of transaction that may be legally delegated by a principal to an agent. Such agency power may include acquisition and disposal of assets, expenditure of the principal's funds and entering into contracts on behalf of the principal. This type of agency would hold a principal accountable for virtually any action by the agent. Universal agency is not very common in typical real estate transactions. An example of universal agency is an adult son or daughter who has been empowered by an elderly parent to conduct all personal and business transactions on the parent's behalf. In this case the parent is held accountable for the actions of the son or daughter in conducting the parent's affairs.

General Agency

The scope of authority in general agency is more restricted than in universal agency. The agent is authorized to conduct an ongoing series of transactions for the principal and can obligate him or her to certain types of contractual agreements. General agency is the relationship that most often exists between a broker and the broker's associates (broker licensees and sales licensees). Brokers authorize associates to act as broker's agents in the course of the brokerage operations. These agents are authorized to act for their brokers in any number of activities that are typical to a brokerage firm. Some of the most frequently performed activities are

- obtaining listings from sellers;
- conducting marketing activities for properties listed by the company;
- entering into buyer representation agreements;
- showing properties to prospective buyers;
- preparing, presenting and negotiating offers to purchase properties; and

- maintaining and transfering a complete singular file of each transaction completed or otherwise terminated.

Considerable authority may be given to the agent by the broker. For example, an agent of the broker can obligate the broker to a listing contract with a seller or to a buyer-representation contract with a buyer. As with universal agency, the broker assumes a considerable amount of liability for the agent's actions. For example, if a broker's agent engages in inappropriate or illegal conduct while acting for the broker, the broker is held responsible for those actions. In addition to liability under general agency law, The Real Estate License Act (TRELA) also holds brokers accountable for the actions of their agents while acting within the scope of the general agency authority that was granted to them.

Because of this extensive responsibility, brokers are usually concerned about engaging conscientious associated licensees and training them to make good decisions and take actions that are not only within the scope of the law but also are honest and ethical. Just one poorly trained or unethical associate who commits an illegal act can jeopardize a broker's entire business. For this reason brokers must satisfy themselves as to the character and integrity of licensees who would like to be associated with the brokerage firm.

Another general agency relationship that frequently occurs in real estate practice is when a broker acts as a property manager for an owner. In most cases the broker conducts a number of transactions for the owner, such as negotiating and signing lease contracts, contracting for maintenance, and initiating eviction lawsuits on behalf of the owner. Frequently the owner is unwilling or unable to perform these functions; therefore, it is necessary to confer on the broker the full authority to carry out these activities.

Special Agency

Special agency, sometimes known as *limited agency,* authorizes the agent to perform only those acts permitted by the principal. Real estate agents are most frequently referred to as *limited* or *special agents;* their scope of authority usually does not extend beyond the terms of a listing agreement or a buyer- or tenant-representation agreement. A well-written listing agreement defines the duties of the broker and the client, and uses distinct well-defined terms rather than the broad, sweeping language of general agency agreements.

A listing agreement authorizes the broker to represent the seller in the marketing of the seller's property. The listing broker is authorized to find a "ready, willing and able" buyer. Generally the broker has no authority to sign contracts for the seller, to initial changes to an offer, to accept offers (even for the full purchase price) on behalf of the seller or to permit early occupancy by a potential buyer or tenant. In exceptional cases, the broker may be appointed as attorney-in-fact under a separately granted power of attorney. Brokers are usually hesitant to accept a power of attorney because of potential conflicts or the appearance of impropriety that can arise as a result of the broker's interest in a transaction. Frequently a family member, a business associate or an attorney will be granted the power of attorney when the buyer or seller is unable to be present to act in his or her own behalf.

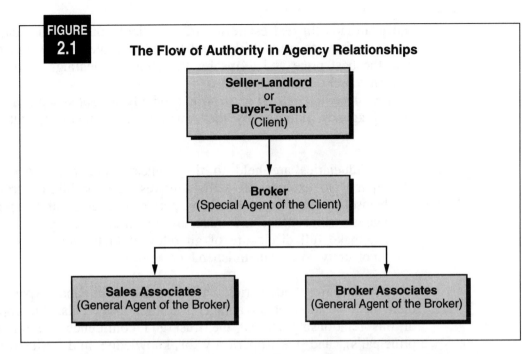

FIGURE 2.1   **The Flow of Authority in Agency Relationships**

Seller-Landlord
or
Buyer-Tenant
(Client)

Broker
(Special Agent of the Client)

Sales Associates
(General Agent of the Broker)

Broker Associates
(General Agent of the Broker)

A buyer- or tenant-representation agreement authorizes the broker to represent the buyer as an agent in purchasing or leasing a property. The agent seeks properties that meet the buyer's or tenant's requirements and then will help negotiate the "best" contract terms and conditions for the buyer or tenant. As when representing sellers, the agent generally has no authority to sign contracts unless a power of attorney has been established.

The Flow of Authority

As shown in Figure 2.1, in a typical real estate transaction there are commonly two levels of agency in operation. One level of agency exists between the associated licensee and the sponsoring broker, and another level between the broker and the buyer or seller. Real estate licensees associated with a broker have a *general agency* relationship with their broker for the operation of the brokerage firm, and brokers have a *special agency* relationship with buyers or sellers for the purchase or sale of property. Because these relationships can be complex and carry legal obligations, it is important that every principal and agent understand the concepts that surround agency relationships.

■ Fiduciary Duties and Responsibilities

Today the broker may play many roles—agent for a seller, agent for a buyer, subagent of a seller, common-law dual agent or statutory intermediary. These roles are discussed in detail in later chapters, but for the moment it is important to know that, regardless of the agency role assumed by the broker, a clear understanding of duties to the client is critical.

If an agency relationship exists, the real estate agent is held to be a *fiduciary.* In classic terms, a fiduciary responsibility implies a position of trust or confidence in which one person—the *fiduciary*—is usually entrusted to hold or manage the assets (in real estate, the property) of another—the *principal* or *client.* Common examples of fiduciaries are trustees, executors and guardians. In real estate terms, the client relies on the real estate agent, as a fiduciary, to give skilled and knowledgeable advice and to help negotiate the best price and terms for the client in dealings with a third person (the *customer*).

Restatement (Second) of Agency, a widely accepted legal authority on the law of agency authored by the American Law Institute, states the following:

> Fiduciaries are held to the highest amount of good faith, are required to exclude all selfish interest, are prohibited from putting themselves in positions where personal interest and representative interest will conflict and must, in any direct dealing with the principal, make full disclosure of all relevant facts and give the latter an opportunity to obtain independent advice.

In lay terms, fiduciaries have special skills and expertise that place them in a position of advantage over their principals. An important aspect of this relationship is that the trust and confidence are on one side (the principal's), and the superiority of knowledge and influence are on the other (the agent's). This is why the fiduciary has special obligations to the principal. The most important obligations a fiduciary owes to a principal can be remembered by using the **"OLD CAR"** memory device:

- **O**bedience
- **L**oyalty
- **D**isclosure
- **C**onfidentiality
- **A**ccounting
- **R**easonable care and diligence

It is important to note that the real estate licensee, when acting as an agent on behalf of either party in the transaction, owes these fiduciary duties *in addition* to whatever duties are specified in the listing contract, the buyer/tenant-representation agreement, TRELA and the TREC Rules. In addition, if the licensee is a REALTOR®, he or she owes the duties outlined in the REALTOR'S® Code of Ethics. The National Association of REALTORS® (NAR) Code of Ethics is generally recognized as representing reasonable and acceptable standards of conduct for any real estate licensee, REALTOR®—or otherwise.

Reasonable Care and Diligence

An agent is hired to do more than merely locate a property or find a ready, willing and able buyer, and an agent's obligations extend beyond simply selling or locating a property. Real estate agents are held to a standard of care that requires, among other things, that they be knowledgeable concerning the land, the title and the physical characteristics of the property being sold.

The agent must use reasonable care and diligence in

- guiding the seller-client to arrive at a reasonable listing price;

- advising the buyer-client to accept a reasonable purchase price for a buyer/client in light of the current market values;

- making reasonable efforts to sell the property, such as holding open houses, advertising, listing with a multiple-listing service (MLS), if customary; and using whatever marketing and advertising means proven to be effective in the specific market area;

- making available properties that meet the buyer's purchasing objectives;

- affirmatively discovering relevant facts and disclosing these facts to the client;

- investigating the material facts related to the sale and asking the seller questions (the duty to question) that will clarify the seller's needs and protect his or her best interests (e.g., "Does your roof leak?");

- preparing and explaining the provisions of the listing form, buyer-representation agreement, purchase contract and other relevant legal documents;

- recommending that the client seek independent expert advisers such as attorneys, inspectors, appraisers and accountants, when appropriate; and

- helping the principals meet deadlines and closing dates.

Agents must exercise care by knowing the laws, financing options and, most importantly, the level of knowledge and expertise the client possesses. An inexperienced client requires vast amounts of information to make the best choices, while clients who have previously bought or sold properties usually are more aware of the basic concepts of ownership. It is important for agents to give their clients the information necessary for them to make informed decisions regarding the purchase or sale of real estate.

Suppose an agent sells a home one week after the listing is signed. Initially, the seller is thrilled. Later, however, the seller may complain that the agent lacked skill and care because the listing price was set too low or the agent failed to obtain better financing terms (this is not meant to suggest that homes that sell quickly are necessarily underpriced). The seller may become angry after discovering that the agent assisted the buyer-customer in obtaining financing that resulted in the seller's paying higher discount points when lower-discount-point options were available. Likewise, a seller who unwittingly closes a transaction a few days before becoming eligible for favorable tax benefits could well complain that the agent failed to exercise reasonable skill by not informing the seller that an early closing would cost thousands of dollars in avoidable taxes.

Similarly, an agent who represents a buyer must exercise reasonable care and diligence on the buyer's behalf. This duty extends beyond giving honest information to a customer—it extends to rendering sound advice and advising the buyer to obtain assistance from experts when appropriate. At the very essence of the fiduciary concept is the fact that a true agent is an "equity preserver" for the client. A buyer's agent preserves equity for the buyer-client by using all of the agent's specialized skills and knowledge in negotiating the least possible price with the best terms.

Agents do not have to meet the high standard of legal knowledge required of attorneys; however, agents do need a basic knowledge of real estate law to qualify for state licenses. Courts impose on agents a duty to know and to explain, in basic terms, the practical effects of key financing terms, contingency clauses, holding title, restrictions and routine contract provisions. In short, agents must spot common problem areas and direct their clients to expert help when the clients require specific advice.

Unlike attorneys, agents do more than act as fiduciaries. Typically, agents are hired to market property. Sometimes these dual responsibilities—that of marketing and that of advising—create practical and ethical dilemmas not normally experienced by other fiduciaries. Recognizing that the agent's income usually depends on a sale, the unprofessional agent could easily justify holding back information, based on the likelihood that the sale will proceed and that certain information would only cloud the client's decision. Nevertheless, the agent must disclose information to the client as part of the fiduciary duty required by law and ethics.

A practical test applied by courts to decide whether an agent has used reasonable skill and care in a given case is, "Would a reasonably efficient broker in the community in a like situation use more care to protect the best interests of the client?" If the answer by the trier of fact (judge or jury) is yes, the agent has been negligent.

 EXAMPLE: Salesperson Jane has just returned from a 3-month vacation in Barbados. She immediately contacts her client, John, to see if he is ready to list his property for sale. He informs her that his company has just finalized his transfer and that he needs to sell his property as soon as possible. She lists his property for $150,000, using her vast list of prior sales in the neighborhood to determine property value. A full price contract is submitted by a buyer's broker the same day the property is listed, and the seller eagerly signs the offer.

After signing the contract John talks with a neighbor, Al, who is also under contract to sell his home. Their homes are very similar in style, amenities and condition, so they compare their selling prices. Al's contract is for $170,000 with basically the same terms and conditions as John's, and he received his offer about 10 days after the property was listed.

? QUESTIONS

1. Why do you think the sales price for John's home is $20,000 less than Al's?

2. What is Jane's liability, if any?

3. Would you do anything different if you were Jane? What? Explain.

Obedience

The agent has an obligation to follow the *lawful* instructions of the client. The agent frequently is asked to obtain a survey, obtain an appraisal or arrange for an inspection for the client. It is important that the *client make decisions about who will provide the services.* The agent then can arrange for the services to be performed. Because the agent cannot act without the client's approval, doing such things as extending closing dates or loan approval dates is not allowed without authorization by the client before the changes are made.

Under no circumstances is an agent allowed to violate the law. Frequently, clients are unaware that a request is illegal. If the client requests an unlawful act, the agent should explain that the request is against the law and that all agents are required to adhere strictly to the law. If the client continues to insist upon the illegal act, the agent should withdraw from the transaction.

 EXAMPLE: Jane has been asked by her good friend, Cecil, to list his property. Jane is delighted to take this listing because the home is in a great neighborhood, close to schools, in wonderful condition and should have an excellent chance of selling quickly at the price and terms that Cecil desires.

After the listing agreement has been signed and Jane is preparing to leave, Cecil clears his throat and says, "Of course you know how I feel about selling my home to a minority. I would like you to do whatever is necessary *not* to show my home to any of 'those folks.'"

At first Jane is stunned. She had no idea that Cecil would make this request. She would really like to take this listing; however, she knows that what he is asking is against the law. Jane has no experience in dealing with this type of situation, and is very unsure how to proceed.

? QUESTIONS

1. What should Jane do?

2. What could she say to convey her point and still be able to maintain the listing?

Loyalty

Agents must always act in the best interest of their clients and must be loyal to the trust placed in them. Once an agreement has been reached between an agent (broker) and a client, *all of the associates of the firm,* whether licensed as salespersons or brokers, will represent the client through the broker. Thus, all licensees associated with the firm will have the same obligations as the broker and must represent the best interests of the client. This means striving to

- obtain the best price and terms possible to satisfy the client's needs; investigate and explain all offers;

- obtain as much relevant information about the other party as possible; and,

- above all, exert maximum effort for the client's benefit.

The agent who acts otherwise is not acting in the best interests of the client. This is a requirement of Texas common law and the Texas Administrative Code (TAC), under the Rules of the Texas Real Estate Commission [22 TAC §535.2(b), 535.156(a),(b) and (c)]. Disloyalty of an agent to the principal or client is not only unethical and unprofessional, it is forbidden and illegal under the law governing real estate licensees. Disloyalty may be grounds for forfeiture of commission, loss of the license to practice, lawsuit for damages incurred by the client, and possible rescission of the sales or lease contract itself.

EXAMPLE: Broker Nancy and her friend, George, owned homes in the same subdivision. Nancy listed George's home when George was transferred to Alaska. Nancy also placed her home on the market about the same time she listed George's home for sale. Nancy showed both her home and George's home to buyer Alicia. Alicia fell in love with George's home and expressed an immediate desire to purchase it for cash. Nancy then persuaded Alicia to purchase her own home instead.

? QUESTIONS

1. Has Nancy breached her fiduciary duty of loyalty to George?

2. How could Nancy have avoided any question of a breach of her fiduciary duty?

Disclosure

A key point related to loyalty is the obligation of the agent to make a full, fair and timely disclosure to the client of all known facts relevant or material to the transaction. A *material* fact is one that a reasonable person might feel is important in choosing a course of action. Important disclosures by an agent to a client include

- the relationship between the client's agent and other parties to the transaction;

- the existence of other offers and the status of the earnest money deposit [22 TAC §535.156(a) and §535.159(b)];

- the buyer's financial condition;

- the agent's true opinion of the property's value [22 TAC §535.16(c);

- any commission split between a listing broker and another broker;

- the meaning of factual statements and business details contained in the contract; and

- all known facts that might affect the status of title to real estate.

Clearly, an agent who has actual knowledge of a property defect is liable to both the client and the customer if the defect is not disclosed. In addition, liability may exist if the agent fails to disclose facts that he or she *should have known* within the range of expertise expected of an agent. Thus, in addition to disclosure, the agent has a duty of discovery and a duty to investigate the many aspects of the transaction as they affect the client's decision making. Texas courts, however, have held that the real estate agent is not liable for *physical* inspection of the property for defects. This is the realm of licensed inspectors, not of brokers and salespersons [*Kubinsky v. Van Zandt Realtors,* 811 S.W.2d 711 (Tex. 1991)].

On the other hand, important facts affecting a client's decision fall within the broker's domain. In one case a buyer offered a seller a property as part of the down payment in the purchase of the seller's property; however, the listing broker failed to verify the appraised value of the property offered by the buyer. As a result, the broker was held liable for failure to disclose information that was important to the seller in making a decision to accept the buyer's offer.

Full disclosure relating to the property. Full disclosure to the client is required, regardless of whether the fact is favorable or unfavorable, whether the fact is found before or after the purchase contract is signed or whether disclosure might prevent the successful completion of the sale. Not only is the client entitled to know the same facts that the agent knows but the client is generally assumed, by law, to know what his or her agent knows. The duty of disclosure is greater to a client than to a customer. A *customer* is *not* entitled to facts about the client or the broker's opinion of value; however, the customer *is* entitled to information regarding material facts about the property, such as

- property defects;

- defects in the title;

- problems relating to the survey;

- flood plain information;

- rights of parties in possession (such as tenants); and

- environmental issues and/or property conditions that would affect the health or safety of occupants.

A *client* is entitled to all of the above *plus* full disclosure of information relating to the transaction and the other party to the transaction, such as

- the broker's opinion of the value of the property;

- possible negotiating strategies or options available to the client;

- motivation of the other party to buy or sell; and

- financial condition of the other party.

It is important that an agent clearly understand the disclosure issues as they relate to a client or a customer. A key distinction is that the interest of the client is paramount, although the customer must, at the same time, be treated honestly and fairly. It should be noted that treating the customer honestly and fairly is usually in the best interest of the client.

Full disclosure of relationships. The real estate agent must disclose to the client any special relationship that may exist between the broker and any of his or her associates and the other parties in the transaction. Because the client may rely on the agent's loyal advice and counsel, it is important to know what interest any agent involved in the transaction may have in the other party's decision. The agent must disclose, for example, whether the prospective buyer or seller is a relative or close friend of one of the broker's salespersons, whether the broker has an agreement with the buyer or seller to be compensated if and when the property is resold or whether the broker is loaning money to the buyer for the down payment.

The agent also must disclose if any compensation is to be received from the referral of business to companies controlled by the broker or others, such as appraisal, termite control, lender, title, escrow and property inspection services. Many brokers offer a number of these services in their offices, thus providing buyers and sellers with "one-stop shopping." When these services are discussed with the client or customer, there must be a disclosure that use of the broker-controlled services is optional.

Full disclosure of other offers. Unless instructed otherwise by the seller, the listing agent should continue to present all offers until the transaction is closed. For rental property, the agent should continue to submit offers until the tenant takes possession of the premises. The agent must submit, or at least communicate, all offers and counteroffers to the client, even those that he or she believes are too low or too high to warrant serious consideration. The offers may be oral or in writing or may or may not be accompanied by earnest money. The listing agent should disclose all offers presented *after* the acceptance of an offer to purchase or lease because the seller or landlord may want to negotiate these offers as secondary contracts. This decision is for the seller or landlord to make.

Although TREC Rule 22 TAC §535.156(a) states that the licensee shall have no duty to submit offers to the principal after the principal has accepted an offer, the contract forms promulgated by TREC on September 22, 1997, provide for the seller to continue to show the property for sale and accept backup offers unless otherwise agreed between the parties. The buyer can object to this provision and attempt to negotiate with the seller to remove the property from the market. If the seller continues to offer the property for sale, it is recommended that the agent warn the seller to handle all subsequent offers strictly as secondary contracts to avoid the danger of lawsuits for breach of contract or for interfering with existing contracts. The buyer has acquired *equitable title* to the property once a contract has been agreed to by all parties. Equitable title is the right of the buyer to expect to complete the sale and receive the title to the property once all the requirements of the contract are met.

Full disclosure of information. The seller's agent must disclose all information that would help the seller develop the best selling strategy, which means disclosing information the agent has about a buyer's level of price resistance or motivation to purchase. For instance, if the seller's agent is aware that the buyer is under pressure to complete a purchase in a short period of time, that information should be disclosed to the seller.

Full disclosure regarding status of earnest money deposits. Many listing agreements authorize the seller's broker to accept an earnest money deposit from the buyer. If the deposit is in the form of a postdated check or a promissory note, the broker must inform the seller. Otherwise, if the buyer defaults and the seller cannot collect on the note, the broker could be liable to the seller for the amount of the deposit to which the seller normally would be entitled.

According to the TREC contract forms, the buyer, not the broker, is responsible for depositing the earnest money with an escrow agent on final signing of the contract by all parties. In practice, in residential sales it is common for the licensee delivering the contract of sale to the title company also to deliver the earnest money check, because the title company is the most common holder of earnest money. For transactions involving other types of earnest money arrangements, it is incumbent on the seller's agent to check periodically with the escrow agent named in the contract to determine the status of the earnest money check and to keep the seller informed of all findings.

If the buyer asks the seller's broker to postpone the deposit of the earnest money check, the seller's broker should disclose this request to the seller and obtain written agreement between the parties to delay the deposit. Otherwise, the licensee holding the earnest money has one of two options: (1) to deposit it according to the contract or (2) to deposit it within a reasonable time, which is defined as "the close of business of the second working day after the execution of the contract by the principals" [22 TAC §535.159(i)].

Full disclosure of buyers financial condition. Frequently, a seller will make a decision to accept or reject a buyer's offer based on the buyer's financial standing. The seller's agent must disclose to the seller all information, good or bad, regarding the buyer's financial condition. This information is usually obtained directly from the buyer or the agent working with the buyer. The only exception is information that a licensee gains during the course of an agency relationship. For example, suppose the buyer had been represented by agent *A* in another transaction, and during this association agent *A* came to know the buyer's financial condition. This information was gained in confidence and cannot be disclosed to the seller, even though the seller is now *A*'s client.

Normally, the seller should make an independent evaluation of the buyer's finances on the basis of data collected from the buyer. Prudent sellers' agents or subagents will inform sellers that because they are not lenders or arrangers of credit, they are not in a position to verify or interpret the financial information supplied by the prospective buyer; however, they will use all possible skill to obtain such information for the seller's evaluation.

Because of the fiduciary relationship between the seller's agent, any subagents and the seller, the seller's agent or subagents must disclose

- any negative information that the agent has concerning the prospective buyer's financial situation. This is especially true when the seller is asked to carry a note for the buyer or allow an assumption of an existing loan that requires that the seller remain liable for repayment of the loan to the lender;

- facts that the buyer states or that the agent has learned independently—for instance, that the buyer has other property that must be sold before closing on the seller's property; and

- any information that affects the buyer's ability to obtain financing or gives the buyer an option to terminate the offer if financing is not obtained.

A buyer's agent has no duty to communicate negative information concerning the buyer's financial strength to the seller. Instead, the buyer's agent has a duty of confidentiality *not* to communicate to the seller the financial strength of the buyer's position unless given permission or direction to do so by the buyer-client. This does not mean the buyer's agent can misrepresent the buyer's financial strength by giving false or misleading information, only that information must not be disclosed unless the buyer gives specific permission.

Full disclosure of property value. Disclosure of property value is a very important part of an agent's fiduciary duty to the client. Real estate agents have a duty to inform their clients of their *opinion of the value* of the real estate being listed or shown. Agents employ many of the same techniques for valuing property as appraisers do, even though agents often have more limited training in appraisal methods. The opinion of a property's value is arrived at through studies of the sales of properties similar to the subject property, the value of the land and improvements and/or the value of the income the property might be expected to produce.

The agent is also liable for disclosure of sales prices of all comparable properties that the agent should have known through a reasonable review. An agent can be held liable to the client and customer for rendering a false opinion of value, because the agent is obligated to keep informed on market conditions. An agent is also liable for giving a wrong opinion of value to a client or customer if the opinion was negligently based on inaccurate comparisons or inaccurate application of appraisal methods [TRELA §15(a)(6)(W); 22 TAC §535.157; 22 TAC §535.156(d); DTPA §17.46(b)(5),(6),(7)]. These duties and the law are especially relevant in cases in which the seller directs the listing agent to underprice or overprice a property to achieve the seller's objectives. For example, the seller may want a particularly fast sale and may suggest that the property be placed on the market for less than market value to achieve this goal. The listing agent should document this request in an attempt to avoid future problems.

When a seller's agent learns of factors that change the value of the property after the listing is signed, disclosure of such factors must be made as soon as possible and certainly before the seller-client decides to accept or reject an offer. The price and terms of the listing may have to be adjusted in accordance with such changed conditions [TRELA §15(a)(6)(V) 22 TAC §535.156(c),(d)].

An agent *does not* have the obligation to give an opinion of value to a customer. Customers will usually form their opinions about the value of a particular property by comparing it with other properties they have seen for sale. Offers that customers submit generally reflect their perception of value based on all of the properties they have seen. Seller's agents have an obligation to encourage buyers to submit offers that are favorable to the seller.

Occasionally agents wish to purchase a property they have listed for a client. According to the rules of TREC, the agent must have given the seller-client an opinion of property value at the time of listing. If the seller's agent later attempts to negotiate an offer to purchase the seller-client's property for his or her own account, it is particularly important to inform the seller of any change in the property's value. It may be particularly advisable for the seller or broker to obtain an appraisal in these circumstances.

Full disclosure of commission split. The listing agent must disclose to the seller the existence of any fee-sharing arrangement with a cooperating broker (also known as the *other broker*). Although the exact amount of any split does not have to be revealed, it is better to disclose fully to the client the amounts to be split, with the rationale for doing so. This disclosure should be in writing, preferably in the listing agreement. [**Note:** It is a violation of TRELA §15(a)(6)(F) for a broker to pay a commission or fees to or divide a commission or fees with *anyone* (including attorneys) not licensed as a real estate broker or salesperson for compensation for services as a real estate agent; however, a broker is not prohibited from reducing a brokerage fee to either principal—buyer or seller.]

Full disclosure of contract provisions. Before signing (executing) any document that is intended to be legally binding, the licensee is obligated to discuss the provisions of the contract with the client and suggest that he or she seek competent legal advice. Competent legal advice is especially important when there are unusual matters or areas of confusion that can best be handled by an attorney. In fact, where it appears that an unusual matter should be resolved by legal counsel or that the document is to be acknowledged and filed of record, the licensee is required, by Texas law, to advise both parties in the transaction to seek legal counsel. Failure to do so is grounds for loss of license [22 TAC §537.11(e)].

Although licensees should not practice law or give legal advice, they are permitted to

- explain the provisions of contracts;

- disclose all pertinent facts of which the licensee has knowledge; and

- explain the meaning of factual or business details.

Of course, licensees who are also licensed attorneys would be allowed to give legal advice. However, rendering legal advice in a transaction where the attorney is also participating as a real estate licensee might create a conflict of interest within the Texas State Bar Association's Code of Ethics.

EXAMPLE: Buyer Brown is considering writing an offer to purchase a property that fits his idea of a perfect home. While reviewing the purchase contract, Brown asks Agent Allen if he will be obligated to purchase the property if he cannot obtain the financing he has asked for in the contract. Agent Allen explains the meaning of the paragraphs regarding financing and asks if Brown would like to seek legal advice for further inquiries.

? QUESTIONS:

1. Did Agent Allen practice law by explaining the terms relating to financing to Buyer Brown?

2. Under what circumstances would Agent Allen be practicing law?

Confidentiality

The duty of loyalty requires that the agent keep confidential any discussions, facts or information about the principal that should not be revealed to others. This is similar to the privileged information concept of a lawyer-client or doctor-patient relationship. The duty of confidentiality owed to a client extends to an affirmative responsibility to withhold from an unrepresented party such confidential information as the client's bargaining position, motivations for selling or buying, opinions of value, marketing and negotiating strategies, the seller's lowest acceptable price or the buyer's highest price and the client's financial position (unless the client is aware of and consents to the disclosure of such information). Licensees are prohibited from disclosing any confidential information gained during an agency relationship *even after the relationship has been terminated.*

EXAMPLE: Agent Maxwell has been working with buyer-customer Taylor for 3 weeks. Finally they find the perfect property for Taylor's business, and he is ready to offer $215,000 for the property, which is $15,000 less than the seller is asking. Maxwell believes that the owner would be happy to accept $195,000 and informs Taylor of his opinion.

? QUESTIONS

1. Has Maxwell breached his duty of confidentiality?

2. If so, what should Maxwell have done to avoid a breach?

There are limits to the duty to maintain confidentiality. Laws prohibit a licensee from withholding information regarding the condition of the property, the condition of the title and other material facts that any prudent person would need to make an informed decision to purchase. The duty of confidentiality is thus modified by a greater duty to the general public. Licensees have a legal requirement and duty to be honest and fair to the customer. For instance, it would be fair and honest for the seller's agent to reveal to the buyer any *known* hazardous conditions, such as the presence of lead-based paint. The customer has the right to pertinent information about the property but not to personal information about the seller.

Accounting

Monies received by a broker as a result of transactions such as purchase contracts or property management agreements are trust funds and are frequently held by the broker for the benefit of the principal. The funds must be held in an account that is separate from the broker's own account(s)—one that does not pay interest unless specifically authorized by the parties. Brokers who hold both their own funds and trust funds in a single account are considered to be *commingling* funds. Commingling is strictly forbidden by TRELA and is grounds for suspension or revocation of the broker's license. To lessen the risk of unintended commingling, brokers might consider having separate trust accounts for sales and for rentals.

Once a contract has been fulfilled or terminated, the broker must deliver the trust funds to the principal or appropriate party. If the funds have not been transferred within a reasonable time after a valid demand has been made, the broker may be subject to license revocation or suspension by TREC. In the event of a contract default, however, the broker or any other entity acting as escrow agent for earnest money may require that all parties sign releases before the earnest money is paid to either party.

As a general practice in Texas, most brokers in residential real estate sales do not hold earnest money in their own trust accounts. Instead, they insist that the principals in the transaction agree on a neutral escrow agent to hold the earnest money. Generally, the escrow agent is the same title company that will close the transaction and provide the title insurance.

■ Summary

In any given transaction, the decision to represent the seller exclusively, the buyer exclusively or both of them at the same time is a serious matter. Agents must understand their fiduciary responsibilities to clients and their general duties of fairness, honesty and good faith to customers. It is easy for salespersons in an automobile showroom to know whom they work for (client-employer) and whom they work with (customer). It is a more complex question in real estate, when salespersons can show a buyer in one day a property listed by their firm, an MLS listing, a For Sale by Owner (FSBO) property or even the salesperson's own home. The various relationships must be understood by all participants in the transaction. One way to understand is to recognize how and when agency relationships are created.

■ Key Points

- Agency occurs when one person, the agent, acts on behalf of another person, the principal (or client).

- There are a variety of agency relationships for agents, buyers and sellers to consider in every transaction.

- There are three general categories of agency: universal, general and special. Each category has a unique set of duties, responsibilities and liabilities for the principals.

- A general agency relationship is common between a broker and sponsored sales associates.

- A general agency relationship is common in property management situations.

- A special agency relationship is common between seller or buyer and the broker for the purchase or sale of property.

- The agent owes the fiduciary obligations to the client of obedience, loyalty, disclosure, confidentiality, accounting and reasonable care and diligence (OLD CAR).

- As a fiduciary, a real estate agent owes greater duties to a client than to a customer, and thus the risk of liability is greater.

- A fiduciary for one party still owes a duty of fairness and honesty to the party for whom the agent is not a fiduciary.

- Principals and licensees are not liable for *unknown* misrepresentations of other parties.

■ Suggestions for Brokers

Company training programs should stress the implications of agency relationships and the fiduciary duties imposed on the licensee when acting as an agent. The broker's associates must understand that unless care is exercised, the firm may become an agent of a principal when agency relationship was not intended. The associate should be instructed on the type of agency relationships promoted by the firm as well as the scope of authority when acting in those agency capacities. Brokers should be ever mindful that they are ultimately responsible for the acts of any broker or sales associate when those associates are acting within the scope of authority given to them by the broker.

■ Quiz

1. General agency commonly exists between the

   A. seller and the broker.
   B. buyer and the broker.
   C. sales associates and the broker.
   D. selling broker and the listing broker.

2. Special agency occurs when

   A. the principal gives an agent a limited authority to act on his or her behalf.
   B. the principal gives an agent authority to act for him or her in the operation of a business.
   C. a person operates a real estate brokerage business.
   D. a person operates a special real estate brokerage business.

3. A broker can buy a property listed with him or her under which of the following conditions?

   A. If a family member secretly purchases the property for more than the asking price
   B. Under no circumstances
   C. Only if the property is listed under an open listing
   D. Only if full disclosure is made to the seller of the broker's involvement as a purchaser

4. Which of the following statements is true of a listing agent?

   A. He or she must present every written offer to the seller.
   B. He or she may refuse to present an offer if it is too low.
   C. He or she must tell the buyer the seller's lowest acceptable price.
   D. He or she may tell the buyer the terms of a counteroffer the seller made yesterday.

5. A salesperson owes all of the following fiduciary duties *except* to

   A. inform the broker and the seller of material facts.
   B. be loyal to the best interests of the client.
   C. prepare a power of attorney for the buyer.
   D. obey the lawful instructions of the broker.

6. A listing agent tells a buyer-customer that the seller is under pressure to sell because of a pending divorce and possible foreclosure. Such disclosure is

   A. acceptable if it results in a sale.
   B. acceptable if no details of the foreclosure are disclosed.
   C. unacceptable because of the fiduciary duty owed the owner.
   D. unacceptable because the listing broker is the agent of the buyer.

7. Sally, as an agent for the seller, listed and subsequently sold George's town house. She did not tell George that a major zoning change in progress would allow business use in the area, thus increasing property values. Which of the following statements is true?

   A. Sally was not required to disclose the change because George never asked her.
   B. Sally was not required to disclose the change if George received his full asking price.
   C. Sally was required to disclose the change because it was a material and pertinent fact.
   D. Sally was required to disclose the change because the zoning laws require notice to all interested persons.

8. Which of the following is not a fiduciary obligation owed to a client?

   A. Obedience
   B. Accounting
   C. Confidentiality
   D. Inspection

9. A material fact is one that

   A. the client considers important.
   B. the customer considers important.
   C. a reasonable person might feel is important.
   D. the listing broker considers important.

10. A customer is entitled to all of the following material facts except

   A. the broker's opinion of value.
   B. the type and age of an existing roof.
   C. the lease termination date of the current occupant.
   D. repairs completed to correct the drainage problems.

■ Discussion Questions

1. What are the main duties a fiduciary owes to the principal?

2. What is the best procedure to use to present multiple offers? Suppose you have two written offers and a buyer telephones that she will better any offer. Do you tell the buyer the amount of the higher offer?

3. Why should you tell the seller about offers received after the seller has already accepted an offer?

4. If you act for the listing broker or as a subagent of the listing broker, how much information can you disclose to the buyer before you begin to act contrary to the best interests of your seller?

5. If you act for the buyer as a buyer's agent, how much information can you disclose to the seller or his or her agents before you begin to act contrary to the best interests of your buyer?

CHAPTER 3

Disclosure and Duties To Third Parties

In the previous chapter we discussed our fiduciary duties to clients, those parties the agent represents. The broker and the client (buyer or seller) are the parties to the agency contract; however, for the agency to be functional, a *third party* must be involved. A third party is the party to a transaction who is *not* represented by the agent. For example, if the licensee is representing a seller, the third party is the buyer. Conversely, if the licensee represents the buyer, the seller is the third party. In some transactions, both principals engage their own agent to represent their individual interests. In this case, the agent representing the seller would consider the buyer the third party. Likewise, the agent representing the buyer would consider the seller the third party. In any event, even though third parties are not clients, they are due certain duties by the licensees.

This chapter addresses the following:

Elements of Misrepresentation
Issue of Reliance
Watching What Is Said

■ DUTIES TO OTHERS (THIRD PARTIES)

Although a broker owes specific fiduciary duties to the client, under Texas Law the broker also owes general duties of honesty and fairness to *all* parties in a transaction. A great deal of confusion concerns the use of the word *fairly,* which remains in the Texas law. Perhaps more to the point for licensees, TREC rules specify that while the primary duty of the agent is to the client, the licensee "shall treat other parties to a transaction fairly" (22 TAC §531.1(1). Remember, *fairly* does not mean *equally* in the context of comparative duties owed to a client versus those owed to a customer. However, when *fair* or *fairly* is used in discussing the treatment of—and comparative duties owed to—one customer versus another customer, the concept of equal treatment is much more relevant. This is particularly germane when applying federal Fair Housing laws to the required treatment of members of protected classes.

Likewise, the listing broker has responsibilities to both seller and buyer, although it is clear that the responsibilities to each are different. The listing broker owes a buyer/customer duties of honesty, fairness, competency, good faith and disclosure of all material facts. While these duties are non-fiduciary in nature, they are strong duties under Texas law.

Moreover, the listing broker and any seller's subagent broker owe the buyer certain statutory duties and other duties under TREC rules of fairness, such as promptly presenting all offers and avoiding misrepresentation and false promises. The fact that the buyer is represented by a broker, does not diminish the duties of the listing broker to the buyer through the buyer's broker.

The duties of fairness to customers are not clearly defined—except where specifically mandated in federal or state laws, such as the Fair Housing Law. Nevertheless, a licensee must be honest at all times and levels when dealing with clients and customers.

■ AVOIDING DISCLOSURE AND MISREPRESENTATION PROBLEMS

The most common complaint of buyers against brokers relates to misrepresentation by brokers or the brokers' associates. The National Association of REALTORS® (NAR) reports that nearly two thirds of all complaints against members result from misrepresentation issues.

Misrepresentations may occur when a licensee makes a false statement to a potential buyer or when a licensee fails to disclose to the buyer important facts about the property. Licensees have a duty to disclose material facts affecting the value and desirability of a property. A buyer frequently asks a broker to describe a property and make representations in connection with a sale. The most common complaint concerns a listing broker's failure to point out material defects the broker knows of—or should have. In California, for instance, court rulings have identified "red flags" that should put the broker on notice that a problem exists—and should be brought to the buyer's attention. Such red flags include evidence of recent mudslides, obvious building code violations and drainage and soil settlement problems. In Texas, the broker, even if licensed as a real estate inspector, is neither expected nor even allowed to function as both broker and inspector in the same transaction. The licensee is, moreover, always responsible for revealing to a prospective buyer important negative facts about a property.

In most cases of liability, a threshold issue concerns the *materiality* of the issue and whether statements were *facts* or *opinions*. The materiality of the issue is based on misrepresentations of *factual matters* and whether such matters are important to reasonably prudent homebuyers in deciding to purchase.

Generally, statements of *opinion* are not considered appropriate grounds for a misrepresentation or fraud suit by a buyer or seller. This is based on the unlikelihood that buyers will rely on a licensee's opinion as the basis for a decision to purchase. Nevertheless, a licensee must take considerable care to clarify whether a statement is merely an opinion or a fact. For example, a licensee's "opinion" regarding easily verifiable factual matters such as the property boundaries could be interpreted by the buyer as a statement of fact. Should the statement prove incorrect, the licensee may be held liable. The licensee is well advised never to give opinions about factual matters. Furthermore, when giving opinions about non-verifiable matters, the licensee should make it unequivocally clear that the statement is an opinion, not based on fact.

To provide better disclosures to buyers, Section 5.008 of the Texas Property Code now requires a seller's disclosure notice for most residential resales. TREC has produced a form for licensees to help sellers meet the requirements under the Property Code (see Figure 3.1.). The form is called *Seller's Disclosure of Property Condition* and while not a *promulgated* form is widely used by licensees. According to TREC, this form "provides a vehicle for disclosure of defects or items in need of repair." Conditions such as the presence of lead-based paint, termite damage and flooding are also addressed. If the notice is not given prior to the effective date of the contract, the purchaser may terminate the contract for any reason within seven days after receiving the notice. TREC contract forms help facilitate compliance with the law. Consistent and proper use of this form gives buyers better information about the property and can help prevent lawsuits against the broker. It is argued that the TREC form lacks provisions of "timely notice" and may be less effective in avoiding litigation than the disclosure form prepared by the Texas Association of REALTORS® (TAR) for their members, which contains such language.

The listing agent will most likely obtain a complete factual statement from the seller by explaining the purpose and importance of the *Seller's Disclosure Form*. The seller (not the agent), should complete the form, and the agent should carefully explain each section of the form to ensure complete compliance with the law. Generally speaking, a good transaction starts with a good listing presentation and full disclosure of all material facts regarding the property. The following case illustrates the importance of the seller's disclosure statement as well as the issue of facts versus opinions.

FIGURE 3.1   **Seller's Disclosure of Property Condition Notice**

APPROVED BY THE TEXAS REAL ESTATE COMMISSION (TREC)   10-25-93

SELLER'S DISCLOSURE OF PROPERTY CONDITION

(SECTION 5.008, TEXAS PROPERTY CODE)

CONCERNING THE PROPERTY AT _____
(Street Address and City)

THIS NOTICE IS A DISCLOSURE OF SELLER'S KNOWLEDGE OF THE CONDITION OF THE PROPERTY AS OF THE DATE SIGNED BY SELLER AND IS NOT A SUBSTITUTE FOR ANY INSPECTIONS OR WARRANTIES THE PURCHASER MAY WISH TO OBTAIN. IT IS NOT A WARRANTY OF ANY KIND BY SELLER OR SELLER'S AGENTS.

Seller ☐ is ☐ is not occupying the Property. If unoccupied, how long since Seller has occupied the Property? _____

1. The Property has the items checked below [Write Yes (Y), No (N), or Unknown (U)]:

__Range	__Oven	__Microwave
__Dishwasher	__Trash Compactor	__Disposal
__Washer/Dryer Hookups	__Window Screens	__Rain Gutters
__Security System	__Fire Detection Equipment	__Intercom System
__TV Antenna	__Cable TV Wiring	__Satellite Dish
__Ceiling Fan(s)	__Attic Fan(s)	__Exhaust Fan(s)
__Central A/C	__Central Heating	__Wall/Window Air Conditioning
__Plumbing System	__Septic System	__Public Sewer System
__Patio/Decking	__Outdoor Grill	__Fences
__Pool	__Sauna	__Spa __Hot Tub
__Pool Equipment	__Pool Heater	__Automatic Lawn Sprinkler System

__Fireplace(s) & Chimney(Woodburning)	__Fireplace(s) & Chimney (Mock)	__Gas Lines (Nat./LP)
__Gas Fixtures	Garage: __Attached __Not Attached	__Carport
Garage Door Opener(s):	__Electronic	__Control(s)
Water Heater:	__Gas	__Electric
Water Supply: __City	__Well __MUD	__Co-op

Roof Type: _____   Age: _____ (approx)

Are you (Seller) aware of any of the above items that are not in working condition, that have known defects, or that are in need of repair? ☐ Yes ☐ No ☐ Unknown. If yes, then describe. (Attach additional sheets if necessary): _____

_____
_____

2. Are you (Seller) aware of any known defects/malfunctions in any of the following? Write Yes (Y) if you are aware, write No (N) if you are not aware.

__Interior Walls	__Ceilings	__Floors
__Exterior Walls	__Doors	__Windows
__Roof	__Foundation/Slab(s)	__Basement
__Walls/Fences	__Driveways	__Sidewalks
__Plumbing/Sewers/Septics	__Electrical Systems	__Lighting Fixtures
__Other Structural Components (Describe)		

_____
_____
_____

01A   TREC No. OP-H

FIGURE 3.1   **Seller's Disclosure of Property Condition Notice (continued)**

Seller's Disclosure Notice Concerning the Property at_____ Page 2   10-25-93
(Street Address and City)

If the answer to any of the above is yes, explain. (Attach additional sheets if necessary): _____
_____
_____

3. Are you (Seller) aware of any of the following conditions? Write Yes (Y) if you are aware, write No (N) if you are not aware.

___Active Termites (includes wood- ___Termite or Wood Rot Damage ___Previous Termite Damage
 destroying insects) Needing Repair

___Previous Termite Treatment ___Previous Flooding ___Improper Drainage

___Water Penetration ___Located in 100-Year Floodplain ___Present Flood Insurance
   Coverage

___Previous Structural or Roof ___Hazardous or Toxic Waste ___Asbestos Components
 Repair

___Urea-formaldehyde Insulation ___Radon Gas ___Lead Based Paint
___Aluminum Wiring ___Previous Fires ___Unplatted Easements
___Landfill, Settling, Soil ___Subsurface Structure or Pits
 Movement, Fault Lines

If the answer to any of the above is yes, explain. (Attach additional sheets if necessary): _____
_____
_____

4. Are you (Seller) aware of any item, equipment, or system in or on the Property that is in need of repair? ☐ Yes (if
you are aware) ☐ No (if you are not aware). If yes, explain (attach additional sheets as necessary). _____
_____

5. Are you (Seller) aware of any of the following? Write Yes (Y) if you are aware, write No (N) if you are not aware.

 ___ Room additions, structural modifications, or other alterations or repairs made without necessary permits or not in compliance
  with building codes in effect at that time.

 ___ Homeowners' Association or maintenance fees or assessments.

 ___ Any "common area" (facilities such as pools, tennis courts, walkways or other areas) co-owned in undivided interest with
  others.

 ___ Any notices of violations of deed restrictions or governmental ordinances affecting the condition or use of the Property.

 ___ Any lawsuits directly or indirectly affecting the Property.

 ___ Any condition on the Property which materially affects the physical health or safety of an individual.

If the answer to any of the above is yes, explain. (Attach additional sheets if necessary): _____
_____
_____

_____ _____ _____ _____
Date   Signature of Seller   Date   Signature of Seller

The undersigned purchaser hereby acknowledges receipt of the foregoing notice.

_____ _____ _____ _____
Date   Signature of Purchaser Date   Signature of Purchaser

01A TREC No. OP-H

EXAMPLE: *Kessler v. Fanning,* 953 S.W.2d 515, (Tex.App.-Fort Worth 1997). The Fannings purchased a property after having received the proper Seller's Disclosure of Property Condition form, which indicated that there were no drainage problems. The Fannings had the property inspected, and no drainage problems were detected even though it was raining at time of the inspection. However, after moving into the property the Fannings discovered drainage problems and sued the sellers, claiming violations of the Texas Deceptive Trade Practices Act (DTPA) for failing to disclose a material fact. The Fannings further claimed that they would not have purchased the home had they known of the drainage problems.

Although other issues had to be decided by the court, a key issue was whether the statements by the seller constituted misrepresentations or merely statements of opinion. The TREC disclosure form used by the sellers states that the form "is not a substitute for inspections or warranties" and that it contains "representations made by the owner(s) based on the owner's knowledge." The sellers claimed that the statements contained in the disclosure form were merely opinions and not statements of fact.

The court found, however, that the statements by the sellers met the three requirements for determining if a statement is a fact rather than opinion in that:

- the statements were specific rather than vague,

- the parties did not possess the same knowledge and

- the representations pertained to past rather than future conditions.

As statements of fact the representations contained in the disclosure form were considered deceptive and misleading. The court found in favor of the buyers.

QUESTIONS

1. Why was the broker not also found liable in this case?

2. The buyers had their own property inspector who indicated no drainage problems. Why was the seller not able to claim that the buyers relied on the inspector rather than their statements?

DISCUSSION

This case illustrates the importance of having the seller write a detailed, disclosure of property condition. The broker was able to show that the statements were those of the seller and that the broker did not know about—nor was it reasonable that he would have known about the drainage problems.

The argument that the buyer relied on the inspection report rather than the seller's disclosure statements may be a defense under some circumstances when no fraud has occurred. Nevertheless, the law states that an independent inspection that might have uncovered fraud does not prevent the recovery for fraudulent misrepresentations.

■ MATERIAL FACTS

One of the more vexing issues for licensees is determining what is, or is not, a material fact relating to a transaction. In the fourth edition of *The Language of Real Estate*, John W. Reilly defines and discusses a material fact as follows:

> Any fact that is relevant to a person making a decision. Agents must disclose all material facts to their clients. Agents must also disclose to buyers material facts about the condition of the property, such as known structural defects, building code violations and hidden dangerous conditions. Brokers are often placed in a no-win situation of trying to evaluate whether a certain fact is material enough that it needs to be disclosed to a prospective buyer, such as the fact that a murder occurred on the property 10 years ago or the fact that the neighbors throw loud parties. It is sometimes difficult to distinguish between "fact" and "opinion." The statement "real property taxes are low" is different from "real property taxes are $500 per year." Even though brokers act in good faith, they may still be liable for failure to exercise reasonable care or competence in ascertaining and communicating pertinent facts that the broker knew or "should have known."

Physical Material Facts

Generally speaking, the physical aspects of the property that may require disclosure are easier to identify than the non-physical issues. Physical issues may relate to any negative condition of the property itself, such as:

- foundation,
- previous flooding,
- roof problems,
- termite infestation or damage,
- electrical,
- plumbing,
- heating, ventilation and air conditioning (HVAC),
- well water and
- septic.

Obviously this list could include virtually any physical component of the property. When licensees know of problems in a property relating to these types of issues, disclosures must be made. As mentioned above, the seller in the *Seller's Disclosure of Property Condition* should reveal the negative condition of any of these types of matters; nevertheless, a buyer should be advised not to rely solely on these disclosures and hire licensed property inspectors and/or other professionals to inspect the property carefully. Further, the buyer should know that such inspections are not warranties and verify only that the inspected equipment was or was not functioning adequately at the time of inspection. The buyer should be informed that warranties are available through *residential service companies* which must be registered through TREC to offer such services in Texas.

Material Facts Relating to Title Issues

As important as the physical issues described above are those relating to the type and quality of title to be conveyed. Types of title may include *fee simple, defeasible fee* and *life estate*. Each of these types of ownership has a different value and the persons acquiring the property should be fully informed about them.

In addition to the type of title a purchaser receives there are concerns regarding the *quality* of the title. Licensees in Texas must advise buyers to determine the quality of the title by obtaining either an attorney's opinion of title, based on an abstract, or a policy of title insurance.

Abstracts of title are condensed versions of all records relating to the subject property beginning with the initial transfer from a sovereign government forward to the present owner. The abstract contains a chronology of all instruments filed into the property records; this may include taxes, judgments, releases and so on. Although abstractors make no judgments relative to the condition or quality of title, they are liable for failing to include or record properly all pertinent data. The abstract is then examined in detail by an attorney who evaluates the facts and submits a written report (opinion of title) on the condition of the title to the purchaser. The report is considered evidence of title for the current owner.

As both abstractor and attorney have liability for mistakes, purchasers often believe that title insurance is not necessary. Purchasers should know, however, that the liability is only for mistakes made to properly filed, truthful records. For example, documents could have been forged, unrecorded claims could exist, unknown heirs might surface—in these instances the property owner would have no recourse. If a purchaser seeks protection from such possibilities, the purchaser should obtain insurance.

Title insurance is a contract between the insurance carrier and the policyholder to indemnify the holder for defects in title up to the policy limits. Note that the insurer does not guarantee continued ownership, only compensation for losses up to the policy limits. Title insurance companies are regulated by the Texas Board of Insurance, and are authorized to issue Standard Texas Policies. The coverages, available endorsements, and exceptions relating to standard Texas policies that should be disclosed to buyers are shown below:

Standard coverage includes:

- Defects found in public records
- Forged documents

- Incompetent grantors
- Incorrect marital statements
- Improperly delivered deeds
- Lack of access to and from land
- Lack of good and indefeasible title

Standard exceptions in Texas policies are:

- Deed restrictions or covenants
- Existing liens listed in policy
- Unrecorded title defects
- Governmental rights of limitation and eminent domain
- Shortages in area or discrepancies in boundaries, encroachments, or overlapping of improvements
- Issues relating to bankruptcy
- Taxes for the current and subsequent years

Additional coverage (endorsements) may be purchased to include:

- Property inspection
- Rights of parties in possession (such as tenant's rights)
- Examination of survey
- Unrecorded liens not known of by policyholder
- EPA lien endorsement (concerning claims relation to EPA violations)
- Homestead or community property or survivorship rights
- Tax liability due to changes in land usage (rollback taxes)

Mortgagee's (lender's) title insurance. Title coverage for the lender is available and usually required when the purchaser secures a new loan on the purchased property. This sometimes is confusing when buyers who have negotiated title policies to be furnished by sellers are charged for a mortgagee's title policy at closing. This policy is a separate policy to ensure that the lender has a valid lien against the property. The amount of coverage is for the original loan amount and coverage decreases as the loan balance decreases, while the owner's title policy is for the sales price and remains constant. For these reasons, as well as the fact that the research is only required once, the price of a mortgagee's policy is considerably less when purchased in connection with an owner's title policy.

Material Facts Relating to Survey Issues

As with defects or flaws in the title to the property, any known problems relating to the physical description of the property must be disclosed. These problems may include discrepancies in the area of the property, boundary lines, encroachments or the overlapping of improvements from one property onto the property of another. Note that these types of problems are specifically excepted from the standard title policy as shown above.

Buyers should be advised not to rely on measurements furnished by the seller, measurements of a licensee or their own measurements, but the measurements of a registered professional land surveyor. Additionally, a buyer should be alerted that previous surveys, perhaps furnished by the seller, should not be relied on; the buyer should obtain a new survey. Surveys are generally required when:

- conveying a portion of a given tract of land,
- obtaining a mortgage loan,
- government entities acquire land through condemnation procedures,
- showing the location of new or existing improvements, and
- determining legal descriptions of properties.

■ STIGMATIZED PROPERTIES

Another type of disclosure issue involves stigmatized properties. Stigma refers to a perception of conditions or events (real or imagined) related to a property that reduce in the marketability or value of the property. Stigmas may be classified as *purely psychological stigmas* or *physical stigmas*.

Purely Psychological Stigmas

Purely psychological stigmas are those that occur as a result of real or imagined events, at the property, that have no actual physical impact on the property or the occupants. An example of this type of stigma is a death occurring on the property as a result of natural causes, accident, murder, suicide or an AIDS-related illness. A stigma may also arise from a notorious event or individual associated with the property. Highly publicized stigmatized properties include the apartment building in which Jeffrey Dahmer housed his victims, the McDonald's restaurant in California, the Luby's restaurant in Killeen, Texas, and O.J. Simpson's home in Buckingham Estates. Of the four, only the Luby's restaurant building is standing today—the others have been demolished as a result of severe stigma although in none of the cases were the buildings physically impacted by the events. In the O.J. Simpson case, the alleged crimes did not even occur on the property, but rather, the stigma arose from the fact that Mr. Simpson lived in the house. The damage to these properties was purely psychological.

Purely psychological stigmas raise a number of issues for licensees including materiality, fact or fiction, duration of the stigma, and laws relating to disclosure of certain events. Suppose it is rumored that Satanic rites have been performed in a property by a previous occupant, or that a murder occurred at a property ten years ago or that a previous occupant had an AIDS-related illness—would these issues require disclosure? The answers to some of these questions may be found in Texas law. In 1993, the Texas legislature passed certain statutes relating to disclosure, later incorporated in to The Real Estate License Act:

SECTION 15E. Notwithstanding any other provision of this Act or any other law, a licensee shall have no duty to inquire about, make a disclosure related to, or release information to whether a:

(1) previous or current occupant of real property had, may have had, has, or may have AIDS, HIV-related illnesses, or HIV infection as defined by the Centers for Disease Control of the U.S. Public Health Service: or

(2) death occurred on a property by natural causes, suicide, or accident unrelated to the condition of the property.

It should be noted that on the issue of AIDS-related disclosures the statutes do not prohibit disclosure, but merely relieve the licensee of a duty to disclose. Further guidelines on this issue may be found in the 1988 Fair Housing Amendment Act, which added persons with handicaps as a protected class. AIDS-HIV-related illnesses are contained within the definition of a handicap. As a result, statements by the Department of Housing and Urban Development (HUD) make it illegal for licensees to make *unsolicited* disclosures regarding an occupant or prior occupant with AIDS-HIV-related problems. In addition, HUD advises that licensees not respond to *direct questions* relating to these matters *even if* the licensee has actual knowledge that an occupant or prior occupant has, or has had an AIDS-HIV-related illness. Although HUD has not produced an acceptable statement, the National Association of REALTORS® in their Legal Liability Series relating to property disclosures, recommends the following response when their members are asked questions relating to these issues:

It is the policy of our firm not to answer inquiries of this nature one way or the other since the firm feels that this information is not material to the transaction. In addition, any type of response to such inquiries by me or other salespeople of our firm may be a violation of the federal fair housing laws. If you believe that this information is relevant to your decision to buy the property, you must pursue this investigation on your own.

In relation to the four classifications of causes of death—natural causes, accident, suicide and homicide—Texas Law, as quoted above, requires that only a homicide be affirmatively disclosed. However, it is reasonable to believe that many buyers might be affected negatively if any type of death has occurred at the property. Remember that any type of death (or other issue) may be disclosed with the permission of the client. A licensee who is concerned about such matters should discuss the issue with the seller and, if not satisfactorily resolved, should consider refusing the listing.

Physical Stigmas

Physical stigmas arise when some negative or detrimental physical or environmental condition exists that may not directly affect the property but may affect the health or safety of the occupants. These conditions may have *real* or *imagined* health-related problems, but in either case the property suffers a loss in marketability or value. Problems in this area may include asbestos, lead hazards, electromagnetic fields (EMFs), radon, chlorofluorocarbon emissions, hazardous waste disposal, underground storage tanks, and soil or groundwater contamination.

Although there is much conjecture regarding the true health risks of many of these problems, property values may be impacted when the public becomes aware of such a condition. In her article, "When Bad Things Happen to Good Properties" (*Tierra Grande,* April 1999) Jennifer Hoffman cites the asbestos scare of the 1970s as an example;

> The fibrous material was commonly used in the construction industry for decades until studies began to demonstrate that the asbestos fibers could infiltrate the lungs—a potentially fatal condition. Hitting the papers, this news caused a near panic in some real estate markets. "Many properties containing asbestos were stigmatized, becoming unmarketable virtually overnight," says Guntermann.

> With more scientific information available, public fear and concern in the real estate community dissipated and became more narrowly focused on a smaller sample of properties than originally suspected.

Although today the presence of asbestos requires disclosure to potential buyers, the stigma is much reduced due to better knowledge and understanding of remedies.

Guidelines for Disclosure of Stigmatized Properties

The National Association of REALTORS®, in their Legal Liability Series, offers their members the following guidelines in the publication Property Disclosures—What You Should Know:

- **Determine whether the information is fact or fiction**. Investigate the validity of the information by checking sources such as newspaper accounts or reports from state or local agencies. Separate rumor form reality. If the stigma is based on rumor and not on facts which can be confirmed, there may be no obligation to disclose. If, on the other hand, the stigma turns out to be factual, e.g., there was in fact a murder on or near the property, you should proceed to the next step.

- **Check state law**. In Texas the law requires disclosure of all physical facts regarding the property. With non-physical matters, the requirement to disclose will hinge on the materiality of the matter.

- **Determine materiality**. To analyze the materiality of a set of facts which may produce a stigma, one must determine whether knowledge of those facts would affect the willingness of a reasonable person in deciding whether to buy the property or the amount of money to offer or pay for the property.

  Most stigmatized property cases involve stigmas that are less sensational than, for example, a multiple-murder on the property.

Less sensational stigmas may or may not impact the market value of the property. Whether or not the problem is a high-profile one, however, it is necessary to assess how reasonable persons would react to the information and if they are less likely to desire to purchase the property.

Alternately, one should consider how the "market" would judge such a property and whether it can be objectively concluded that the market value of the property is less because of the property's history. If this analysis results in the conclusion that the facts and stigma may have an impact on the buying decision of prospective purchasers, the facts creating the stigma are probably material and should be disclosed.

- **Discuss disclosure with the sellers**. A listing agent who concludes that the stigma-producing facts are material and need to be disclosed should also discuss with sellers the basis for his conclusions and his intended course of action. The sellers need and deserve to understand the salesperson's analysis and why the particular facts may affect the marketing and sale of their property and, thus, must be disclosed. Often sellers can understand the problem better if they are asked to consider themselves in the position of a prospective purchaser and whether or not they would want the factual information before deciding to purchase or what to offer for the property. Discussing the matter with the sellers up front avoids objections and controversy later about why the particular facts were disclosed to prospective purchasers.

- If the sellers refuse to agree to disclose what the listing broker (or a subagent working with the listing broker) has determined to be a material factor regarding the property, the agents should strongly consider terminating the listing or other involvement in the transaction.

Although such guidelines are helpful, the licensee should seek competent legal counsel whenever there is doubt regarding disclosure issues. The following case illustrates the difficulty of determining the materiality of facts regarding stigmatized property.

 EXAMPLE: *Sanchez v. Guerrero*, 885 S.W.2d 487 (Tex. App.—El Paso, 1994). The Guerreros purchased a VA foreclosed property through broker Sanchez. After closing the Guerreros discovered that a prior occupant of the property had been accused (although acquitted) of child molestation in the property. Upon learning this information, the new buyers moved out and later sold the property at a loss. The Guerreros then sued Sanchez, alleging that the broker was aware of the circumstance and willfully withheld the information in order to induce them to buy the property. The suit brought under the Texas Deceptive Trade Practices Act was won by the Guerreros, finding that the broker took advantage of the buyer's lack of knowledge of real estate to a grossly unfair degree and supported a claim for mental anguish as well as damages. The jury awarded the Guerreros $120,000 in actual damages, $20,000 for closing costs, and $100,000 for mental anguish.

? QUESTIONS?

1. What implication does this have for licensees regarding disclosure of events that may not have happened but apparently created a stigmatized property?

2. What types of crimes that may or may not have occurred on the property must be disclosed?

3. Would the broker be exposed to a potential libel suit from the acquitted defendant for disclosing this information to the Guerreros?

DISCUSSION

Unfortunately, this case raises more questions than it resolves. The fact that a prior occupant had been accused of a notorious crime, even though acquitted was sufficient to create a stigma which would have required disclosure by the broker. The broker admitted knowledge of the circumstances surrounding the property, but felt that the alleged crime had no direct or physical impact on the property and therefore did not need to be disclosed. Further, the defendant argued that as the accused had been acquitted it would have been inappropriate and potentially libelous to make such a disclosure. The court disagreed on the basis that the information was public knowledge and that the story had been reported in the media. All in all, a very troubling case for Texas brokers.

Megan's Law and SB 1650. A related issue to *Sanchez v. Guerrero* is the federal law concerning the registration of individuals convicted of child molestation and other dangerous sex crimes. The federal government now requires states to register sex offenders living in their communities. The federal law requiring such registration is commonly known as Megan's Law.

Current Texas law (SB1650) requires released sex offenders to register with local law enforcement agencies and be photographed and fingerprinted. This information must be submitted to superintendents of public schools and to the administrators of private primary and secondary schools in the district where the offender resides. Additionally, enforcement officials must publish in a local newspaper information regarding the offender including the name, age and gender, a brief description of the offense, the street name, zip code and municipality of residence and the person's risk level generally. If the individual is determined to be high risk (level 1) then notices must be mailed by the Texas Department of Safety to each residential address within three blocks in a subdivided area, or within one mile in an area that is not subdivided.

Some states, including Texas, have given specific exemptions to some real estate licensees from any requirement to disclose such matters, leaving the issue to law enforcement. The Texas rule exempts owners of single-family residences and the owner's agents from a duty to disclose information relating to sex offenders [SB 1650 § 4(e)] to prospective buyers or tenants. Interestingly, no mention is made of the duties relating to an agent of a buyer.

As the requirements for disclosure are not specifically defined for some licensees, the issue falls under the general rules for disclosure of material facts to potential purchasers regarding a property. It would appear, then, that an agent other than a seller's agent, who knows that a registered sex offender lives in close proximity to a subject property must disclose this information. Such disclosures should be approached with great care, citing the source of information and warning that the information may be incorrect or incomplete. A licensee is cautioned from making any related statements based on rumor or hearsay.

Even when a licensee has no specific knowledge that a sex offender lives in close proximity, it may be advisable to add this issue to a general checklist of items that may be of concern to prospective buyers, including guidance on where to obtain such information. Such sources include local law enforcement agencies and lists published on Internet websites.

Licensees should be aware that Megan's Law is controversial and is being challenged as a violation of an individual's constitutional right to privacy. The information provided here is general and is based on laws at time of publication. These laws are subject to change, and licensees should seek competent legal counsel when dealing with these matters.

Prohibited Disclosures to Third Parties

Licensees should take care during disclosure to avoid volunteering information about or responding to questions relating to protected classes under federal, state or local fair housing laws. Prohibited disclosures relate to race, color, religion, sex, national origin, familial status or handicap. Such questions may be asked by buyers in relation to specific owners and/or properties, or neighborhoods in general. If the potential buyers have concerns relating to these matters, they should be advised to seek information through their own independent investigations.

In addition to the matters described above, care must be taken not to volunteer to the buyer so much information that the client's negotiating position is compromised. Suppose the licensee knows that the sellers are anxious to sell as they have just completed the purchase of another home. If the broker discloses this information and the prospective buyer chooses to offer substantially less than the listing price, the seller can claim that the listing broker acted contrary to the seller's best interests and cancel the listing. The buyer obviously would like to know that the seller is considering a price reduction, but the buyer is not entitled to disclosure of this information.

What if the seller orders the listing broker not to disclose a material fact, such as a basement that floods? If such an order is given early in the listing period, the broker should decline the listing and refuse to work with this seller. But if the order comes two days before closing, after the broker has fully performed his or her obligations, should the broker disregard the instruction, make the disclosure and protect the earned commission, even if the disclosure prevents the sale? Whenever full and fair disclosure of a material fact is not made, the real estate agent is at risk. The broker has an independent duty to the buyer to take reasonable steps to avoid giving the buyer false information or concealing material facts. Seek immediate legal counsel in these situations. It is not a good idea to continue to market the property until you have resolved the problem.

Liability for Misrepresentation

To file a successful misrepresentation claim against a broker, the plaintiff must prove that

- the broker made a misstatement (oral or written) to the buyer or failed to disclose a material fact to the buyer;
- the broker either knew or should have known that the statement was not accurate or that certain undisclosed information should have been disclosed;
- the buyer reasonably relied on such statement and
- the buyer was damaged as a result.

Element of reliance. Courts have held that the buyer is entitled to relief if the representation was a material inducement to the contract, even though the buyer may have made efforts to discover the truth and did not rely wholly on the representation. Also, "agency is no defense"; that is, it is generally not a defense that the broker merely passed along information that the seller provided—for example, the amount of taxes or the connection to the sewer system. The seller has a duty not to misrepresent, and the broker's duty stems from the seller's duty.

In fixing liability or in applying remedies, it makes no difference whether the misrepresentation was intentional or negligent. The most common remedies available include:

- monetary damages,
- rescission of the contract, and
- forfeiture of the broker's commission.

Watch What Is Said

Brokers must carefully consider their statements to buyers and sellers. The broker is considered the real estate expert; therefore, the consumer relies on what the broker says, even when the broker does not act as the buyer's agent. Following is a short list of broker statements that *never* should be made:

- No need to get a title search. I sold this same property last year, and there was no title problem.
- Don't worry, the seller told me by phone I could sign the contract for her.
- If it helps you make up your mind about the price to offer on my listing, the seller countered a $130,000 offer last week with $135,000.

- I won't be able to present your offer until the seller decides on the offer submitted yesterday.

- I can't present your offer yet. We have a contract working.

- I can't/won't present your offer with that type of contingency clause in there.

- Go ahead and make an offer. If you can't get financing, you don't have to buy anyway and you'll still get your earnest money back.

- I can't submit your offer without earnest money. It's not legal.

- Trust me. I can word a contingency clause in such a way that you can back out whenever you want.

■ Summary

In addition to the fiduciary duties owed to a client a licensee must be aware of duties to third parties to the agency transaction. These duties include honesty, fairness, and a duty to disclose material facts regarding the property.

Material facts are important facts that may affect the decision to purchase or the price to offer. These facts may relate to physical attributes, title and survey problems, as well as certain stigmas that may have been attached to the property. These stigmas may be *purely psychological,* stemming from events that may have occurred in the property but that do not directly affect the structure, such as a death on the property. Other sources of stigma are *physical psychological* issues relating to environmental or other conditions surrounding the property that may affect the health or safety of the occupants, such as electromagnetic fields or radon gas.

Licensees should be constantly alert for circumstances or conditions that require disclosure and ensure that such disclosures are made in writing. In matters where the licensee is unsure of a disclosure issue, the licensee should consult a competent attorney.

■ Key Points

- An agency contract is a two-party agreement in which the client engages an agent to represent his or her interests; however, agency becomes functional due to a *third party*, the party to the transaction who is not represented by the agent.

- Licensees should take considerable care in avoiding misrepresentations to clients or third parties. Misrepresentations may occur by misstatements or by the omission of important facts by the licensee.

- While duties owed to a third party are not fiduciary duties, they are strong and include a duty to treat the third party fairly and honestly. In addition, the licensee is obligated to disclose any *material facts* regarding the property that might affect the buyer's decision to purchase the property or the amount the buyer would be willing to pay.

- Licensees should be certain that affected residential sellers complete the "Seller's Disclosure of Property Condition" form in complete detail and that, whenever possible, the potential buyer receives a copy before signing an offer to purchase.

- Material facts are those facts that would affect the buyer's decision to buy, or the amount of money to be offered for the property and include:

  - Physical condition

  - Title issues

  - Survey issues

  - Stigmatized properties

- Stigmas may be created from *purely psychological* sources such as the reaction of a purchaser to a death that may have occurred on the property, or from *physical conditions* outside the property that may have negative health or safety impact on the occupants. Examples of physical stigmas are exposure to radon gas or electromagnetic fields.

- The National Association of REALTORS® suggests the following guidelines when dealing with stigmatized properties:

  - Determine whether the information is fact or fiction

  - Check state law

  - Determine materiality

  - Discuss disclosure with the seller

- Although a licensee has a duty to disclose material facts to a third party, care should be exercised not to disclose confidential non-material information to a third party that could be detrimental to the best interest of the client.

■ Suggestions for Brokers

Research indicates that a key reason for complaints against licensees across the nation relates to misrepresentation or omission of important information to clients and customers. In response to this problem, brokers should encourage associated licensees to participate in continuing education efforts in this area. Further, a well designed, ongoing legal issue program is strongly recommended as a part of company training. Keep in mind that the laws governing disclosure are of a dynamic nature and must be reviewed carefully and frequently.

■ Quiz

1. Title Insurance Companies in Texas are regulated by the

    A. Texas Board of Insurance.
    B. Texas Real Estate Commission.
    C. Texas Attorney General.
    D. U.S. Attorney General.

2. Title Coverage for the lender is called

    A. Mortgagor's Title Insurance.
    B. Mortgage Company Title Insurance.
    C. Title Commitment.
    D. Mortgagee's Title Insurance.

3. The buyer should only rely on measurements furnished by

    A. the seller's previous survey.
    B. the listing agent.
    C. the registered professional land surveyor.
    D. all of the above.

4. On the issue of AIDS related disclosures

    A. the statutes prohibit disclosure.
    B. the statutes do not prohibit disclosure.
    C. the licensee may follow their best judgment.
    D. HUD requires the licensee to respond to a direct question from the buyer.

5. Under Megan's Law, states:

    A. may choose to ignore Megan's Law.
    B. must develop procedures for registering sex offenders.
    C. must require licensees to disclose registered sex offenders.
    D. may not develop their own rules relating to registration of sex offenders.

6. An agent of the buyer should disclose information regarding a convicted child molester in close proximity to a subject property

    A. if they have actual knowledge.
    B. if the seller gives authorization to disclose.
    C. even if it is only rumor.
    D. only if the buyer asks.

7. A seller states that he will list his home with you only if you do not reveal to prospective buyers that the police have twice raided the house next door for suspected drug activity. You should

    A. take the listing as long as there was no conviction.
    B. take the listing but reveal the information to prospective buyers.
    C. decline the listing and refuse to work with this seller.
    D. refer the seller to another agent in your office and take a referral fee.

8. The listing agent tells the buyer that the seller installed a new air conditioner as agreed in the contract, when in fact the seller only refurbished the existing air conditioner. The licensee is

   A. not liable since his misrepresentation was not intentional.
   B. not liable since his misrepresentation was not negligent.
   C. not liable since he only passed on the seller's representation.
   D. liable.

9. A property whose value or marketability has been affected by conditions or events related to the property

   A. is considered unsaleable.
   B. is considered stigmatized.
   C. is considered valueless by appraisers.
   D. may not legally be sold until the condition is corrected.

10. A property whose value has been diminished by a murder occurring on the property has suffered which of the following?

   A. Physical stigma   C. Incurable obsolescence
   B. Curable obsolescence   D. Purely psychological stigma

■ Discussion Questions

1. Presume that you have learned from a neighbor that a property that you are attempting to list was the site of a death that occurred by natural causes. How would you approach the seller regarding this matter?

2. List the conditions or circumstances regarding a property that you consider to be important in making a decision to purchase. Compare your list with others.

3. In reference to question 2, how do the comparative lists illustrate the difficulty in determining the *materiality* of an issue?

Creation and Termination of Agency

Few people, including many licensees, know the acts, conditions, expectations and statements that can unintentionally turn an ordinary broker into an agent for one or more parties. It is in the best interests of all parties to a real estate transaction to understand the rules that govern agency. This is particularly important for licensees to enable them to establish when their responsibilities begin and which set of legal duties they owe—and to whom. Many professional publications, standards of professional conduct and state licensing laws focus on the strict fulfillment of the rules of conduct for an agent. However, few offer exact determinations of when an agency relationship is created and to whom fiduciary duties are owed.

Licensees must know and understand the dynamics of agency and are responsible for strict compliance with the law of agency. This chapter introduces the concepts of how and when agency is created as well as how the relationship may be terminated. This knowledge will lay the foundation for understanding one of the most vital aspects of real estate practice today.

This chapter addresses the following:

How and When Agency Is Created
Express Agency
> *Implied Agency*
> *Ostensible Agency or Agency by Estoppel*
> *Agency by Ratification*
> *Gratuitous Agency and Compensation*

Important Issues
> *Legal Effect*
> *Constructive or Imputed Notice*
> *Professional and Ethical Responsibility*

How Agency Is Terminated
> *Time*
> *Actions of Principals and Agents*
> *Operation of Law*

Duties of Agency That Continue

■ How and When Agency is Created

We know that an agency relationship generally is created when one person authorizes another to act on his or her behalf and to exercise some degree of authority and discretion while acting in this capacity. In most cases, the agreement must be mutual; that is, the principal must authorize the agent to act on his or her behalf, and the agent must agree to do so. The agent may be empowered to do many of the things the principal could do but has chosen not to do. Typically, the agency relationship is created by some spoken or written agreement between the parties, but as will be shown, agency can be created by other, less formal means.

The fact that a person licensed as a real estate broker or salesperson performs a service for a consumer is not, by itself, sufficient to create an agency relationship. A real estate licensee's role is to give valuable service both to clients and to customers. The creation of an agency relationship requires more than just giving benefits and services. It requires *consent and control.* Once created, the agency relationship requires that the licensee place the interest of the client above his or her personal interests in the transaction. The licensee, as an agent, becomes an advocate of the principal in dealing with third parties and is obligated to protect the interests of that person.

As stated earlier, an agency relationship ideally results from mutual consent between the principal and the agent. In this case the agent agrees to act on the principal's behalf and is subject to the principal's control. Formalities, are not required, however, and an agent does not need a license, written contract or receipt of a commission or fee for an agency relationship to exist (see Figure 4.1).

While it is desirable for the agent and the principal to enter into a written agreement, it is not required. Most states, including Texas, require a written agreement, if the broker wants to have the option of bringing a lawsuit for a commission should the client default on the agreement. Texas also requires written permission to perform specific acts, such as advertising or placing the broker's sign on the property.

FIGURE
4.1

Elements *Not* Essential To Create an Agency Relationship

Not Essential for Agency

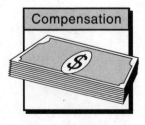
Compensation

Writing

Contract

License

Agency can be created by an oral agreement between the agent and the principal. The prudent broker will, however, establish a written contract as soon as possible. The written agreement should, at a minimum, address the issues relating to the duties of the agent and principal and the expectations for compensation, and it should be sufficient to protect the interests of both parties.

Some form of authorization from the principal is needed for the agent to act on behalf of the principal in dealing with others. The principal must delegate authority to act to the agent and the agent must consent to act, or no agency exists. Licensees should be clear about their authority to act for others.

Specific authorization may come in different forms—express or implied—and by different means—words, actions or, in some cases, by inaction. Agency may be classified as

- express agency

- implied agency,

- ostensible agency or agency by estoppel,

- agency by ratification or

- gratuitous agency.

It would be helpful for you to refer to Figure 4.2 during your study of these topics.

Express Agency

Express agency is the agency relationship that is created when a principal engages or employs an agent to act for him or her. In legal terms, the word *express* means *clear, definite, explicit, unmistakable* and *unambiguous*. In carrying out the duties of an express agency agreement, the agent acquires *express authority* to act for the principal. In practice this authority is created when a principal authorizes an agent to act for him or her by specifying certain acts, functions or duties that the agent should perform. Remember that these instructions may be either written or oral. Generally, the more specific the agreement, the better for both the agent and the principal. Some states require such an agreement of representation to be in writing under both the licensing law and other laws relating to oral versus written contracts. In Texas, the authorization may be in writing or by an oral agreement between the principal and the broker. The obligations of the agent (broker) and the principal are the same, whether the agreement is in writing or oral; however, if a broker wishes to have the right to bring a lawsuit for payment of a commission or fee for services, the agreement *must* be in writing. The agreement can be a simple note or memorandum that includes an agreement to compensate the broker for services performed.

The two most common express agency agreements used by brokers in sales transactions are written *listing contracts* and *buyer representation contracts*. Generically, these agreements are referred to as *broker employment agreements*. In written listing contracts the broker is authorized to represent a seller or landlord in the sale or lease of that principal's property. The

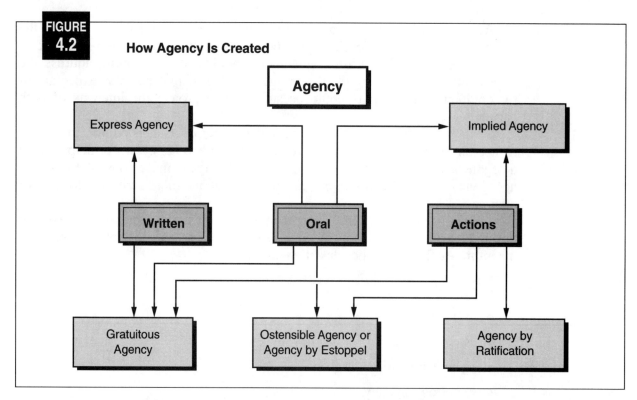

FIGURE 4.2

How Agency Is Created

written *buyer-tenant representation agreement* employs the broker to represent the buyer or tenant in the purchase or lease of a property. These written agency contracts are usually quite detailed. They attempt to clarify the rights and obligations of both the principal and the agent and include provisions for compensation when the agent's duties have been performed. These contracts will be discussed in detail in a later chapter.

Implied authority (not to be confused with implied agency) is a concept that is applicable to both express agency and implied agency (discussed below). Implied authority is authority not specifically granted to the agent but necessary or *customary* if the agent is to perform his or her agency duties, and it is implied by the principal's actions. Due to the varied functions required of real estate agents, it is unlikely that the entire scope of an agent's activities could be stated in an express written agreement such as a listing agreement. The agent, therefore, may also acquire certain authority to act for the principal by implied authority. For example, a listing contract may not specifically outline each and every tool that the agent may employ in marketing the property. However, when owners instruct agents to make their best efforts to sell their properties, it is implied that the agents have the authority to advertise, conduct open houses, distribute flyers and so on. Note that this type of authority is created *between the agent and principal* and does not require some third party's reliance or actions to become operational.

Implied Agency

Implied agency (not to be confused with implied authority) occurs when there is no express agreement that the broker will act as an agent for a party. The actions or words of the broker and the party may lead the party to believe that the broker is representing the party's interests. This often occurs when a licensee who is working with a buyer-customer with no intended representation makes statements or performs actions that lead the customer to believe the licensee has become the customer's agent.

In the past licensees were not accustomed to discussing and confirming whom they represented when meeting with third parties. As a result, unrepresented buyers often assumed that licensees who were showing them properties were the buyer's representatives. Those buyers were unaware of the fact that the licensees legally represented the sellers.

Courts generally look to the actions of a broker and to the reliance by a buyer on a licensee to determine if an implied agency relationship existed between broker and buyer. Because formalities are not required, courts may hold that an agency arrangement was implied, based on the intentions of the broker and the alleged principal, as shown by their actions and/or words. Even though a broker is the seller's agent, the broker could be held to be acting as the buyer's agent as well. Courts will ask the question, "Did the broker act under the alleged principal's direction and control?"

 EXAMPLE: Buyer Betty contacts Bay Realty, seeking to purchase a four-unit rental building. Sally, a licensee with Bay Realty, agrees to work with Betty; however, Betty signs no representation contract. Sally shows ten properties listed by her company and other real estate companies and negotiates unsuccessfully on two of those properties. During the negotiations Sally gives advice and opinions to Betty Buyer. After the two unsuccessful attempts to negotiate a purchase, Sally tells Betty not to despair, as she is sure that she can locate the "perfect property." Sally continues to seek, and ultimately finds, a four-unit rental building that suits Betty's needs and qualifications. Sally then obtains the listing on the four-unit building from owner Harry on behalf of Bay Realty. Betty Buyer and the seller enter into a contract for the purchase of the property.

? QUESTIONS

1. Did Sally represent Betty during the negotiation on the two unsuccessful contracts? If so, when did the representation begin?

2. Did Sally's actions imply to Betty that Sally represented her? If so, what actions would give this impression?

Disclosure and clarification should lessen the chances of creating an implied agency. However, a licensee who behaves like a buyer's agent, even though bound to an express written agreement to represent the seller, nevertheless will be deemed an implied agent of the buyer. Licensees must be careful of their actions, even after they disclose their agency arrangements in writing. The conduct of the parties can result in the creation of an agency relationship, even if a written agreement asserts that no agency exists or that the parties never intended for an agency relationship to exist.

Ostensible Agency or Agency by Estoppel

The word *ostensible* means "for all appearances." In agency law, *ostensible agency* and *agency by estoppel* (when a court does not allow a principal to deny that agency existed) are based on a third party's being led to believe that a licensee was acting as an agent of another party. If the actions of a principal led a reasonable person to assume that a licensee was acting on his or her behalf, then ostensible agency or agency by estoppel could have occurred. In that event, a court would likely prevent the principal from denying that an agency relationship existed. In effect, if a principal allows a licensee to "walk like an agent, talk like an agent and act like an agent," third parties will reasonably be allowed to presume that the licensee *is an agent* for that principal.

This concept could apply either before a formal agency agreement is created or after it expires. For example, presume that a seller allows his or her "former agent" to show and advertise his or her property after the listing contract expires. During this period of "unofficial representation" a buyer purchases the property and, after closing, discovers that the licensee has made misrepresentations regarding the property. The buyer later sues the seller, claiming misrepresentations were made by the licensee while acting as an agent of the seller. The seller then claims that because the listing contract had terminated, the licensee was not the seller's agent and the buyer cannot hold the seller liable for the misrepresentations made by the licensee. Under these circumstances, the court is likely to hold that, based on the doctrine of estoppel, the seller cannot deny the agency relationship still existed. The seller allowed the buyer to *believe* that an agency relationship continued to exist between him or her and the licensee, and the buyers were justified in relying on that belief.

 EXAMPLE: *Wilson v. Donze,* 692 S.W.2d 735 (Tex. Ct. App.—Fort Worth 1985). Ken Wilson, the owner of Ken/Car Investments, Inc., approached Anthony and Lena Donze in May asking if their home was for sale. The Donzes informed Wilson that they did not do business with brokers and did not pay commissions. Wilson said he would get the commission from the buyers if he could sell their home. The Donzes agreed to allow him to show the property and told him that they wanted $85,000 for the home.

On June 1, Powers, another real estate broker acting with Wilson, wrote an offer from the Bullards for $100,000, telling the Bullards that it would probably take $115,000 to purchase the home. On June 2, Wilson presented a contract to the Donzes for $85,000, naming Ken/Car Investments, Inc., trustee or assigns, as the purchasers; the contract was accepted by the Donzes. Also on June 2, the Bullards were informed by Powers that their offer had been rejected and that it would indeed take $115,000 to purchase the property; they agreed.

The Donzes and the Bullards met only once after the contracts were signed and both assumed that the contract was between them, and not Ken/Car, even though Ken/Car Investments, Inc., trustee or assigns, was named as the purchaser on the Donze's contract and Ken Wilson, trustee as the seller on the Bullard's contract. No one clarified to the Donzes or Wilsons that this was a "pass through" transaction. Ken Wilson believed that he had done no wrong because the Donzes received what they wanted for the sale of the property, and the Bullards were willing to pay $115,000.

The court held that Ken Wilson was a broker for the Donzes and that he breached his fiduciary duty by not obtaining the best price for them. The jury awarded $24,900 in actual damages and $35,000 in punitive damages. The court of appeals upheld the jury's decision.

? QUESTIONS

1. When did Ken Wilson become an agent for the Donzes?

2. How could Ken Wilson have avoided this problem?

Agency by Ratification

Agency by ratification occurs when a principal gains some benefit from a previously unauthorized act of an agent and the principal, on learning of the act, does not deny that the agent had authority to perform such an act on his or her behalf. The principal ratifies the action of the agent by accepting the benefits that come from the action. A principal has an affirmative duty to reject any unauthorized acts of an agent; otherwise the principal may be held liable for the consequences of the agent's actions. Under the ratification theory, the principal is considered to have approved the agency if he or she accepts the benefits of an agent's previously unauthorized act. This is *agency after the fact.* There are four elements to look for in this concept:

1. The agent performs an unauthorized act.

2. The principal subsequently learns of the act.

3. The principal does not repudiate (deny) the agent's authority to act.

4. The principal benefits from the act.

EXAMPLE: Daniel, from Action Realty, tried unsuccessfully to obtain a listing on a warehouse from Harry. Daniel went to Harry one day and told him that he had a number of interested buyers, but Harry would not give him a listing. Nevertheless, Daniel showed several buyers the property. When Daniel brought in an offer from a buyer, Harry accepted the offer, which contained a provision for him to pay Daniel. Harry asked Daniel to monitor the closing. Subsequently, the buyer brought a lawsuit against Harry to cancel the purchase contract because of a misrepresentation made by Daniel. Harry argued that Daniel was not his agent because he did not sign a listing agreement. A court likely would hold that Harry ratified or affirmed the agency by signing the contract of sale and asking Daniel to monitor the closing, and he is therefore bound by Daniel's misrepresentation.

? **QUESTIONS**

1. What actions should Harry have taken to ensure that Daniel did not represent him?

2. What could Daniel have done to secure his position as Harry's agent?

Gratuitous Agency and Compensation

The most common notion of real estate agency has been frequently expressed as, "You are the agent of the person who pays you." In the past, when asked what the determining factor was in creating an agency, most real estate licensees answered that it is payment of the fee. However, the payment of a commission is not the sole factor in creating an agency relationship. In fact, by contract, the seller could agree to pay all of the buyer's broker's fee, just like the seller sometimes agrees to pay the loan discount points on the buyer's loan or the cost of the professional home inspection. Also, by contract, the buyer could agree to pay the brokerage fees and/or any of the seller's closing expenses. An agency relationship can exist without regard to who pays the fee: the seller, the buyer, both or neither. Texas law, like most state agency disclosure laws, confirms the common-law rule that *payment of the fee does not determine agency.*

The agency relationship that is created when the agent provides brokerage services and charges no fee is known as *gratuitous agency.* Thus, a gratuitous agent giving free advice, perhaps to build goodwill, could be held liable when giving the wrong advice. For example, an agent working without charge could be liable for bad advice if he or she were asked for and gave an opinion about the need to obtain an inspection or title insurance. If the agent's opinion were subsequently relied on and resulted in a loss to the principal, the agent could be held liable just as he or she would have been if a fee or commission had been charged.

Licensees are often placed in positions where they are asked their opinions regarding real estate matters. Many licensees will say that once they obtained a real estate license they never could go to a gathering of people without someone asking their advice about real estate. While it is flattering to be asked for advice, it is also *very risky* to offer advice without being fully informed about the situation. This is particulary true in the arena of helping a "For Sale by Owner" who "only needs a simple question answered."

Despite the fact that payment of the commission does not necessarily determine agency, prudent licensees should discuss and document whom they represent and who pays whom. A clear disclosure can dispel any notion that the licensee represented the person who paid the broker's commission when the licensee did not. If no agency documentation exists, courts will probably use the commission payment as evidence of the intended agency relationship, especially if the person paying the fee is the one claiming that an agency existed. Without clear evidence to the contrary, the broker will have difficulty proving no agency existed. Note that this could apply either to a buyer who pays the commission or to a seller who pays the commission.

EXAMPLE: *Kelly v. Roussalis,* 776 P.2d. 1016 (Wyo. 1989). John Roussalis called Gus Kelly of McNamara Realty to show him a property located on South Poplar, because Gus had worked with him on several other real estate transactions. The house was listed with another firm, and the asking price was $600,000. John said that he would like to pay less and that he would need to sell his current home before purchasing another. Gus had heard that the seller was having financial problems and thought the South Poplar house might go into foreclosure. He suggested that John might be able to buy the property for less at a foreclosure sale.

Subsequently a property in the name of the same person who owned the South Poplar property was posted for foreclosure. John asked Gus if this was the South Poplar property that he had seen, and Gus told him that it was, without checking to verify the information.

Gus then helped John purchase the property by accompanying him to the foreclosure sale— even though Gus's company had a policy of not attending foreclosure sales. Gus bid $150,000 for John and won the final sale, obtained a check from the bank and paid the sheriff, only to find out that the property John had been successful in buying was not the South Poplar property.

John sued Gus and McNamara Realty for negligence. Gus said he was just being a friend and not an agent. John won the suit, and Gus and McNamara Realty appealed. The state Supreme Court upheld the lower court's decision, saying that Gus did not exercise the care expected of real estate agents. The court also held McNamara Realty responsible for Gus's actions.

? QUESTIONS

1. When did Gus become an agent for Roussalis?

2. How did the fact that no fee was being paid affect the outcome?

3. What steps should Gus and his broker have taken to prevent this problem?

■ Important Issues

Why is it so important to determine *in every case* whether an agency relationship has, in fact, been created? The main reasons are legal effect, constructive or imputed notice, professional and ethical responsibility and quality of representation.

Legal Effect

The agent stands in the shoes of the principal and carries out those duties agreed on in the agency contract. The agent speaks, listens and acts for the principal. This is the very essence of the word *represents* when used in the context of the agency relationship.

Because the agent acts on behalf of the principal, the principal may be responsible for or bound to the agent's statements within the scope of the agency. That is, anything done to further the principal's objective to sell or purchase may be assumed to be done with the knowledge and approval of the principal. This is true whether the words or actions are fraudulent, negligent or innocent. The statements, omissions, admissions and misrepresentations made by the agent or subagent may be attributed to the principal, even though the principal may be unaware of them. The reasoning behind this ruling is that principals should not be allowed to benefit from the negligent acts of their agents and subagents.

Recent changes resulting from reform in Texas contract law now will not, presumably, hold principals responsible for the unauthorized acts of their agents unless they are actually aware of the acts. There is, however, little case law to reflect how the courts will interpret these changes. In any event, the principal should make an informed decision regarding the agent he or she selects for representation.

A recent judicial trend expands agent liability in the area of negligence. Courts often base decisions on the fact that an agent knew or should have known certain information, such as that the sewer wasn't connected, the roof leaked or the property was located in a flood-prone area. The listing agent's failure to discover obvious defects and disclose such defects to the buyer may be termed *negligence*. However, in Texas, the courts have found that agents who did not know of latent defects were not bound to the same extent as real estate inspectors and are, in fact, prohibited from acting as inspectors and brokers in the same transaction. In the landmark case, *Kubinsky v. Van Zandt,* the broker appropriately was not found to have known in a "should have known" situation. A few courts in the United States have held that brokers *and their principals* are liable for the brokers' innocent misrepresentations.

 EXAMPLE: Agent Charlie lists a home in an exclusive area of town. Although the property is near the shoreline and at a relatively low elevation, the property has never flooded. However, mortgage lenders require flood insurance when making loans in the area. Charlie finds a buyer, and the seller agrees to "owner finance" the property. Neither Charlie nor the seller advises the purchaser as to the issue of possible flooding. Six months after the sale the property floods following a torrential downpour. The new purchaser has not secured flood insurance, and the loss is devastating. Charlie claims no fault since he was not aware of the potential problem.

? QUESTIONS

1. Is this something that Charlie "should have known"?

2. Is the seller obligated to disclose this type of information?

3. What should Charlie have done differently, if anything?

Constructive or Imputed Notice

In the course of a real estate transaction licensees are required to give notice to buyers and sellers regarding matters such as acceptance or rejection of offers to buy or sell, withdrawal of offers or removal of a property from the market. Time is important in negotiations of offers, and proper notice may determine who is the rightful purchaser of a property—particularly when more than one offer is being negotiated.

It is important for everyone involved in a real estate transaction to know who is representing whom, so that when notifications are required, it may be determined when a legal notification actually occurred. In practice, licensees often find themselves involved in disputes over issues of notification to buyers and sellers as well as to other licensees involved in the transaction.

Once the buyer and seller have reached an agreement and all parties have signed the contract, it must be delivered to all principals, *or their agents,* to become enforceable. Most contracts have a number of details that must be completed to process the sale. Frequently there are deadlines for the delivery of inspection reports, approval of the buyer's financing or a title commitment.

Many licensees erroneously believe that an agent must actually tell his or her principal before notice is effective. In reality, the knowledge of or notice to the agent is binding on the principal, *even if the information is never conveyed to the principal.* Notifying the agent is regarded as actually notifying the principal. This is called *constructive* or *imputed notice.* The following case is somewhat complex; nevertheless, it demonstrates the importance of properly notifying each party and making sure that all parties are aware of whom each agent is representing.

 EXAMPLE: *Stortroen v. Beneficial Finance Company,* 736 P.2d 391 (Colo. 1987). Beneficial Finance entered into a listing agreement with Olthoff Realty Company to sell a property it owned. Olthoff placed the property in the local multiple-listing service (MLS). Mary Panio, an associate with Foremost Realty, saw the listing in the MLS and subsequently showed the home to the Stortroens, who had expressed an interest in selling their home and purchasing a larger one. After touring the home, the Stortroens asked Mary to prepare and present an offer for $105,000 to the seller. Because the Stortroens needed to sell their current home before buying another one, they made the offer contingent on selling and closing the sale of their present home. The contingency also stated that Beneficial would keep the home on the market and give the Stortroens 72 hours to remove the contingency on notification that Beneficial Finance had received another acceptable offer.

Beneficial's representative, Donald Reh, reviewed the contract and instructed Olthoff to increase the sales price to $110,000 and to state in the counteroffer that acceptance by the buyer would be "evidenced by the Purchaser's signature hereon; and if seller receives notice of such acceptance on or before 9 PM 2-3-84."

While the offer from the Stortroens was being negotiated, the Carellis also toured the home and submitted an offer for $112,000 on Friday, February 3, 1984, through their agent. Olthoff informed Beneficial's Mr. Reh of the second offer and was told by him to have the Carellis' agent bring the offer directly to him. Mr. Reh reviewed the contract and told Olthoff to withdraw the counteroffer to the Stortroens and accept the offer from the Carellis.

Olthoff tried contacting Mary Panio but was unable to speak to her personally, so he left messages at her office and her home informing her that the counteroffer with Beneficial had been withdrawn. Olthoff told Reh about the messages to Panio, whereupon Reh signed the offer from the Carellis.

Before she received the messages from Olthoff, Mary Panio presented the counteroffer to the Stortroens. The Stortroens agreed to the terms of the counteroffer and signed it at about 4:10 P.M. on Friday, February 3. On returning to her office with the signed counteroffer, Mary received the messages from Olthoff.

On Saturday, February 4, Mary Panio obtained a withdrawal of the contingency from the Stortroens. On Monday, February 6, Mary delivered the signed offer and the withdrawal of the contingency to Olthoff. Subsequently, the Stortroens filed their contract into record at the County Clerk's office—thereby placing a cloud on the title to Beneficial's property.

The Carellis moved into the home on a month-to-month lease because they didn't want to close on the property while there was a cloud on the title. The Stortroens brought suit against Beneficial for specific performance of the contract and against the Carellis to vacate the premises. The Carellis brought suit against Beneficial and a complaint against Olthoff.

The District Court found in favor of Beneficial and against Stortroen, saying that Mary Panio was acting as a representative of the buyer. Thus, when the counteroffer and the contingency were signed by the Stortroens and given to Panio, this was not considered to be notification of acceptance to Beneficial.

The Supreme Court was asked to render a decision regarding whom Mary Panio was representing. They found that she was representing Beneficial Finance through the agreement of subagency (working with the buyer but representing the seller) offered through the MLS. Therefore, when the counteroffer from Beneficial was accepted and signed by the Stortroens in the presence of Mary, *constructive notice to Beneficial had been officially made.* This decision made the Stortroens the prevailing party.

This case illustrates how licensees can run into enormous problems when notification is required. Technically, once all parties have signed the offer, it becomes an enforceable contract, but only when all parties *or their agents* have received notification (thus, constructive notice). If Mary had been representing the buyers—not the seller through a subagency agreement—notice would been considered to be effective only when she delivered it to Olthoff Realty.

Professional and Ethical Responsibility

Real estate licensees acting as agents owe general duties of good faith, fairness and honesty to all with whom they deal. But when acting as agents and subagents, licensees owe a far greater degree of care and loyalty to a principal than they do to a third person. In general, a customer is entitled to honesty, fairness, accurate information and material facts concerning a property. A client is entitled to accurate information, opinions and advice about the significance of facts and information, the alternative courses of action available and the recommendations of the agent. The best interests of the client must be kept in mind at all times.

■ How Agency Is Terminated

Except in the case of an agency coupled with a broker's interest in the transaction (partial ownership), an agency relationship may be terminated at any time for any of the following reasons:

- Lapse of the time specified in the agreement
- Lapse of a reasonable time if no time is specified
- Completion of the purpose of the agency
- Mutual rescission
- Revocation by the principal
- Agent's renunciation
- Abandonment of the agreement by the agent
- Incapacity or death of either the agent or the principal
- Bankruptcy of the owner if title is transferred to the receiver
- Condemnation or destruction of the premises
- Agent's breach of duties to the principal

Time

The Real Estate License Act (TRELA) does not specifically address the length of time appropriate for listing or buyer/tenant agency contracts. It does, however, state that an agent may not enter into these contracts without a definite termination or expiration date that requires no action on the part of the principal (there are exceptions for certain types of property management contracts). Likewise, a contract may not automatically renew itself into perpetuity (forever). Failure to provide for a definite termination date may be grounds for revocation or suspension of the agent's real estate license.

Although TRELA does not limit the term of these agency agreements, it is inherent in agency law that such agreements must be for *reasonable* periods of time. In practice, the length of listing and buyer representation contracts are negotiated between the broker and the principal. Typically, these negotiations depend on the type of property, market conditions and motivation of the sellers or buyers.

Actions of Principals and Agents

The *actions* of a principal or agent may terminate the agency in a variety of ways. These include

- accomplishment of the agency objective,
- rescission,
- revocation,
- renunciation,
- abandonment by the agent and
- breach of the agent's duty to the principal.

The agency agreement was entered into for a specific purpose. When that *purpose has been accomplished,* the agency terminates. The house is sold for the seller, or the prospective buyer client purchases a property. Neither the agent nor the principal needs to take any action for the agency to end.

Other actions by the parties could include rescission by the parties, revocation by the principal or *renunciation* by the agent. With *rescission,* the parties mutually agree to cancel the agency relationship, thereby releasing both parties from any obligations or duties. If, however, a principal *revokes* the agency without cause, the principal may be liable for any damages suffered by the agent. Likewise, if an agent *renounces* the agency relationship and refuses to represent the principal further, the principal may attempt to recover any damages caused by the action of the agent.

Two other methods by which action (or inaction) by the principal or agent terminates agency are abandonment or breach of duty by the agent. For example, if an agent enters into a listing contract with a seller and then makes no effort to market the property, the agency relationship may be terminated by the principal due to *abandonment.* Finally, *a breach of the agent's duty to the principal* allows the principal to terminate the agency relationship and also provides other legal remedies for the agent's principal, such as a lawsuit for damages suffered as a result of the breach.

Operation of Law

In addition to acts of the parties to the agency relationship, certain circumstances will cause the agency to terminate by law. Unless the agent has an ownership or contractual interest in the property (known as *agency coupled with an interest*), *incapacity* or *death* of the agent or principal will terminate the agency relationship. Other examples of termination by law include *bankruptcy* of the principal that results in the property's being taken into receivership, the property's being taken by the government through *condemnation* or the *destruction* of the property.

■ Duties of Agency That Continue

Even though the agency relationship may have appeared to terminate by action of time, actions of the parties or operation of law—the duty of *confidentiality* of information remains after the termination of the agreement. Under no circumstances can a licensee disclose confidential information that was gained during the course of the agency contract unless authorized to do so by the principal. Frequently an agent who has listed and/or sold a property for a seller subsequently is asked to show that seller other property to purchase. Whether or not the agent has a formal agency agreement with the former client, he or she cannot disclose any information that was gained during the previous relationship with the former client without that client's authorization.

 EXAMPLE: Christian from Executive Realty listed and sold one of Judy's investment homes. Three weeks after closing, Judy asks Christian to show her possible replacement properties. She does not ask to be represented by Christian. He knows that Judy has $30,000 from the sale of her other property to invest in new properties. He also knows that for personal reasons Judy must invest this money quickly. Christian shows Judy one of his listings—one that he believes she will consider to be an excellent investment. She tours the property and proceeds to write an offer that is substantially below the list price.

? **QUESTIONS**

1. Is Judy still Christian's client?

2. How much information is Christian allowed to give the seller about Judy?

3. Will Christian have to disclose his former agency relationship with Judy to the seller?

■ Summary

Real estate licensees need to be aware of the variety of positions relative to agency that a broker can have in a real estate transaction. Because no formalities are required to create an agency relationship, one can be found to exist when none was ever intended. The existence of an agency relationship can have a significant impact on issues of liability, notice, responsibility and quality of representation. By becoming more aware of agency issues, the real estate licensee can better define and control agency relationships, thus ensuring that working relationships intentionally created are the most effective and successful while better reducing the possibility of risk.

Subsequent chapters examine in depth each of the agency alternatives. Brokers have to evaluate which alternative is best. Today, companies must consider many factors in developing their agency policies. One thing is certain: no perfect solution exists.

■ Key Points

- The payment of a fee does not determine agency.

- An agency can be created expressly, by implication, by estoppel, by ratification or gratuitously, with or without a written agreement.

- A *customer* is entitled to accurate information and material facts; a *client* is entitled to accurate information, opinions, and advice.

Courts look at not only the documents creating agency but also the acts of the agent and the parties. The duty of confidentiality continues after the termination of an agency.

■ Suggestions for Brokers

Develop a company policy covering which agency alternative the company prefers, which services the broker or sales and broker associates may extend to customers and which services they must or must not provide to clients. It should be policy that any variations must be reported to the managing broker, as when a salesperson in a large, exclusively seller-agency-oriented firm attempts to represent a buyer in locating a property.

■ Quiz

1. Which of the following is required to create an agency relationship?

   A. Compensation
   B. A contract
   C. A real estate license
   D. A belief that the relationship exists

2. Express agency

   A. is created by the principal's actions.
   B. is always in writing.
   C. can be a verbal agreement.
   D. is ambiguous.

3. Implied authority

   A. is specifically given in a listing contract.
   B. is not specifically given to an agent.
   C. is the same as implied agency.
   D. is a part of every contract.

4. Agency based on a third party's being led to believe that a licensee was acting as an agent of another party is

   A. express agency.
   B. implied agency.
   C. ostensible agency.
   D. agency by ratification.

5. To become enforceable, a contract must be signed and delivered to

   A. all principals and their agents.
   B. all principals or their agents.
   C. the mortgagor's lender.
   D. the closing office.

6. Which of the following statements is true regarding termination of agency for time?

   A. Unlike seller agency, a contract for buyer agency does not require a definite termination date.
   B. TRELA mandates a maximum of 180 days for residential listings.
   C. A contract for seller or buyer agency may not automatically renew itself into perpetuity.
   D. All property management contracts require a definite termination date.

7. You entered into an agency agreement with and successfully found a home for a buyer. To terminate the agency you

   A. need take no action.
   B. must wait until closing.
   C. must notify the buyer in writing.
   D. must notify the seller in writing.

8. Which of the following statements is true regarding the determination of whom the broker represents?

   A. Whoever pays the commission is the principal.
   B. The principal must sign a written agreement for an agency to exist.
   C. It is important to decide whether the buyer or the seller is the broker's principal because the broker will owe the principal a higher standard of care and more extensive duties.
   D. The broker must be paid a commission for an agency to exist.

9. Notice to an agent that is considered notice to the principal is known as

   A. ostensible notice.   C. constructive notice.
   B. implied notice.   D. unintended notice.

10. Duties that continue after the termination of agency include the duty

   A. to continue to present offers to the seller.
   B. to continue to advertise the property.
   C. not to disclose confidential information.
   D. to offer advice and opinions.

■ Discussion Questions

1. What two essential elements are necessary to create an agency?

2. Compare and contrast implied and express agency.

3. When is gratuitous agency most likely to occur?

CHAPTER 5

Seller Agency

Until recently the traditional viewpoint in real estate brokerage has been that the real estate licensee, when acting as an agent in a transaction, represented the seller. In fact, until 1988, when the first written agency disclosure was required in Texas, most licensees, clients and customers gave very little thought to who represented whom. This agency disclosure requirement had the effect of raising the awareness of both the public and the licensees. With the increased awareness of the dynamics of the agency relationship comes the necessity to adequately identify the responsibilities agents assume when they agree to represent a party to a real estate transaction. In this chapter we explore the agent's responsibility to the seller and identify how these responsibilities translate into our dealings with the buyer-customer.

This chapter addresses the following:

Express and Implied Agreements
Types of Listing Agreements
Listing Agreements
Advantages of Seller Agency
Approaches to Representing Sellers
Exclusive Seller Agency
In-House Sales
Cooperative Sales
Exclusive Seller Agency in Practice
Advantages and Disadvantages of Exclusive Seller Agency
Nonexclusive Seller Agency
Advantages and Disadvantages of Nonexclusive Seller Agency
Disclosure Issues
Disclosure of Seller's Agent to Seller
Disclosure of Seller's Agent to Buyer

■ Express and Implied Agreements

The most common and easily recognized agency relationship in real estate is that between the seller (client) and the listing broker (agent). The relationship is usually evidenced by a written agreement called a *listing agreement,* typically an *exclusive-right-to-sell* listing. (This and other types of listing agreements are discussed later in this Chapter.) Listing agreements establish the working agency relationship between the seller and the broker. Although the actual listing agreement is frequently presented and signed by an associate of the broker on the broker's behalf, the agency relationship and all the rights and obligations of the agreement fall to the broker. As shown in Chapter 2, these duties flow through the broker to all the associated licensees of the broker. Additionally, if other licensees not associated with the firm are permitted to represent the seller through the listing broker, the duties of the other licensees to the seller will be the same as those of the listing broker. This arrangement is known as *sub-agency* and is covered in detail in Chapter 7.

Listing agreements, as well as other agency agreements, may be either oral or in writing. However, The Real Estate License Act (TRELA) states that "an action may not be brought in a court in this state for the recovery of a commission for the sale or purchase of real estate unless the promise or agreement on which the action is brought, or some note or memorandum thereof, is in writing and signed by the party to be charged or signed by a person lawfully authorized by the party to sign it" [TRELA §20(b)].

In other words, properties may be listed orally, but if the seller refuses to pay an orally agreed-on commission, the broker cannot look to the courts to compel the seller to pay. An oral listing agreement and commission entitlement may, however, be enforced against third parties who attempt to tortuously (wrongfully) interfere with them (for example, a licensee from another firm who attempts to list a property during the term of an oral listing).

Neither a written contract nor an oral agreement to pay a fee is necessary to create an agency relationship with the seller; the words and conduct of the parties may create an agency relationship. A listing created in this manner is called an *implied agency,* and a broker may be surprised when a court finds an agency relationship when the broker intended none. This implied agency could be a result of a previous relationship with the principal. For example, a licensee has represented a buyer in acquiring a new home and then "unofficially" helps the principal sell another property. Under these circumstances it is assumed that the licensee has a close working relationship with the former client that is likely to continue after the previous contract is fulfilled or has terminated. Buyers who have been clients of a broker thus may continue to be clients when they subsequently sell a property with the unofficial help of the broker, even though no written listing agreement has been signed.

Once an agency relationship is created with the seller, the law imposes a number of fiduciary duties on the seller's agent, the most important one being that the agent must protect and promote the best interests of the seller. The interests of the seller must be placed above those of anyone else, including the agent's own interests. The seller's agent owes absolute allegiance to the seller.

■ Listing Agreements

The listing agreement between the broker and the seller creates an express agency relationship—it is essentially a broker's employment contract. Typically, this agreement is a contract that establishes the rights and obligations of both principals to the agreement—the seller and the broker. The seller gives permission and authority to the broker to act as his or her agent and generally agrees to pay compensation (a fee or commission) for the service the broker renders. The broker agrees to represent the seller, market the property and place the seller's interests above all others. Compensation is usually conditioned on the broker producing a ready, willing and able buyer at the price and terms stated in the listing agreement.

The parties to a listing contract are the broker and the seller. The listing contract is an agreement to market the property and to seek qualified buyers; it is not a contract to "sell" the property. Once a qualified buyer has submitted a contract that meets the price and terms stated in the listing contract, the broker has fulfilled his or her obligation. If the seller elects *not to sell,* he or she technically owes the broker the stated compensation. The buyer has no recourse if the seller decides to remove the property from the market after the buyer has presented an offer but *before* a contract of sale is signed. Remember: the only signed contract at this point is between the listing broker and the seller—no one else (buyer or any other broker involved) has the right to sue under the terms of the listing agreement, because they do not have a signed contract with the seller.

 EXAMPLE: Broker James, Precision Realty, obtained a listing contract from Joyce to sell her home for $115,000 cash or with a conventional loan. James marketed the home, and three weeks after he listed the property, a full-price cash offer was submitted by a buyer with the resources needed to fulfill the terms of the offer. James met with Joyce later that evening and presented the offer. After discussing the terms and projected proceeds, it appeared that Joyce was prepared to sign the offer; however, at the last moment she had a change of heart and decided not to sell the property after all.

? QUESTIONS

1. Is the broker entitled to a fee or commission?

2. If this contract offer was written by another agency, could the other broker sue Joyce?

3. What, if any, legal recourse might the buyer have against Joyce?

🔍 DISCUSSION

Under the terms of most listing contracts the broker is entitled to a fee or commission once a ready, willing and able buyer makes an offer that meets the price and terms stated in the listing contract. If the listing contract is in writing, the broker can seek the compensation and even go so far as to bring a lawsuit against the seller, if necessary. If the contract is taken orally, the broker has no recourse.

If the *purchase contract* were written by another agency, Precision Realty would have the same right to seek compensation as it would have if the sale had been in-house. However, the broker from the other firm would have no recourse because the *listing contract* was between Precision Realty and the seller. The decision to pursue the seller for compensation is one that can be made *only* by the listing broker.

Although the listing broker may have the right to bring legal action against the seller, this may not prove to be the best solution for the broker. The time, energy, expense and possible damage to the broker's reputation may far outweigh the potential benefits.

Because the offer to purchase was not signed, the buyer has little recourse other than to pursue the seller on the basis of fraudulent advertising. While sellers can always remove their properties from the market, it might raise questions if they later were to sell the property to someone else under terms similar to the first contract offer. Of particular concern would be issues of discrimination, which could arise (under the Civil Rights Act) if it could be shown that the seller's reason for rejecting the first offer was based on the buyer's being a member of a protected class.

Types of Listing Agreements

There are three generally recognized types of listing agreements that brokers and sellers can enter into:

1. exclusive-right-to-sell,

2. exclusive-agency and

3. open listings.

The type of listing the broker and the seller select depends on the circumstances surrounding the seller's motivation to sell and the broker's policies regarding listings.

The *exclusive-right-to-sell* listing offers the broker the greatest amount of security and, in many cases, offers the seller the greatest amount of service. Under this agreement the broker is entitled to the stated fee or commission no matter who sells the property—even if it is the seller. The seller also benefits by offering the maximum protection to the broker because the broker then can afford to invest time and money in promoting the property with the assurance that he or she will be paid regardless of who finds the buyer. It can be very costly for a broker to market listings and to operate a general brokerage business.

Most brokers avoid listings that do not have a reasonable chance to sell or that do not fairly compensate the broker for expenses. The brokerage business is just like any other business; it must pay for operations and give its investors a fair return on their money. The exclusive-right-to-sell listing gives the broker a greater opportunity to realize those goals. A broker holding an exclusive-right-to-sell listing usually will agree to let other brokers

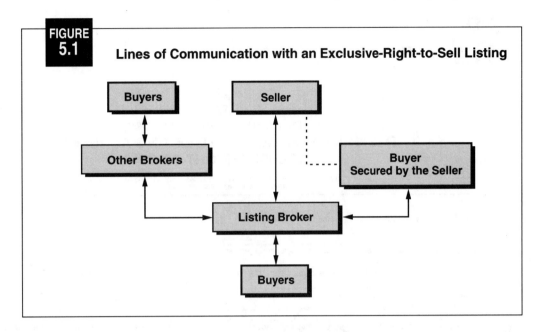

FIGURE 5.1 Lines of Communication with an Exclusive-Right-to-Sell Listing

negotiate with the seller through him or her. The listing broker typically agrees to pay the other broker some part or percentage of the commission paid to him or her by the seller. When brokers agree to cooperate in this manner, sellers gain wider exposure for their properties. Figure 5.1 depicts the lines of communication and negotiation in an exclusive-right-to-sell listing, and Figure 5.2 is an example of an exclusive-right-to-sell listing *agreement*.

An *exclusive-agency listing* allows sellers to reserve the right to sell a property themselves without the obligation to pay a commission or fee if successful. Under an exclusive-agency listing a seller can do this and still have the property listed by a broker. If, however, another brokerage firm secures a buyer, it must present the contract through the listing brokerage; it cannot go directly to the seller. Hence the name *exclusive agency*—indicating that another agency cannot work directly with the seller.

As with the exclusive-right-to-sell listing, the listing broker may allow other brokers to negotiate through him or her. Thus, if any broker finds a buyer, the listing broker is entitled to a fee that will be shared with the selling broker. A seller should be made aware that with this type of listing the broker may not be able to justify the same level of advertising and promotion because the seller still may secure his or her own buyer. In that case the broker would not be entitled to a commission. Figure 5.3 illustrates the exclusive-agency listing.

Open listings generally entitle the broker to compensation only if he or she is the *procuring cause* (the person who secures the offer from the buyer) of the sale or lease of the property. The open listing does not give any broker the exclusive right to offer the property for sale; rather, it allows the owner of the property to give one or more brokers the same opportunity simultaneously, but only the broker who produces an accepted contract is compensated. The open listing also allows the seller to continue to seek potential buyers and to negotiate independently of the broker. If successful, the seller does not owe any broker a commission. A listing generally is considered to be an open listing unless its terms clearly indicate that both parties intend a more exclusive agreement.

FIGURE 5.2

TAR Exclusive Right-to-Sell Listing

TEXAS ASSOCIATION OF REALTORS®

RESIDENTIAL REAL ESTATE LISTING AGREEMENT
EXCLUSIVE RIGHT TO SELL

USE OF THIS FORM BY PERSONS WHO ARE NOT MEMBERS OF THE TEXAS ASSOCIATION OF REALTORS® IS NOT AUTHORIZED.
©Texas Association of REALTORS®, Inc. 1998

1. **PARTIES:** The parties to this agreement (this Listing) are _____ _____ (Seller) and _____ (Broker). Seller appoints Broker as Seller's sole and exclusive agent and grants to Broker the exclusive right to sell the Property.

2. **PROPERTY:** All property described below is called "the Property." The Property is described as: _____
   (legal description) in the City of_____ , _____ County, Texas, known as _____ *(address and zip code)*, or as described on attached exhibit, together with the following items, if any: curtains and rods, draperies and rods, valances, blinds, window shades, screens, shutters, awnings, wall-to-wall carpeting, mirrors fixed in place, ceiling fans, attic fans, mail boxes, television antennas and satellite dish system with controls and equipment, permanently installed heating and air-conditioning units, window air conditioning units, built-in security and fire detection equipment, plumbing and lighting fixtures including chandeliers, water softener and filters, stove, built-in kitchen equipment, garage door openers with affixed and remote controls, built-in cleaning equipment, all swimming pool equipment and maintenance accessories, shrubbery, landscaping, permanently installed outdoor cooking equipment, built-in fireplace screens, artificial fireplace logs, and all other property owned by Seller and attached to the above described real property except the following property which is not included: _____ _____ . The Property ☐ is ☐ is not subject to a mandatory membership in an owners' association. *(If Property is a condominium use Condominium Addendum).*

3. **LISTING PRICE:** Seller lists the Property for the gross amount of _____ (Listing Price) and agrees to sell the Property for the Listing Price or any other price acceptable to Seller. Seller will pay all typical closing costs charged to sellers of residential real property in Texas (seller's typical closing costs are those set forth in the residential contracts promulgated by the Texas Real Estate Commission).

4. **TERM:** This Listing commences on _____ (Commencement Date) and ends at 11:59 p.m. on _____ (Expiration Date). If Seller enters into a binding written contract to sell the Property before the Commencement Date, this Listing will not commence and will be void.

5. **BROKER'S FEE:**

   A. <u>Fee</u>: When earned and payable, Seller will pay Broker a fee of:

   ☐ (1) _____% of the sales price. In the event of exchange or breach of this Listing, the Listing Price will be the sales price for purposes of computing Broker's Fee.

   ☐ (2) _____ .

   B. <u>Earned</u>: Broker's Fee is earned when any one of the following occurs during the term of this Listing:

   (1) Seller sells, exchanges, agrees to sell, or agrees to exchange the Property to anyone at any price on any terms;
   (2) Broker individually or in cooperation with another broker procures a buyer ready, willing, and able to buy the Property at the Listing Price or at any other price acceptable to Seller; or
   (3) Seller breaches this Listing (including but not limited to Seller selling or leasing the Property without Broker's consent).

   C. <u>Payable</u>: Once earned, Broker's Fee is payable, either during term of this Listing or after its expiration or termination, at the earlier of:

   (1) the closing and funding of any sale or exchange of the Property;
   (2) Seller's refusal to sell the Property after Broker's Fee has been earned;
   (3) Seller's breach of this Listing; or
   (4) at such time as otherwise set forth in this Listing.

   Broker's Fee is <u>not</u> payable if a sale of the Property does not close or fund as a result of: (i) Seller's failure, without fault of Seller, to deliver a title policy to a buyer; (ii) loss of ownership due to foreclosure or other legal proceeding; or (iii) Seller's

(TAR-1101) 8-01-98   Initialed for Identification by Broker/Associate _____ and Seller _____, _____   Page 1 of 6

FIGURE 5.2   TAR Exclusive Right-to-Sell Listing (continued)

Residential Listing concerning _____

failure to restore the Property, as a result of a casualty loss, to its previous condition by the closing date set forth in a contract for the sale of the Property.

   D.   Protection Period: If within _____ days after this Listing ends (the Protection Period), Seller enters into a contract to sell the Property or sells, exchanges or otherwise transfers a legal or equitable interest (excluding a lease with no right to purchase) in the Property to any person whose attention has been called to the Property by Broker, any other broker, or Seller during the term of this Listing, Seller will pay Broker an amount equal to the Broker's Fee stated in Paragraph 5A, provided Broker, prior to or within ten (10) days after this Listing ends, has delivered or sent to Seller written notice specifying the names of the persons whose attention has been called to the Property during the term of this Listing. If during the Protection Period such sale, exchange or transfer occurs while the Property is listed exclusively with another Texas licensed real estate broker, this provision will not apply and Seller will not be obligated to pay Broker the amount specified. The term "person" is broadly construed to include any individual or entity in any capacity.

   E.   Other Fees:

      (1)   If a buyer, with whom Seller has entered into a contract for the sale of the Property during the term of this Listing, breaches such a contract and Seller receives earnest money or a portion thereof as liquidated damages, Seller will pay Broker the lesser of one-half of such amount or the amount of Broker's Fee stated in Paragraph 5A. Any amount paid under this Paragraph 5E(1) is in addition to any amount that Broker may be entitled to receive for subsequently selling the Property.

      (2)   If Seller collects the sales price and/or damages either by suit, compromise, settlement or otherwise from a buyer who breached a contract for the sale of the Property entered into during the term of this Listing, Seller will pay Broker, after deducting attorneys' fees and other expenses of collection, an amount equal to the lesser of one-half of the amount collected after deductions or the amount of the Broker's Fee stated in Paragraph 5A. Any amount paid under this Paragraph 5E(2) is in addition to any amount that Broker may be entitled to receive for subsequently selling the Property.

      (3)   Transaction Fees: _____

   F.   County: All amounts payable to Broker are to be paid in cash in _____ County, Texas.

   G.   Escrow Authorization: Seller authorizes, and Broker may so instruct, any escrow or closing agent authorized to close a transaction for the purchase or acquisition of the Property to collect and disburse to Broker all amounts payable to Broker under this Listing.

6.   LISTING SERVICES (*choose only one*):

☐   A.   Broker will file this Listing with the following Multiple Listing Services (MLS) or other listing services: _____
            _____.

      (1)   Broker will file this Listing with the named listing services within the earlier of: (a) the time required by the rules or regulations of the named MLS or listing service; (b) 4 days after the Commencement Date of this Listing. **Seller may review the information about the Property prior to its submission to MLS or other listing service.**

      (2)   Seller authorizes Broker to place information about the Property on the Internet either directly or through a program of the MLS or other listing service.

      (3)   Seller authorizes Broker, upon a final and closed sale of the Property, to submit information about this Listing, the sale of the Property, and contract terms to the named MLS or listing services for publication to subscribers for market evaluation or appraisal purposes and for disclosure of such information to such persons as Broker deems appropriate, including the appraisal district. Any information or data, including information about a sale, becomes the property of the named MLS or listing services for all purposes. **NOTICE: Submission of information to MLS insures that persons who use and benefit from MLS also contribute information.**

☐   B.   Broker will not file this Listing with a Multiple Listing Service or any other listing service.

7.   ACCESS TO THE PROPERTY:

   A.   Authorizing access: Authorizing access to the Property means giving permission to another person to enter the Property, disclosing any security codes affecting the Property to such person, and lending a key to the Property to such person either directly or through a keybox. To facilitate the showing and sale of the Property, Seller instructs Broker and Broker's associates to: (1) access the Property at reasonable times; and (2) authorize other brokers, inspectors, appraisers, and repair persons to access the Property at reasonable times.

   B.   Scheduling Companies: Broker may engage the following company to schedule appointments and to authorize others to access the Property: _____.

(TAR-1101) 8-01-98   Initialed for Identification by Broker/Associate _____ and Seller _____, _____   Page 2 of 6

FIGURE
5.2

TAR Exclusive Right-to-Sell Listing (continued)

Residential Listing concerning _____

C. Keybox:

NOTICE: **A keybox is a locked container placed on the Property in which a key to the Property is placed. Keyboxes make it more convenient for cooperating brokers and their associates, home inspectors, appraisers, and repair persons to facilitate the showing, inspecting, and repairing of the Property. The keybox is locked and opened by a special combination, key, or a programmed access card so that whoever possesses the special combination, key, or the access card to the keybox has access to the Property at any time, even in Seller's absence. The use of the keybox will probably increase the number of showings, but involves risks (such as unauthorized entry, theft, property damage, or personal injury). Neither the Association of REALTORS® nor MLS requires the use of a keybox. Please discuss the advantages and disadvantages of keyboxes with your Broker, insurance agent, and/or attorney.**

(1) Broker ❑ is   ❑ is not   authorized to place a keybox containing a key to the Property on the Property.

(2) If the Property is occupied by a tenant at any time during this Listing, Seller will furnish Broker a written statement, signed by all tenants, authorizing the use of a keybox or Broker may remove any keybox from the Property.

D. Liability: Seller will protect, defend, indemnify and hold Broker, Broker's associates, other brokers and their associates, and any keybox provider harmless from any damages or claims arising from authorizing access to the Property or the use of a keybox including, but not limited to, damages to or loss of real or personal property or personal injury not caused by Broker's negligence. Seller assumes all risk of any loss, damage, and injury. Broker advises Seller to obtain personal property insurance.

8. **REQUIRED DISCLOSURES:**

A. If applicable, Seller will deliver the following disclosures or notices to Broker. Seller must complete the required disclosures or notices to the best of Seller's knowledge and belief. Seller authorizes Broker and Broker's associates to furnish prospective buyers and other brokers with copies of all applicable disclosures or notices.

❑   (1) Seller's Disclosure Notice (§5.008, Texas Property Code).
❑   (2) Addendum for Seller's Disclosure of Information on Lead-Based Paint and Lead-Based Paint Hazard (required by federal law if Property was built before 1978).
❑   (3) Resale Certificate for Property Subject to Mandatory Membership in an Owner's Association (contractual).
❑   (4) MUD Disclosure Notice (Chapter 49, Texas Water Code).
❑   (5) New Home Insulation Addendum (FTC Regulations if Property is a new home).
❑   (6) Condominium Resale Certificate and copies of Condominium Documents (Chapter 82, Texas Property Code - see attached Condominium Addendum).
❑   (7) Addendum for Property Located Seaward of the Gulf Intracoastal Waterway (§61.025, Texas Natural Resources Code).
❑   (8) Addendum for Coastal Area Property (§33.135, Texas Natural Resources Code).
❑   (9) any disclosures or addenda required by a relocation company or Seller's employer.
❑   (10)_____.

B. Seller represents that the applicable notices and disclosures will be completed to the best of Seller's knowledge and belief and that Seller has disclosed all known material defects and material facts affecting the Property in the applicable disclosures or notices.

C. Seller agrees to amend the applicable notices and disclosures if any material change occurs during the term of this Listing.

D. Seller will protect, defend, indemnify and hold Broker, Broker's associates, and any other brokers or their associates harmless from any damages, costs, attorney's fees or expenses arising from Seller's failure to disclose any material or relevant information or the giving of any incorrect information to Broker, Broker's associates, any other brokers or their associates, or prospective buyers.

9. **COOPERATION WITH OTHER BROKERS:** Cooperating with and compensating other brokers means that Broker will allow other brokers to show the Property to prospective buyers and if another broker procures an acceptable offer, Broker will pay the other broker part of the Broker's Fee described in Paragraph 5A. Broker will determine the terms and conditions of offers to cooperate with and compensate other brokers. Broker will offer cooperation and compensation (*choose only one*):

❑   A. only to buyer agents.
❑   B. only to subagents of Broker.
❑   C. to both buyer agents and Broker's subagents.

**FIGURE
5.2**   **TAR Exclusive Right-to-Sell Listing (continued)**

Residential Listing concerning _____

10. AGENCY RELATIONSHIPS:

   A. Seller acknowledges receipt of the attached exhibit entitled **"Information About Brokerage Services,"** which is incorporated in this Listing for all purposes.

   B. Broker will exclusively represent Seller in negotiations for the sale of the Property unless Seller authorizes Broker, as set forth below, to act as an intermediary in the event Broker also represents a buyer who offers to purchase the Property *(choose (1) or (2))*.

   ☐ (1) <u>Intermediary Relationship Authorized</u>: Seller authorizes Broker to show the Property to prospective buyers Broker has agreed to represent. If Broker represents a buyer who offers to buy the Property, Seller authorizes Broker to act as an intermediary between the buyer and Seller, to present any offer such buyer may wish to make, and to assist both Seller and buyer in negotiations for the sale of the Property. Broker's compensation will be paid by Seller as provided in Paragraph 5. **If Broker acts as an intermediary between Seller and a buyer, Broker:**

   (a) **may not disclose to the buyer that the Seller will accept a price less than the asking price (Listing Price) unless otherwise instructed in a separate writing by the Seller;**
   (b) **may not disclose to Seller that the buyer will pay a price greater than the price submitted in a written offer to Seller unless otherwise instructed in a separate writing by the buyer;**
   (c) **may not disclose any confidential information or any information Seller or the buyer specifically instructs Broker in writing not to disclose unless otherwise instructed in a separate writing by the respective party or required to disclose the information by the Real Estate License Act or a court order or if the information materially relates to the condition of the Property;**
   (d) **shall treat all parties to the transaction honestly; and**
   (e) **shall comply with the Real Estate License Act.**

   If Broker acts as an intermediary, Broker may appoint a licensed associate(s) of Broker to communicate with, carry out instructions of, and provide opinions and advice during negotiations to Seller and appoint another licensed associate(s) for the same purposes to a buyer.

   ☐ (2) <u>Intermediary Relationship not Authorized</u>: Broker will exclusively represent Seller and may not act as an intermediary between Seller and a buyer. Seller understands *(choose only one)*:

   ☐ (a) Broker exclusively represents sellers and does not represent buyers.
   ☐ (b) Broker represents both buyers and sellers. However, Broker will not show the Property to any buyer Broker represents.

   C. During the term of this Listing or after its termination, Broker may not knowingly disclose information obtained in confidence from Seller except as authorized by Seller or required by law. Broker may not disclose to Seller any information obtained in confidence regarding any other person Broker represents or may have represented except as required by law.

11. BROKER'S AUTHORITY: Broker is not authorized to execute any document in the name of or on behalf of Seller with respect to the Property. Broker will make reasonable efforts and act diligently to sell the Property. Seller authorizes Broker and Broker's associates to:

   A. advertise the Property by means and methods as Broker determines;
   B. place a "For Sale" sign on the Property;
   C. remove from the Property all other signs offering the Property for sale or lease;
   D. furnish comparative marketing and sales information about other properties to prospective buyers;
   E. disseminate information about the Property to other brokers and their associates;
   F. enter the Property at reasonable times to show the Property to prospective buyers;
   G. obtain information from any holder of any note secured by a lien on the Property;
   H. upon a final and closed sale of the Property, disclose the sales price and terms of sale to other brokers, appraisers, or other real estate professionals; and
   I. accept earnest money and deposit the earnest money in trust in accordance with the terms of a contract for the sale of the Property.

12. SELLER'S REPRESENTATIONS: Seller represents that:

   A. Seller has fee simple title to and peaceable possession of the Property and all its improvements and fixtures thereon, unless rented, and the legal capacity to convey the Property;
   B. Seller is not now a party to a listing agreement with another broker for the sale, exchange or lease of the Property;
   C. any pool or spa and any required enclosures, fences, gates, and latches comply with all applicable laws and ordinances;
   D. no person or entity has any right to purchase, lease, or acquire the Property by virtue of an option, right of first refusal, or other agreement;
   E. there are no delinquencies or defaults under any deed of trust, mortgage, or other encumbrance on the Property;

(TAR-1101) 8-01-98   Initialed for Identification by Broker/Associate _____ and Seller _____, _____   Page 4 of 6

FIGURE
5.2

TAR Exclusive Right-to-Sell Listing (continued)

Residential Listing concerning _____

   F. the Property is not subject to the jurisdiction of any court; and
   G. all information relating to the Property provided to Broker by Seller is true and correct.

13. SELLER'S ADDITIONAL PROMISES: Seller agrees to:

   A. cooperate fully in good faith with Broker to facilitate the showing and marketing of the Property;
   B. not rent or lease the Property during the term of this Listing without the prior written approval of Broker;
   C. not negotiate with any prospective buyer who may contact Seller directly, but refer all prospective buyers to Broker;
   D. not enter into a listing agreement with another broker for the sale, exchange or lease of the Property to become effective during the term of this Listing;
   E. employ a pool maintenance company, if there is a pool on the Property and the Property is or becomes vacant, to maintain the pool and all required enclosures in compliance with all applicable laws and ordinances; and
   F. provide Broker with copies of all leases or rental agreements, if any, pertaining to the Property and advise Broker of any tenants moving in or out of the Property.

14. LIMITATION OF LIABILITY: If the Property is or becomes vacant during the term of this Listing, Seller must notify Seller's casualty insurance company and request a "Vacancy Clause" to cover the Property. Broker is not responsible for the security of the Property nor for inspecting the Property on any periodic basis. Broker is not responsible or liable in any manner for personal injury to any person or for loss or damage to any person's real or personal property resulting from: (i) acts of third parties; (ii) vandalism; (iii) theft; (iv) freezing water pipes; (v) a dangerous condition on the Property; (vi) the Property's non-compliance with any law or ordinance; and (vii) any act or omission not caused by Broker's negligence. Seller agrees to protect, defend, indemnify, and hold Broker harmless from any liability for which Broker is not responsible under this Listing.

15. IRS: The Internal Revenue Service (IRS) requires a closing agent to report the gross sales price, Seller's tax identification number and other required information to the IRS. Seller will provide to any closing agent such information at the time of closing. IRS requires a buyer of real property to withhold a percentage of the sales price from Seller if Seller is a foreign person. A foreign person includes nonresident aliens, foreign corporations, foreign partnerships, foreign trusts, or foreign estates. In most sales, Seller will be required to deliver an affidavit that Seller is not a foreign person. Seller certifies that Seller ❑ is ❑ is not a foreign person.

16. SPECIAL PROVISIONS:

17. DEFAULT: If Seller breaches this Listing (including but not limited to leasing or selling the Property without Broker's knowledge and consent), Seller is in default and will be liable to Broker for the amount of the Broker's Fee specified in Paragraph 5A. If Broker breaches this Listing, Broker is in default and Seller may exercise any remedy at law.

18. MEDIATION: The parties agree to negotiate in good faith in an effort to resolve any dispute related to this Listing that may arise between the parties. If the dispute cannot be resolved by negotiation, the dispute will be submitted to mediation before resorting to arbitration or litigation. If the need for mediation arises, the parties to the dispute will choose a mutually acceptable mediator and will share the cost of mediation equally.

19. ATTORNEYS' FEES: If Seller or Broker is a prevailing party in any legal proceeding brought as a result of a dispute under this Listing or any transaction related to or contemplated by this Listing, such party will be entitled to recover from the non-prevailing party all costs of such proceeding and reasonable attorneys' fees.

20. NOTICES: All notices must be in writing and are effective when hand-delivered, mailed, or sent by facsimile transmission to:

Broker at _____ Seller at_____
Phone ( ) Phone ( )
Fax ( ) Fax ( )

(TAR-1101) 8-01-98   Initialed for Identification by Broker/Associate _____ and Seller _____, _____   Page 5 of 6

FIGURE
5.2   **TAR Exclusive Right-to-Sell Listing (continued)**

Residential Listing concerning _____

21. AGREEMENT OF PARTIES:

A. Addenda: Addenda and other related documents which are part of this Listing are: **Information About Brokerage Services, those disclosures or notices marked in Paragraph 8, and** _____

B. Entire Agreement: This Listing contains the entire agreement between the parties and may not be changed except by written agreement.

C. Assignability: This Listing may not be assigned by either party without the written approval of the other party.

D. Binding Effect: This Listing is binding upon the parties, their heirs, administrators, executors, successors, and permitted assigns.

E. Joint and Several: All Sellers executing this Listing are jointly and severally liable for the performance of all its terms

F. Governing Law: The laws of the State of Texas govern the interpretation, validity, performance, and enforcement of this Listing.

G. Severability: If any clause in this Listing is found to be invalid or unenforceable by a court of law, the remainder of this Listing will not be affected and all other provisions of this Listing will remain valid and enforceable.

22. ADDITIONAL NOTICES:

A. **Broker's Fees, or the sharing of fees between brokers are not fixed, controlled, recommended, suggested, or maintained by the Association of REALTORS®, MLS, or any listing service. Brokerage fees are set by individual firms and may be negotiable.**

B. Fair housing laws require the Property to be shown and made available for sale to all persons without regard to race, color, religion, national origin, sex, disability or familial status. Local ordinances may provide for additional protected classes (e.g., creed, status as a student, marital status, sexual orientation, or age).

C. Whether a keybox is authorized or not, Seller is advised to safeguard and remove jewelry and other valuables from the Property.

D. City ordinances, codes, and statutes may regulate the safety and maintenance of certain items in the Property (for example, swimming pools, septic systems, etc.). Non-compliance with the ordinances, codes, and statutes may delay a transaction and may result in fines, penalties, and liability to Seller.

E. Unless expressly agreed otherwise, Broker will submit all offers received by Broker for the sale of the Property, including any back-up offers Broker receives after Seller has entered into a binding contract to sell the Property. However, Broker is not obligated to continue to market the Property after Seller has entered into a binding contract to sell the Property, unless specifically requested by Seller in writing.

F. Residential service contracts are available from licensed residential service companies. A residential service contract is an agreement whereby the residential service company may repair or replace the appliances or the electrical, plumbing, heating, cooling, or other systems. The purchase of a residential service contract is optional. Residential service contracts cover different items and are available from various companies. Some residential service contracts may cover the Seller during the listing period.

G. **Broker cannot give legal advice. This is intended to be a legally binding agreement. READ IT CAREFULLY. If you do not understand the effect of this Listing, consult your attorney BEFORE signing.**

_____   _____   _____   _____
Broker's Printed Name   License No.   Seller's Signature   Date

By: _____   _____   _____
       Broker's or Associate's Signature   Date   Seller's Signature   Date

_____   _____
Seller's Soc. Sec. Nos.   or Tax I.D. Nos.

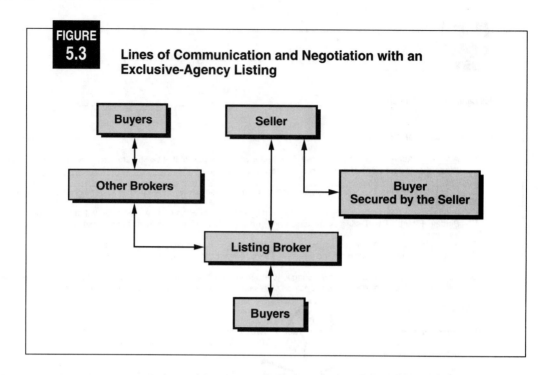

FIGURE 5.3

Lines of Communication and Negotiation with an Exclusive-Agency Listing

Depending on the terms of a specific open listing, the broker may be entitled to a commission if he or she produces an offer from a buyer that meets or exceeds the exact terms of the listing and the owner refuses to sell. The buyer, however, has no rights under the broker's listing agreement to force the owner to sell the property, even if the buyer's offer meets or exceeds the terms of the listing agreement.

One disadvantage of the open listing is that a broker and his or her associates may expend a great deal of energy and time advertising and showing a property, only to have another broker provide the actual buyer and receive the commission. For this reason, most brokers generally will not advertise open listings; however, they will show the properties to buyers in the course of showing other properties.

Most multiple-listing service (MLS) systems refuse to take open listings because of the potential for disputes over procuring cause and commission entitlements. The only broker entitled to a commission under an open listing agreement is the one who procures the buyer. Any broker procuring a buyer for the seller who does not have an open listing agreement with that seller is merely a volunteer, as far as the seller is concerned.

While open listings are not common in residential sales, they are common in the sale of commercial properties and farm and ranch properties. Figure 5.4 shows the lines of communication and negotiation in an open listing.

Net listings relate to the way the broker is paid rather than the type of agency agreement. Any of the agency agreements mentioned previously could be used in a net listing. With these types of listings sellers determine the amount of money they will accept after the costs of sale; the broker receives the remainder as a commission.

This type of listing may present some legal and ethical problems, particularly with an inexperienced seller. Net listings are not illegal in Texas. However, two specific rules of the commission are especially designed to curb potential abuse.

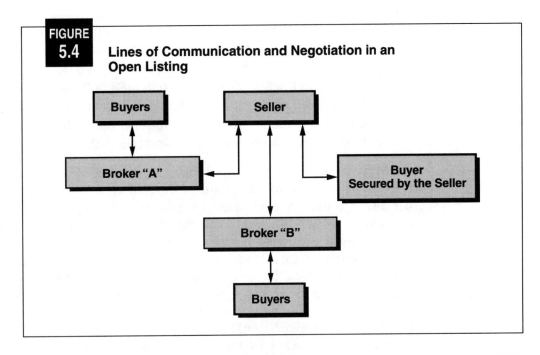

FIGURE 5.4 Lines of Communication and Negotiation in an Open Listing

1. 22 TAC §535.16(b): A "net listing" is a listing agreement in which the broker's commission is the difference ("net") between the sales proceeds and an amount desired by the owner of the real property. A broker may not take net listings unless the principal requires a net listing and the principal appears to be familiar with current market values of real property. When a broker accepts a listing, the broker enters into a fiduciary relationship with the principal, whereby the broker is obligated to make diligent efforts to obtain the best price possible for the principal. The use of a net listing places an upper limit on the principal's expectancy and places the broker's interest above the principal's interest with reference to obtaining the best possible price. If a net listing is used, a broker should modify the listing agreement so as to assure the principal of not less than the principal's desired price and to limit the broker to a specified maximum commission.

2. 22 TAC §535.16(c): A real estate licensee is obligated to advise a property owner as to the licensee's opinion of the market value of a property when negotiating a listing or offering to purchase the property for the licensee's own account as a result of contact made while acting as a real estate agent.

For many years, the Texas Real Estate Commission (TREC) has warned licensees that TREC officially discourages taking net listings because of their possible manipulation and harm to the public, which TREC is designed to protect. In some cases, however, it is the broker rather than the seller who ends up with less money as a result of a net listing.

EXAMPLE: Susan took a net listing on Gertrude's property. The asking price was $85,000, the closing costs were expected to be $6,000 and Gertrude had a loan balance of $69,000. The net listing agreement called for Gertrude to receive $4,000 in cash at closing.

After marketing the property for six months, Gertrude accepted an offer of $81,000 for her property. Susan received $2,000 as her brokerage fee because all costs of sale ($69,000 note + $6,000 closing costs) and the seller's agreed-on net ($4,000) were deducted before Susan's fee could be calculated. If Susan and Gertrude had agreed on the 7 percent commission her firm had established as its commission fee, she would have earned $5,670.

Most would agree that the broker in the preceding example should have been more careful to safeguard her position in the transaction. However, because a broker is considered to have the expertise to conduct business in a manner that is consistent with the desired outcomes, this transaction may have been one that met her objectives.

The situation that causes the greatest concern is one in which the broker earns an unusually large commission relative to the property being sold. The question in these cases is whether the broker took unfair advantage of a naive seller who was unaware of the real value of the property. Such actions by the broker would be regarded as clear examples of breaching the fiduciary duties owed to the client by the broker. The following example illustrates the problem that concerns most state regulators.

EXAMPLE: Phillip, the broker for Action Real Estate, has been called by Elvin and Elma Jones to list their property. The Joneses have lived in their present home for 60 years and have decided to move to California to be close to their grandchildren. During the listing presentation Mr. and Mrs. Jones tell Phillip that they would like to receive $75,000 cash for their home, and if he can guarantee them that amount they will be absolutely delighted with the sale. In fact, they are quite willing for Phillip to keep whatever amount he can obtain over the $75,000 plus closing costs and repairs. Phillip attempts to tell the Joneses that he believes that the home will sell for at least $150,000, but the Joneses are not impressed and tell him, "Just get us $75,000 to take to California and we will be very happy." The Joneses sign the listing agreement. The home subsequently sells for $160,000. At closing the Joneses receive their $75,000, the closing costs and repairs cost $15,000 and Phillip receives $65,000! One week later the grandchildren call and threaten to bring a lawsuit against Action Real Estate for fraud.

? QUESTIONS

1. How could Action Real Estate have avoided this situation?

2. Could Phillip refuse to take the listing for Action Real Estate?

✎ DISCUSSION

This example appears to be a gross exaggeration; unfortunately, however, there have been many such situations. Action Real Estate could have avoided this problem by insisting on a percentage commission, especially because it was obvious that there was an enormous disparity between what the sellers desired to net and the potential net profit.

Action Real Estate should make sure that it has a clearly written policy regarding net listings that carefully follows TREC rules. At minimum, the broker should be notified by the associate that the sellers desire a net listing so that the final decision can be made by the broker, not the associate. If the sellers continue to insist on the net listing, the broker may refuse to enter into the agreement (knowing that a potential lawsuit is almost guaranteed) or give full disclosures that are signed by the sellers. The broker may suggest that family members enter into the discussion, although many sellers might reject this proposal, believing that it would be an unwelcome intrusion.

A *one-time-showing agreement* allows the terms of the agreement to apply to a specific buyer only. This frequently is used in situations where the seller is offering the property "for sale by owner" but is agreeable to allowing a licensee to show the property to a single potential buyer. If an acceptable contract of sale is entered into between that buyer and the seller, the broker will receive a commission according to the terms of the agreement.

It is important that the relationship between the seller and the agent as well as the relationship between the buyer and the agent be fully understood and *disclosed*. Numerous court cases have resulted from misunderstandings of who represented whom in these situations. Licensees are frequently unaware that their obligation to the seller under a one-time-showing agreement may be the same as under any other agency agreement.

■ Benefits of Seller Agency Relationships

Agency Benefits to Seller or Landlord

The following are some of the benefits to sellers and landlords who are represented by agents instead of representing themselves in a sale or leasing transaction.

Reaching buyers through broad marketing. *Reaching buyers through marketing efforts* has long been one of the most valuable services that real estate professionals have offered sellers. Sellers generally do not have the expertise or the funds to advertise effectively. When a broker has numerous agency contracts with sellers, advertising can be combined to give each seller's property the greatest possible exposure to the market. Brokers who are members of the MLS also market to other real estate professionals in their areas through this medium. The Internet has become a powerful means for brokers to advertise their listings. Many licensees as well as professional real estate organizations have begun to develop Web sites on the Internet that provide valuable new conduits for advertising. Although there are several Internet listing services available, the National Association of REALTORS® (NAR®) realtor.com Internet site has received considerable attention from real estate professionals and the public since it began posting listings from local boards of REALTORS® from around the country.

Receiving advice and opinions that inform the seller or landlord. *Giving advice and opinions* is another of the basic services that an agent offers to the seller. Licensees are considered to be the "experts" in the field of real estate, and sellers and landlords are anxious to receive information about all aspects of listing and selling or leasing their properties. The information that licensees provide allows sellers to make informed decisions about their transactions. Licensees have an obligation to be knowledgeable about market conditions, financing conditions for buyers and tenants and all other aspects of the real estate market that affect their clients.

Assistance in contract negotiations. *Assistance in contract negotiations* for the seller/landlord also represents another key benefit to the seller in seller representation. Sellers' agents may be able to greatly assist sellers during negotiations by giving helpful advice relating to pricing, favorable financing options, counteroffers and other terms and conditions of a sale. Many sellers are unprepared for the many details of contract negotiations and must rely on their agents for such assistance.

Confidentiality. When agents represents the seller they are obligated to keep confidential the negotiating position of the seller/landlord and all other information that might compromise the owner's interests; except those aspects that must legally be disclosed such as property or title condition. If the owner is selling or renting the property himself or herself, and the licensee has obtained information in a manner that was not confidential, that licensee is under no obligation withhold the information from a prospective buyer/tenant. In fact, if the buyer/tenant is a client, that licensee has an affirmative duty to disclose all information that might be relevant in his or her client's decision to purchase or lease.

Benefits to Seller or Landlord's Agents

The seller/landlord's agent can expect certain benefits from a seller/landlord agency that would not be available to them when the owner represents him or herself.

Greater understanding of the circumstances of the sale/lease. When a licensee is attempting to locate property for a buyer customer he or she will often show owner listed properties. Without an understanding of the circumstance of the sale or lease the licensee may lose the potential sale or lease due to a lack of important information that would aid in facilitating the transaction.

Incentive to market the property. With an Exclusive Right to Sell/Lease or an Exclusive Agency agreement, the agent will feel more comfortable marketing the property, since there is a reasonable expectation that the property will sell or be leased and a commission will follow. Without some expectation of a return, as perhaps with an open listing, an agent may find it necessary to reserve scarce advertising dollars for other more promising opportunities. Sellers should be made aware of these limitations when deciding on the type of listing agreement into which they are entering.

No conflict of loyalties. A seller/landlord's agent will feel free to be an advocate for the seller/landlord. There should be no conflict of interest when showing buyer-customers, as the agent's loyalty is strictly to the owner. The agent must always be fair and honest with the buyer, however; the owner's interests will be the primary focus of the agent during negotiations.

Limited liability for the acts of the buyer's broker. When the buyer employs his or her own agent, the owner's agent is not responsible for the actions of that agent. This can be particularly important when a buyer's agent gives misinformation or makes a misstatement of a material fact without the knowledge of the listing agent. Texas law gives some protection from the acts of other brokers and their agents, however, when a buyer employs his or her own agent there may be a more clearly defined separation of liability.

■ Approaches to Representing Sellers

Brokers have several options when deciding on company policy regarding seller agency. These options include

- *exclusive seller representation,* in which brokers and associates represent sellers only, whether they are showing buyers properties listed by their own companies (in-house sales) or properties listed by other brokers (cooperative sales);

- *nonexclusive seller representation,* in which brokers and their associates represent sellers on all in-house transactions but may represent *buyers* when selling the listings of other brokers;

- *subagency,* which may involve permitting brokers and associates from other firms to represent a listing broker's sellers through their firms or permitting a broker's associates to represent sellers listed by other firms through those listing brokers;

- *dual agency,* in which the broker represents both buyer and seller in the same transaction; or

- *intermediary,* in which the broker may act as an agent of both buyer and seller but with reduced representation to both while negotiating a transaction between the parties.

Although *subagency, dual agency* and *intermediary* relationships are covered in detail in later chapters, these working definitions will be helpful as we discuss seller agency in this chapter.

■ Exclusive Seller Agency

Some real estate brokerage firms represent only sellers. In this situation the seller is always the client, the buyer is always the customer. Until the increased acceptance of buyer agency, exclusive seller agency was the traditional and predominate type of practice. In Texas, some traditional brokerages have made the transition to other forms of agency representation, whereas other firms retain their commitment to represent sellers exclusively.

These exclusive seller agencies encourage buyers and tenants who want representation to seek buyers' or tenants' brokers, appraisers or attorneys. The broker usually offers to work with buyers or tenants in the purchase or lease of property as long as they realize that the broker and all licensed associates of the firm represent the interests of the sellers and landlords.

Licensees working in firms representing sellers exclusively must be careful not to convey the impression that the buyer is being represented. A variety of situations can arise for licensees working in exclusive seller agency firms. Brokers and associates should have a clear understanding of their duties when conducting *in-house sales* as well as *cooperative sales* involving other brokers.

Many firms today find that it is beneficial to represent people generally rather than people classified by their relationship to the property in question—that is, a broker may wish to represent a person whether that person sells, buys or leases a property. As a result, exclusive seller agency is no longer the majority practice.

In-House Sales

A large number of residential real estate transactions involve the services of two brokers in a cooperative sale. However, a significant number of sales are in-house sales, especially in those real estate firms with large market shares. In-house sales involve only one broker, although several associates from the same brokerage firm may participate. In an in-house sale, brokers and their associates offering exclusive seller agency will treat buyers as customers, not clients.

When a seller lists a property with a broker, the seller expects—and Texas law demands—that everyone associated with the brokerage firm use his or her best efforts to produce a ready, willing and able buyer. In a firm offering exclusive seller agency, the broker, the associate taking the listing and all associates in the firm work exclusively for the seller to find a buyer.

Many brokers prefer to sell their listings in-house because of the control they maintain over the transactions and because of the prospect of earning the full commission. Some firms offer the selling associate a greater share of the commission as an incentive for producing an in-house sale. This incentive may motivate some associates to look primarily toward in-house listings, something that *may not* be in the best interests of every prospective buyer.

Cooperative Sales

Because significant numbers of transactions occur between two brokerage firms, particularly in large metropolitan areas with active MLSs, licensees should understand the roles they play in cooperative sales. The brokers, and all associates of those brokers who offer exclusive seller representation will *always* seek to act as subagents of the listing broker's client when selling another broker's listing. Should the other broker not offer subagency, the exclusive seller agent could not show the property.

Exclusive Seller Agency in Practice

In the following examples assume that Sally is a top salesperson for Bay Realty, a multioffice firm offering exclusive seller agency.

***EXAMPLE 1:* Sally as the listing associate.** Sally successfully acquires for Bay Realty an exclusive listing of a three-bedroom town house from her friend George. At the first open house conducted by Sally, prospective buyer Betty discusses the property with Sally. Sally initially discloses to Betty that she is an agent of the seller and furnishes Betty with a written TREC statement regarding information about brokerage services. Later that night Sally prepares an offer from Betty on George's property, which is later accepted by George.

? QUESTIONS

1. Because Sally represents the seller through Bay Realty, must she suggest that Betty use another brokerage firm that would represent Betty's interest?

2. Would Bay Realty's agency role change if Betty were referred to a different licensee within the firm?

Q DISCUSSION

In this case, Bay Realty clearly represents George only. No facts indicate that Bay Realty has become an implied agent of Betty because of any of Sally's actions. No law prohibits in-house sales or requires that Sally suggest that the buyer hire another broker to prepare the offer. Sally can show the property, explain its features and deliver the buyer's offer without creating any implied agency with the buyer—in fact, that's her job. However, Sally must tell Betty that she is the agent of the seller and that she does not represent Betty. Also, unless Betty is represented by an agent, Sally must present Betty with a written statement regarding representation responsibilities as required by TRELA §15C. This statement must be presented at the first face-to-face meeting between Sally and Betty. Otherwise, the disclosure is not timely and may fail to protect Sally in case of a later lawsuit.

***EXAMPLE 2:* Sally as the selling associate with no prior relationship with the buyer.** Bay Realty has a policy of exclusive seller representation. Sally is the licensee on duty when Bob Brown walks in and asks about available properties. Sally checks Bay Realty's listings and finds a property on Main Street listed by Carol, from a branch office of Bay Realty, and one on King Street listed by Tom, from Southside Realty on the other side of town. Sally makes appointments to show Bob both properties.

? QUESTIONS

1. Because Sally is not the listing agent on the Main Street property, will she be free to represent Bob on this property?

2. When Sally shows the properties, how will her duties to Bob and to the sellers differ when she shows the Main Street property from when she shows the King Street Property?

DISCUSSION

Sally must remember that Bay Realty is the agent of the seller of the Main Street property and will be the subagents of the sellers of the King Street property. Even though an associated licensee other than Sally took the listing on the Main Street property, Sally is bound to act in the best interests of the seller. Because Bay Realty represents sellers exclusively, the same thing is true on the King Street property. Sally should be careful not to give Bob the impression that she can represent him in negotiations regarding *any* property. She can do this by giving Bob the written statement required by TRELA §15C, discussing it with him, and disclosing her agency relationship with the sellers. In an exclusive seller agency firm, Sally should treat Bob as a customer, not as a client.

 EXAMPLE 3: **Sally as the selling associate with prior relationship with buyer.** Sally, as listing agent, has just negotiated a completed sales contract on George's town house. She has opened escrow by placing the contract and earnest money with the escrow agent named in the contract. George is extremely pleased with Sally's professional attitude and skills and asks her to find a suitable replacement property. Sally is well aware of George's needs and wants, as well as his financial resources and favorite bargaining techniques. Sally knows a perfect property for George, and it happens to be listed with Bay Realty through Tom, another Bay Realty salesperson.

Sally knows from experience that when satisfied clients like George sell their homes and buy replacement properties in the same locality, the client typically works with the same listing agent (Sally, in this case). It is natural for George to think that Sally is still his agent. Sally recognizes that the seller of the new home might find it useful, in negotiations, to know how much cash George will receive from his recent sale and when George is planning to move. This seller, like most sellers, wants to learn as much information as possible from the agent about the buyer, especially if the offer is contingent on financing.

? **QUESTIONS**

1. If Sally is to represent the new seller on behalf of Bay Realty, should Sally disclose these useful facts to the seller?

2. Would such disclosure surprise George or violate any fiduciary duty to him?

 DISCUSSION

This in-house "turn around" sale, so common in today's market, can present some confusing agency relationship questions. Is Bay Realty now representing two parties? Is George a client in the listing of his town house and a customer in buying the replacement property? Is it understandable for George to expect he'll continue to receive client-level services, even though his status has changed from seller to buyer?

It would be the path of least resistance for Sally to keep quiet, to avoid raising any of these questions, to simply proceed to do the best job for both parties and hope all goes well. This too often happens in the real world of real estate, especially with real estate licensees who regard themselves primarily as facilitators who help work out differences between buyers and sellers and bring a transaction to a successful close. The correct approach, though, is to clarify each relationship through discussion and disclosure to the buyer and the seller.

Because Bay Realty represents sellers *exclusively,* George must be made fully aware that in the purchase transaction he will be receiving the reduced services extended to buyer-customers and will not enjoy client status. Sally also must inform the seller of the home that George is interested in purchasing that because of a prior client relationship with George, there might be financial information known to Sally regarding George that she cannot disclose to the seller. Even with the informed consent of both parties, Bay Realty may be on shaky ground. Changing George's status from client to customer may be difficult at best.

If either George or the seller is not in agreement with Bay Realty's role in the transaction, Sally should not proceed until the agency issues are resolved. One possible alternative is to refer George to another firm offering buyers' brokerage services so he can get representation in the purchase of the home. In this scenario, Sally or any licensee within Bay Realty still would be prohibited from disclosing George's financial circumstances to the seller because that information was gained during a client relationship with George. Before continuing with the transaction, the seller must give informed consent to Sally and Bay Realty.

Advantages and Disadvantages of Exclusive Seller Agency

Some advantages of exclusive seller agency are as follows:

- It reduces chances of conflicts of interest that may arise by mixing dual representation or buyer agency in the same firm, especially if the brokerage has a considerable number of licensed associates and listings.

- Sellers receive 100 percent loyalty and confidentiality, with someone advocating their best interests and providing expert advice.

- It may be more comfortable and familiar to licensees trained as sellers' agents.

- It is a proven method of compensation in cooperating sales transactions.

- Agency lines are clarified in the in-house sale.

Some disadvantages of exclusive seller agency include the following:

- It does not satisfy the needs of qualified buyers seeking representation.

- An increased potential exists for undisclosed representation of more than one party (may be an implied buyer agency).

- The broker may lose buyers who want representation.

■ Nonexclusive Seller Agency

Rather than choosing to represent sellers exclusively, many firms wish to represent buyers and sellers, but *not* in the same transaction. This means that the brokerage firm will engage buyers in representation agreements, but will show only properties listed by other brokers to their buyer clients. (Buyer representation is covered in detail in Chapter 6.) An advantage of nonexclusive over exclusive seller representation is that the broker at least can offer representation services to buyers on properties not listed by the firm. The obvious disadvantage of this form of nonexclusive seller representation is that a buyer wishing to be represented by the firm cannot be shown any property listed by that firm. This may work to the disadvantage of the buyer, the seller and the firm. That is, the buyer may not have access to a desirable property, the seller may miss a sale and the firm is unable to earn a commission.

In an effort to overcome the problem of not being able to show represented buyers properties listed in-house, some brokers have an understanding with buyers to show properties listed with their firms *prior* to entering into a buyer representation agreement. If after viewing the firm's listings a suitable property has not been found, the broker and buyer then enter into a buyer representation agreement in which the broker agrees to represent the buyer on all properties listed by other brokers. If such an arrangement is undertaken by the broker, the buyer must be made fully aware of the lack of representation that will occur if they choose to negotiate on any property listed by the brokerage firm. In addition, the broker who wishes to avoid situations that involve representing more than one party in a transaction must be prepared to deal with a possible dilemma if a buyer who has entered into a representation agreement later decides to negotiate on a listing held by the firm.

 EXAMPLE: Reconsider Example 2 above, "Sally as the selling agent with no prior relationship with the buyer." Sally wishes to show Bob, a potential buyer, the Main Street property, listed by a fellow associate of Bay Realty and the King Street property, listed by Southside Realty. In this scenario, however, presume that Bay Realty offers both seller agency and buyer agency (nonexclusive representation), but does not offer services to buyers represented by the firm on properties listed by the firm. Further presume that Bob would like to be represented as a buyer-client.

? QUESTIONS

1. What role can Sally play when showing Bob the Main Street property (in-house transaction)?

2. What role can Sally play when showing Bob the King Street property listed by Southside Realty?

3. At what point should Sally and Bay Realty agree to represent Bob?

4. How will circumstances change if Bob decides to reconsider the Main Street property after Bay Realty agrees to represent him?

Q DISCUSSION

Keep in mind that Bay Realty, while offering representation to both sellers and buyers, will not act as representatives of both parties in the same transaction. Of course, Bob first must be made aware of the services that may be offered to buyers and sellers by brokers and, more specifically, the services offered by Bay Realty. Bob should understand that neither Sally nor any other associate of Bay Realty can represent him on the Main Street property or on any other property listed by Bay Realty. However, because Bay Realty does not limit representation to sellers, it could represent him as a client on either the King Street property or any other property listed by another broker who allows cooperation by brokers who represent buyers.

After a thorough discussion of these alternatives, if Bob wishes to view any property listed by Bay Realty, he should do this *before* he enters into a representation agreement with Bay Realty. If no suitable property is found, then Bay Realty and Bob could enter into a representation agreement for properties listed by other brokers. If Bob is not satisfied with customer status on Bay Realty's listings, he should be referred to another brokerage firm that will offer the desired representation.

The most difficult situation would occur if Bob decided to negotiate on a listing of Bay Realty after it agreed to represent him. Because Bay Realty does not offer representation to buyers and sellers in the same transaction, it could consider one of the following options:

- Rescind the representation agreement with Bob and show the properties to him as a customer, notifying the sellers that Bob is a *prior client* and that the seller may not receive full disclosure regarding Bob's financial status or other matters gained in confidence;

- Rescind the listing agreement with the seller and show Bob the property as a client while serving the seller as a customer, notifying Bob that the seller is a *prior client* and that he may not receive full disclosure regarding the seller's matters; or

- Refer Bob to another brokerage firm and represent the seller only. When addressing issues of representation, the broker should keep in mind that principals must always be in agreement before proceeding. Sellers who enter into listing agreements with brokers, must be informed as to the various roles that licensees may play. It is *sellers* who must decide whether to authorize brokers to represent buyers as well as themselves when showing their properties.

Advantages and Disadvantages of Nonexclusive Seller Agency

Some of the advantages of nonexclusive seller agency are as follows:

- Offers sellers full representation under listing agreements
- Permits the broker to offer full representation services to buyers on properties not listed by the broker
- Permits the "turn around" sale, where the seller as a prior client could be represented when desiring to purchase a home from the list-ing firm, so long as the desired property is not listed by the firm

The *disadvantages* of nonexclusive seller agency include the following:

- Disallows in-house sales to buyers and sellers demanding representation
- May create confusion among buyers and sellers as to what role the licensee is playing
- Sometimes creates difficult situations of attempting to change pre-existing agency roles with buyers or sellers
- May require referring business to other brokers

■ Disclosure Issues

Disclosures of Seller's Agent to Seller

Before signing the listing agreement, the listing agent should provide the seller with the written statement required by TRELA §15C, which describes the services that the seller may expect from a seller's agent, a buyer's agent and an intermediary. TRELA requires that the listing agent provide this statement at the first face-to-face meeting with the seller—that is, the first meeting at which a "substantive discussion occurs with respect to the specific real property." In addition, the seller's agent should attempt to provide as much information to the seller as is reasonable to ensure that the seller is fully informed regarding matters such as

- general company policies regarding cooperating with other brokers,
- the fact that buyer/tenant agents represent the buyer/tenant, even if paid by the listing broker or the seller, and
- the possibility, if any, of the listing agent's acting as an agent for both the seller and a buyer.

The licensee obtaining the listing also should discuss with the seller whether an MLS will be used and whether a blanket offer allowing other brokers to represent the seller through the listing broker will be permitted by the seller.

TREC rules require that a real estate licensee give the seller the licensees opinion of market value of the property at the time of negotiating a listing. If the licensee expects to receive compensation from more than one party or to represent buyers as well as the seller in a transaction, the source of compensation and consent to the arrangement must be expressed in writing. These and other disclosures can be made either in the listing agreement or in a special addendum to the listing agreement.

Disclosures of Seller's Agent to Buyer

The seller's agent must disclose to the buyer that the brokerage represents the seller, not the buyer. To facilitate this required disclosure, some firms have the buyer read and acknowledge a customer letter that outlines what the licensee can and cannot do for the buyer while acting as an agent of the seller. This letter could soften the tone of the disclosure, but should not diminish the intent.

Early information and disclosure is the best policy. But keep in mind that state law prevails. If the buyer is not represented by an agent, the written information statement required by TRELA §15C must be provided at the first face-to-face meeting with the buyer. This statement, known as the "Information about Brokerage Services" notice, contains state-mandated language relating to the various roles that a broker may play in a transaction. In addition, the agent must disclose to the buyer that the agent is the seller's representative at the time of the first contact with the buyer. This *agency disclosure* may be oral or written.

Remember, the seller's agent dealing with a buyer cannot provide advice regarding the buyer's purchase decision that may be considered adverse to the seller's best interests unless it is information that the licensee is required, by law, to supply, such as a known defect in the property.

The seller's agent also should make clear to the buyer-customer that the licensee works on behalf of the seller on all negotiable issues. It is important to note at this point that almost every term or condition in any potential sales contract is fully negotiable between the buyer and the seller. The fact that TREC-promulgated forms for contracts may call for certain costs to be paid by the buyer and other costs to be paid by the seller in no way prohibits principals in the transaction from reallocating those costs to the other party through negotiation.

It is the licensee's legal obligation to make the contract conform to the intent of the principals. Therefore, licensees may add factual statements and business details desired by the principals and should strike from the contract only those items desired by them [22 TAC §537.11(d)]. A fine line exists here between modifying the contract to "conform the instrument to the intent of the parties" and engaging in the unauthorized practice of law. All Texas licensees should be thoroughly familiar with the provisions and implications of TRELA §16 and 22 TAC §537.11 before they attempt to assist in contract negotiations.

A nonrepresented buyer should deal with the seller's agent as though dealing or negotiating directly with the seller. The buyer should be told in the initial interview not to disclose anything to the seller's agent that the buyer would not tell the seller. Additionally, the buyer should be told not to expect to receive any information from the seller's agent that the seller would not want to tell the buyer directly. The seller's agent must be careful in responding to questions such as "How low will the seller go?" "Will the seller take less?" "How can I get the seller to compromise on terms and come down in price?" Questions like these should elicit carefully rehearsed answers so that the agent appears professional and competent, replies honestly and fairly and is not disloyal to the client or misleading to the customer.

■ Summary

The broker who consistently acts in the sole capacity of a seller's agent has little trouble distinguishing the client from the customer. Until the early 1990s, firms with large shares of the market often chose this type of relationship to lessen the risk of conflicts of loyalty in selling their own listings. However, with the passage of laws requiring better information and disclosures to the parties, buyers and sellers are becoming more aware of agency options. As a result, many Texas firms are experimenting with a variety of policies. Some firms have clearly stated policies of not offering cooperation with other brokers except on an individual, case-by-case basis. Great care should be exercised, both with in-house sales and cooperative sales, to avoid conduct that could be interpreted to create implied agencies with the buyers if none is intended. Supervising brokers can and should develop policies and procedures and competently train licensed associates to act consistently with company policy.

■ Key Points

- Expressed listing agreements can be written or oral.
- Implied listing agreements are created by words or conduct of the parties.
- Early disclosure of seller agency helps lessen the chance that the buyer will claim later that the broker also represented the buyer.
- Written disclosures and brochures help clarify that the buyer is the customer and the seller is the client. Warning: Do not substitute the word *impartially* or *equally* for its sometime synonym *fairly* in the context of how an agent for the seller-client will treat the buyer-customer. The customer must be treated fairly by law, but not impartially or equally, relative to the client.

■ Suggestions for Brokers

Review with your licensed associates the types of services they can provide to accommodate at least some of the needs of the buyer while remembering that they act as agents of the seller.

To ensure that your licensed associates do not accidentally create an implied or accidental agency with the buyer, require that the associates have the buyer acknowledge *in writing* that your firm and your associate act as agents of the seller, not as agents of the buyer.

Develop a company policy regarding net listing that includes the TREC requirements for disclosure.

■ Quiz

1. A listing broker owes which of the following duties to the prospective buyer-customer?

   A. Loyalty
   B. Obedience
   C. Agency disclosure
   D. All of the above

2. A broker who does not wish to represent buyers under any circumstances is practicing

   A. dual agency.
   B. intermediary brokerage.
   C. nonexclusive seller agency.
   D. exclusive seller agency.

3. A listing broker normally can do all of the following *except*

   A. sell the listing broker's own listings.
   B. advertise listed properties.
   C. hold open houses.
   D. split fees with a buyer's broker without the seller's knowledge.

4. A buyer approaches Broker Smith, an exclusive seller's agent, and requests to be represented in the purchase of a home. Broker Smith should

   A. explain that there are no real benefits to buyer representation.
   B. explain that while he cannot personally work with the buyer, one of his associates may do so.
   C. describe the services that the buyer may receive as a customer, but if the buyer still wants representation, refer the buyer to a buyer's broker.
   D. show the buyer only properties listed by other brokers.

5. A net listing requires that the

   A. seller accept the net amount of money remaining after all costs of sale.
   B. seller independently determine the value of the property.
   C. agent advise the seller of the value of the property.
   D. agent limit the amount of commission charged.

6. The listing that allows the seller to list with several brokers is the

   A. exclusive right to sell.
   B. exclusive agency.
   C. open listing.
   D. net agency.

7. A listing agreement that applies only to a specific buyer is called

   A. an exclusive right to sell.
   B. a net agency agreement.
   C. an exclusive agency agreement.
   D. a one-time-showing agreement.

8. A subagent brings a full-priced offer to purchase to the listing broker but is later informed that the seller has elected not to sell the property. The subagent

   A. has no right to sue under the terms of the listing agreement.
   B. may file suit against the listing broker for his commission.
   C. may force the listing broker to file suit against his client.
   D. may file suit against the seller for his commission.

9. The seller says he will list with you as long as he gets enough to pay his loan balance and closing costs. Your commission will be anything above those costs. This is an example of

A. an open listing.
B. a one-time showing agreement.
C. a net listing.
D. a fixed commission listing.

10. If the broker chooses nonexclusive seller agency as an office policy, then a represented buyer who wishes to be shown a property listed by that broker

A. may only be represented if the broker acts as an intermediary.
B. may only be represented if the broker acts as a dual agent.
C. must be referred to another broker if they insist on continued representation.
D. should insist on continued representation by that broker since Texas law permits buyer representation.

■ Discussion Questions

1. Why can't licensed associates take listings with them when they transfer to new firms?

2. In exclusive seller agency brokerage firms, what is the best way to handle a transaction in which the seller wants help in finding a replacement property?

3. How would you offer to help a prospective buyer you meet at an open house and still remain loyal to the seller?

4. What should the associate of a listing broker say when the nonrepresented buyer asks common questions such as

   ■ How low will the seller go?

   ■ Do you think the property is worth what the seller is asking?

   ■ Are there any other offers on the property?

   ■ Have you had any contracts that fell through?

6

Buyer Agency

Although this chapter refers to buyer agency, it should be noted that tenants may be represented by brokers as well. By substituting tenant for buyer and landlord for seller, the licensee can apply the same principles to the leasing of real estate. Buyer agency exists when the broker represents the buyer exclusively in the real estate transaction. Buyer agency is not a revolutionary business practice. For decades, brokers have been employed to represent buyers. Buyer representation has been regularly practiced in commercial real estate transactions for the better part of this century. Brokers also have represented themselves, their business ventures, their relatives and undisclosed principals in the acquisition of real estate. In residential transactions, however, it has been less common to employ a broker under written contract to represent the buyer in the selection, negotiation or acquisition of real estate. Although attitudes are changing today, brokers have generally treated buyers—theoretically, at least—as customers, not as clients.

Residential consumers have begun to see that they can benefit from client-quality representation, whether they are buyers or sellers. In the 1970s and 1980s, some residential brokers began to offer their services to buyers. This has become a rapidly growing market segment; many brokers now offer client-level service to buyers. Other brokers continue to offer only customer-level service to buyers. Many licensees do not understand the basic differences between conduct and duties of agency when representing sellers, buyers or both. This chapter explores the factors that affect the broker's decision to treat certain buyers as clients (rather than as customers) or as one of two clients.

This chapter addresses the following:

Deciding To Represent the Buyer
    Factors To Consider
Myths about Buyer Agency
The Creation of Buyer Agency
    Representation Agreements
    Advantages and Disadvantages of Exclusive Buyer Agency

■ Deciding to Represent the Buyer

When a prospective buyer enters a broker's office asking to see homes for sale, the broker does not necessarily have to represent the buyer in an agency capacity, even if the broker specializes in representing buyers. A seller's agent spends a considerable amount of time leading up to the listing of the seller's property. Likewise, a buyer's agent spends time discussing the buyer's preferences and qualifications.

In some cases, a licensee may not feel comfortable in a fiduciary relationship with a particular buyer. This may be because of preexisting agency relationships the company may have with sellers or because of an analysis of this particular buyer in terms of the buyer's cash, credit or capacity to buy, seriousness in buying or incompatible personality traits. Nevertheless, the licensee still may want to serve that same buyer as a customer. In addition, some licensees choose to spend time showing a buyer properties listed in the multiple-listing service (MLS) with other brokers and choose to act as a subagent of the seller. It is *not necessary* that a broker create an agency relationship to help a buyer locate a property.

The professional licensee recognizes that adequately representing a buyer is a significant responsibility. The licensee is held to a higher standard of care in working with a client than with a customer. If the buyer feels the licensee has given poor advice, the buyer may threaten to sue the agent for breach of fiduciary duty. The buyer might ask, "Who got me into this deal, anyway?" Deciding to offer client-level services, whether the client is the seller or the buyer, is a serious business decision with significant legal and economic consequences. For this reason, many brokers and their associates prefer to work with most buyer prospects on a customer-level basis and with only select buyers on a client-level basis.

Factors to Consider

Unless company policy does not permit buyer representation, nothing prevents a licensee from showing properties to a buyer as a client, provided the licensee clarifies his or her role early in the transaction. When working with a buyer, the licensee should decide, disclose and obtain necessary consents to act. Licensees can act as agents of buyers, subagents of sellers (a licensee not associated with the listing broker but representing the seller through the listing broker) or perhaps agents for both parties. In deciding whether to represent the buyer, licensees should keep several points in mind:

- The broker, not the licensed associate of the broker, is the primary agent of the buyer. If the broker represents the seller, dual representation questions will arise if the broker's associate acts in such a way as to give the impression that he or she represents the buyer. As with seller's listings, if the associated licensee who obtained a buyer's representation agreement leaves the brokerage firm, the agreement remains with the firm. A buyer's representation agreement cannot be transferred automatically to the new brokerage firm with which the licensee is now affiliated.

- The real estate licensee can, with proper disclosures, provide valuable services to a buyer without creating an agency relationship. This is especially true with in-house sales. Real estate firms that wish to avoid representing more than one party develop ways to accommodate some of the needs of buyers in a seller-oriented service business without crossing into agency representation of buyers.

- Few brokers are exclusively buyers' brokers. Even though some brokers start out representing buyers only, those brokers often find that satisfied buyers eventually turn into sellers and want the brokers to list their properties for sale. The practice of representing either buyers or sellers exclusively is known as *exclusive single agency,* and some brokers feel that this practice may avoid potential conflicts that may arise when representing buyers and sellers.

- Buyers' brokers can, with proper authority, appoint subagents to help in the search for the right property. This is especially useful in long-distance transactions, for example, when employees of nationwide companies are transferred and relocated.

■ Myths about Buyer Agency

Early on, certain myths created obstacles to the widespread acceptance of licensees representing buyers as clients. Acknowledgment by the National Association of REALTORS® (NAR®) and other professional real estate organizations of buyer brokerage as a viable business arrangement has helped to dispel these myths, but some—such as the following—survive:

- Buyer agency is illegal.

- Buyer agency is prohibited by MLS rules.

- Buyer agency does not permit the seller to pay the commission, nor does it allow the listing broker to split commissions with the buyer's agent.

- Buyer agency is not recognized by lenders.

- Buyer agency increases the risk of procuring-cause disputes.

- Buyer agency is too complicated for the average buyer or seller to understand.

- Buyer agency must be created by written agreement to be lawful.

■ The Creation of Buyer Agency

A buyer-agency relationship can be created by verbal agreement or by implication and may be expressed orally or in writing. Texas requires only an intermediary agreement to be in writing. The requirement that some note or memorandum of an agreement to pay a commission be in writing is a limiting requirement only if the Texas broker wishes to pursue legal action for the recovery of any agreed commission. While a written agreement is certainly preferable for any type of agency agreement, many express buyer agency and listing agreements are oral, with written confirmation noted in the sales contract.

Representation Agreements

A buyer's agent should clarify the types of services to be offered to the buyer-client (in addition to the traditional services rendered by real estate licensees to buyer-customers). These could include such tasks as

- providing data relating to market values,

- assistance in determining favorable financing,

- the structuring of the offer to purchase,

- advice during contract negotiations and

- assistance in investment analyses.

The buyer's agent should mention the potential need for the buyer to consult with legal, tax and other expert advisers.

Buyer-representation agreements can take many forms, depending on what the buyer and the buyer's agent want and are able to negotiate. Even if a licensee decides not to work as an agent with the buyer, the licensee and the buyer may enter into a general written understanding of their working relationship. This can be especially useful in large real estate firms that have many listings and need to avoid claims that the broker has illegally represented more than one party. Under one arrangement, the buyer agrees to work exclusively with the licensee and recognizes that the licensee renders specified *customer*-level services. Under this arrangement the licensee is acting as an agent or a subagent of the seller and generally will be paid by the seller.

Buyers' brokers frequently develop their own buyer-representation agreement forms. Brokers who draft their working agreements without good legal counsel may be taking unnecessary risks, but they are not considered to be engaged in the unauthorized practice of law by so doing. In commercial transactions that involve large commissions, brokers often have their attorneys prepare comprehensive listing agreements. The Texas Real Estate Commission (TREC) has no state-approved or promulgated form for agency agreements, listing agreements, buyer-representation agreements or agreements for representing more than one party. However, the Texas Association of REALTORS® (TAR) and local REALTORS® associations do have such forms, for use by their members only.

In some residential real estate transactions, the form used by the buyer's broker is not comprehensive, unlike those that may be found in big commercial transactions or the more carefully crafted agreements of the exclusive buyer's broker firms. These more generalized agreements are designed to encourage trust and understanding, although they typically may not enable the real estate agent to prevail in a lawsuit. Control of the client arises from the trust relationship itself, not from a supposedly ironclad agreement. Still, the form should be specific on essential items to minimize misunderstandings and disputes.

Some of the key points to consider in any buyer's broker agreements are

- exclusivity of representation,
- termination date,
- conflicts of interest,
- role of the agent and
- compensation and/or fees.

More comprehensive buyer-representation agreements are as protective as well-written exclusive-right-to-sell listing agreements. For example, most buyer's agent agreements have an enforceable exclusive-right-to-purchase clause that allows the broker legal recourse for compensation if the buyer purchases a property without compensating the broker during the period of the agreement, even if the broker did not show the buyer the property. A sample buyer representation agreement is shown in Figure 6.1.

Exclusive right to purchase. Novice buyers' agents are sometimes uncomfortable asking buyers to sign exclusive representation agreements. Some develop a nonexclusive agreement containing an automatic right-to-

FIGURE 6.1

TAR Buyer/Tenant Representation Agreement

EQUAL HOUSING
OPPORTUNITY

TEXAS ASSOCIATION OF REALTORS®
RESIDENTIAL BUYER/TENANT REPRESENTATION AGREEMENT
EXCLUSIVE RIGHT TO PURCHASE/LEASE

REALTOR®

THIS FORM IS FURNISHED BY THE TEXAS ASSOCIATION OF REALTORS® FOR
USE BY ITS MEMBERS. USE OF THIS FORM BY PERSONS NOT MEMBERS
OF THE TEXAS ASSOCIATION OF REALTORS® IS NOT AUTHORIZED.
©Texas Association of REALTORS®,Inc., 1995

1.   PARTIES: The parties to this agreement are
_____(Client) and
_____ (Broker).

2.   APPOINTMENT: In consideration for services to be performed by Broker, Client grants to Broker the exclusive right to act as Client's real estate agent under the terms of this agreement to locate and acquire property for Client in the Market Area. The term "property" means any interest in real estate whether freehold, leasehold, nonfreehold, or an option.

3.   MARKET AREA: Market Area is defined as that area located within the perimeter boundaries of the following areas:
_____
_____
_____
_____ and within the State of Texas.

4.   TERM: This agreement shall commence on _____
_____
(Commencement Date) and terminate at the earlier of: (i) 11:59 p.m. on
_____ (Termination Date);
or (ii) the closing and funding of Client's purchase of property in the Market Area, or upon Client's execution of a binding lease for property in the Market Area. If at the time this agreement is to terminate there is a pending contract for the purchase of property in the Market Area in effect between Client and a seller and the transaction described in such a contract has not closed, Broker's Compensation is earned and shall be payable according to paragraph 8.

5.   BROKER'S OBLIGATIONS Broker shall: (a) use diligence in locating suitable property for Client to purchase or lease within the Market Area; (b) assist Client in negotiating the purchase or lease of suitable property within the Market Area; and (c) use Broker's best efforts to procure the purchase or lease of suitable property within the Market Area on terms acceptable to Client.

6.   CLIENT'S OBLIGATIONS: Client shall: (a) conduct all attempts to locate suitable property to purchase or lease in the Market Area exclusively through Broker; (b) negotiate the purchase or lease of property in the Market Area exclusively through Broker; (c) refer to Broker all inquiries about purchasing or leasing property in the Market Area received from real estate brokers, salesmen, prospective sellers or landlords, or others; (d) inform other real estate brokers, salesmen, and prospective sellers or landlords with whom Client may have contact during the term of this agreement, that Client is subject to this agreement; (e) timely pay to Broker all due compensation in accordance with this agreement; and (f) pay the Retainer to Broker upon final execution of this agreement.

7.   CLIENT'S REPRESENTATIONS: Client represents that: (a) the undersigned person has the legal capacity and authority to bind Client to this agreement; (b) Client is not now a party to another Buyer or Tenant Representation Agreement with another real estate broker for the purchase or lease of property in the Market Area; and (c) all information relating to Client's ability to purchase or lease property in the Market Area given by Client to Broker is true and correct.

8.   BROKER'S COMPENSATION:

NOTICE: §15(a)(6)(D) of the Real Estate License Act prohibits a broker from receiving compensation from more than one party except with the full knowledge and consent of all parties.

(a)   Broker's compensation shall be paid as follows *(choose all paragraphs that apply):*

❑   (1) <u>Fee Paid by Client</u>: If Client purchases property in the Market Area during the term of this agreement, including any renewal or extension, Client shall pay Broker a fee of: (i) $_____; or (ii) _____% of the gross purchase price of the property. If Client leases property in the Market Area during the term of this agreement, including any renewal or extension, Client shall pay Broker a fee of: (i) $_____; or (ii) _____% of all rents to be paid for the term of the lease. Broker's fee under this paragraph is earned when Client enters into a binding written contract for the purchase or lease of property in the Market Area and is payable upon the earlier of: (i) the closing of the purchase of the property; (ii) Client's execution of a lease of the property; (iii) Client's breach of a written contract to purchase or lease a property; or (iv) Client's breach of this agreement.

❑   (2) <u>Fee Paid by Seller or Landlord</u>: If Client purchases property in the Market Area during the term of this agreement, including any renewal or extension, Broker shall seek compensation from the seller or the seller's broker in the amount of: (i) $_____; or (ii) _____% of the gross purchase price of the property. If Client leases property in the Market Area during the term of this agreement, including any renewal or extension, Broker shall seek compensation from the landlord or the landlord's broker in the amount of: (i) $_____; or (ii) _____% of all rents to be paid for the term of the lease. <u>If a seller or landlord, or their broker, refuses to pay Broker's compensation in the amount specified in this agreement, Client shall pay to Broker the amount of Broker's compensation specified less any amounts received from the seller or landlord, or their brokers.</u> Broker's fee under this paragraph is earned when Client enters into a binding written contract for the purchase or lease of property in the Market Area and is payable upon the earlier of: (i) the closing of the purchase of the property; (ii) the execution of a lease of the property; (iii) Client's breach of a written contract to purchase or lease a property; or (iv) Client's breach of this agreement.

❑   (3) <u>Other</u>: _____
_____ .

❑   (4) <u>Broker's Hourly Rate</u>: Client shall pay Broker compensation at the rate of $_____ per hour (Broker's Hourly Rate). If Broker receives a fee pursuant to paragraph 8(a)(1), (2), or (3) Broker ❑ shall ❑ shall not refund the

(TAR- 039) 1-1-96   Initialed for Identification: _____, _____ Client and _____ Broker/Associate   Page 1 of 3

FIGURE 6.1
TAR Buyer/Tenant Representation Agreement (continued)

amounts paid or payable to Broker for Broker's Hourly Rate upon Broker's receipt of the fee. Broker's Hourly Rate is earned when Broker's services are rendered and payable when billed to Client.

☐ (5) Retainer: Upon execution of this agreement Client shall pay to Broker a non-refundable retainer for Broker's services in the amount of $_____. THE RETAINER IS NOT REFUNDABLE with the exception that Broker shall refund the retainer to Client upon Broker's receipt of all other compensation due under this agreement.

(b) Excess compensation: If Broker's compensation is to be paid by a seller, landlord, or their brokers pursuant to paragraph 8(a)(2) and a seller, landlord, or their brokers offer marketing incentives, bonuses, or additional compensation to Broker in excess of the amount of Broker's compensation specified in this agreement, Broker may retain the excess.

(c) Protection Period: If within _____ days after the termination of this agreement (the Protection Period), Client or a Related Party enters into a contract to purchase or lease a legal or equitable interest in property in the Market Area which was called to the attention of Client or a Related Party by Broker, any other broker, or Client during the term of this agreement, Client shall pay to Broker all Broker's compensation under this agreement, in cash at the time the purchase closes or the lease is executed, provided Broker, prior to or within five (5) days after termination of this agreement, has sent to Client written notice specifying the addresses or locations of the properties called to the attention of Client by Broker, any other broker, or Client. If during the term of this Protection Period Client has entered into another Buyer/Tenant Representation Agreement with another Texas-licensed real estate broker at the time the purchase or lease is negotiated, this paragraph shall not apply and Client shall not be obligated to pay Broker's Compensation. "Related Party" means any assignee of Client, any family member or relation of Client, any officer, director, or partner of Client, and any entity owned or controlled, in whole or part, by Client.

(d) County: Client shall pay all compensation to Broker under this agreement in _____ County, Texas, when due and payable.

9. COOPERATING BROKERS: Client authorizes Broker to share or divide Broker's Compensation, on terms and conditions as Broker determines, with any licensed real estate broker or brokers who assist Broker in locating or acquiring property for Client within the Market Area.

10. CLIENT'S IDENTITY: Unless otherwise agreed in writing, Broker may disclose the identity of Client to a prospective seller, landlord, or their agents.

11. COMPETING CLIENTS: Client acknowledges that Broker may represent other prospective buyers or tenants seeking to purchase or lease properties that may meet Client's criteria. Client agrees that Broker may, during the term of this agreement or after its termination, represent such other prospects, show the same properties to other prospects shown to Client, and act as a real estate agent for other prospective buyers or tenants in negotiations for the purchase or lease of the same properties Client may seek to purchase or lease. If Broker submits offers by competing buyers or tenants for the purchase or lease of the same property Client has offered or stands ready to offer to purchase or lease, Broker shall notify Client of the conflicting offers, but shall not disclose any material terms or conditions of any offers made by competing buyers or tenants. Within 3 days after receipt of notice of competing buyers or tenants from Broker, Client may object to the conflict and terminate this agreement in writing or waive any objections to any conflict by reason of competing buyers or tenants. Failure

to object within the time specified shall be deemed to be Client's waiver of any objections under this paragraph.

12. AGENCY RELATIONSHIPS:

(a) Client acknowledges receipt of the attached exhibit entitled **"Information About Brokerage Services",** which is incorporated in this agreement for all purposes.

(b) Broker shall exclusively represent Client in negotiations for the purchase or lease of property in the Market Area unless Client authorizes Broker, as set forth below, to act as an intermediary in the event Broker also represents a seller or landlord of property that Client wishes to offer to purchase or lease (choose (1) or (2)):

☐ (1) Intermediary Relationship Authorized: Client authorizes Broker to show to Client properties which Broker has listed for sale or lease. If Client wishes to purchase or lease any property Broker has listed for sale or lease, Client authorizes Broker to act as an intermediary between Client and the seller or landlord, to present any offers Client may wish to make on such property, and to assist both Client and the seller or landlord in negotiations for the sale or lease of such property. In such an event and notwithstanding paragraph 8 and any other provision of this agreement to the contrary, Broker's compensation shall be paid by the seller or landlord in accordance with the terms of Broker's listing agreement with the seller or landlord, unless all parties agree otherwise. **If Broker acts as an intermediary between Client and a seller or landlord, Broker:**

(i) **may not disclose to the buyer or tenant that the seller or landlord will accept a price less than the asking price unless otherwise instructed in a separate writing by the seller or landlord;**

(ii) **may not disclose to the seller or landlord that the buyer or tenant will pay a price greater than the price submitted in a written offer to the seller or landlord unless otherwise instructed in a separate writing by the buyer or tenant;**

(iii) **may not disclose any confidential information or any information a seller or landlord or a buyer or tenant specifically instructs Broker in writing not to disclose unless otherwise instructed in a separate writing by the respective party or required to disclose the information by the Real Estate License Act or a court order or if the information materially relates to the condition of the Property;**

(iv) **shall treat all parties to the transaction honestly; and**

(v) **shall comply with the Real Estate License Act.**

If Broker acts as an intermediary, Broker may appoint a licensed associate(s) of Broker to communicate with, carry out instructions of, and provide opinions and advice during negotiation to Client and another licensed associate(s) to the seller or landlord for the same purposes.

☐ (2) Intermediary Relationship not Authorized: Broker and Broker's associates shall exclusively represent Client and shall not act as an intermediary between Client and a seller or landlord. Client understands (choose (i) or (ii)):

☐ (i) Broker exclusively represents buyers or tenants of real property and does not represent sellers or landlords.

FIGURE 6.1   TAR Buyer/Tenant Representation Agreement (continued)

(ii) Broker represents both buyers (tenants) and sellers (landlords) of real property. However, Broker shall not show to Client any properties Broker lists for sale or lease.

(c) Broker shall not knowingly during the term of this agreement or after its termination, disclose information obtained in confidence from Client except as authorized by Client or required by law. Broker shall not disclose to Client any information obtained in confidence regarding any other person Broker represents or may have represented except as required by law.

13. ESCROW AUTHORIZATION: Client authorizes any escrow or closing agent authorized to close a transaction for the purchase or lease of property contemplated in this agreement to collect and disburse to Broker the Broker's Compensation due under this agreement.

14. DEFAULT: If either party breaches or fails to comply with this agreement or makes a false representation in this agreement, the party shall be in default. The non-defaulting party may seek any relief provided by law.

15. SPECIAL PROVISIONS:

16. MEDIATION: The parties agree to negotiate in good faith in an effort to resolve any dispute related to this agreement that may arise between the parties. If the dispute cannot be resolved by negotiation, the dispute shall be submitted to mediation before resorting to arbitration or litigation. If the need for mediation arises, the parties to the dispute shall choose a mutually acceptable mediator and shall share the cost of mediation equally.

17. ATTORNEYS' FEES: If Client or Broker is a prevailing party in any legal proceeding brought as a result of a dispute under this agreement or any transaction related to or contemplated by this agreement, such party shall be entitled to recover from the non-prevailing party all costs of such proceeding and reasonable attorneys' fees.

18. NOTICES: All notices shall be in writing and effective when hand-delivered, mailed, or sent by facsimile transmission to:

Client at _____

Phone (___) _____ Fax (___) _____

Broker at _____

Phone (___) _____ Fax (___) _____

19. AGREEMENT OF PARTIES: Addenda and other related documents which are part of this agreement are: Information About Brokerage Services; ❏ _____ .

This agreement contains the entire agreement between Client and Broker and may not be changed except by written agreement. This agreement may not be assigned by either party without the written permission of the other party. This agreement is binding upon the parties, their heirs, administrators, executors, successors, and permitted assigns. All Clients executing this agreement shall be jointly and severally liable for the performance of all its terms. Should any clause in this agreement be found invalid or unenforceable by a court of law, the remainder of this agreement shall not be affected and all other provisions of this agreement shall remain valid and enforceable to the fullest extent permitted by law.

20. ADDITIONAL NOTICES:

(a) Broker and Client are required by law to perform under this agreement without regard to race, color, religion, national origin, marital status, sex, disability, or familial status.

(b) If Client purchases property, Client should have an abstract covering the property examined by an attorney of Client's choice or obtain a policy of title insurance.

(c) Broker is a member of the _____ . Association or Board of REALTORS®. Broker fees are not fixed, controlled, recommended, suggested, or maintained by the Association of REALTORS®. The amount Broker is paid is negotiable.

(d) Broker is not qualified to render property inspections, or surveys. Client should seek experts to render such services. Broker is obliged to disclose any material defect in a property known to Broker. Selection of inspectors and repairmen is the responsibility of the parties to a contract or lease and not the Broker.

(e) Broker cannot give legal advice. This is intended to be a legally binding agreement. READ IT CAREFULLY. If you do not understand the effect of this agreement, consult your attorney BEFORE signing.

_____   _____
Client's Signature   Date

_____   _____
Client's Signature   Date

_____   _____
Broker's Printed Name   License No.

By: _____   _____
     Broker's or Associate's Signature   Date

terminate provision. More experienced buyers' agents already have developed their counseling skills to a point where they are as comfortable in securing buyer's agent exclusive representation agreements as seller's agents are in securing exclusive-right-to-sell listings from sellers.

Agents know that an exclusive-right-to-sell or exclusive-right-to-buy agreement means better control over the transaction and provides a better means for the buyer's agent to protect the agent's investment of time, energy and skill. They also know that an "open" buyer-agency agreement can lead to the same type of procuring-cause disagreements between brokers and buyers as can occur in seller open-listing situations.

The buyer must make the same choice as the seller in an open listing: Does the buyer-client want more agents working on his or her behalf, but with less commitment, motivation or knowledge of the buyer's needs? It is also much more important for the agent to have exclusive-agency rights when the agent is compensated by a contingent fee rather than by an hourly fee.

Termination date. Both the agent and the buyer should be clear as to when the agency relationship will terminate. A specific termination date on any buyer-representation contract is required by Texas state licensing law. The expiration period is fully negotiable and can be longer or shorter than in a listing agreement with a seller. If the agent wants to be covered for a sale that takes place on a certain property after the agreement expires, the agent should insert an extending *carryover clause* to specify the protection period and the procedures for registering prospects. The agreement may be terminated at any time by mutual consent of the agent and principal.

Conflicts of interest. A problem exists if the buyer wants to purchase a property already listed by the broker or another associate in the same office. If the broker has a buyer-representation agreement with the buyer, under Texas law all licensees associated with that broker also represent the buyer and must act in that buyer's best interests in any transaction. To attempt to avoid conflicts that may result when representing more than one party, the buyer-representation agreement may contain a withdrawal provision whereby the agreement becomes void in any transaction in which a conflict arises. In this case the buyer would be free to seek outside representation or counsel in making the offer and is not obligated to pay a fee or commission. The seller then would compensate the broker.

Another method to consider is renouncing one or the other agency relationship. Some brokers use the LIFO approach (last in, first out), in which the broker represents, for a single transaction only, the buyer or the seller, depending on who signed the representation agreement first. The last one in can choose self-representation or find outside representation and is not obligated to pay the broker any fee. All of these approaches have risks in that once agency is begun, it is not simple to disengage one part of the relationship or to avoid its consequences.

Some brokerage firms have developed a practice of representing buyers in the purchase of all properties except those listed with the firms. In this fashion, in-house listings are shown first, before buyer representation begins. If no acceptable in-house listings are found, the agent then enters into a buyer-representation agreement and thereafter works solely as a buyer's agent when showing properties listed by other brokers. This practice reduces the possibility of transactions involving two represented parties while preserving the opportunity for the agent to make an in-house sale.

Of course, this leads to an obvious problem if a buyer now represented by the firm wants to reconsider a property listed by the firm that had been seen earlier or if a new listing acquired by the broker meets the buyer's needs. If the broker does not wish to represent both parties, either the buyer or the seller would have to agree to cancel his or her agency agreement and allow the agent to act as the sole agent of the other party.

Because some risk does arise when a party terminates agency and reverts to customer status, some agents may choose to terminate both agreements and refer the parties to other agents. From a practical perspective, few agents wish to lose business by referring their buyers and sellers to other agents. Instead, agents take measures to minimize their risk through careful practice, making sure the parties fully understand the changing roles of the agent.

Other firms that specialize in representing buyers take the position that they will not actively solicit listings to sell. They will, however, occasionally list a property for one of their satisfied buyer-clients who now wants to sell a property. They also will register a seller's property with the understanding that this property will be exposed to their buyer-clients. There is a clear disclaimer of agency with the seller, and no fee is required to register the property.

Another conflict may arise if more than one buyer-client is interested in the same property. This is the reverse of the situation of a listing broker working with a customer who is interested in more than one of the broker's listings in the same location. Some buyer-representation agreements contain a disclosure that the buyer's agent may enter into agreements with other buyers to locate property, making it possible that two or more buyers will be interested in the same property. If this should occur, the buyer's agent might seek an agreement authorizing the broker to show the property to all buyer-clients, with the understanding that

- none of the buyer-clients will consider the arrangement to be a conflict of interest and
- all such multiple interests will be strictly confidential to the agent.

Remember that in the business of real estate, no form of agency is so pure that potential conflicts of interest cannot arise. If a broker decides beforehand how to handle possible conflicts, some serious problems may be avoided.

Advantages and Disadvantages of Exclusive Buyer Agency

There is a more dramatic solution to the above-mentioned potential conflicts of interest: some brokers have chosen to limit their practice to *exclusive buyer agency*. This indicates that the broker represents *only* buyers and will not list a seller's property for sale, whereas most brokers who offer buyer representation also will offer representation services to sellers. The brokers who practice exclusive buyer agency promote themselves to buyers both aggressively and successfully.

Some of the advantages of exclusive buyer agency are the following:

- It reduces the possibility of the unauthorized representation of more than one party because exclusive buyers' brokers do not take listings.

- Buyers have greater confidence that they will see all the properties available from every source.

- Buyers have greater confidence that they will receive 100 percent undivided loyalty and expert advice on all property negotiations.

- Buyer loyalty to the agent increases under an exclusive buyer-representation agreement.

- Exclusive buyer agency tends to prevent lapses or mistakes in negotiating objectives and styles that often occur when brokers switch back and forth from one role to the other, as do brokers who practice non-exclusive agency.

- An exclusive buyer's agent is more likely to be able to charge and collect retainer fees because buyers are sure of the 100 percent commitment they receive from the broker.

The disadvantages of exclusive buyer agency include the following:

- Buyers sometimes want to sell; however, the firms will not take the listings.

- Because the company has no listings, the possibility of earning commissions from both the listing side and the selling side of the business is eliminated.

- A potential conflict of interest arises if two buyer-clients want to make offers on the same property.

Exclusive buyer agency raises compensation issues, such as who pays the fee and whether listing brokers will cooperate and split any fees.

Single property. A broker may wish to contract to represent a buyer with respect to a single property only. This is similar to obtaining a single-party listing (one-time listing agreement) from a seller for the sale of an otherwise unlisted property so that the agent can offer the property to a specific buyer. To contractually represent (list) a buyer in this case, the broker should prepare a brief letter agreement after first determining that the buyer is unaware of any similar property in the general location. For example, the agent might ask whether the buyer has been shown any large apartment buildings in the midtown area. If not, the buyer agrees to pay a fee to the broker if the buyer purchases a specific property. The agent does not reveal the exact location of this property until the agreement is signed. This technique has proved helpful when the seller refuses to list a particular commercial property and the buyer does not want client status in regard to any other property except the one to be shown.

■ Benefits of Buyer-Agency Relationships

Agency Benefits to Buyer or Tenant

Following are some of the benefits to the buyer (or tenant) who receive client-level services.

Tailored buyer-representation contract. In a buyer-representation (or tenant-representation) agreement with the broker, the buyer can tailor the agent's services to meet the buyer's needs and adjust the compensation accordingly. This applies not only to large national companies seeking housing for relocated employees or sites for chain stores or restaurants but also to purchasers seeking residences or investment opportunities. In some cases, the buyer has already identified the property and the financing and wants the agent to handle the negotiations.

Access to a larger marketplace. In practice, traditional agents frequently limit their search of properties to those properties in which the broker's commission is protected. Thus, they limit their search to properties listed in-house or in the MLS. The buyer's agent whose guarantee of commission is protected, although not necessarily paid, by a buyer-client is motivated to show the buyer all available properties that meet the stated requirements, including

- open-listing properties;
- properties exclusively listed with other brokers;
- for-sale-by-owner properties;
- foreclosure and probate sales;
- sales by lenders of real estate owned properties;
- sales by trusts and pension plans;
- properties owned by a government agency; and
- properties not yet on the market.

Stronger negotiating strategy. The buyer's agent views the entire transaction from the buyer's perspective, without the divided and diminished loyalty that would be demanded of an agent representing more than one party. Therefore, the buyer is in a stronger negotiating position. Also, the buyer may want the protection of an agent in dealings with an unrepresented owner. Some buyers fear that the reason an owner does not list with a broker is because something is wrong with the property.

Fiduciary responsibility of the agent. Under Texas licensing laws and the common law, the buyer's agent is held to a higher standard of skill and care in dealing with the buyer than is a subagent of the seller or the seller's listing agent, who works with the buyer on a customer basis. Buyers' agents have an affirmative duty to their clients to thoroughly investigate and completely disclose all facts that bear on a buyer's decision to buy. On the other hand, buyers' agents have a duty to be honest and deal fairly—not equally or impartially—with sellers, but they owe no duty to advise and counsel sellers.

The buyer's agent is held to the same standard of performance in dealing with the buyer that the listing broker is held to in dealing with the seller. There is nothing unique about the responsibility and duties of the buyer's agent. There is no new fiduciary duty or ethical responsibility that the buyer's agent must learn. What is different is that the agent owes conventional common, statutory and administrative law fiduciary duties to a different group of participants, namely buyers. The quantity and quality of client-level services are at least the same as those a listing agent would give sellers. It is simply the other side of the representation coin. Buyers are, quite simply, not legally entitled to this level of service unless they retain their own real estate agents to represent them.

Confidentiality. Confidentiality can be especially important when the buyer wishes to remain anonymous. For example, Sarah, a movie star, considers purchasing a new mansion. If the seller learns the identity of the intended buyer, the seller may likely hold firm or increase the asking price. A buyer's agent acting for an undisclosed principal may be able to negotiate a better price and better terms for the anonymous buyer.

More counseling, less selling. As opposed to persuasion to buy, the buyer can expect to receive more counseling, expert opinion, advocacy and advice regarding the acquisition decision. When an agent is hired by the seller under an exclusive-right-to-sell listing, the agent's emphasis is on selling the property. When the buyer hires an agent under an exclusive-right-to-represent agreement, the agent does not sell a house, he or she assists a buyer in purchasing a house. In a very real sense, the buyer's agent is a purchasing agent, not a selling agent. This agent's emphasis is on helping the client evaluate different properties and alternative courses of action, then getting the best deal possible once having elected to go forward with negotiations on a property.

A buyer's agent might recommend inspection of a home at random times of the day and perhaps might check with the neighbors to gain more complete information about the property or the seller. Buyers' agents do their best to find out things about a property that the seller or the listing agent might not want to disclose or might not feel obligated to disclose, such as excess noise, sewage odors, high energy costs, traffic congestion or unauthorized seller improvements. Buyers also expect their agents to review any proposed contract to determine whether unfavorable provisionsnecessitate hiring a real estate attorney. To illustrate the level of service due a client, consider the following example.

 EXAMPLE: George refers Betty to Sally of Bay Realty. Betty is interested in looking at properties. Betty says she wants someone to represent her best interests, and if she works well with Sally, she will purchase other properties through Sally. Sally decides to work with Betty on a client basis. Betty indicates she will pay Sally for her help and advice or will see that Sally is paid by the seller as a condition of any subsequent contract. She signs an exclusive buyer-representation agreement. Sally shows Betty a country property listed in the

MLS with Sam of Main Realty, and Betty decides to buy it. Sally properly notifies Sam that she disclaims any subagency to Sam and states that she and Bay Realty represent the buyer and not the seller.

? QUESTIONS

In the course of negotiations, Sally deals with a number of important items, such as (1) price and appraised value; (2) seller financing; (3) earnest money, amount and default remedies; (4) condition of property; (5) contingencies; and (6) fixtures and inventory. How should Sally treat each item, recognizing that her primary allegiance is to Betty?

DISCUSSION

Sally must be honest and make appropriate disclosure to the seller; as Betty's agent, however, she owes a greater duty of skill, care and disclosure to protect Betty's best interests. Sally can advise Betty how she might persuade the seller to modify the terms and reduce the selling price and what alternative courses of action Betty might take. Sally should handle each item as follows:

- **Price and appraised value.** Sally should analyze the property and the seller's position to obtain the lowest realistic price for Betty. She should do a competitive market analysis (CMA) on the property and should consider getting Betty's permission to submit the CMA, along with any lower offer on the property, to the seller. Sally may ask to see any appraisals that have been made and may suggest obtaining another appraisal to support a lower price offer. Sally, as the buyer's agent, legally negotiates with the seller for a lower price. She would not do so as a subagent. In a buyer's market, Sally might suggest that Betty prepare two offers and not reveal the higher offer unless and until the seller rejects the first offer. A subagent who did that would breach his or her fiduciary duties.

- **Seller financing.** Sally need not suggest that Betty submit tax returns and a credit report unless these are requested by the seller. Sally might suggest seeking legal advice regarding favorable financing terms, such as: no due-on-sale clause, no prepayment penalty, liberal grace periods and minimal late charges, default remedies limited to judicial foreclosure with no deficiency against Betty (nonrecourse) or deferred interest.

- **Earnest money.** Sally can suggest that the earnest money be relatively modest or be reflected in an unsecured note. Conversely, she might suggest a substantial earnest money deposit to convey the buyer's serious intent to purchase the property.

- **Condition of property.** Sally might suggest seeking the advice of an attorney regarding the use of additional clauses addressing such items as a property inspection that makes the purchase contingent on Betty's satisfaction; a requirement that the seller pay for a residential service contract; and written warranties regarding roofing, plumbing and termites.

- **Contingencies.** Sally can explain the meaning of standard contingency clauses as they appear in TREC-promulgated addenda. Of course, she should be very careful not to engage in the unauthorized practice of law when dealing with contingencies and should never add any language of her own.

- **Fixtures and inventory.** Sally may advise Betty to request in her offer additional personal property for the same purchase price, such as paintings and Oriental rugs. Sally should review any written inventory list before the offer is prepared and check to see that no substitution of items occurs.

- **Other items.** As a buyer's agent, Sally must be careful not to reveal to the seller or listing agent facts regarding Betty's bargaining position, for example, plans to buy adjoining parcels or adjoining condominium apartment units or that a resale buyer waits in the wings. Sally has no duty to disclose the name of the buyer or that Sally might lend Betty money to make the down payment. However, in Texas, if Sally is being paid by Betty and also expects to be paid by Sam, that fact must be clearly disclosed and consented to by all parties or Sally and/or Bay Realty could face TREC disciplinary hearings and possible loss of license [TRELA §15(a)(6)(D)].

Sally must use her skill to research and investigate the contemplated acquisition. She must advise Betty of any facts relevant to the purchase decision that can be used to negotiate better terms (for example, that the seller is near foreclosure, is filing for divorce or has already bought a new home; the property is about to be rezoned; the neighbors are unruly; or the house was burglarized four times last year).

Sally can accept an incentive fee for obtaining a reduction in the listed price. But, again, if Sally receives compensation from more than one party in the transaction, that fact must be agreed upon by all parties.

Sally must do more than produce copies of relevant documents for Betty. She must be sure Betty understands the impact on her purchase decision of key provisions in the documents. If she feels it is necessary, Sally should recommend that Betty obtain legal, title or property inspection advice from outside experts.

Sally has a duty to express any doubts she may have about the suitability of the property for Betty, especially if she feels that the property is, in Sally's opinion, overpriced.

Benefits to Buyers' Agents

The buyer's agent can expect certain benefits from an agency relationship with a buyer.

Greater client loyalty. Traditionally, real estate agents work with "wandering" buyers on the chance of earning a fee, sometimes even if the chance is remote. With an exclusive-right-to-purchase representation agreement, the agent has greater control and little fear of losing the buyer to an owner or to another brokerage. For many of the same reasons that traditional brokers seldom take open listings (oral or written) with sellers, buyer agents may be reluctant to do so as well.

Avoid conflict of loyalty. The buyer's agent should feel no ethical discomfort or hesitancy in withholding from the seller information on the buyer's future plans for the property, including immediate resale or obtaining options on adjoining properties. Nor should the buyer's agent be reluctant to disclose to the buyer the broker's opinion that the property is overpriced or that the seller's terms are unrealistic. As a matter of fact, the agent is duty-bound to express such opinions to a buyer client.

Within the bounds of honesty and fairness to the seller, the buyer's agent can develop with the buyer a negotiating strategy that promotes the buyer's best interests at all times and seeks to obtain reasonable concessions from the seller. Healthy and complete negotiations are not as likely in traditional real estate transactions, where agents represent sellers' interests only. While a buyer and seller are not hostile in the sense of a plaintiff and defendant in a lawsuit, they do have competing interests. The buyer's agent will be able to represent the buyer's best interests in this spirit of competition while negotiating honestly to arrive at a transaction agreeable to both the buyer and the seller.

In addition to price, many other items must be negotiated in every transaction. Among these are

- initial and additional earnest money deposits;
- down payment;
- seller financing;
- interest rate;
- due date;
- sales price;
- commissions;
- terms;
- home warranty;
- termite report;
- assessments;
- appraisal;
- closing costs;

- title report;

- possession date;

- impound, reserve or escrow account on the seller's loan (in assumption situations);

- title and escrow agent;

- personal property and inventory;

- discount points;

- repairs;

- inspection contingencies;

- hazard insurance;

- default remedies and

- extensions.

During the offer and counteroffer stage of the transaction, any one of these items can provide an opportunity for conflict between the buyer and the seller and, thus, a deal-making compromise. The buyer's agent is able to negotiate all of these items on the buyer's behalf. Neither a listing agent nor a cooperating agent acting as the *seller's* subagent has the legal ability to negotiate on the buyer's behalf.

No liability for acts of the listing broker. Because a buyer's agent has no agency relationship with either the seller or the listing broker, the buyer's agent is not vicariously liable for their acts. In addition, buyer's agents tend either to verify information about the property given by the listing broker or to require that the seller give certain warranties or representations concerning such conditions of a property as roof, plumbing and boundary concerns. This reduces the agent's exposure to claims for misrepresentation, for concealment of material defects or for failure to ascertain material facts. Although changes in Texas law have reduced the broker's liability for the unknown acts of other brokers, it is felt that a buyer's agent is clearly separated from the acts of the listing broker. This may have the effect of further reducing the chance of the buyer's agent being sued for things that are not the agent's fault. However, in Texas, the buyer's agent does have an increased responsibility to the buyer-client to use due diligence to discover problems that may adversely affect the client.

■ Fee Arrangements

An entire book could be written on all the possible methods of compensating a buyer's broker. Keep in mind that the broker's first concern is to become comfortable with the agency relationship that exists and the types of services to be provided. The mechanics of compensation seem to fall into place once the agency relationship is clearly understood. Often, the buyer's broker's fee is paid out of the sales proceeds, either through an authorized commission split or through a credit from the seller to the buyer at closing.

Seller-oriented brokers can benefit from understanding the methods by which buyers' brokers structure their compensation arrangements. Because listing brokers will receive offers from buyers represented by their own brokers, each listing broker should become acquainted with how the offers may be structured and how fees are handled. The following sections summarize the ways in which buyers' brokers can be paid for their services. The way in which fees are to be paid should be stated in writing and clearly understood well in advance to avoid potential conflict between the buyer and the broker.

Retainer Fee

Regardless of how a broker is compensated, some brokers feel more comfortable obtaining advance payments. This can serve as a screening device to determine whether a buyer is serious about buying. However, some states have extensive restrictions on advance fees. For example, in California the broker cannot withdraw monies from retainer trust accounts to cover hourly fees until several days after an accounting has been made to a client for services performed, and statements must be sent every calendar quarter and at termination. In Texas, however, no such requirement exists.

If a retainer fee is to be taken, some benefit or service must accrue to the person paying the fee; otherwise, it may be considered one of the two unconscionable acts under the Texas Deceptive Trade Practices and Consumer Protection Act. If no research is done for the client, no houses shown, no counseling and advising or any other service performed and the client cancels the agreement, it may be difficult for the broker to justify keeping the retainer fee.

If the retainer fee from the buyer is retained by the broker and the transaction closes with the buyer's broker being compensated from the seller's side of the transaction, the broker technically receives compensation from both parties, a fact that must be disclosed and consented to by all parties. Some brokers choose to refund the retainer fee on closing to avoid this problem and make as much cash available for the buyer as possible. Tax counsel should be consulted regarding the deductibility of the retainer portion as a professional fee.

When deciding to require a retainer fee, the broker should establish a consistent office policy. In other words, the broker should not decide selectively that some buyers must pay a retainer fee and others will not be required to do so.

Seller-Paid Fee

No legal or ethical barrier prohibits the seller from paying the buyer's broker fee or authorizing the listing broker to share fees with the buyer's broker. Either is a matter of contract and may be handled in advance by appropriate language in both the seller's listing agreement and the buyer-representation agreement. Substantial legal authority backs up the proposition that the payment of fees does not determine whom a licensee represents. As long as the agency relationship is clear and explicit, it does not matter legally whether the buyer or the seller pays the fee. If the agency is unclear, however, a court will likely consider who paid the fee to be an important factor in determining who is the agent's principal.

Currently, in residential sales, the traditional commission-sharing arrangement between the listing broker and the other broker is the most widely accepted method of compensation for the buyer's broker. In essence, the seller is notified of the arrangement and agrees that the other broker represents the buyer and that the commission may be split between the listing broker and the buyer's broker. This tends to keep the transaction simple. However, there is some precedent to support the notion that this practice may create conflicts of interest and misunderstandings, especially regarding procuring-cause issues.

In Texas, some buyer broker specialists are using and promoting the practice of the buyer's inserting a condition in the sales contract that requires that the seller pay the buyer's broker on behalf of the buyer or reimburse the buyer for brokerage expenses at closing so that the buyer may pay his or her broker. The broker should not draft these conditional terms.

Traditionally, the buyer's broker receives a share of the commission from the listing broker out of the sales proceeds. However, two alternative methods of providing compensation exist:

1. the listing broker agrees to reduce the commission by the amount of the usual split with the cooperating broker so that the seller either can reduce the price by a like amount (the *net offer approach*) or can give an offsetting credit on the buyer's closing statement in the amount of the cooperating broker's share.

2. the buyer's broker receives the amount of the fee negotiated with the buyer. If the amount offered by the seller to the cooperating broker exceeds the fee that the buyer is obligated to pay, any difference is credited to the buyer. If the amount is not sufficient to pay the fee, the buyer pays the difference to the broker.

When employing compensation methods that differ from the traditional splitting of the listing broker's fee, cover letters should be drafted and accompany the offer to explain this arrangement to both the listing agent and the seller. The inherent problem with this approach is a lack of sophistication on the part of sellers, buyers and some brokers, making such agreements difficult to negotiate, particularly in residential transactions.

Commission Split

In a number of states, real estate agents do not use formal written agreements to represent buyers. Commissions are normally paid out of an authorized commission split with the listing broker or by the seller's crediting the buyer with a specified amount out of the sales proceeds. There usually is a written acknowledgment of buyer representation in the state-required agency disclosure form, with a written confirmation also included in the purchase agreement. (Note that Texas does not have such a form.) The preferred practice is to use a formal written buyer-representation agreement that addresses the issues of exclusivity, compensation, scope of services, termination and conflicts of interest.

In Texas, no state-approved or state-promulgated form covers buyer representation, seller representation, or representation of more than one party. The Texas Association of REALTORS®, however, produces such forms for its membership. Some of the larger local REALTOR® associations also have developed separate forms for their own local memberships.

A buyer's broker, if planning on a traditional fee-split method, must determine from the listing broker, at initial contact, whether the listing broker is authorized and willing to split the commission with the buyer's broker (as opposed to a subagent of the seller). If the listing broker is not authorized to split the commission, the buyer's broker should advise the buyer of that fact. The buyer then may decide to reduce the offering price to a net amount that reflects that the buyer is to pay his or her broker's fee. The seller and the listing broker will have to reach their own agreement on whether to reduce the listing broker's commission.

Now that most MLSs accept listings in which sellers can offer cooperation regarding commissions but not subagency, there will be an increased general acceptance by sellers, buyers and brokers of such commission-splitting arrangements. Sellers primarily are concerned with selling their property and netting a certain amount of money from the sales proceeds. Most sellers are much less concerned about whether their brokers split commissions with someone labeled either as a buyer's broker or as a subagent of the seller. In fact, sellers often feel that the other broker, even if described as a subagent, actually works for the buyer. Some sellers feel that compensation for both the listing broker and the selling broker is already part of the listing and purchase price; that is, they feel there really are two fees—the listing fee and the selling fee.

EXAMPLE: In *LA&N Interests, Inc. v. Fish,* a buyer's broker and his licensed associate felt that they had been unjustly deprived of a commission in a transaction and sued their client and the competing broker to recover their commission and damages for interference with their buyer's brokerage agreement. The buyer-client bought a property with the assistance of another broker, and the buyer's broker was paid nothing, even though the buyer's broker had an exclusive-agency representation agreement with the buyer. The buyer's brokerage agreement with the buyer-client clearly stated that the client "shall have no liability or obligation to pay a Professional Service Fee to [the buyer's broker]" but rather that the seller would pay the buyer's broker fee. This flaw—assuming that some party other than the client would pay the commission—led to the broker's not being able to recover from his client. Neither was he able to recover from the seller, who had never agreed to pay him in the first place.

Although a listing broker typically voluntarily reduces his or her share of the commission if another broker as subagent finds the buyer, a few listing brokers adamantly resist such a reduction or split if a buyer's broker is involved. In the first instance, why should a seller or a listing broker consent to a split? Simply because it is more likely to lead to a sale of the listed property. The listing broker, some sellers reason, should not be paid twice as much just because the buyer works with a buyer's broker instead of a seller's subagent.

EXAMPLE: Assume that the seller signs an exclusive listing agreement with a 7 percent commission. Most of the transaction participants expect that the 7 percent commission will cover all the sales commissions involved, with the listing broker and the other broker each earning 3.5 percent. Most sellers would refuse to sign if the total commissions were 10.5 percent, with the listing broker receiving 7 percent.

Why would a broker not consent to a split commission? When the listing broker sees an opportunity to obtain a full rather than a reduced commission. If the listing agreement contains a clause permitting such a split with a buyer's broker, listing brokers who are REALTORS® should reconsider this refusal in view of the ethical restrictions in the NAR® Code of Ethics. These articles require that the broker cooperate with other brokers and act in the best interests of the client at all times. If the listing broker's refusal to share commissions results in too low an offer, or no offer at all, the seller may have grounds for complaint, especially if it appears the broker's sole motivation was to receive a greater fee than usual in a cooperative sale.

In any event, an agent's fiduciary duty of full disclosure to his or her client under TREC Rules requires that the listing broker advise the seller of the general company policy regarding cooperation and compensation of buyer's agents. In brief, listing brokers should do everything possible to make it easy for the buyer's broker to show the seller's property and make an offer.

Buyer-Paid Fee

The buyer may elect to pay the commission directly to his or her broker. This may avoid any implication of seller agency or conflict of interest that may be present when the seller pays the brokerage fee. An experienced buyer's broker, not wanting a nonclient to control payment, may prefer being paid directly by the buyer rather than receiving a commission split from the listing broker or being paid directly by the seller at closing. Buyer-paid compensation can take several forms, such as an hourly rate, a percentage fee or a flat fee.

 EXAMPLE: Sam, the listing broker, and Carol, the other broker representing the seller through the listing broker as a subagent of the seller, agree on a 50-50 commission split. The property is a commercial warehouse not listed in the MLS. The listing commission is 5 percent. The offer is submitted at $1 million on a $1.2 million listing. The seller accepts the offer, provided that Sam reduces his fee to 4 percent. Sam agrees to do so, but fails to inform Carol. Carol now receives $24,000 instead of $30,000.

Hourly rate. Under this arrangement, the agent is, in essence, a consultant, charging a noncontingent hourly rate. It is payable regardless of whether a title transfer is contemplated, for example, when a consultant advises on whether to develop a shopping center or a commercial office building. A variation may be an hourly fee that is applied against an incentive fee if the agent finds the right property for the buyer. This requires that an agent keep time sheets and be diligent in his or her record-keeping and billing practices.

Percentage fee. A buyer's agent may charge a percentage fee based on the selling price of the property bought by his or her client, just as most listing agents do. The obvious problem the percentage fee creates is the appearance of a potential conflict of interest because the higher the purchase price, the greater the fee, making the percentage fee seem seller-oriented. The prime benefit of the percentage fee is that real estate licensees and clients are accustomed to this arrangement.

Many buyers' agents begin by charging buyers on a percentage basis and later progress into charging flat fees (discussed below). Other agents combine an hourly rate with a percentage of the purchase price. Rates may vary when the seller is not represented by a listing broker because the buyer's agent may have to do more of the background work and handle negotiations with the seller.

Flat fees (contingent or noncontingent). A buyer's agent is sometimes compensated on a flat fee, payable if a buyer purchases a property located through the agent. The amount of the flat fee is based on the estimate by the agent of the work and skills involved, the potential fee that will be paid by the seller and the probability of success.

A *contingent flat fee* often is based on what the buyer will pay for the agent's services, depending on the price range of the home or an estimate of the amount of work involved.

 EXAMPLE: Betty is looking for a property in the $175,000 to $225,000 range. A cooperating broker might expect to receive a fee of $6,000 on a $200,000 sale. Carol, a buyer's broker, charges the buyer a $6,000 flat contingent fee. Whether Betty selects a property for $175,000 or for $225,000, the fee to Carol remains $6,000.

Another method is the *noncontingent flat fee.* The agent predicts the amount of work necessary to accomplish the client's objectives and then sets a flat fee. This approach is seldom used unless the agent has gained a great deal of experience in representing buyers.

Some buyer-representation agreements provide that the buyer is obligated to pay the fee but is entitled to a credit for any amounts the seller agrees to pay. Thus, the buyer would not pay the buyer's broker fee in the usual MLS sale, although the buyer might pay the fee directly if the agent located an unlisted property, a builder-owned house or a for-sale-by-owner property. An experienced buyer's agent might encourage the client to make such a stipulation, just as the client might base a sale on the condition that the seller fixes the roof.

Disclosure of fee. A buyer's broker paid directly by the buyer might disclose the exact amount of the fee on the offer to purchase. In this way, the seller and the listing broker have a clear understanding of what fees are being paid. It is easier for the seller to see that the net proceeds will be about the same with a gross price offer. The seller could be paying both brokers or could accept a net price offer, with the buyer paying the buyer's broker's commission and the seller paying the listing broker a reduced commission.

An argument can be made for not disclosing the amount of fees on the offer to purchase based on confidentiality. If, in fact, the buyer's broker has contracted to receive less than the typical commission split, the amount of the difference could accrue to the buyer's benefit.

Net Purchase Price

The net purchase price is the sales price reduced by the buyer's brokerage fee. A theory supporting the net price method is that the buyer has only a certain amount for the down payment. A portion of that money no longer will be deducted from the seller's proceeds to pay the other broker but now will be used to pay the buyer's broker. The restructured brokerage fees will not increase the acquisition costs. The overall transaction will not change, even if a loan is involved. If accepted, a net offer may result in lower title and closing costs, which are now based on the lower purchase price.

 EXAMPLE: Betty makes a full price offer to the seller on a $100,000 listing in the following way: a net purchase price of $97,300, plus Betty agrees to pay Carol, her buyer's broker, a cash fee of $2,700. The seller acknowledges that the buyer's broker represents the buyer and not the seller in this transaction. Carol inserts a provision in the sales contract that the buyer agrees to pay the sum of $97,300 to the seller and $2,700 to Carol for services rendered.

Lenders. The amount of a maximum loan is based on a percentage of the purchase price plus the buyer's broker's commission. The commission is thus paid from the loan proceeds rather than from the buyer's personal cash. A different approach is used in a net offer situation. So that a lender will add to the sales price a buyer's broker's commission as an acquisition cost, the broker might provide the lender with a copy of the purchase contract in which the buyer acknowledges the buyer's broker's commission. This makes it easier for a lender to visualize the economic adjustments made in the transaction.

Federal Housing Administration (FHA) regulations specifically authorize an add-back to the purchase price of the buyer's broker's fee under Section 532 of the National Housing Act. The notable exception is a Department of Veterans Affairs (VA) loan. The VA does not allow lenders to include buyer's broker's fees in the loans to be paid by veteran purchasers. This position is based on the belief that

- the buyer's broker's fee may increase the acquisition cost;

- buyers are adequately protected by the requirement to furnish a certificate of reasonable value and reasonable closing costs and by access to many properties through general advertising and

- selling brokers, although representing sellers, do not ignore buyers' interests.

Note that no VA rule prohibits the buyer's broker from receiving a seller-approved commission split from the listing broker. Thus, a VA transaction can include a buyer's broker, but the broker must be compensated by or through the seller. This is similar to the seller's paying the points on the buyer's loan.

Gross Price

An alternative method of buyer's broker compensation that is gaining some acceptance in residential sales transactions is the gross price method. The buyer pays the gross purchase price. The purchase contract provides that the seller then pays the buyer's broker's commission. The seller acknowledges and accepts that the buyer's broker solely represents the buyer and not the seller, despite the payment of the fee by the seller. To ease the listing broker's and seller's concerns, some brokers add that this fee is the sole compensation of the buyer's broker in the transaction. Texas licensees should recall that it is grounds for loss of license to be paid by more than one party to a transaction without the full knowledge and consent of all parties.

This method satisfies all outside participants in the transaction, such as appraisers, lenders and insurers, and it is easier to finance the contract amount. This method helps reduce the concerns over excess commission expense and double charging, and it seems easier for the seller to understand and respond to a customary sales price offer. The seller's main difficulty is psychological: The seller and the listing broker may feel that while they pay the buyer's broker's fee, the buyer receives the services. This flaw is less serious when using the gross price method of fee payment, where a buyer's broker's commission can be built into the contract price through the terms of the buyer's offer. As a consequence, the cash required, the mortgage amount, the net proceeds to the seller and the sales price are approximately the same as they would be in the traditional sale, in which both brokers represent the seller and both commissions are included in the contract price. To avoid loan underwriting problems, some brokers include the following language in the purchase contract: "Seller credits $ [dollar amount] toward buyer's expenses listed on the closing statement."

Some advantages of the sellers paying the commission are that it

- clears up questions of who works for whom and who pays whom;
- protects the buyer's agent from the listing agent's breaches and other chances of losing commissions because of badly crafted listing agreements;
- protects the buyer-client from having to pay the broker's commission at closing if the seller refuses to pay, but provides the option to do so should the situation require;
- allows no reasonable basis for procuring-cause disputes;
- presents no suggestion of interfering with the listing broker's commission agreement with the seller;
- works equally well for listed, unlisted, builder, MLS or non-MLS properties;

- places responsibility for securing the compensation of the buyer's broker directly on the shoulders of the client whose interests were served by the broker and

- does not trigger the TRELA §15(a)(6)(D) prohibition concerning payment from more than one party in the transaction without knowledge and consent of both, unless the buyer's broker has collected a retainer fee from the buyer in advance.

Some disadvantages are that it

- is relatively untested in the courts in Texas;

- may change expected tax advantages for the parties and

- may cause some confusion among lenders until it is widely recognized, thus impeding some transactions.

It is important for brokers to understand compensation alternatives when they consider representing buyers. Many brokers working with buyer prospects now realize that they need not give away their time and expertise. Brokers should study the different methods of representation and develop their skills so that they can comfortably discuss with buyers and listing brokers the amounts and various methods of compensation. For assistance in this area, many buyers' broker books and seminars are helpful. (One such source is *Buyer Agency,* 3rd Edition, by Gail Lyons and Don Harlan, Dearborn Financial Publishing, Inc.®, 1993.)

■ Written Notification of Compensation to Broker

Regardless of who will be responsible for the payment of fees or commissions to the broker, it is strongly advised that such agreements be in writing. Although Texas law does not require that listing contracts or buyer-representation contracts be in writing, a broker will have no legal recourse against a seller or buyer who refuses to pay a fee unless the agreement was written.

In addition to written buyer or seller commission agreements, brokers are also advised to have written agreements relating to fee splits between cooperating brokers. Most multiple-listing services (MLSs) require that listing brokers disclose all fee arrangements to other brokers when the property is published in the MLS. In addition, the "Broker Information and Ratification of Fee" section that appears at the bottom of a standard TREC contract form spells out under what conditions and in what amounts any compensation will be paid from the listing broker to the other broker.

The following example shows the need for comprehensive commission agreements.

 EXAMPLE: *Trammel Crow Company No. 60, et al. v. William Jefferson Harkinson* (40 Tex. Sup. Ct. J. 425, 1997). A broker acting as a tenant's agent located a commercial rental space for the client. Subsequently, the client went around the broker and negotiated a lease directly with the property owner, who was represented by a different broker. The owner's agent was paid according to the representation agreement between the owner and the listing broker, which did not address payment of a commission to a tenant's broker.

The tenant's broker sought payment of a commission from the owner's broker. The Supreme Court found that the tenant's broker was not entitled to a commission, since there was no contract between the tenant's broker and the property owner.

Comment: If the tenant's broker had had a clause in the tenant's representation agreement that required payment by the tenant, in the event the owners did not agree to pay the tenant's broker may have had a legitimate claim for a commission from the tenant, unless there were other issues that precluded payment.

■ Procuring Cause

Occasionally, more than one real estate licensee works with a buyer in locating a property. Without a clearly written agreement, disputes may arise over which licensee was the procuring cause of the sale and thus is entitled to a share of the commission. These disputes are sometimes resolved in arbitration using guidelines such as those developed by NAR®.

In Texas, when a buyer or tenant in a commercial or residential transaction desires representation and contracts with a buyer's broker or tenant representative, procuring cause will generally becomes a legal nonissue. This is true even if the buyer or tenant was first shown a property by the listing or leasing agent or their subagents and even if negotiations have begun. However, creating an agency relationship will not, in itself, prevent claims filed asserting procurement by another licensee.

■ Purchase Agreement

Attorneys representing buyers often view TREC-promulgated contract forms for residential sales as being seller-oriented or at least as containing some buyer compromises. Therefore, some buyers prefer to work with their own attorneys to develop acceptable purchase agreements. Such an agreement could be similar in format to the standard purchase contract, except that it is prepared from the buyer's perspective. Other buyer agents prefer to use a special buyer's addendum, which can be attached to the standard form of purchase agreement.

When assisting a buyer with the preparation of an offer to purchase, the buyer's agent should keep in mind that

- the agent is not an attorney and must avoid the unauthorized practice of law;

- any complicated drafting should be left to an attorney, although it may be appropriate for the agent to suggest various negotiating strategies and certain contingencies and financing techniques that should be incorporated into the offer;

- the offer should not be so one-sided as to be unfair or unrealistic; and

- although the agent should help the buyer evaluate key contract terms, the agent should not decide what is best for the buyer.

What follows is a list of important items for the buyer's agent to consider before preparing an offer to purchase. Some of the items will influence price negotiations. Some states, including Texas, require the use of pre-approved forms, and this requirement may affect the ability of a buyer's agent to use some of these suggestions.

Again, keep in mind that the TREC contract forms may be adjusted to conform to the intent of the principals, not necessarily rigidly copied. It should be noted, however, that modifications to a promulgated form should be at the direction of the principal—*not at the discretion of the agent.* (Also remember that this chapter looks at these contract terms from the point of view of the buyer and buyer's agent. Many of these statements would be reversed in the negotiating strategy of the seller's agent or subagent.)

Earnest Money Deposit

In Texas, earnest money is not essential to the validity of a contract. A real estate contract in Texas is just as valid without as with earnest money. Earnest money is not the consideration necessary to make the contract valid. It is money or something else of value, usually to be held in escrow by a third party, to be given to the seller in the event of the buyer's default on the contract before closing.

Earnest money is meant to provide a nonjudicial remedy for damages incurred by the seller because of the buyer's default. It is an alternative remedy to a lawsuit for damages, specific performance, injunction or other legal action. However, its major significance is that a seller does not have to go to court to get the earnest money; that is why earnest money is referred to as a *nonjudicial remedy.* Traditionally, the buyer gives the earnest money check to the broker to accompany the offer and to be deposited by the broker. Currently TREC-promulgated forms do not indicate that necessity, stating only that the buyer shall deposit the earnest money with the escrow agent named in the contract "upon execution of this contract by both parties."

Buyer's brokers should keep the following in mind when their clients agree to deposit earnest money in the course of a transaction:

- Discuss with the buyer-client the strategy of depositing a large amount of earnest money as a negotiation tool to drive down the sales price, giving an offer (in the eyes of the seller) an advantage over competing offers without such security. Remember, though, that a large deposit also increases the buyer-client's potential financial loss. If the buyer-client is risk-averse, he or she might want to keep the initial deposit low, with any additional deposit to be made 10 to 15 days (or within some other acceptable time period) after the seller accepts the offer. If a substantial deposit is made, suggest that the client consider the use of an interest-bearing account to benefit the buyer.

- Avoid giving the deposit directly to the seller. As stated earlier, TREC contract forms do not provide for sellers or sellers' agents or subagents to deposit earnest money. Nor do they provide for earnest money checks to be carried back and forth with the contract documents. They are to be deposited by buyers or designated licensees on execution of the contract by both parties unless otherwise agreed. If done differently, the contract should specify exactly how it will be handled. The selection of the escrow agent in the contract is a fully negotiable item; however, the issue must be agreed on by the parties or no enforceable contract exists.

- Where appropriate, request that the seller deposit a sufficient sum of earnest money to cover any closing and title cancellation charges, buyer's moving and storage expenses and some money for the buyer's broker if the contract is terminated due to the seller's default. If the buyer-representation agreement calls for the broker to get half of any earnest money put up and forfeited by the seller, the amount requested must be doubled; otherwise, the buyer will not receive enough to cover reasonable potential damages.

Assignability

In Texas, most standard contracts are assignable unless otherwise stated. An assignable contract is one in which the rights to the contract can be given, or assigned, to some other party. Of course, the parties should understand this clearly before entering into any negotiations.

Seller Financing

If the buyer asks the seller to carry back a note and mortgage or a similar security instrument, such as a deed of trust or an installment sales contract, the buyer should specify in the purchase agreement the key provisions to be inserted in the financing document for the buyer's benefit. These might include the following:

- no prepayment penalty,

- no due-on-sale clause,

- nonrecourse liability (the seller's remedy is to foreclose on the property without the buyer being personally liable for any deficiency),

- extended grace periods and

- deferral of interest.

Depending on the terms of the seller-provided financing (maturity date, interest rate and amount of down payment), the buyer should be flexible in selecting the offering price. These provisions are provided for in a TREC-promulgated addendum for seller financing that should be the only form used, unless the buyer's or seller's attorney drafts another addendum. Don't try to create them in the special provisions paragraph of the contract. Such action is grounds for loss of license and basis for lawsuit by the client if the terms are drafted incorrectly and lead to damage to the buyer. Notwithstanding this caution, the buyer-client, as a party to the purchase contract, has the right to insert any desired provision in a contract offer. The client's agent must follow the client's instructions, but when substantial modifications are made, the agent should advise the client to seek competent legal advice first.

Contract Acceptance

The seller's acceptance of the offer is effective only if delivered in writing to the buyer or the buyer's agent. This gives the buyer the longest time possible in which to revoke the offer if he or she so chooses, for whatever reason.

Extended Closing

For their own protection, buyers should consider whether they want to be given the contractual right to extend closing dates beyond those in the TREC form if they have difficulty arranging financing or otherwise meeting the closing dates.

Inspection

The buyer's offer could be made contingent on one or more professional inspections. If there are problems with the condition of the property, the buyer may be justified in canceling the contract, based on the results of the inspection. The TREC-promulgated sales contracts provide for an option fee to be paid by the buyer to the seller, giving the buyer the unrestricted right to inspect and the unrestricted right to terminate the contract for some agreed-on time period after the acceptance of the offer.

The contract provides boxes that may be checked indicating that if the property is purchased, the option fee will or will not be credited to the buyer. A buyer's agent or seller's agent or subagent attempting to create his or her own version of this provision will be engaging in the unauthorized practice of law. Keep in mind, however, that a principal or an attorney acting for a client may use alternative inspection language in addendums. Likewise, professional organizations such as the Texas Association of REALTORS® may create alternative inspection addendum forms for optional use by their members.

Property Condition

The seller should submit a property condition disclosure report for the buyer's approval. A buyer's agent may counsel his or her buyer-client to require that the seller agree to the following:

- No personal property items will be substituted for those at the property when it was shown and that were expected, by the buyer, to be included in the purchase price.

- The property is in the same or the required improved condition at the time of possession by the buyer as so contracted.

- The property is clear of debris, and the appliances and the plumbing, heating and electrical systems are in good working condition.

- All required building permits have been issued.

- All adverse environmental conditions will be removed.

- The present use is lawful.

TREC contract forms already include some of these concerns. Texas law requires that most sellers furnish buyers with a Seller's Disclosure of Property Condition in accordance with Section 5.008 of the Texas Property Code. TREC has produced an approved, but not promulgated, form that licensees may use to meet this Property Code requirement. Sellers subject to this disclosure requirement to the buyer must do so by the time specified in the Property Code or the transaction may be subject to rescission by the buyer. A licensee who fails to make his or her client aware of the necessity and availability of this form for use could face a lawsuit from a damaged client and loss of license under TRELA §15(a)(6)(W).

Pests

The buyer may want to require that the seller agree to pay for a pest-clearance report from a licensed exterminator chosen by the buyer, and the seller may agree to repair all pest damage or to treat the home if necessary. The seller may be required to treat for fleas and/or termites and other wood-infesting organisms, using care not to use chemicals that may make the dwelling unsafe after use.

Assessments

The seller should agree to pay all assessments at closing, on the theory that the enhanced value of these improvements has been reflected in the sales price. Suppose that an assessment is outstanding at a low interest rate (a $20,000 sewer assessment payable in ten years at 6 percent, for example). Rather than have the seller pay off the assessment, consider having the buyer assume the assessment and lower the purchase price accordingly or credit the amount against the down payment.

Title Matters

The seller should agree to correct any title defect by a certain date; in fact, the closing can be postponed at the buyer's election to allow the defect to be cleared. The buyer may want to consider paying for the owner's title insurance policy to have the nonnegotiable right under the Real Estate Settlement Procedures Act (RESPA), to choose the title insurer. Under RESPA, regardless of who pays for the title policy, the buyer cannot be required to use a specific title insurer as a condition of sale. By the same token, a seller cannot be forced to pay for a title policy. Thus, from a practical perspective, the party paying for the policy usually chooses the title insurer.

Financing and Other Contingencies

Financing contingencies should be structured so that the buyer has enough time to perform. It is appropriate to make the contract subject to the review and approval of the buyer's attorney or tax adviser. If the buyer cannot meet a contingency, such as obtaining loan approval, the buyer should have the choice to cancel, extend or waive the condition and proceed to close, perhaps obtaining funds from another source.

If the property increases in value after the offer is accepted and before title transfers, the buyer who didn't qualify for financing could benefit by waiving the contingency and assigning his or her rights in the contract to another buyer for a profit. The buyer should use reasonable efforts to meet the contingency and not use the contingency clause as a bad-faith means to tie up the seller's property.

Miscellaneous Checklist

In a seller's market, the buyer may not be in a good position to demand too many concessions from the seller. The buyer's agent should consider covering some of the following items with the client for possible inclusion in a purchase contract for the buyer's benefit:

- The buyer is permitted occupancy prior to closing.

- The buyer is granted a right of first refusal to acquire any adjoining property owned by the seller.

- The buyer is given credit for any impound (escrow) accounts on assumed mortgages.

- The buyer is given the right to lock in points on a loan.

- The seller pays the appraisal fees and points on the loan.

- The buyer can extend the satisfaction date of any seller-provided financing.

- The buyer-borrower is given the right of first refusal if the seller discounts the sale of any purchase-money mortgage that the seller carried back.

- The seller agrees to allow the buyer-borrower to substitute collateral on any seller-provided financing.

- The seller provides a corporate resolution if the seller is a corporation, indicating, among other things, who is duly authorized by the corporation to sign all necessary documents on behalf of the corporation.

- The seller covers the buyer's expenses if the seller refuses to close on time.

- The seller permits the buyer to show the property to prospective tenants prior to closing.

- The seller allows the buyer reasonable access to the property to permit inspection by buyer's representatives such as interior designers and architects.

The seller's agent or subagent should urge the seller to consider resisting any or all of these concessions unless his or her seller-client gains some exceptional benefit in return. Sometimes an overly aggressive buyer agent gives advice that works to the buyer's disadvantage in the negotiations. The buyer must keep in mind that each concession requested from the seller may result in refusal of an offer and the possible loss to the buyer of a desirable property. Similarly, overly aggressive listing agents may give sellers negotiating advice such as rejecting an offer or encouraging sellers to make harsh counteroffers that are unacceptable to buyers and actually harm the sellers. In both examples the agents may have gone beyond their legitimate roles and breached fiduciary duties to their clients.

■ Buyer's Broker Disclosures

Disclosures to Buyer

Before entering into a buyer-representation agreement, the real estate agent is required by TRELA §15(a)(6)(D) and §15C to make an oral or a written disclosure of any agency representation relationships the broker may have with parties whose properties the buyer may be interested in considering. In addition, TRELA §15C requires that the broker provide the buyer with a written statement describing seller agency, buyer agency and intermediary brokerage. Although law no longer requires it, the broker probably should make any agency disclosures in writing and try to obtain the signature of the buyer acknowledging receipt of the disclosures and the written statement.

Disclosures to Seller or Listing Broker

TRELA §15C requires that agents disclose their representative capacities to other parties and to the agents of other parties at the time of first contact. When dealing with listing brokers, the buyer's broker also should be careful to reject any offer of subagency that may have been made.

The NAR® Code of Ethics and Standard of Practice requires that the buyer's agent disclose that relationship to the listing agent at first contact and provide written confirmation of that disclosure no later than the signing of the purchase agreement. As soon as the buyer's agent calls for an appointment, the buyer's agent should inform the listing broker that the buyer's agent represents the buyer and rejects any offer of subagency made. If the property is not listed, the buyer's agent should disclose the relationship to the seller at first contact and make any requests for compensation from the seller at that time.

Buyers as Customers

Although this chapter has focused on buyer agency, not every buyer wants to be represented by an agent. Some buyers appreciate the flexibility of dealing with several brokers and avoiding commitments and loyalties to any one of them. Such buyers who work with a number of brokers may acquire enough facts to enable them to make a decision, such as information about property values and seller motivation, although they may be unaware of any fiduciary duties owed to the seller or landlord by the broker. Others enjoy the "free ride" given by many brokers, each hoping that the buyer will make an offer to purchase through him or her. Still other buyers prefer to deal directly with the listing broker because they hope to obtain some inside information that they can use to make the best deal or because they fear they may lose the opportunity to buy the home they really want if they make an offer through another agent. This fear of missed opportunity may be based on the time factor involved in presenting an offer in a seller's market. Another concern is that an unprofessional listing agent might produce an equivalent or a better offer in-house after having first seen the buyer's offer submitted by the buyer's agent.

■ Summary

In the past, in the majority of real estate transactions the seller was represented by a real estate agent, but the buyer was not. Today, primarily owing to better disclosure and information that agents are required to provide, many buyers now seek the same level of client service that sellers typically receive from agents. The decision to represent a buyer is a serious one because the agent will be held to a high standard of care and will owe fiduciary duties to the buyer. Both the agent and the buyer must weigh the various benefits of buyer representation. It is strongly recommended that brokers use a written buyer-agency agreement and carefully discuss alternative methods of compensation. In helping the buyer or the buyer's attorney prepare the purchase agreement, the agent should consider the negotiable aspects of the transaction from the buyer's perspective.

■ Key Points

- Whether to represent the buyer is an important decision because the agent then owes the full range of fiduciary responsibilities. The real estate licensee may want to be selective and not represent every buyer who walks in the front door.

- Buyer brokerage does not mean that the broker is in the business of representing buyers only. Most buyer's agents regard buyer agency as one of the options available to them in single-agency or nonexclusive-agency practices.

- Not every buyer wants or needs representation. Some prefer to represent themselves, especially those not wanting to risk a missed opportunity in a fast-moving seller's market.

- Written buyer-representation agreements are preferable to oral ones.

- In showing buyers in-house listings, brokers must take care to avoid unintentional and unauthorized representation of more than one party. If such representation is to be authorized, the broker must make full disclosure of the potential conflicts of interest to both buyer and seller.

- A buyer's agent must disclose to the listing broker at initial contact that the licensee is a buyer's agent and must clearly reject any offer of subagency. Frequently, the listing broker will be authorized to share fees with buyer's agents and allow them equal access to property for showing.

- Buyer's agents in Texas should seriously consider benefits and drawbacks of being compensated by buyers/tenants rather than by sellers/landlords, as is the most common practice in Texas today.

■ Suggestions for Brokers

Establish an office policy on how to handle an offer received from a buyer's agent on one of your listings. Discuss with the seller the possibility that you will receive offers from buyers' agents and that these offers may require a commission split or an adjustment in the offering price when the buyer will pay the buyer's agent directly. Discuss the net effect these offers will have on the seller's position, and advise the seller accordingly.

■ Quiz

1. When a buyer's agent shows a property listed through an MLS, the agent is the fiduciary of which of the following?

   A. Buyer   C. Seller
   B. Buyer's broker   D. MLS

2. Buyer agency

   A. must be created with a written buyer's representation agreement.
   B. may be created by the actions of a licensee as well as by written agreements.
   C. while legal, is seldom practiced by brokers in Texas.
   D. excludes the possibility of a brokerage firm's obtaining listings from sellers.

3. Which of the following is (are) true regarding buyer agency?

   A. Buyer agency is illegal.
   B. Buyer agency is not recognized by lenders.
   C. Buyer agency increases the risk of procuring-cause disputes.
   D. None of the above

4. Which of the following requires that a buyer purchase only through a particular broker?

   A. The buyer pays the broker a commission.
   B. The buyer signed an exclusive representation agreement.
   C. The buyer asked the agent to help negotiate the purchase of an already identified property.
   D. The buyer signed an open buyer-representation agreement.

5. Buyer-representation agreements

   A. are promulgated forms available from TREC.
   B. impose duties on buyers' brokers similar to those that listing agreements impose on sellers' brokers.
   C. differ from listing agreements in that listings require definite termination dates while buyer-representation agreements do not.
   D. in order to be binding, must provide that the buyer compensate the broker for the representation services.

6. The increase in buyer representation is due primarily to

   A. better disclosure and information required of brokers.
   B. the infusion of more buyers into the marketplace.
   C. brokers seeking and promoting compensation by both parties.
   D. All of the above.

7. In which of the following cases must a real estate broker obtain a written agreement with a buyer?

   A. The broker is to act as a buyer's agent
   B. The broker wishes to take legal action against a buyer for commission.
   C. Both of the above
   D. Neither of the above

8. Which of the following are possible benefits of buyer agency?

    A. Greater client loyalty
    B. Better protection against conflicts of loyalty
    C. No liability for acts of the listing broker
    D. All of the above

9. Which of the following would be a disadvantage of exclusive buyer agency?

    A. The broker would not be able to list a property owned by their buyer-client.
    B. The broker could never earn full commission on an in-house sale.
    C. There is a potential conflict of interest if two buyer-clients wish to offer on the same property.
    D. All of the above are potential disadvantages.

10. The listing broker has agreed to pay the cooperating broker a fee of 2 percent of the sales price. The buyer is represented and has agreed in writing to pay her broker a nonrefundable $2,000 flat fee.

    A. All parties must be notified of the compensation agreement between the buyer and her broker.
    B. As an agent of the buyer, the broker has no duty to disclose the dual compensation.
    C. The broker for the buyer may disclose the dual compensation only if authorized to do so by his client.
    D. The dual compensation must be disclosed only if it impacts on the ultimate tax advantage of the buyer.

■ Discussion Questions

1. Can a buyer's broker participate in the MLS and receive a share of the listing broker's commission?

2. Why would a listing broker reduce a portion of the sales commission so the seller could credit that portion to the buyer for payment of the buyer's broker's commission?

3. How could a buyer's broker handle conflicts of interest involving in-house sales?

4. Name at least four important elements of a well-drafted buyer's broker-representation agreement.

5. Name at least five important points for a buyer's broker to cover in a purchase contract.

CHAPTER 7

Subagency

One of the least understood agency relationships is subagency. In 1996 The Real Estate License Act (TRELA) was amended to define a subagent as "a licensee who represents a principal through cooperation with and consent of a broker representing the principal and who is *not* (emphasis added) sponsored by or associated with the principal's broker." A subagent is appointed by an agent, with the informed consent of the agent's principal. Typically, a subagent is a real estate broker authorized by a listing broker, under the authority granted by the seller, to perform functions on the seller's behalf. Less frequently, a buyer's broker or tenant's representative appoints a subagent to perform functions on the buyer's or tenant's behalf, especially in the area of opinions of value. On other occasions, the buyer's broker refers clients to buyers' brokers located in different geographic areas or to buyers' brokers or tenant representatives who specialize in certain properties.

This chapter focuses on the relationship between the listing broker and the cooperating or other broker, also called the selling broker, the one who actually finds the ready, willing and able buyer. Remember, a buyer's broker should not be referred to as a *selling broker, cooperating broker* or *subagent of the listing broker.* Buyers' brokers do not procure ready, willing and able buyers for sellers. Instead, they procure suitable properties for buyer clients. Buyers' brokers should not be the target of procuring-cause grievances of listing agents or subagents because buyers' brokers are under separate contracts to buyers, not to sellers or sellers' agents.

This chapter addresses the following:

Establishing Status: Subagent or Buyer's Broker?
Creation of Subagency
Selective Offers of Subagency
Blanket Offers of Subagency (MLS)
Rejecting Subagency
No Offer of Subagency
Subagency Optional
Sellers and Subagency

■ Establishing Status: Subagent or Buyer's Broker?

Transactions usually start from two positions quite independent of each other. A buyer begins to consider buying and then starts taking action to buy. Meanwhile, a seller starts to consider selling and later starts taking action to sell. A transaction is the result of these two independent forces meeting. During the marketing of a property by the seller's broker, the buyer frequently visits the property with another broker or a licensed associate of another broker, who may be called the *other broker, cooperating broker, selling broker* or *buyer's broker*. Who is this other broker? Whom does the other broker represent?

The status of the other broker should be established as early as possible. Whether the other broker is a seller's subagent or a buyer's broker can be critical. If held to be a *seller's subagent,* the other broker owes fiduciary duties and primary allegiance to the seller and the seller may be vicariously liable for his or her subagent's conduct toward third parties if such conduct was misleading or fraudulent *and* the seller was aware of the conduct. If held to be a *buyer's broker,* the other broker owes fiduciary duties and primary allegiance to the buyer.

■ Creation of Subagency

Like any agency relationship, the subagency relationship is created by the consent of those involved. Only when a valid subagency is created does the law impose fiduciary duties and liabilities on the subagent. Subagency may be created expressly by agreement or implicitly by words, conduct or custom. Subagency may be created within or apart from the framework of a multiple-listing service (MLS). Even within the MLS, subagency is not automatic. The seller has the option to offer subagency. On the other hand, the listing broker has the option to condition the taking of a listing on whether the seller will allow or insist on subagency or some other form of representation. Also, any other broker in the transaction can reject any offer of subagency made and can elect to work with the buyer on a client basis as the buyer's agent.

Selective Offers of Subagency

Subagency can be created outside the framework of an MLS. While many listing brokers are members of an MLS, there are thousands of listings in the small towns and rural areas of Texas that have no MLS systems. Further, MLS systems do not require that certain types of properties be listed. Commercial properties, new project sales, business opportunities,

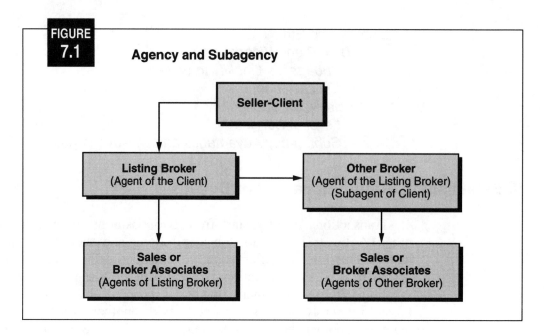

long-term leases and vacant land typically fall into this voluntary category. Still, listing brokers may decide to work with other brokers on a selective basis to help in the search for buyers for these types of properties.

Rather than talk in terms of a formal offer of subagency, brokers may talk of cooperating in a transaction and sharing or splitting the commission. This type of informal understanding is particularly dangerous because it is often unclear as to whom the other broker represents or who is responsible for payment of compensation. In a recent case, a Texas commercial broker failed to recover a commission in a $9 million transaction because he was unable to convincingly establish whose agent he was, whose best interests he acted in and who was supposed to pay him. Instead of the $270,000 commission he sued for, he settled for $40,000. Had the commercial broker known and practiced the principles set out by law, there might have been a decidedly different outcome.

Listing brokers and the other brokers involved in a transaction often have separate commission agreements among themselves that serve as a basis for the subagency relationship. Such agreements are often silent as to the agency duties and tend to cover only how the commission is to be split. Brokers who work cooperatively frequently operate without any specific written or oral agreement; however, a written arrangement is preferable.

The listing broker usually works with a number of subagents, yet only the subagent who procures the sale is entitled to a share of the commission as the procuring cause. This arrangement is similar to an open listing. As in any situation where more than one broker works with a single buyer, the possibility exists that procuring-cause disputes may arise between different selling, cooperating or other brokers, with two or more of the other brokers each claiming a right to share the commission with the listing broker.

In the model in Figure 7.1 notice that *associates of the listing broker are not subagents.* Wording in the TRELA leaves room for speculation about the proper term to describe an associate of another broker when that other broker is acting as a subagent of the listing broker's client. It is clear, however, that the associate is an agent of the subagent broker and will carry out the duties of a subagent. In other words, when a broker is acting as a subagent, the associates of the subagent broker will have the same obligations to the listing broker's client as would the subagent broker.

EXAMPLE: Broker Jeff of South Side Realty tells brokers Bob and Aileen, each from different companies, about a commercial office building listed for sale with South Side Realty. The seller authorized Jeff in the listing agreement to use subagents. Bob and Aileen each separately agree to help market the property. Both Bob and Aileen are now subagents of the seller and are acting through Jeff's South Side Realty.

If Bob finds the buyer who eventually buys the building, Bob is entitled to a previously agreed-on share of South Side's listing commission, and Aileen receives nothing for her efforts. However, if Aileen originally showed the building to the buyer but the buyer enlisted Bob to write up the offer, both Aileen and Bob might involve South Side Realty in a dispute over which one of them was the procuring cause of the sale and thus is entitled to share in the commission.

On the other hand, if Bob was a buyer's broker in this situation, any claim by Aileen that she was the procuring cause would be directed to the listing broker and would not affect Bob or his compensation because Bob's agency relationship is with the buyer. Bob's right to a commission would come from his buyer-client negotiating Bob's payment as a part of the contract with the seller and would be independent of the listing agent's listing agreement or offers of compensation or cooperation to other brokers.

Blanket Offers of Subagency (MLS)

Residential properties are typically listed in an areawide MLS. A seller often lists property with a licensed associate of a broker who is a member of the local MLS. The seller expects that the property will receive the widest possible exposure to potential buyers through the efforts of hundreds of local real estate licensees. An MLS is a convenient way to offer subagency and arrange to share commissions.

Until the late 1970s, the MLS was defined as a system created for the orderly dissemination and compilation of listing information. MLS regulations, written under guidelines formulated by the National Association of REALTORS®, were modified to provide that by submitting a property to the MLS through the broker, the seller authorizes the broker to make a blanket offer of subagency to the other members of the MLS.

The other broker accepts the blanket offer by showing the property to the buyer and by procuring an offer to purchase. No rule establishes exactly when the subagency offer is accepted, other than that acceptance is based on performance. If no written acceptance of the subagency offer exists, there may be a question as to whether the subagency offer is accepted at the time a property is shown or only when an offer is produced.

One uncertainty is the effect of the other broker's accepting subagency from a listing broker while showing one of that broker's listings to a buyer-customer, then later returning with a second buyer who is already a buyer-client.

 EXAMPLE: Suppose Sandra, a subagent of the seller, shows customer Alice a property listed in the MLS. Alice decides she does not like the house. The next week, Sandra looks for a home for her buyer-client Patty, with whom she and Shoreline Realty have a written buyer-agency agreement.

? QUESTIONS

1. Can Sandra serve Patty as a buyer's agent with respect to the home she showed Alice, or will her earlier subagency to the seller, with Alice as a prospective customer, make her a representative of both parties?

2. Can Sandra tell Patty that the seller agreed to reduce the asking price for Alice?

DISCUSSION

It would seem that subagency applies to the person, not the property. Thus, the earlier subagency does not apply to a later transaction. If it did, after Sandra showed Alice the property, all of Shoreline Realty's associates would become subagents of the seller until that property was sold. On the other hand, the argument can be made that when Sandra first showed the home she may have learned confidential information from the listing agent, who believed Sandra to be accepting the blanket offer of subagency. The listing agent would have had good reason to believe Sandra was accepting subagency by showing the house without clearly rejecting the offer of subagency. Therefore, the listing agent would have been acting within the proper scope of her duty if she conveyed to Sandra confidential information with regard to the seller's motivations and negotiating position. (Information "leaks" often occur through comments from listing agents who believe the other broker has accepted subagency.)

Once entrusted with information about the seller (actually or constructively, intentionally or accidentally) while in a subagency capacity, the entire brokerage becomes the subagent of the listing broker. Should the licensee—or anyone in the entire brokerage—now represent a buyer without full disclosure of the potential conflicts and consent of all the parties? Provided that both the seller and the buyer-client are informed of the situation, nothing would prevent Sandra from showing the buyer-client the property with the consent of both parties. Everyone should be made aware, however, that any confidential information that has been learned in a subagency capacity *cannot* be disclosed to the buyer. The buyer-client, on learning of this prohibition, may prefer to use another broker who is not limited in the services that can be provided.

Information learned as an agent or subagent must be kept confidential in the future, even when working with a buyer-client. However, the buyer-client should be informed of the prior subagency relationship with the seller and should be told that there may be information about the property or the seller that cannot be disclosed. A buyer who insists on full disclosure should be referred to a licensee who has not worked as a subagent on this particular property. In practice a subagent will probably not have any more information than a buyer's agent because sellers' agents have become very careful about disclosing confidential information.

By accepting the offer of subagency, the other broker owes complete fiduciary duties and loyalty to the seller. Any real estate agent acting as a subagent of the seller must relate to both buyer and seller exactly as if the subagent's company had taken the listing. The subagent must be careful not to act for the buyer in any manner adverse to the seller's best interests. This may be a problem if the subagent has developed close ties with the buyer. By the same token, the subagent rarely meets the seller and usually knows little about the seller's needs. The subagent's main source of information will be what is revealed in the MLS or what is discussed with the listing agent.

Rejecting Subagency

It is not mandatory for another broker to accept an offer of subagency. Listing a property in an MLS may permit subagency but does not automatically create it or require it. Unless disclosed on the first contact with the listing agency, it is presumed that the listing broker offers subagency on behalf of the seller and that those cooperating members who attempt to find a buyer for a listed property are subagents of the seller. However, these are only presumptions. Therefore, all brokers would do well to clarify agency relationships *before* acting, not after. Other brokers and buyers are free to arrange their legal relationships as they see fit, so long as adequate disclosure is made. Under the new MLS systems, the seller can direct the broker to offer subagency on a blanket basis or not allow the broker to offer subagency at all. The broker, with the consent of the seller, may offer compensation to subagents or buyers' agents.

The other broker may reject the offer of subagency and work as a buyer's broker, if the seller has consented to cooperation with buyers' agents. A common example of this is when other brokers decide to buy property listed in the MLS for their own account. If the other broker wishes to reject subagency, it is extremely important to notify the listing broker and the seller that he or she is not a subagent of the seller. It is important to immediately disclaim any subagency in the transaction and obtain a clear understanding with the listing broker and seller regarding the payment of commission.

No Offer of Subagency

Just as some MLS brokers decide not to accept the offer of subagency, some sellers decide not to authorize subagency on a blanket basis. Sellers often carefully select their own listing brokers. They may not want other brokers representing them in a transaction, especially brokers they do not know. While these sellers want the market exposure of an MLS, they feel that other brokers acting as subagents do not actively work to obtain the most favorable terms for them but instead try to get the best terms and conditions for buyers. The common perception is that the other broker represents the buyer. However, as long as other brokers accept and practice subagency correctly, sellers should not object because they thereby enjoy the benefits of having two brokerage firms represent their interests.

In the past, listings in which the sellers did not want other brokers or an MLS involved in the sale were called *office exclusives.* Today, many sellers want their brokers to submit their listings to an MLS so they can benefit from the wide exposure of their property. These sellers prefer the use of a blanket offer of cooperation (in the form of a commission split), but no subagency.

Subagency Optional

All board of REALTORS® MLSs have been required to amend their regulations to delete mandatory offers of subagency and to make offers of subagency optional. Participants submitting listings to the MLS must, however, offer cooperation to other MLS participants in the form of a subagency or cooperation with buyers' agents or other licensees. All offers of subagency or cooperation made through an MLS must include an offer of compensation. Sellers are now free to have their listing brokers submit the listings to the MLS and offer cooperation and fee splitting, as always, but they are also free not to offer subagency if that choice is deemed by the seller not to offer benefits. A seller can always direct the broker to make a blanket offer of subagency, as was once the customary practice, and if the listing broker chooses to take the listing under that condition, the listing broker will offer subagency.

When other agents take buyers to listings where no subagency is offered, they must be clear about their agency status. However, when the other agent comes to a property with a buyer-customer and has not clarified the relationships, that other agent may be in the middle of the transaction as a licensee without a defined role in the transaction. If the seller is not permitting subagency and the buyer does not want to be represented as a client, the broker has reached an impasse.

Nothing in the license act addresses a nonagency status, and in fact, §535.1(c) of the Rules of the Texas Real Estate Commission states that TRELA *is an agency law.* Therefore it is presumed that in a brokerage transaction the licensee, while acting under the provisions of the act, is the agent of someone—the buyer, the seller or both.

Some states provide for nonagency status for real estate licensees who may provide real estate services as *transactional brokers, facilitators* or *middlemen.* A broker in Texas attempting to maintain a nonagency status will find no comfort in TRELA if a dispute arises in the transaction. Likewise, the courts have determined that a broker, while attempting to act as a middleman, may become an agent if he or she attempts to perform any services on behalf of a property owner. [See *West v. Touchstone,* 620 S.W.2d 687 (Tex.Civ.App.—Dallas 1981).]

Regardless of the role of the other agent, the compensation between the listing broker and the other broker must be specified within the MLS framework if offered through the MLS. Keep in mind, however, that in Texas more than half of all real estate licensees are not REALTORS® and many who are REALTORS® are not members of any formal or NAR®-sanctioned MLS system. Therefore, they are not subject to MLS rules on listings. Brokers bringing buyers to builder's homes or for-sale-by-owner (FSBO) homes need to have a very clear understanding of the agency relationships and compensation agreements with all the parties before any work begins.

Sellers and Subagency

The seller enjoys several benefits when the use of subagents is authorized and the subagency is carried out properly. Theoretically, in addition to the listing broker, all members of the MLS will act on the seller's behalf to find and qualify buyers. All brokers will owe the seller their fiduciary duties and professional skills. Furthermore, this increased exposure may hasten the sale of the property. The seller can direct the listing broker to exert better control by imposing on subagents special requirements for showing, presenting offers, depositing earnest money, registering buyers and opening escrow.

EXAMPLE: The listing on George's house by Sam's firm, Supreme Realty, recently expired. George then listed the home with Main Realty, which submitted the listing to the local MLS. Sam meets Susan, and George's home is perfect for Susan. Because of Sam's prior client relationship with George, it would be advisable for Sam to treat the buyer, Susan, as a customer and work on this property as a subagent of the seller, George, with the express consent of George and Main Realty.

If, however, Susan requires representation and Sam undertakes to act as her agent, she should be fully informed that Sam has previously acted as an agent for George (the seller) and that there may be certain confidential information learned about George that cannot be disclosed. Remember: Anytime a client may receive anything less than full fiduciary duties, the client *must* be so informed.

■ Liability and Ethics

No one can make an informed decision to choose or not to choose subagency without first becoming aware of the legal and practical consequences of a subagency relationship. Often, the outcome of a court case turns on whether the other broker is found to be a subagent of the seller or an agent of the buyer. Sellers and listing brokers have at times refused subagency on the basis of potential liability created by a subagent over whom the listing broker may have no control or about whom he has no knowledge. Some of these issues have recently been resolved by the Texas Legislature, as shown below.

S.B. 489 and Vicarious Liability

In addition to major changes in the agency provisions of the TRELA, Senate Bill 489 also addressed the liability of parties and agents for the acts of others (vicarious liability). The TRELA has been amended in §15F as follows:

(a) A party is not liable for a misrepresentation or a concealment of a material factor made by a licensee in a real estate transaction unless the party knew of the falsity of the misrepresentation or concealment and failed to disclose the party's knowledge of the falsity of the misrepresentation or concealment.

(b) A licensee is not liable for a misrepresentation or concealment of a material fact made by a party in a real estate transaction unless the licensee knew of the falsity of the misrepresentation or concealment and failed to disclose the licensee's knowledge of the falsity of the misrepresentation or concealment.

(c) A party or a licensee is not liable for a misrepresentation or a concealment of a material fact made by a subagent in a real estate transaction unless the party or licensee knew of the falsity of the misrepresentation or concealment and failed to disclose the party's or licensee's knowledge of the falsity of the misrepresentation or concealment.

(d) The provision of this section shall prevail over common law and any other law. This section does not diminish a real estate broker's responsibility for the acts or omissions of the broker's salespersons associated with or acting for the real estate broker, as provided by Section 1 of this Act.

(e) In this section, "licensee," "subagent," and "party" have the meaning assigned to those terms by Section 15C of this Act.

With these new provisions, many brokers who previously were reluctant to extend subagency to other brokers may be more inclined to do so.

Following is an example that should help clarify the role of the subagent and the importance of promptly disclosing agency status.

 EXAMPLE: Jeff, the listing agent from Southside Realty, tells subagent Sally of Bay Realty that the roof leaks. Sally fails to tell buyer Betty, who doesn't discover this fact until the first rainy spell after closing.

? QUESTION

Who is potentially liable for failing to disclose a known material fact?

DISCUSSION

The seller, Jeff, Southside Realty, Sally and Bay Realty are all potentially liable. If Jeff, Southside Realty and the seller were all held liable for Sally's negligence, they would have claims for indemnification against Sally and Bay Realty. The general rule is that both the listing broker and the seller may be liable for the faults of their authorized subagent. However, TRELA §15F(c) exempts both the seller and the listing broker from liability for misrepresentation by a subagent unless they were aware of such misrepresentation. The result would be different if Sally and Bay Realty had been buyer Betty's agents; Betty then would have bought with the constructive or imputed notice that the roof leaked because Betty's own buyer's agent, Sally, had been told of the leak. Also, Sally's negligence then would not be imputed to Southside Realty, because Bay Realty was not its agent. However, Betty would have a claim against Bay Realty because of Sally's negligence.

Subagent's Liability to Seller

Subagents need to consider their legal and ethical responsibilities to the seller. For example, as a buyer's agent presenting an offer on a Department of Veterans Affairs (VA) loan assumption, a broker is under no legal duty to suggest that the seller require from the buyer a substitution of eligibility or release of liability (from both the VA and the lender). A subagent, however, is legally obligated to point out to the seller the risks involved in accepting such an offer.

Likewise, the subagent, as well as the listing broker, could be liable to the seller of a dilapidated old house for failure to advise (or recommend that an attorney be consulted) on the appropriate use of an "as is" clause or the fact that the seller may have to make repairs if a Federal Housing Administration (FHA) loan is involved.

Similarly, a buyer's agent has no duty to point out the risks to the seller of accepting a wraparound mortgage or an installment land sales contract of sale in which the buyer does not agree to pay any prepayment penalties on the seller's underlying loan. As a subagent of the seller, however, an agent is obligated to point out any risks to the seller that are evident to the ordinary agent, even if the buyer instructed the agent to remain silent regarding such risks. Likewise, as a seller's subagent, an agent would be remiss if he or she were to fail to point out to the seller the risks involved in accepting, as partial payment, a note from a recently formed corporation without any personal guaranty from the principals of the corporation. A buyer's agent is under no similar duty toward the seller.

Ethical Concerns

Brokers who serve as subagents are sometimes confronted with difficult ethical questions. Consider the following examples, in which Sally and Bay Realty act as the seller's subagents on a property listed in the MLS by Jeff of South Side Realty.

 EXAMPLE: Sally learns that Betty Buyer has an option to purchase the two parcels on both sides of the listed property. Betty is trying to consolidate and subdivide the three lots, hoping to "double their value." The seller asks Sally, "Is the buyer's offer her best offer, or should I hold out for more?"

? **QUESTION**

What does Sally tell the seller?

DISCUSSION

As a seller's subagent, Sally has a fiduciary duty of full disclosure to the seller of all material facts. She is also obligated under 22 TAC (Texas Administrative Code) §535.156(a) and (c) to "convey to the principal all known information which would affect the principal's decision on whether or not to accept or reject offers," and Sally "has an affirmative duty to keep the principal informed at all times of significant information applicable to the transaction or transactions in which the licensee is acting as an agent for the principal." She is further required under 22 TAC §(535.2(b) to "negotiate the best possible transaction for the principal, the person the licensee has agreed to represent." Armed with Sally's information about Betty's consolidation plans, the seller might well decide to hold out for a better offer, especially if the seller is not under great pressure to sell. This example is also useful in understanding the dilemma of an agent representing both parties.

EXAMPLE: Jeff listed Carol's home for sale. Carol asks Jeff to find her another home. Jeff locates a perfect home. The seller is George, who is the broker/owner of Success Realty. George is offering seller financing on his property. Jeff is aware that Carol has had credit problems.

QUESTION

What disclosures should be made to George?

DISCUSSION

The answer depends on the agency role that Jeff is assuming in the second transaction. If Jeff is attempting to act as a subagent of George, he would be required to disclose the negative information about Carol.

The real question is whether it is practical or legally possible to work with Carol as an agent in the sale of her property and simultaneously as a subagent of the seller of the property that Carol is attempting to buy?

While it may be technically possible to do so, this would create a very difficult situation for Jeff. It would be much better to serve Carol as a buyer's agent in the purchase of George's home. In this case Jeff would have no obligation to disclose Carol's past financial problems to George, and Jeff could give Carol full agency representation services in both transactions.

■ Deciding on Subagency

While other brokers outside the listing firm should recognize the potential liability of being a subagent, the more important question for the other broker working with a *buyer* is, "How effective am I for the buyer when I act in the capacity of a subagent?" Often, the answer depends on how real estate licensees perceive their roles: whether as facilitators and marketing specialists or as negotiators and representatives of clients. Some brokers and associates, as subagents of the seller in a cooperative sales transaction, feel very comfortable in limiting their roles with buyers to providing accurate and honest customer-level service and actually negotiating for the seller's best interests. They also feel assured of having an enforceable right to receive compensation once the listing brokers are paid by the sellers—that is, of course, if they have made the appropriate agreements.

Other licensees feel less comfortable and less effective as subagents. They often sense a hesitation or resistance on the part of buyers (or tenants) to trust or rely on them as professionals, especially when they point out that they represent the owner (or landlord). These licensees feel they can demonstrate more of their talents and creative skills when they represent and negotiate on behalf of the buyer as client. This is especially true if prospective buyers (or tenants) are unsophisticated investors or business owners with plenty of disposable income but little negotiating ability or experience as far as real estate is concerned. These licensees find success in carefully screening prospective buyers (and tenants) and electing to work for a few on a client/agent basis.

A broker should consider several factors when deciding whether to be a subagent.

- Some licensees find difficulty in explaining subagency to buyers, especially if a buyer expects the broker to protect and promote the buyer's best interests.

- A subagent cannot be too aggressive in furthering the buyer's interests for fear of being disloyal to the seller. The subagent would feel an ethical discomfort if, in his or her opinion, the seller's listing was overpriced, the seller's terms were unreasonable or better properties were available. A seller's subagent must withhold negative opinions because of the duty of loyalty to the seller.

- A subagent of the seller must immediately disclose all pertinent facts to the listing broker, both before and after the contract is signed. TREC Rules require full disclosure of all material information to a client. This includes information about the buyer's ability to pay, the buyer's plans to resell for a profit or the buyer's willingness to offer a higher price. This can have a chilling effect on the working relationship with the buyer.

- Sellers' subagents know that they may not be told all the pertinent facts about a property or a seller. The competent listing agent and seller are unlikely to tell the subagent anything that they do not want the buyer to know.

- The subagent has no contractual relationship with the seller and cannot sue the seller if the seller cancels the sale and the listing broker elects not to pursue the seller for the commission. Neither is the subagent protected if the listing broker breaches his or her fiduciary duties to the seller and the seller refuses to pay the compensation. If the listing broker's agreement is invalid or unenforceable and the seller refuses to pay, the subagent will get part of nothing.

- Subagency has functioned as a viable role for many brokers for many years. These brokers feel comfortable and confident that the buyer, as customer, can receive excellent service without a necessity for agency representation—especially in noncomplex residential transactions.

- As long as the licensee clearly explains the choices, limitations and risks associated with subagency to the buyer, the buyer can choose the level of service that best meets his or her particular requirements.

Level of Service

To make an informed decision to act as a subagent, the real estate licensee must understand the different levels of services rendered to a client and to a customer. A real estate licensee often decides to treat the buyer as a customer, in which case a subagency relationship with the seller may be appropriate. Occasionally, however, a licensee may want to represent and negotiate for a particular buyer as a client, in which case subagency with the seller is not appropriate. This is more likely when the buyer is a former client or a quality prospect, one whom the licensee wants to represent and does not want to lose. To gain a better understanding of the level of service to be given to a buyer customer by a subagent consider the following example.

 EXAMPLE: George, a former client, refers Harry to Sally of Bay Realty. Harry is interested in looking at expensive homes. Bay Realty has no high-priced listings, but several expensive homes are listed in the local MLS. Harry mentions that he has talked to five other brokers and will be talking to several others. Sally decides to work with Harry on a customer basis. Sally shows Harry a property listed in the MLS with Sam of Main Realty, and Harry decides to buy it.

? QUESTION

In the course of negotiations, Sally deals with a number of important items, such as (1) price and appraised value; (2) seller financing; (3) earnest money, amount and default remedies; (4) condition of property; (5) contingencies; and (6) fixtures and inventory. How should Sally treat each item, recognizing that her primary allegiance is to the seller?

✎ DISCUSSION

Sally must be honest with Harry and make appropriate disclosures; as a subagent of the seller, however, Sally owes a duty of loyalty to only the seller and a much higher degree of skill, care and disclosure to the seller than to the buyer. Sally should handle each item as follows:

Price and appraised value. Sally must try to obtain the highest price and best terms for the seller consistent with the seller's preferred terms. Sally should not show Harry a competitive market analysis (CMA) and probably is not obligated to disclose any previous lower appraised value. Sally should not suggest or encourage starting with a low offer to test the seller. She has a legal and ethical obligation to attempt to get the best transaction possible for the seller.

Seller financing. While Sally can mention the types of provisions commonly found in mortgages, she should not encourage terms unfavorable to the seller. Sally should encourage the seller to request a financial statement and credit report on Harry and point out any negative features of the buyer's qualifications to the seller, such as repeated late payments.

Earnest money. Sally should try to obtain a sufficient amount of earnest deposit to protect the seller in case of default. The seller should have the choice of remedies in the event of the buyer's default.

Condition of property. Sally should disclose all known and reasonably discoverable material defects to Harry and inform him that he is responsible for inspecting the property to make sure it meets his specifications. If appropriate, Sally might be obligated to suggest that the seller seek an attorney's advice about using an "as is" clause to limit the seller's exposure to liability for obvious defects in a run-down property. (*Note:* "As is" is not a defense against deceptive trade practices or against the failure to reveal defects known by either the seller or the seller's agents.)

Contingencies. Sally should ensure that contingencies are worded clearly. Neither Sam nor Sally should draft any language regarding contingencies or conditions in contracts that affect the legal rights of the parties to the contracts. They should stick to using TREC-promulgated addenda or recommend that the parties get legal counsel on any added wording that the buyer may require to be included. [See 22 TAC §537.11(b), (c) and (d) for more detail on this issue.] Sally must advise the seller, usually through the listing broker, of her opinion as to the reasonableness of the offer. Any doubts should be shared with Sally's client, the seller. Sally may need to advise the seller, through Sam or with Sam present, to consider making a counteroffer with time limits for performance of the contingency or within a specified time for the right of first refusal, in case the seller receives another offer during the contingency period.

Fixtures. Sally must point out to the seller any personal property included in Harry's offer that is not included in the listing, such as a portable microwave oven or a satellite dish.

Other items. Sally must be careful not to disclose facts that may compromise the seller's position (for example, that the seller is near foreclosure or bankruptcy or that the property is overpriced). However, Sally must disclose to Harry any material conditions that may affect value or desirability, such as building code violations or lack of legal access, about which Sally actually knows or reasonably should know.

Sally, as well as Sam, must disclose to the seller such pertinent facts as

- a proposed favorable rezoning that may increase the value of the property,

- Harry has secured a resale buyer once the property has been subdivided,

- Harry is the brother of Sally,

- Harry will pay more than the offering price or

- the undisclosed buyer is a business competitor of the seller and is using Harry as a straw man to make the offer to buy.

Sally cannot agree to accept bonus money from Harry for obtaining a reduction in the listed price. Nor can she consider offers of future listings of Harry's five rental properties "if she'll treat him right on this deal."

Sally must respond as accurately as she can to Harry's questions about easements, loans or restrictions on the property. Sally might give Harry copies of all relevant documents, such as loan assumption papers, declarations of restrictions, title reports, easements and deeds. Sally should be careful not to act as Harry's adviser in interpreting such documents, although Sally can suggest that Harry have other experts review these documents on his behalf. Sally should take care to follow through on promises she or the seller makes, such as promises to obtain adequate insurance coverage for Harry and to make necessary repairs. Failure to do as promised could result in the seller's being liable for Sally's carelessness (for example, if the uninsured home were to burn to the ground two days after closing).

Subagency Advantages and Disadvantages

Some of the advantages of subagency are as follows:

- Subagency established the traditional basis for the other broker's compensation.

- With subagency, there is no need to obtain written agreement from the buyer as may be required in other forms of representation.

- The customer may be advantaged by not being contractually bound to use only one broker to assist him or her or to have to pay for assistance the customer may never use.

- Subagency enables the seller to be represented by two brokerage companies.

Some of the disadvantages of subagency are as follows:

- Sellers' subagent must give information statements about brokerage services and disclose their agency relationships with sellers to buyer-customers. This potentially could cause buyers to seek someone who can legally represent their interests. Less frequently, any buyer's sub-agent must also give any seller-customer the same required notice.

- A subagent may find it too easy to act like the customer's "agent," leading the customer to believe that he or she is a client being represented by the licensee.

- The seller and listing broker might be liable for acts of the seller's subagent, although under current law this liability has been reduced.

- The subagent owes fiduciary duties to the listing broker and an unknown seller.

- Confusing relationships, disclosures and conflicts arise if the licensee acts as subagent with one buyer and buyer's agent with another buyer on the same property.

■ Summary

In the majority of residential real estate transactions, an agent other than the listing agent procures the buyer. It is important to make an early decision about whether the other agent is a subagent of the seller or an agent of the buyer. This depends on whether subagency was offered and whether it was accepted. If accepted, the subagent owes client-level services to the seller and customer-level services to the buyer.

■ Key Points

- A seller's subagent owes a general duty of fairness and honesty to the buyer (customer), but owes full fiduciary duties to the seller (client).

- Under an MLS, subagency is no longer automatic; the offering of subagency is optional, and a buyer's agent is free to reject an offer of subagency.

- As a matter of routine, the listing office should clarify subagency status of any other broker.

- Some brokers don't feel very effective as subagents, especially if they favor the buyer in a transaction.

- Some cooperating brokers prefer to treat certain buyers as customers, and thus, subagency to the seller is the appropriate relationship.

- It is easy to appear to treat the buyer as a client, leading the buyer to believe he or she is a client, and thus create an accidental undisclosed agency relationship.

■ Suggestions for Brokers

When you act as the nonlisting or other broker, decide whether you prefer to represent the buyer or to represent the seller as a subagent. Choose what works best for you, and to be safe, get the informed written consent of all parties to act in that manner. Note that the offer of subagency is no longer automatic, and even if it is given, an offer of subagency can be rejected. Because principals may incur some liability by the acts of their subagents, listing brokers should tell sellers of the risks, as well as the benefits, of using subagents.

■ Quiz

1. The listing broker can direct the other broker acting as a subagent to do all of the following *except*

   A. register buyers to lessen procuring-cause problems for the listing broker.
   B. show the property only in the evening.
   C. obtain earnest money deposits only in the form of cashiers' or certified checks.
   D. act as a fiduciary to the buyer.

2. Any broker in a transaction

   A. must accept an offer of subagency.
   B. must accept an offer of buyer agency.
   C. can reject any offer of subagency.
   D. must do all of the above.

3. George lists his house with Sally of Bay Realty, a member of the local Board of REALTORS® MLS. Subagency is offered and not disclaimed. Betty arrives in town and goes to Jeff of South Side Realty for help in buying a home. Jeff shows her George's house and helps Betty with an offer, which is accepted by George. Who does Jeff primarily represent?

   A. George   C. Sally
   B. Betty   D. The MLS

4. A local Multiple Listing Service (MLS) may be accessed by

   A. anyone licensed by TREC.
   B. any REALTOR® associate representing the buyer.
   C. any REALTOR® associate representing the seller.
   D. any REALTOR® associate who is a member of that MLS.

5. Three different subagents show a property to the same buyer over a span of two weeks. Which subagent is entitled to a share of the commission?

   A. The subagent who procures the sale.
   B. The subagent who first showed the property to the buyer.
   C. The subagent who last showed the property to the buyer.
   D. All three subagents above receive an equal share of the commission.

6. It is always in the seller's best interest to refuse to offer subagency to other brokers in order to reduce liability to the seller.

   A. True
   B. False
   C. True only when the property is located in a large community.
   D. False because the seller never has liability for anyone in a real estate transaction.

7. The subagent's fiduciary duties to a listing broker's client

   A. are substantially reduced from those of the listing broker.
   B. are the same as the listing broker's duties.
   C. depend on the situation.
   D. do not exist.

8. Subagency agreements

   A. are often blanket agreements offered through MLSs.
   B. are never required because TRELA provides for automatic subagency.
   C. can be entered into by associated licensees of the firm, according to the TAC.
   D. must be signed by the cooperating brokers in each transaction, according to TRELA.

9. Brokers are responsible for the negligent acts of subagents

   A. under no circumstances.
   B. to the extent that they knew of the negligent acts.
   C. no matter whether they knew of the negligent acts or not.
   D. only when they encourage the subagent to commit a negligent act.

10. A buyer asks a broker, who is the subagent of the listing broker, whether the seller would accept $4,000 less than the asking price. The listing broker already has told the subagent that the seller will take $5,000 less. Which of the following is the best response for the subagent?

    A. "Go ahead and make the offer because the seller needs to sell before the bank forecloses."
    B. "You may make the offer, and we'll see what the seller says. But remember, you may want to make your very best offer the first time because we don't discuss the existence or nonexistence of other offers."
    C. "I can't present an offer that is less than the asking price."
    D. "If I get the seller to accept this low offer, I want a $1,000 bonus. But remember, you may want to make your very best offer the first time because we don't discuss the existence or nonexistence of other offers."

■ Discussion Questions

1. Does a subagent owe the seller any different fiduciary duties from those owed by the listing broker?

2. Can a subagent sue the seller for a commission if the seller defaults and the listing broker elects not to sue? Why or why not?

3. What are the pros and cons of a seller offering subagency to other brokers?

4. What are some of the differences between client-level services and customer-level services?

5. Do you feel more effective as a real estate agent working with a buyer when you are a subagent or a buyer's broker?

CHAPTER 8

Representing More Than One Party in a Transaction: Dual Agency and Intermediary Brokerage

For many years brokers have been accustomed to representing only one principal in a transaction. Traditionally, the seller was represented by an agent and treated as a client, whereas the buyer was not represented by an agent and was treated as a customer. The growth of buyer representation, however, has created new issues for brokers, who now are faced with the prospect of a buyer being represented by the firm and wishing to purchase a property listed by the same firm. The specter of representing both principals in a single transaction raises many questions about potentially conflicting duties. How, for example, can a broker place the interests of his or her client above all others if, in fact, there are *two* clients, each entitled to the fiduciary duties created by agency relationships with the broker?

This chapter explores the issues of dual agency and the status of intermediary brokerage and compares and contrasts the concepts and the duties of each. Students should have a clear understanding of these concepts before they become involved in a real estate transaction that involves dual representation of any type.

This chapter addresses the following:

The Path from Dual Agency to Intermediary
Representation of More Than One Party in a Transaction
    Conflicting Positions
    Common Law Dual Agency (Implied and Express)
    Volatile Issues
Former Statutory Dual Agency Rules in Texas
    Duties of the Statutory Dual Agent
S.B. 489 and Intermediary Brokerage
    The Appointment Process
    Appointed Licensee—Who and When?
    Status of Intermediary Brokers and Appointed Licensees
Nonresidential Intermediary Applications
    Exchanges
    Syndications

■ The Path From Dual Agency to Intermediary Brokerage

Texas has always recognized the concept of *common-law dual agency;* however, the common-law rules are complicated and often appear contradictory. As a result, this arrangement has long been discouraged by the Texas Real Estate Commission (TREC). In 1993, the legislature, in an effort to assist brokers in dual representation, authorized a modified form of this practice—*statutory dual agency.* The Real Estate License Act (TRELA) was amended to outline the specific duties of a broker who was functioning in this new form of dual representation. Even with the statutory guidelines, many felt that this form of representation was inherently dangerous, and TREC did not recommend the practice.

Effective January 1, 1996, the language relating to statutory dual agency was removed from TRELA and replaced by a new form of relationship between the broker and two represented parties. This practice is known as *intermediary brokerage.*

To understand the intermediary duties of a broker, it is helpful to trace the evolution of this status from its beginning and to understand the pressures and concepts that caused this evolution. From this starting point it becomes clearer why intermediary brokerage sometimes appears to have the same duties as the former statutory dual agency.

■ Representation of More Than One Party in a Transaction

The broker may, by accident or design, become the agent for both buyer and seller in the same transaction. In the past, these actions were governed by common law and, for a while, by a statutory form of dual agency for real estate licensees. *Common law* is law that has evolved by custom or precedent set by the courts as contrasted with *statutory law,* which is enacted by legislatures. In either case, when licensees undertake to represent more than one principal in the same transaction, they should be fully informed of their duties and obligations and fully aware of the possible conflicts of interest.

In general, the agent representing more than one principal owes to *each principal the same fiduciary duties* of obedience, loyalty, disclosure, confidentially, accounting and reasonable care. Because the agent cannot possibly provide full client-level service to both, the agent must alert each client that he or she will receive less than full representation. The agent cannot presume that each client will be satisfied just because the transaction closes and the agent is helpful and honest. Both clients must understand what level of service each will waive (and thus fail to receive) when they consent to multiple representation.

It is sometimes difficult to define in specific terms the responsibilities that an agent owes to a buyer and to a seller when both are being represented by the same agent. Much depends on the type of agency services that are *expected* by the respective principals. For example, if the parties expect the agent to act impartially, giving neither party advice or opinions, one party later might claim that the agent favored the other party during the transaction. On the other hand, the seller and buyer who give informed consent to have a broker direct one associate in the firm to *negotiate on the seller's behalf* and another associate from the same firm to *negotiate on the buyer's behalf* have, arguably, agreed to a limited agency. Therefore, they have waived any challenge to the brokerage's dual representation. Nevertheless, brokers attempting to represent more than one principal must be careful to act in a manner consistent with the principals' instructions.

A key issue in representing more than one party in a transaction is to obtain the informed consent of both. Unfortunately, a licensee may become the agent of both parties without intending to do so, thus creating an illegal and potentially dangerous type of agency known as *undisclosed dual agency*. Licensees should take measures to avoid a dual representation that is unintended or created by accident.

Conflicting Positions

The positions of buyer and seller are inherently in conflict, at least on some issues. The two of them may be very friendly and share the goal of making a transaction work. In law, however, their interests are considered distinct and adverse, and each may need protection of these interests. The objectives of the buyer and seller are seldom identical in a transaction. The agent is placed in the delicate position of using any knowledge about either side in a way to attempt to please both sides and complete the transaction. It may appear that one side does not receive full representation because the agent may find it impossible to remain totally neutral.

A disgruntled buyer or seller may decide at any time to challenge the agent's actions. In hindsight, either client may later assert that the agent violated the trust given him or her because the representation tipped in favor of the other client. The provisions in a contract that benefit one side may burden the other. If the agent wants to represent the interests of more than one party in a transaction, the agent is expected and required to maintain a delicate balance and avoid the risk of sacrificing the interests of one client for those of the other.

Conflicting expectations of two represented parties may make the agent's job difficult, especially because a real estate transaction is characterized by negotiation of price within a reasonable range. The process of negotiation is an expected and usual part of consummating a transaction. Fortunately, many transactions, particularly in residential sales, are typified by negotiations based on fair market value. Such negotiations do not necessarily create adversarial win-lose situations but, rather, set the stage for win-win transactions. While this is desirable in all transactions, it becomes a requirement in transactions in which more than one party is represented by a broker. The ultimate issue is whether the buyer and the seller can benefit best by having a single broker represent both parties. If so, multiple representation is lawful, provided both clients give their informed consent.

Common-Law Dual Agency (Implied and Express)

Chapter 4 discussed agency relationships that are created by actions or conduct in regard to a principal rather than by some express agreement. This is referred to as *implied agency,* and it imposes the full burden of agency duties on the agent. Sometimes this implied agency is intentional, but more often than not, it is accidental. The classic example is that of nonrepresented buyers being led to believe that a licensee is acting as an agent for them, when in fact the licensee is an agent of the seller. When this occurs, a form of dual representation arises, known as *undisclosed, nonconsensual dual agency.* The effect is to create an illegal form of agency whereby the broker (through his or her own actions or the actions of an associated licensee) unknowingly becomes an agent of both buyer and seller without their knowledge and consent. Interestingly, in most of these situations the buyer, the seller and the broker are unaware that dual agency is occurring. This situation exposes the broker to considerable liability from both principals and is clearly a position to be avoided by the broker, if not by the principals themselves.

Consensual dual agency, whereby the broker knowingly becomes an agent of both principals with their express knowledge and consent, has long been established as a legal (if somewhat confusing) form of agency in Texas under *common law.* An in-depth discussion of common-law dual agency is beyond the scope of this text; the rules are complicated, ambiguous and appear to impose conflicting duties on the agent. Because of the potential for a misunderstanding between the broker and the clients, most brokers avoid intentionally entering into dual-agency transactions. This topic is discussed in greater detail later in this chapter.

Volatile Issues

As long as both buyer and seller are happy with the transaction, the question of dual agency probably will not arise. But if either party becomes unhappy, for whatever reason, even months after closing, dual agency may provide the mechanism to undo the transaction, recover commissions from the offending broker, seek money damages and result in revocation of broker licensure. It is no legal defense that the dual agency was unintended or was performed with all good intentions to help both buyer and seller. Buyers and sellers generally neither know nor care about the subject of dual agency until someone wants to back out of a transaction and consults an attorney. It is then that a principal often finds that he or she did not receive the required (and appropriate) level of service. Dual-agency cases have a high rate of success for plaintiffs (the person bringing the suit) and high monetary rewards.

As you can see, dual agency, even when disclosed and intended, may be risky, despite the fact that in some cases neither party loses and both, perhaps, gain. Mutual gain might occur, for example, if the dual agent discloses the seller's urgency to sell and also the buyer's recent profitable cash sale of another property. These and other confidential disclosures may actually speed up acceptance of an agreement on price and terms fully acceptable to both parties. Nevertheless, a dual agent takes a calculated risk whenever concealing or revealing information that potentially compromises the position of one of the principals. The principal later may argue in court that the agent's loyalty was improperly directed to the transaction itself and the compensation to be derived from it and not in the client's best interests.

It should be noted that the TREC, while not prohibiting dual agency, does not encourage the practice. Licensees need to be well informed on the issues relating to the potential problems and follow the statutory guidelines carefully when attempting such representation.

■ Former Statutory Dual Agency Rules in Texas

In an effort to clarify the dual-agency role for both the public and licensees, the Texas legislature passed an amendment to TRELA §15C, effective September 1, 1993, that created a modified form of dual agency. It established specific guidelines for brokers when acting as dual agents and limited the liability of common-law dual-agency practice. Although the statute has been repealed and TRELA no longer addresses dual agency, it is important to look at the provisions of the statute to better understand the *intermediary brokerage rules* discussed in the following sections.

Duties of the Statutory Dual Agent

Specifically, the state provided that a broker, when acting as an agent for more than one party, should

- not disclose to the Buyer or Tenant that the Seller or Landlord would accept a price less than the asking price unless otherwise instructed in a separate writing by the Seller or Landlord;

- not disclose to the Seller or Landlord that the Buyer or Tenant would pay a price greater than the price submitted in the written offer to the Seller or Landlord unless otherwise instructed in a separate writing by the Buyer or Tenant;

- not disclose any confidential information or any information a party specifically instructs a real estate broker in writing not to disclose unless otherwise instructed in a separate writing by the respective party or required to disclose such information by law and

- treat all parties to the transaction honestly and impartially, so as not to favor one party to the disadvantage of the other party.

Many brokers who had refused to practice dual agency under the old common-law rules found some comfort in the specific language of the statute, and the practice of statutory dual agency became more common in the real estate industry in Texas. Still, this form of *limited agency* had its drawbacks for both brokers and principals. From the broker's perspective it created a delicate balancing act in which the broker and all the involved sales associates were required to remain totally impartial during the transaction. As a result the broker and the associates could offer no advice or opinions to *either party* during the transactions that might act to the disadvantage of the other party. The broker was exposed to liability if either party felt that the other party was given any preferential treatment during the course of the transaction.

Limitations of the broker's services. From the principals' perspective, neither the buyer nor seller could expect the same level of service from the broker as when the broker acted as a single agent for either. The seller, when represented solely by the agent, received the full advice and opinions of the agent when negotiating offers from nonrepresented buyers. In the dual-agency transaction, however, that same seller now found that the agent could provide factual information but no preferential advice or opinions during negotiations. The buyer who had become accustomed to full representation experienced the same reduction in the services provided by the agent. Many principals found that this limited form of agency was not exactly what they thought they had bargained for and were dissatisfied with the transaction.

It was critical for the broker, when acting as a statutory dual agent, to be certain that both the associated licensees and the principals fully understood the limitations of this form of agency and that all parties agreed to the terms. Unfortunately, case law has illustrated that in some transactions the brokers, the associates and/or the principals had no clue.

■ S.B. 489 and Intermediary Brokerage

Recognizing the inherent shortcomings and the limitations created by the statutory dual agency, the Texas legislature passed Senate Bill 489, which, among other things, eliminated statutory dual agency and amended TRELA to substitute statutory *intermediary brokerage.* Effective January 1, 1996, TRELA §15C authorized brokers to act on behalf of both parties to a transaction in an intermediary role as follows:

(h) A real estate broker may act as an intermediary between the parties if:

(1) the real estate broker obtains written consent from each party to the transaction for the real estate broker to act as an intermediary in the transaction and

(2) the written consent of the parties under Subdivision (1) of this subsection states the source of any expected compensation to the real estate broker.

(i) A written listing agreement to represent a seller or landlord or a written agreement to represent a buyer or tenant that also authorizes a real estate broker to act as an intermediary in a transaction is sufficient to establish written consent of the party to the transaction if the written agreement sets forth, in conspicuous bold or underlined print, the real estate broker's obligations under Subsection (j) of this section.

(j) A real estate broker who acts as an intermediary between parties in a transaction

(1) may not disclose to the buyer or tenant that the seller or landlord will accept a price less than the asking price unless otherwise instructed in a separate writing by the seller or landlord;

(2) may not disclose to the seller or landlord that the buyer or tenant will pay a price greater than the price submitted in a written

offer to the seller or landlord unless otherwise instructed in a separate writing by the buyer or tenant;

(3) may not disclose any confidential information or any information a party specifically instructs the real estate broker in writing not to disclose unless otherwise instructed in a separate writing by the respective party or required to disclose such information by this Act or a court order or if the information materially relates to the condition of the property;

(4) shall treat all parties to the transaction honestly; and

(5) shall comply with this Act.

(k) If a real estate broker obtains the consent of the parties to act as an intermediary in a transaction in compliance with this section, the real estate broker may appoint, by providing written notice to the parties, one or more licensees associated with the broker to communicate with and carry out instructions of one party and one or more other licensees associated with the broker to communicate with and carry out instructions of the other party or parties. A real estate broker may appoint a licensee to communicate with and carry out instructions of a party under this subsection only if the written consent of the parties under Subsection (h) or (i) of this section authorizes the broker to make the appointment. The real estate broker and the appointed licensees shall comply with Subsection (j) of this section. However, during negotiations, an appointed licensee may provide opinions and advice to the party to whom the licensee is appointed.

(l) The duties of a licensee acting as an intermediary provided by this section supersede and are in lieu of a licensee's duties under common law or any other law.

Consider how this might work in practice. The statute requires written permission from both parties before the broker may act as an intermediary, and the agreement must disclose any source of compensation expected by the broker. This is accomplished in a listing contract with a seller or a written buyer-representation contract with a buyer. The respective agreements give the seller or buyer the option of authorizing the broker to act as an intermediary. These agreements are considered sufficient by TREC, as long as the broker's compensation is clarified.

If the intermediary situation arises, the broker cannot disclose:

- the highest price a buyer might pay, until authorized to do so in writing;

- the minimum price a seller will take, unless authorized to do so in writing;

- confidential information about either party, unless the parties authorize it or law requires a disclosure.

Finally, the broker shall treat all parties to the transaction honestly and fairly, while complying with the act.

Sound familiar? At least to this point, the intermediary brokerage language is almost identical to the former language regarding statutory dual agency. A broker accustomed to acting as a dual agent under the statutory provisions would see no practical difference between the two. In fact, many brokers mistakenly believe that *intermediary* is simply another term for a dual agent. However, the language in TRELA §15C(k), as amended by S.B. 489, provides the major departure from the old dual-agency statute by providing for the *appointment* of licensees to assist buyers and sellers in an intermediary transaction by offering advice and opinions during negotiations.

The Appointment Process

The ability of the broker to make appointments is the *key difference* between statutory dual agency and the intermediary status. This enhances the level of service that can be given to represented buyers and sellers during in-house transactions.

As you recall, one of the major drawbacks in dual-agency arrangements is the reduction of services that can be provided to the principals. When acting as an agent for either buyer or seller, full fiduciary duties must be given to the principal the agent represents. Clients are entitled to accurate information and can look to their agents for advice and opinions during the negotiations. The advice and opinions given clients are designed to place the broker's clients in the best negotiating position and offer clients the best advantage in meeting their goals. In dual agency, with two clients, the agents are restricted from giving such advice to either client, creating a form of limited agency.

Under dual agency, buyers and sellers, accustomed to the full-service representation of single agency, saw dramatic reductions in the level of service that the broker could provide. Although information could be given to each party, no preferential advice or opinions could be given to either, and both parties had to be treated equally.

Advice and opinions from appointed licensees. In the intermediary transaction, *if one or more licensees are **appointed** to the seller and different licensees are **appointed** to the buyer, the principals are able to receive services similar to those of single agency.* Although other legal distinctions may exist between an intermediary broker and a dual agent, the practical difference between the former statutory dual agent and the current intermediary broker lies in the ability to expand the limited services of the former statutory dual agent through the *appointment process* afforded the new intermediary broker. Thus, the appointed licensee is freed from the limitations placed on the former statutory dual agent, which required an absolute balance between the parties and prohibited giving preferential negotiating advice or opinions to either. The appointed licensees (not the intermediary) may now give to their respective principals services similar to those given when acting as a single agent. In other words, an appointed licensee may give the party to whom he or she has been appointed advice and opinions that may not be in the best interest of the other party. Keep in mind, however, that the appointed licensee is still prohibited from disclosing how little a seller may accept, how much a buyer may be willing to pay or any other confidential information about either party. In addition, appointees must treat the parties fairly and comply with TRELA.

Appointed Licensees—Who and When?

The appointment process raises several questions for brokers who wish to extend the company's services to buyer and seller clients through the appointment process. First, remember that before appointments may be made, the broker must have the written consent of both parties to act as an intermediary and their permission to make appointments. The statute provides that with this written consent the broker may appoint *one or more* associated licensees to work with the buyer and *different* licensees to work with the seller. The broker cannot appoint himself or herself to either and must maintain the role of the intermediary. Thus a broker who works alone or a broker with only one associate *cannot* make appointments and must conduct the transaction as an intermediary. If no appointments are made, any involved associates are required to carry out the same duties as the intermediary broker—no preferential advice or opinions to either party are permitted.

Timing of the appointments and notification to the principals are important. Until a buyer who is represented by the firm wishes to negotiate on a property *listed by the firm,* no potential for an intermediary transaction exists and therefore appointments need not be made. Likewise, if the broker has chosen not to make appointments, the involved associates carry out the transaction as if they were intermediaries, offering neither advice nor opinions to buyer or seller during negotiations that might work to the disadvantage of the other party.

It is extremely important that parties clearly understand that during an intermediary transaction no preferential advice or opinions can be given by the associates working with the principals, *unless appointments are made.* If, however, the parties wish to have an associate appointed to each of them, thereby gaining the expanded advice and opinions of the associate, the appointment must be made *before* such advice or opinions are given to either party. The broker, or an authorized representative of the broker, must make the appointments, and written notification of these appointments must be given to both the buyer and the seller. Note that while the actual appointments of the licensees may be made orally, the notification to the parties announcing the appointments and identifying the appointees must be given to the buyer and the seller in writing. Neither the statute nor TREC provides specific language for the notification. Members of the Texas Association of REALTORS® may use form TAR-027, "*Notification of Intermediary Relationship*" (see Figure 8.1), to indicate that an intermediary transaction is occurring and whether appointments are to be made in order to identify the appointed licensees. Licensees who are not members of TAR® should develop in-house forms to give similar notice to the parties. Unless appointments are made, the broker is not required to notify the parties that an intermediary transaction is occurring, although the prudent broker will make it clear to the parties, preferably in writing, that an intermediary transaction is taking place.

An obvious timing problem may arise if an intermediary transaction occurs during the absence of the broker and no appointments have been made. If this occurred, the licensee associate could not give advice or opinions until the appointment process had been completed. Clearly, this might be too late because the negotiations might be completed before the broker was available to make the required appointments. One solution might be

FIGURE 8.1

Notification of Intermediary Relationship

EQUAL HOUSING OPPORTUNITY

REALTOR®

TEXAS ASSOCIATION OF REALTORS®
NOTIFICATION OF INTERMEDIARY RELATIONSHIP
THIS FORM IS FURNISHED BY THE TEXAS ASSOCIATION OF REALTORS®
FOR USE BY ITS MEMBERS. USE OF THIS FORM BY PERSONS WHO ARE NOT MEMBERS
OF THE TEXAS ASSOCIATION OF REALTORS® IS NOT AUTHORIZED.
©Texas Association of REALTORS®, Inc. 1995

*Use this form **only if** written listing and buyer representation agreements were signed authorizing the possibility of an intermediary relationship. May be used to remind buyer and seller that broker will act as an intermediary.*

NOTICE TO: _____ *(Seller/Landlord)*

_____ *(Buyer/Tenant)*

FROM: _____ *(Brokerage Firm)*

RE: _____ *(Property)*

DATE: _____

Please take notice that this firm represents the above named Seller or Landlord under a written listing agreement and also represents the above named Buyer or Tenant under a written Buyer or Tenant Representation Agreement. Please recall that the paragraphs entitled "Agency Relationships" in both the Listing Agreement and the Buyer/Tenant Representation Agreement authorized this firm to act as an intermediary in the event a buyer or tenant that the firm represents wishes to make an offer to purchase or lease a property listed by the firm. When we present the offer from the Buyer or Tenant to purchase or lease the Property we will act in accordance with the provisions of the Listing Agreement and Buyer/Tenant Representation Agreement concerning Agency Relationships.

Broker ❑ will ❑ will not appoint licensed associates to communicate with, carry out instructions of, and provide opinions and advice during negotiations to each party. If Broker is to make such appointments, the parties are hereby notified that _____ _____ is appointed to Seller or Landlord and_____ is appointed to Buyer or Tenant.

We also wish to inform you of the following additional information _____ _____

(disclose any relevant information that may affect a person's decision to authorize broker to act as an intermediary; e.g., existence of personal, prior business, or contemplated future business relationships).

If you have any questions or objections to the information contained in this notice, please notify us immediately. We appreciate your acknowledgement of and consent to this notice by signing below.

CONSENT: As previously authorized, I reaffirm my consent for the above named Broker to act as an intermediary in this transaction and to any of the appointments or statements made in this notice.

Buyer or Tenant	**Date**	**Seller or Landlord**	**Date**
Buyer or Tenant	**Date**	**Seller or Landlord**	**Date**

(TAR - 027) 1-1-96   Page 1 of 1 for the broker to give the authority to make appointments to others in the firm. Another possibility could be to *preappoint* listing associates to work as appointees to sellers—and selling associates working under buyer-representation contracts to work as appointees to buyers—should an intermediary transaction arise. Keep in mind that a preappointment would have no effect until an intermediary transaction actually occurred. The parties still would have to be furnished with written notice of the appointments as soon as the intermediary transaction was undertaken.

Who Is to be appointed? The appointees could be any licensees of the firm other than the broker. However, in a practical sense it would be most common for the associate who obtained the listing to be appointed to the seller and the associate who obtained the buyer-representation contract to be appointed to the buyer. Exceptions might be where listing agents sold their own listings to buyers with whom they were working under the terms of a buyer-representation contract. For appointments to be made in these circumstances, a second licensee would be required to enter the transaction, to be appointed to either buyer or seller, because the statute requires that *different* licensees be appointed to buyer and seller. Would this indicate, then, that a licensee could not participate on both sides of the transaction and receive the increased commission? No; the practical solution might be for the broker to decline to make appointments and to instruct the associate to conduct the transaction as an intermediary transaction, giving no preferential advice or opinions to either party. In any event a broker should have a well-reasoned, written office policy to avoid confusion and conflict within the office regarding these matters.

The following examples and short questions and answers may help illustrate how and when an intermediary transaction may arise and when appointments may be made.

 EXAMPLE 1: Broker Able has listed Seller Sharp's house. The listing agreement permits Able to act as an intermediary if the occasion arises. Customer Jones, an unrepresented buyer, asks Able to present an offer on the Sharp property.

? QUESTION

What kind of agency relationships will be operational?

🖐 DISCUSSION

Because Customer Jones has no representation agreement, Broker Able simply will act as the agent for the seller, giving Seller Sharp full representation services while treating Customer Jones fairly and honestly. Note in Figure 8.2 that the broker can give preferential advice and opinions to the seller, thereby tipping the scale in favor of the seller.

 EXAMPLE 2: Broker Able has entered into a buyer-representation agreement with Buyer Baker. The buyer-representation agreement permits Able to act as an intermediary should the occasion arise. Baker, a represented buyer, wishes to negotiate a contract on Seller Sharp's house.

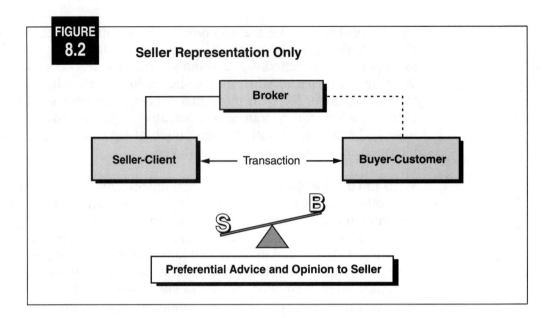

FIGURE 8.2 Seller Representation Only

Broker

Seller-Client ← Transaction → Buyer-Customer

Preferential Advice and Opinion to Seller

? QUESTION

What is Broker Able's position in the transaction?

DISCUSSION

Because the listing agreement with the seller *and* the written buyer's-representation agreement authorized Broker Able to act as an intermediary, the intermediary brokerage relationship will become operational without requiring further notice to the principals. *(Although the statutes do not require notice to the principals when the intermediary transaction begins, a prudent broker will advise the principals that an intermediary agency is in place.)*

Throughout the transaction, Broker Able must carefully adhere to the requirements of intermediary brokerage. Because Broker Able operates alone, no appointments may be made, and the principals will receive the limited services permitted by the intermediary rules. Both parties must be treated honestly and fairly, but no advice or opinions may be given to either party in the negotiations. Observers of this transaction would see no difference between this intermediary transaction and the former statutory dual-agency transaction if both were performed correctly. Note that in Example 2, the scale must be kept in balance, as shown in Figure 8.3. No preferential advice or opinions can be given to either seller or buyer.

EXAMPLE 3: Broker Able hires a new sales associate, Sally Lightfoot, who promptly engages Buyer Smith in a buyer-representation agreement. The written agreement authorizes Able to act as an intermediary and to make appointments when appropriate. Buyer Smith becomes interested in and wishes to make an offer to purchase Seller Sharp's house, currently listed by Broker Able.

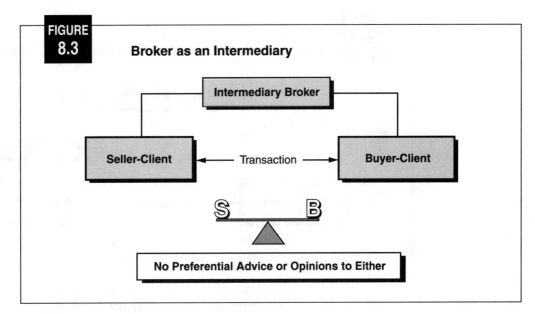

FIGURE 8.3

Broker as an Intermediary

Intermediary Broker

Seller-Client ←— Transaction —→ Buyer-Client

S   B

No Preferential Advice or Opinions to Either

? QUESTION

What will be the roles of Able and Sally in the transaction?

DISCUSSION

Broker Able will act as an intermediary and will direct Sally to act as Able's agent and carry out the duties of an intermediary but she will not be considered "appointed." Both Able and Sally must remain impartial. No preferential advice or opinions may be given to either Buyer Smith or Seller Sharp. The principal's interests must be kept in strict balance.

? QUESTION

May Broker Able make appointments in this transaction?

DISCUSSION

No. Able has only one sales associate; therefore, the appointment process is inappropriate. A broker with more than one associate may appoint *different associates* to the buyer and seller; the broker cannot be appointed to either.

? QUESTION

Could Able appoint Sally to Buyer Smith and simply serve Seller Sharp as an intermediary?

DISCUSSION

No. The statutes prohibit appointments to only one side of the transaction. If a licensee is appointed to the buyer, a different licensee must be appointed to the seller. For example, Figure 8.4 shows the scale's being maintained in balance by both the broker and the sales licensee.

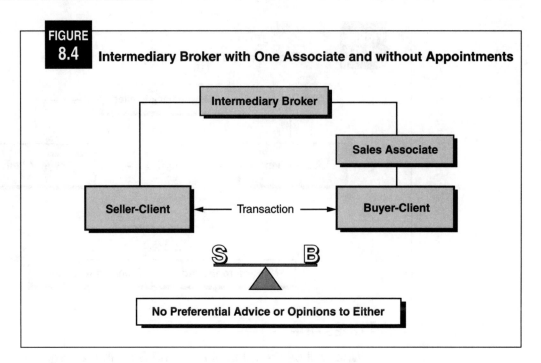

FIGURE 8.4 Intermediary Broker with One Associate and without Appointments

EXAMPLE 4: Broker Able hires another associate, JimBob Brown, who lists a home owned by Seller Anxious. The listing agreement authorizes Broker Able to act as an intermediary and to make appointments if appropriate. Sally, who represented Buyer Smith in an unsuccessful attempt to purchase the Sharp property (Example 3) wishes to make an offer on the Anxious property.

? QUESTION

What are the potential roles of Broker Able?

✒ DISCUSSION

Broker Able may complete the transaction as an intermediary with or without making appointments.

? QUESTION

If no appointments are made, what will be the roles of Sally and JimBob?

✒ DISCUSSION

Sally and JimBob will be instructed to carry out the duties of their intermediary broker. Neither associate may give advice or opinions to the principals with whom they are working. Both principals must be treated exactly the same. Figure 8.5 illustrates this option. Note that the broker and both associates are required to keep the scale in balance. No advice or opinions are given to either party.

? QUESTION

If Broker Able wishes to make appointments, how is this accomplished?

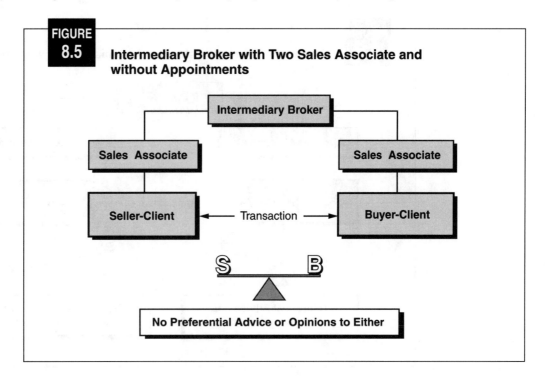

FIGURE 8.5 Intermediary Broker with Two Sales Associate and without Appointments

DISCUSSION

Broker Able will advise Sally that she is the appointed associate for Buyer Smith and will advise JimBob that he is the appointed associate for Seller Anxious. In addition, both principals must receive *written* notification of the appointments naming the licensee appointed to the other party. (See Figure 8.1, TAR® notification form 027.) Keep in mind that the identities of the parties must be disclosed to each other.

QUESTION

How will the appointments change the roles of Broker Able and her associates Sally and JimBob?

DISCUSSION

Broker Able's role will not change. She will carry out her duties as an intermediary, being careful not to take any action that would favor one party over the other. However, the roles of the appointed licensees change. Sally will now be permitted to give advice and opinions to Buyer Smith and assist in the negotiations. JimBob will now be able to give similar services to Seller Anxious. Figure 8.6 depicts the intermediary transaction with appointments. Note what while the broker must maintain a balanced scale, the appointed licensees will be able to give advice and opinions during the negotiations to attempt to tip their individual scales in favor of the principal to whom they have been appointed. The parties and the appointed associates must be aware that the intermediary broker is prohibited from providing preferential advice or opinion to either party.

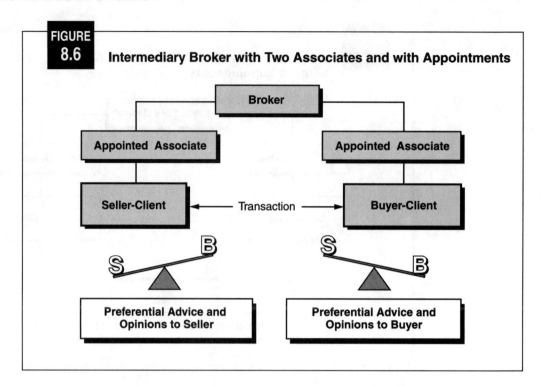

FIGURE 8.6 Intermediary Broker with Two Associates and with Appointments

EXAMPLE 5: Sally Lightfoot, an agent of Broker Able, is working with Buyer Smith, a buyer represented by the company. Smith wishes to negotiate on a property owned by Seller Jones. Sally is also the listing agent for the Jones property. Both representation contracts permit Broker Able to act as an intermediary and to make appointments.

? QUESTION

If Able wishes to conduct an intermediary transaction, what options are available regarding appointments?

Q DISCUSSION

If Able wished to make appointments, Sally could be appointed to either the buyer or the seller, but a *different associate* would have to be appointed to the other party. This would require the involvement of a new associate in the transaction, possibly causing concern for the principals. In addition, Sally might be required to share some commission with the other associate, depending on company policy. The practical solution for the broker and associate would be not to make appointments. Although the broker is authorized to decide if appointments are to be made or not, the broker should consider whether this solution is also in the best interests of the parties involved.

? QUESTION

If no appointments are made, how would this change the roles that Able and Sally could play?

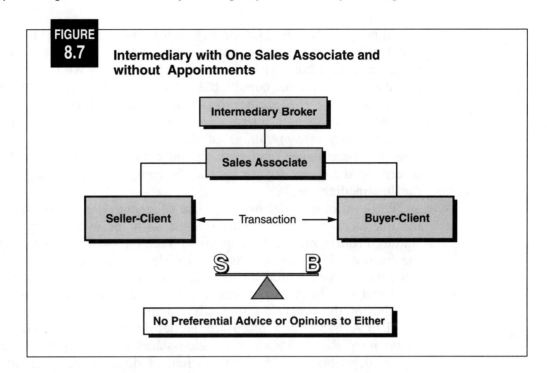

FIGURE 8.7 Intermediary with One Sales Associate and without Appointments

DISCUSSION

Broker Able would remain as the intermediary and instruct Sally to carry out the duties of the intermediary while working with both the buyer and the seller. No new associate would be required to enter the transaction. Figure 8.7 shows the transaction without appointments. Again, the broker and the sales licensee must keep the scales in balance. It would be best for the broker to confirm this choice with the principals to ensure that they would agree with the decision not to make appointments.

Status of Intermediary Brokers and Appointed Licensees

Intermediary brokerage is a relatively new concept in Texas real estate law. Consequently, many questions remain unanswered regarding the nature of this form of brokerage. Such questions relate to the nature of the agency relationship, representation issues and fiduciary duties, if any. The general interpretation of the TREC is as follows:

- An intermediary is an agent, but with different duties from those of a single agent.

- Subject to the limitations imposed by TRELA §15C(j), an intermediary offers a limited form of representation to the parties. This representation may be broadened by the use of "appointed associates."

- As an intermediary, although the scope of agency is more limited, certain fiduciary duties are imposed on the agent.

- The license act has no provision for a broker to "opt out" of an agency relationship when acting as an intermediary.

Although TRELA §15C(m)(2) states that an intermediary "*may* be an agent of the parties to the transaction," at least for the purposes of negotiating the transaction, TREC's interpretation of the word *may* is taken to be permissive rather than conditional. That is to say, the use of *may* confirms the authority of the broker to act as an agent rather than to suggest an alternative nonagency intermediary relationship. Keep in mind that these represent only *interpretations* of the statute. The statutory language is not clear on these issues, and perhaps the courts will be required to ultimately determine the agency capacity and fiduciary duties—if any—that accrue to the intermediary broker.

While attorneys debate the issue of agency versus nonagency status of the intermediary, brokers must grapple with the everyday application of the statute. From a practical perspective, TREC has offered some guidelines for the licensee. Until the courts, the legislature or TREC changes these opinions, the licensee would be well advised to follow these interpretations. The label that we attach to the broker may be less important than a clear understanding of the broker's duties when acting as an intermediary as described in TRELA §15C, and discussed earlier in this chapter. Some direction is found in §TRELA 15C(k)(L), which states that the duties of an intermediary, as described in §15C, "are in lieu of duties under common law or any other law." But as we have just seen, the explicit duties described in the statute are very limited: conditional nondisclosure, honesty and compliance with the License Act. No doubt many of the questions surrounding intermediary brokerage will be resolved by the issuance of TREC regulations and by interpretation of this law in the courts. In the meantime, licensees should exercise caution when attempting to act in an intermediary role and understand the possible pitfalls as well as the potential benefits.

With any new law, there are bound to be many unanswered questions. Only time will provide the answers. The new Texas intermediary brokerage statute is an attempt to resolve a complex problem that has been a significant issue in the real estate community for years: the specific duties, responsibilities and liabilities of real estate licensees with respect to the parties in a transaction. Whether the Texas legislature has succeeded in the resolution of this issue remains to be seen.

Keep in mind that the intermediary provisions of S.B. 489 will affect only a minority of real estate transactions. Only during in-house transactions involving a represented buyer *and* a represented seller will the intermediary circumstance arise, and then only when all parties have agreed, in writing, to the arrangement. Although few of the licensee's transactions may involve the intermediary rules, if a broker attempts to undertake a single intermediary transaction, there should be a clear understanding as to how the broker should proceed. In an attempt to clarify some of the issues surrounding the intermediary law, TREC, through its legal counsel, has compiled the list of frequently asked questions from licensees that are found in Appendix B. The responses are those of the commissioners through the general counsel for TREC.

■ CONCERNS RELATED TO INTERMEDIARY PRACTICE

Even with the guidelines provided by statute and the rules of TREC many brokers and attorneys feel that the spector of attempting to represent more than one party in a transaction presents too may legal and ethical problems to be practical. The TREC in no way recommends intermediary practice and only provides certain guidelines and suggestions for brokers who choose to offer intermediary services.

Consider, for example, that in an intermediary transaction appointments have been made to the respective parties. The appointed associates are now permitted to give advice and opinions to their party which may not be in the best interest of the other party. Still, confidential information must be kept confidential. How far may the appointed associate go as an advocate? At what point will the associate violate confidentiality? What if one party feels that the associated appointed to the other party is more experienced or competent and that they are now at a disadvantage during negotiations? These and many other issues have yet to be resolved, and understandably many brokers are very leery of this type of practice.

Certainly before attempting intermediary practice, a broker should carefully study the law, and determine company policy regarding procedures. Once established, the policies and procedures should be reviewed by an attorney competent in this area of law. Finally, a company training program should be developed and delivered to ensure that the policies and procedures are properly implemented.

 EXAMPLE: Kelly, a first-time buyer, engaged Jackie, through her broker, to act as a buyer's agent. In the process of finding a suitable home Kelly became interested in a property listed by Jackie. The buyer's representation agreement authorized Jackie's broker to act as an intermediary should the potential arise.

During the negotiations Kelly complained to Jackie that it appeared that all the advice and opinions were being offered to the seller rather than to her. In fact, the only advice offered to the buyer was that she should pay full-price for the property, and meet all other demands made by the seller. After the complaint from the buyer, Jackie told Kelly that if Kelly didn't like the way she was being represented that Kelly's broker would represent Kelly and Jackie would represent the seller.

Subsequently, Kelly's broker, by phone, informed Kelly that he would represent her interests rather than the seller's and again recommended that at least a full price offer be tendered, and never spoke with Kelly again. After several negotiations through Jackie, Kelly ended up paying slightly more than full asking price. Later she complained again that all the emphasis seemed to be placed on the seller's need rather than her own, but ultimately closed on the transaction, paying more than market value.

? QUESTIONS

1. Is it permissible for a listing associate to negotiate the sale of her own listing to a buyer whom she also represents through her broker?

2. In the above example, how should the process of making appointments be handled?

3. What issues arose when the broker, in effect, appointed the listing agent to the seller and told the buyer that he would represent her interests rather than the seller's?

DISCUSSION

This example illustrates the lack of understanding of the intermediary statutes and points to the fact that brokers who do not understand the role of an intermediary should not attempt the practice.

In reference to the first question above, nothing prevents a listing associate from negotiating a sale of that listing to a represented buyer. However, in this case no appointments could be made and neither the seller or buyer should receive any advice or opinions that would act to the disadvantage of the other party.

If, in reference to the second question, appointments are to be made, one or more associates of the broker may be appointed to give advice and opinions to one party and one or more *other associates* of the broker could have been appointed to offer advice and opinions to the other party [TRELA §15C(k)]. Once the appointments were made, both parties should receive written notification of the respective appointments naming the appointed associates. Under no circumstance should this broker attempt to appoint himself to either party.

A number of legal and ethical questions arise from this example and clearly point out the dangers of attempting to act as an intermediary without fully understanding the rules. In addition to demonstrating the lack of understanding the fundamentals of intermediary brokerage, the broker by claiming to represent the buyer rather than the seller in the transaction violated fiduciary duties to the seller whom he had originally agreed to represent in the listing contract.

■ Nonresidential Intermediary Applications

The representation of more than one party is not confined to residential transactions, and brokers should be alert to the potential for undisclosed dual-representation issues arising in real estate exchanges; syndications; and farm and ranch, industrial, special-use and commercial property transactions. Keep in mind that in any of the transactions the statutory "information about brokerage services" notice must be given to the parties and an agency disclosure made prior to the beginning of the transaction.

Exchanges

Some brokers help owners exchange property under the Internal Revenue Code of 1986, Section 1031, "Tax-Deferred Exchange Provisions." Clear disclosure must be made when only a single broker is involved with more than one party to an exchange. An intermediary relationship would probably best serve the interests of the parties as well as those of the broker. With one agent and two commissions at stake, the nonprofessional broker has ample temptation to compromise the interests of either or both parties. Often more than one broker is involved in an exchange.

Syndications

Possible undisclosed dual-representation problems may arise in several situations in which the general partner of a limited partnership syndication is also a broker. Examples follow:

- The general partner sells or leases partnership property for a fee to be paid by the partnership.

- The general partner sells his or her own property to the partnership for a fee.

- The general partner, on behalf of the partnership, buys property listed with another firm and seeks a commission split.

- The general partner, on behalf of the partnership, buys unlisted property and seeks compensation from the seller-owner.

The general partner has fiduciary obligations to the other general partners and limited partners. The broker should represent and be paid by the partnership only, unless full disclosure is made and written consent is obtained from all principals and brokers involved.

Commercial Leasing Agent

Brokers involved in commercial real estate leasing may find themselves in situations where both parties desire representation. Leasing agents often work under exclusive-right-to-lease listings from developers or building owners. Usually, an MLS does not require the listing of commercial leases. In commercial leasing a great deal of negotiation regarding lease terms and concessions frequently occurs between the owner and the potential lessee. The leasing agent is usually at the center of such negotiations and should be careful to ensure that both owner and lessee understand the role of the leasing agent.

Many times, the lessee is sophisticated and is represented by an attorney or an accountant; the lessee should not look to the owner's leasing agent for advice of a legal or financial nature. Often the principals complete their own negotiations and look to the broker as an effective go-between. The lessee looks to the leasing agent more for accurate information and figures, especially about market trends and economic factors, typically not within the attorney's field of expertise.

For those cases when the lessee has no adviser and looks to the leasing agent for negotiating advice and opinions, a cautious leasing agent will have the owner and lessee consent to an intermediary agreement permitting appointments. The broker might further recommend that the lessor and lessee each obtain legal counsel.

Leasing agents may work with lessees to locate and evaluate specific sites. It is not unusual for a leasing agent to approach the owner of an unlisted building. In these no-listing transactions, there should be a clear written understanding as to whom the leasing agent represents, especially when the owner is asked to pay the commission. There is no difference between residential and commercial licensees regarding agency disclosure requirements.

■ Intentional versus Unintended Dual Representation

In considering the representation of more than one party to a transaction, one must determine whether such representation is intentional or unintentional. Because S.B. 489 has removed only the statutory provisions for dual agency, a broker may, with the consent of both parties, choose to act as a common-law dual agent rather than as an intermediary. An intentional representation of more than one party as an intermediary may present some serious business risks, but it does provide the broker an opportunity to discuss the pros and cons of multiple representation and obtain written consent designed to minimize risk. In addition, the specific requirements to act as an intermediary are stated in the law.

A common-law dual agent has, however, no such statutory authorization and, as stated earlier, the unclear common-law rules create a fertile field for conflicts of interest. Today, it is hard to envision a scenario in which a broker would intentionally act as a dual agent. The chief concerns, however, focus on the *unintended* or *accidental* representation of more than one party. A broker who doesn't know that multiple representation is occurring has no contractual way to minimize the risks inherent in the dual representation and by default will become an *undisclosed dual agent* subject to common-law rules. While any form of undisclosed agency violates the statutes, undisclosed dual agency is particularly troublesome. Some common dual-agency situations are outlined in the chart shown as Figure 8.8. The letters and numbers in the following list correspond to those on the figure.

A. Sellers often list property with a listing broker under an exclusive-right-to-sell listing. The listing broker and the broker's entire staff represent the seller.

B. No dual-agency problem exists if clear disclosure, consent and conduct indicate that

1. the listing broker represents only the seller. The buyer is a customer and the seller is a client.

2. the cooperating (other) broker is a buyer's broker. The seller is a customer of the buyer's broker and the buyer is a client.

3. the listing broker acts as an intermediary after full disclosure and with written consent of all parties.

C. A dual-agency problem exists if the dual agency arises because of inadequate or no disclosure that

1. the listing broker represents both buyer and seller.

2. two licensed associates from the same brokerage are attempting to represent the buyer and seller separately.

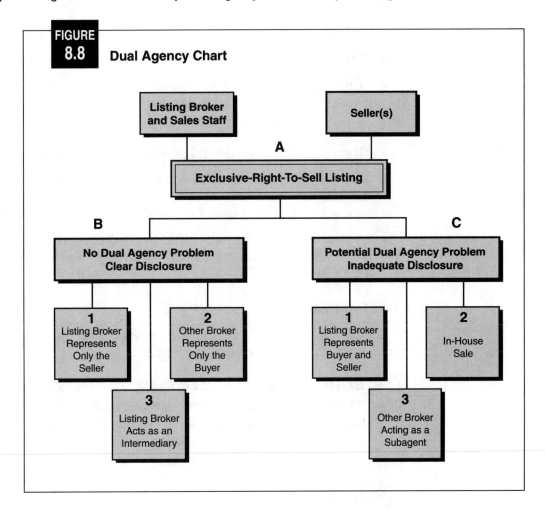

FIGURE 8.8 Dual Agency Chart

3. the cooperating (other) broker has declared himself or herself as a subagent of the seller but his or her conduct creates an agency relationship with a buyer.

Most commonly, unintended dual agency occurs in one of the following contexts:

- The listing broker or licensed associate represents both the buyer and the seller.

- Separate associates from the listing office (an in-house sale) represent the buyer and the seller.

- Another broker represents the buyer and also acts as a subagent of the seller.

- The real estate licensee acts as a buyer or a seller.

The conduct of the listing broker's licensed associate may be such that the buyer is led to believe that the associate represents the buyer. In his or her zeal to develop rapport with the buyer prospect, the salesperson sometimes gives the buyer that impression. In its handbook, *Who Is My Client?*, NAR® lists the following examples of statements often used by real estate brokers that can create implied agency relationships with buyers:

- "I'll take care of everything. I'll handle the sale for you."

- "I'll see if I can get the seller to come down on the price."

- "This listing has been on the market for six months. That tells me it's overpriced. Let's offer $80,000 and see what they say."

- "I'll get you the best deal I possibly can."

- "Trust me. I'm sure the seller won't counter at that price."

- "If the seller is going to insist on a full-price sale, I think you should tell him no. Then we can try an offer on that house your wife liked so much. I'm sure those sellers will be more realistic."

- "If they insist on the full $100,000, I'll remind them that the furnace is 15 years old and the carpet is fraying. That should justify at least a $3,000 reduction."

Prior Relationships

Sometimes a dual representation arises based on a prior relationship between the listing broker and the buyer.

 EXAMPLE: Mike of Prospect Realty lists George's house. Mike has represented Linda on several sales and purchases of property. Mike tells Linda about the house, and Linda wants Mike to prepare an offer at 10 percent below the asking price. Linda mentions she'll pay near the asking price, if necessary.

? QUESTION

Whom does Mike represent?

DISCUSSION

As the listing salesperson, Mike owes primary allegiance to George, the seller. Based on his prior relationship with Linda, however, Mike may, under implied agency principles, also be held to represent Linda. This could put Mike's firm, Prospect Realty, into an unintended dual-representation role.

Mike's options are either to disclose the prior relationship and obtain consents from Linda, George and the broker of Prospect Realty permitting an intermediary transaction or to disclaim any agency to Linda. The second option requires clarification to Linda that Mike can work with her, but only on a customer basis, because Mike would be the agent of the seller only.

If Mike is acting through his broker in an intermediary role or as a lawful dual agent, he has a duty to Linda not to reveal her bargaining intentions. Neither can Mike tell Linda that his other principal, George, will take $10,000 less than the listed price or reveal any of George's other bargaining intentions. These usually inappropriate duties are the norm of intermediary brokerage, and mutually exclusive duties are the dilemma of the intermediary. With clear disclosure and consents, Mike, under the first option, may be authorized to keep confidential his discussions regarding price and terms. On the other hand, if Mike disclaims an agency relationship with Linda, under the second option he would have to tell George that Linda has expressed a willingness to increase her first offer. Had Mike followed proper information and disclosure procedures, the options would have been discussed at first contact with Linda. If the second option were selected, Linda should have been advised not to disclose any bargaining information that she did not want George to know. In either event, Mike should tell George about his prior business relationship with Linda.

In-House Sale

Even though the selling salesperson working with a represented buyer in an in-house sale is someone other than the listing salesperson, a dual representation exists because the employing broker has become an intermediary or a dual agent through the conduct of the two salespersons.

 EXAMPLE: Joe, a salesperson with Pacesetter Realty, lists Harry's house. Kathy, also of Pacesetter Realty, has been looking for two months to find the right house for her client, Lisa. She shows Lisa the house that Joe listed. Lisa loves it and wants Kathy to negotiate on her behalf for a lower price, a long closing period and favorable financing terms. Lisa wants Kathy secretly to look for a resale buyer at a quick profit, ideally in a back-to-back closing.

? QUESTION

Who represents whom?

🔍 DISCUSSION

Unless Pacesetter Realty has written consent to act as an intermediary, it now represents both the seller and the buyer as an undisclosed dual agent. The knowledge possessed by both Joe and Kathy will be imputed to Pacesetter Realty and to each other. Pacesetter Realty is still the broker and would, therefore, be advocating for both sides against each other. The only logical conclusion is that Pacesetter Realty has become an unlawful dual agent. The danger here is of actually trading inside information within the same office.

The best answer may lie in the intermediary transaction with appointments. Joe, the listing agent, would be appointed to give advice and opinions to Seller George, thereby protecting George's interests. Kathy, working with represented Buyer Lisa, would be appointed to assist Lisa with advice and opinions toward meeting her goals. Because in the intermediary agreement both parties have agreed that certain information may be kept confidential, the fact that Lisa is hoping to resell quickly at a profit is moot.

Some brokers are not aware that this two-salesperson situation in an in-house sale creates a dual-representation conflict and, therefore, will not attempt to obtain proper consents. The broker may believe that both buyer and seller will be treated fairly and that each will receive full representation from their respective associates.

The broker often becomes aware of the conflict for the first time when served with notice of a lawsuit. It is then that the listing broker discovers, for example, that the salesperson never told the seller that the real reason for extending the closing date was to close the sale of the buyer's home, which was also listed by the broker. The seller then claims a breach of fiduciary duty because the broker failed to point out the seller's options in agreeing to an extension (for example, as a condition for extending, the seller possibly could have asked for compensating concessions). Trying to reverse unintended dual agency by attempting to get an intermediary agreement at the point of a lawsuit comes too late to protect the broker.

Cooperating or Other Broker

The other broker in the transaction often acts as the agent of the buyer in negotiations to acquire a property listed in an MLS. If subagency is offered and the broker fails to disclaim the offer of subagency, the other broker may be deemed to be the subagent of the seller and the implied agent of the buyer.

 EXAMPLE: Patricia of Supreme Real Estate checks the MLS book in her search of a home for Nancy Sue. She sees an interesting house and calls Jeff from South Side Realty about his listing. She makes arrangements to see the property and subsequently submits Nancy Sue's offer. The negotiations are long and hard, but after a series of four different offers and counteroffers, the seller agrees to Nancy Sue's offer. Before closing, Nancy Sue gets cold feet and asks for a return of her deposit money.

? QUESTION

Does Nancy Sue have a valid claim for rescission of the contract based on undisclosed dual representation?

DISCUSSION

Even though it may have no relevance to the true reason why Nancy Sue wants to back out of the contract, she might assert that she relied on the fact that she believed that Patricia was her agent. Later, Nancy Sue alleges she discovered that Patricia and Supreme Real Estate were really subagents of the seller. Because Supreme Real Estate acted as an undisclosed dual representative, she argues, either the buyer or the seller can legally refuse to close, even though no damages are proven. Patricia should have clarified her agency status to both Nancy Sue and Jeff when she first contacted Jeff to view the property. Under typical MLS rules, if subagency is offered, according to current Texas common law, Patricia will probably be presumed to be the subagent of the seller unless she rejects the offer of subagency and declares that she is a buyer's agent. As a subagent, Patricia must act as a subagent, taking care to protect the interest of the seller and not act as an agent of the buyer. In this case, she negotiated hard for Nancy Sue, and it may very well be that Patricia and Supreme Real Estate were unintended agents of Nancy Sue, as well as intended agents of the seller through the subagency rules.

Real estate licensees should note that professional liability often is based on the law of agency and the failure of a licensee to live up to the duties of an agent when held to be acting as one. Subagency may complicate this problem by creating an unintended dual representation with an inherent conflict of interest.

Broker as Principal

Brokers should be especially alert to dual-representation problems when they or their associates or employees, licensed or otherwise, buy or sell property for their own accounts. This can happen in several contexts.

Buying an in-house listing. On occasion, a broker or one of the broker's associates decides to make an offer on one of the broker's own listings. As a general rule, brokers should not purchase their own listings, especially if they are real bargains. The risks to the professional image of the broker are too great, not to mention the risks of loss of commission for breach of the duties of good faith and loyalty and loss of license under TRELA rules and regulations. To minimize exposure to liability, brokers desiring to purchase in-house listings should recommend that sellers obtain confirming appraisals and retain other consultants or advisers.

 EXAMPLE: Debra lists her home with broker Sid for $100,000. After six months of marketing, Debra has received only one offer, for $75,000. Sid offers to pay $95,000 by way of an assumption of the $80,000 first mortgage and further agrees to reduce the 7 percent listing fee to 3.5 percent. Five days before closing, Sid meets Betty, a recent arrival to town, who buys the home from Sid for $110,000 five days after closing.

? QUESTION

Did Sid breach a fiduciary duty to Debra?

🔍 DISCUSSION

Sid probably did breach his fiduciary duty if he did not inform Debra immediately on learning of Betty's offer. TREC Rule 22 TAC §535.156 requires that a broker "must put the interest of his [or her] principal above his [or her] own interest" and that the broker has "an affirmative duty to keep his [or her] principal informed at all times of significant information applicable to the transaction." TREC Rules 22 TAC §535.2(f) and §535.16 require that Sid obtain the best possible transaction and the best possible price.

Even if, technically, Sid were found to have breached no fiduciary duty, the appearance of wrongdoing is there. Sid may have a difficult time proving to a jury that he acted in Debra's best interests, particularly if the home's appraised value exceeded the listing price.

At best, there will always be a doubt in Debra's mind as to whether Sid stole a profit opportunity from her. Even if Betty had not appeared until a few days after closing, Sid would have a tough time convincing a jury that he didn't knowingly underprice the house at the time of the listing, which would be not only an additional breach of fiduciary duty but also a deceptive trade practice.

Sid should offer to return to Debra all or a fair portion of the quick profit or allow Debra the opportunity to sell directly to Betty. Such an attitude enhances the broker's professional standing in the community. In fact, it may enhance the broker's reputation so much that it more than makes up for the temporary loss of revenue. However, whether it is more profitable is not an appropriate standard by which to measure moral conduct. It is easy for brokers to *say* they promote their clients' best interests above anyone else's, including their own. It is much more effective to demonstrate this. (See *Wilson v. Donze,* 692 S.W.2d 735 [Tex. App. 2 Dist. 1985]. In this case, the broker had a duty to obtain the best price possible, even above the asking price. Though the seller ultimately determines the list price, the broker's duty is still to obtain the best possible price.)

The risks of a lawsuit increase if the licensee buying an in-house listing competes against offers submitted by other licensees on behalf of buyers or by buyers' agents on behalf of their clients. The listing agent has an unfair competitive advantage over other buyers because the agent knows all the bids. Section 15(a)(6)(V) of the License Act, which prohibits dealing in bad faith and dishonest dealings, also applies. The listing agent should reveal to other buyers the price and terms of any prior or subsequent offer made by the listing agent. Otherwise, the agent risks possible action by a buyer for breach of the general duties of fairness and honesty. Such an action could be based on failure to present the buyer's offer in a timely manner, failure to notify the buyer after the agent outbid the buyer or failure to reveal information the buyer might have used to justify a more attractive offering price, such as a pending beneficial zoning change.

State licensing law often requires that a real estate licensee disclose in writing his or her true position when offering to buy property listed with the broker. Although TRELA §15(a)(6)(J) requires this disclosure, it does not require that it be in writing. (The necessity for this disclosure also applies when the buyer is related to the listing agent in some way—for example, a family member, as a member of a corporation or as a business partner). As the buyer, the listing agent must remember that unless the agency has been terminated, the broker is still a fiduciary of the seller. The agent must act primarily for the benefit of the seller and owes the seller the standard duties of full disclosure, skill and care, in addition to honesty and fairness. There may a question as to whether a broker can represent himself or herself in buying a client's property and continue to place that client's interests first. A jury might also find it difficult to accept.

Buying property listed in an MLS. A licensee may decide to purchase a property listed in an MLS by another firm. The licensee should disclaim any subagency to the seller. Otherwise, the seller may claim that the licensee-buyer owed fiduciary duties to the seller under any MLS offer of subagency. Note that licensees are not normal consumers and may be required, under agency law, to disclose their opinions of value or of the likelihood of future appreciation [22 TAC §535.16(c)].

Sellers have won cases against cooperating brokers who bought for their own accounts. The success of these suits has been based on failure by licensees to disclose the true market value (one week after purchase of a property, for example, a licensee listed it on a financial statement as having a $20,000 greater value) or to disclose that a simple subdivision of the property would increase its market value (in one case, by 25 percent). The sellers won because the other agent owed fiduciary duties to the sellers based on the rules of subagency. These cases might have turned out differently had the licensee rejected subagency from the beginning, made all proper disclosures and documented them before proceeding.

If a commission split will occur, the listing agent should fully disclose this fact. This amount is often used as part of the down payment. The cooperating broker should disclose in the purchase contract that the receipt of such split does not create an agency relationship between the other licensee (the buyer) and the seller. It is much safer for the licensee-buyer to disclaim subagency, deduct the fee from the offering price and not participate in the fee paid by the seller.

Buying from The FSBO. Licensees buying FSBO ("for sale by owner") properties should disclaim any agency relationship with the sellers and should not approach the sellers under the guise of representing the sellers' best interests or listing the properties. Otherwise, they may be deemed agents of the sellers. If the licensees are deemed agents, they will be held to a higher standard of care with a greater duty of disclosure to sellers [22 TAC §535.16(c)].

The FSBO seller often agrees to pay a reduced commission to the licensee-buyer as a courtesy fee. The seller may later argue that the payment of a fee to the licensee-buyer was enough to create an agency relationship. At a minimum, the licensee buying for his or her own account should insert disclaimer language, such as, "Seller understands that buyer is a Texas real estate licensee buying for the licensee's own account and is not acting as an agent of the seller. Seller is not relying on the licensee for any advice or counsel regarding the sale. The licensee has advised seller that seller is free to obtain an independent consultant or agent to represent the seller's interest."

Licensed associates buying properties for their own accounts. Some realty firms prohibit or limit the right of their associates to buy properties listed with the firms. In some cases, a property must be offered to the public for at least 45 days before anyone in-house can make an offer on the property. These firms believe that the risk of alienating clients and prospective buyers outweighs any benefits to the brokerage firms.

If an associate does offer to buy property listed with his or her broker, the contract should clearly state that the seller understands that the buyer is associated with the listing broker.

If the associate buys property listed in the MLS (offering subagency) and receives a commission split, both the associate and the broker are considered subagents of the seller unless they clearly disclaim any agency relationship. As subagents, both would owe complete fiduciary duties to the seller. Another approach, thought by some to be somewhat safer for the associate-buyer, would be to take a buyer's agent position, offer a lower net price and not participate in any fee paid by the seller. The associate would have to discuss compensation with the cooperating broker, who normally would expect to receive a portion of the commission split from the listing broker.

Selling licensee's own property. Licensees who sell their own properties must disclose to prospective purchasers that they are licensed brokers or salespersons. For the protection of both the brokers and the buyers, licensees also should make clear to buyers that they are not acting as agents for the buyers and that the buyers are free to seek independent representation. This is true regardless of whether a licensee has a full, a partial or no ownership position in the brokerage firm or is involved in another business relationship, such as being part of an investment group that owns the property [TRELA §15(a)(3); 22 TAC §535.144].

Some brokers limit the number of properties owned by associates that can be sold at reduced commission rates. Brokers fear that associates will create the impression of spending valuable time competing for qualified buyers with sellers who have listed properties with the brokers. Other brokers prohibit their associates from marketing their personally owned properties to past or present clients to avoid any impression of impropriety. Associates should always inform their brokers of any intention to sell their own properties.

Adopting the Buyer

If no other broker is involved, the listing agent often spends a good deal of time with the buyer both before and after the contract is signed. A clear conflict arises in a back-to-back sale if the agent signs a listing with the buyer to resell the property before an offer has been made. More likely, however, is a situation in which an agent "adopts" a buyer during the closing process, agreeing, for example, to list other properties of the buyer, to cooperatively develop a property or to perform any other actions that may create an implied or express conflict of interest or representation agreement with the buyer.

Suppose the listing agent is asked by a buyer prior to closing to look for a resale buyer at $10,000 more than the contract price. While there is nothing illegal about taking a listing from a buyer after the contract is signed, the listing agent ethically and legally must disclose the dual representation to the seller. The seller might feel, in retrospect, that the agent, before the contract was signed, failed to disclose the existence of a resale buyer and possible higher selling price so that the agent could make a double commission.

Again, the intermediary role might be in the best interest of all parties, especially the broker. The principals would, by agreement, not be entitled to full disclosure. Both principals could have a licensee appointed to give advice and opinions and protect their individual interests while maintaining confidential negotiating details. It is best to discuss the possibility of future representation of a buyer before the agent begins to work with the buyer. If representation in a future transaction is contemplated, it is wise to enter into a buyer-representation contract for the first transaction. If, as in this case, the first transaction involves a property listed by the broker, the broker could, with the written consent of both buyer and seller, conduct the first transaction as an intermediary and the second resale transaction as a single agent for the buyer who has now become the seller.

A key ingredient in all the preceding scenarios is a full and complete disclosure of the role the broker is to play. When parties agree to allow a broker to act in any capacity that gives any principal less than the full fiduciary duties of an agent, the principals should be fully informed of the limitations and give their *informed consent*.

■ Summary

S.B. 489, which became effective January 1, 1996, made sweeping changes in the area involving representation of more than one party to a transaction. Statutory dual agency has been removed and replaced with intermediary brokerage. The statutory intermediary brokerage status in Texas presents a possible solution to the problems inherent in trying to represent both sides in a transaction. The key distinction between the old statutory dual agent and the intermediary broker lies in the ability of the intermediary to offer a broader range of services to represented buyers and sellers during in-house transactions. These extended services are accomplished through allowing appointed licensees of the broker to give preferential advice and opinions to the party to whom the licensee has been appointed, while the intermediary broker remains neutral throughout the transaction.

Undisclosed dual representation is a clear breach of an agent's fiduciary duty of loyalty. Even when an agent intends to act as a dual agent, such representation is unlawful if adequate disclosure is not given to both the buyer and the seller and unless consents are obtained from both. Most dual agencies, however, are accidental and arise because of the conduct of the licensees. Brokers need to establish internal management controls to lessen the risks of both unintended and underdisclosed dual representation.

■ Key Points

- If properly entered into and conducted, consensual dual agency, while not practical, is lawful; however, undisclosed or underdisclosed dual agency is illegal.

- It is possible to sell your own listing without creating dual agency or intermediary brokerage, provided the buyer remains a customer.

- Intermediary brokerage, with the option of appointed licensees for each party, is authorized in Texas and became effective in January 1996. Theoretically, an intermediary broker may act as an agent for both parties, but the broker's duties differ from those the broker assumes when acting as a single agent for either party. The duties and obligations of the intermediary are limited to those set out in TRELA §15C. The purpose of the new statute is to extend greater services to represented buyers and sellers in in-house transactions. It also is designed to reduce the liability of brokers when they conduct transactions in which both principals are represented by the same broker. This new law has yet to be fully interpreted by TREC regulations or by decisions of the courts.

- A broker who expects to become an intermediary should lay a foundation early by discussing the possibility of an intermediary transaction with in-house sales at the initial interviews with both the potential seller and the potential buyer. The possibility of an intermediary transaction should never be sprung on a client after a relationship is established. Consent to conduct an intermediary transaction should be authorized in the listing contract or in a buyer-representation contract.

- In comparison with single agency, the intermediary brokerage practice offers reduced services to the parties in the transaction. However, this shortcoming has been reduced by the ability of the broker to appoint associates to the buyer and seller for the intermediary transaction. These appointed associates may give preferential advice and opinion to their respective parties during the transaction.

- Although the intermediary broker may be exposed to legal liability if he or she fails to follow the intermediary guidelines carefully, the broker may benefit from this practice through in-house sales to represented buyers.

■ Suggestions for Brokers

A broker who is considering offering intermediary services to buyers and sellers should fully understand the requirements of the intermediary and develop a company policy regarding such practices. In addition, the broker should address the issue of appointed associates and be prepared to train associates who may be involved in such transactions.

■ Quiz

1. An associate of a broker, while working with a nonrepresented buyer, begins to give advice and opinions to the buyer during negotiations with a seller represented by the broker. Most likely the broker has become a(n)

   A. single agent of the buyer.   C. undisclosed dual agent.
   B. intermediary.   D. facilitator.

2. Currently, dual agency is

   A. illegal in Texas.
   B. permitted under statutory rules.
   C. encouraged by TREC.
   D. permitted under common-law rules.

3. The major difference between dual agency and intermediary status is that with intermediary status

   A. appointed licensees can give advice and opinions.
   B. agents have the same restrictions as the broker.
   C. the broker can give advice and opinions.
   D. confidential information can be relayed.

4. If an intermediary situation arises the broker cannot disclose

   A. the highest price the buyer might pay, until authorized to do so in writing.
   B. the minimum price a seller will take, unless authorized to do so in writing.
   C. confidential information of either party, unless the parties authorize it or law requires disclosure.
   D. Any of the above

5. In a transaction involving "appointed associates" which of the following is true?

   A. Associates may be appointed to either the buyer or the seller.
   B. The broker may be appointed to the buyer, while an associate is appointed to the seller.
   C. Written notification of the intermediary transaction and the appointed associates must be given to both parties.
   D. Written notification and identification of the appointed associates must be given to both parties.

6. Broker Able's represented buyer wishes to negotiate on a property listed by Broker Smith in a different firm. During this transaction which broker(s) may act as an intermediary?

   A. Broker Able   C. Neither Able nor Smith
   B. Broker Smith   D. Both Able and Smith

7. In an intermediary transaction, if a broker appoints an associate to the seller

   A. an associate also must be appointed to the buyer.
   B. the broker must take an appointment to the buyer.
   C. the same associate also must be appointed to the buyer.
   D. the broker must appoint someone from another firm to the buyer.

8. Unintentional dual representation can occur when

   A. another broker acts as a subagent and represents the buyer.
   B. the listing broker represents both the buyer and seller.
   C. a licensee acts as a buyer or a seller.
   D. All of the above

9. A small company consists of a broker and one associate. During an intermediary transaction the

   A. broker may be appointed to one party and the associate may be appointed to the other party.
   B. broker is prohibited from making appointments.
   C. associate may be appointed to both parties.
   D. broker may be appointed to both parties.

10. An associate who has listed a property shows a represented buyer that same property and an intermediary transaction develops.

   A. The associate may be appointed to both the seller and the buyer.
   B. The associate may be appointed to either the seller or the buyer.
   C. The associate may *not* be appointed to either the seller or the buyer.
   D. The associate may appoint another associate to work with the buyer.

■ Discussion Questions

1. What are the key differences between the former statutory dual agent and the current intermediary broker?

2. Why might a broker make or not make appointments in an intermediary transaction?

3. What issues should be considered in office policy regarding appointed associates in an intermediary transaction?

CHAPTER 9

Single Agency

By some within the real estate industry, the term *agency* is now being modified with the adjective *single*. *Single agency* is not a recognized legal term; it is a descriptive term that, on the surface, appears to distinguish *dual agency* or *intermediary brokerage* from *agency*. The broker practicing *single agency* or *nonspecific client-based agency* must understand the specific procedural and position features of both representing sellers and representing buyers.

This chapter presents an overview of the following agency practice issues applied to a broker who has decided to practice single agency without limiting the broker's client base to only one category of clients.

This chapter addresses the following:

Practicing Single Agency
Counseling Sessions Prior to Engagement
Conflicts of Interest
Hybrid Approach
Advantages and Disadvantages

■ Practicing Single Agency

Many brokers and their associates are becoming more comfortable with the concepts of representing buyers as well as sellers; nevertheless, a considerable number are unwilling to represent both parties in a single transaction. These brokers are termed *single agents*. Unlike brokers who represent only buyers or only sellers exclusively, single-agency brokers and their associates represent either buyer or seller, either tenant or landlord, or only one party to an exchange of property, but never *both* in the same transaction. Single-agency brokerage is oriented more toward the person in the transaction rather than toward that person's relationship to the property. That is, the broker focuses on the person's needs, whether that person buys, sells, leases, exchanges, develops or builds real estate.

The single-agency type of brokerage practice appeals to the real estate professional interested in long-term broker-client relationships in which the agent becomes part of the family advisory team, similar to the relationship with a family doctor, a lawyer and an accountant.

In some cases, the single-agency broker is paid directly by the broker's client, be it buyer, seller, tenant or landlord. In other cases, the single-agency broker is compensated indirectly by the other party as a condition of the contract or is paid by an authorized commission split from the broker representing the other side in the transaction.

James B. Warkentin, in *Buyer Brokering: How To Represent and Get Paid by the Buyer,* describes single agency as follows:

> Single agency means that each principal can choose to be represented by their own broker or to represent themselves. Since all listed sellers have their own broker, this area is not a problem. It is the buyer who needs the choice of being a client of his [or her] own broker or representing himself [or herself]. At this time, the vast majority of buyers are customers and are not given a choice. In essence, this means that client quality services are available to sellers and customer quality services are available to buyers. Client quality services are always greater than customer quality services. This is in the nature of the relationship. For example, you are a client with your attorney, a customer with a new car salesperson.

Some licensees confuse the concept of a single-agency with the inability of a single-agency broker to conduct an in-house transaction. Any nonrepresented buyer might purchase any listing held by a single-agency broker without creating a conflict for the broker. The seller would be represented as the client, and the buyer would be treated as the customer. While a single-agency broker often works *with* both sides, that broker will not work *for* both sides. The dedicated single-agency broker will not, in any given transaction, act in a representative capacity for both the buyer and the seller or both the landlord and the tenant. The single-agency broker usually attempts to maintain an ongoing, long-term, agency relationship with a client.

 EXAMPLE: Broker Bob lists and sells Sara's house while representing Sara as a seller's agent. During this transaction, Bob locates a new home for Sara that is listed by another broker. As a single agent Broker Bob would most likely wish to continue his agency relationship with Sara during this new transaction and represent Sara as a buyer's agent. Unless Bob acts as an agent for Sara in the second transaction, he would be in the position of simultaneously treating Sara as a client in the sale of her home and as a customer in the second transaction. In the second transaction Broker Bob would be acting as a subagent of the listing broker. This is not an illegal relationship; however, many questions relating to fiduciary duties might arise.

If Broker Bob worked only as an *exclusive buyer's agent,* he would not have listed Sara's house and could have served her only in the purchase of the new home, thus eliminating the possibility of earning two commissions in the transactions. Conversely, if Broker Bob operated only as an *exclusive*

seller's agent, he would have served Sara as her agent in the sale of her home but could not change his role to become Sara's agent when she became a purchaser of the new property. Although this would make it possible to earn a second commission, it would be contrary to the goals of a broker wishing to maintain pure single agency.

The advantage, then, of single agency for the broker in this example is that the broker practicing single agency can continue to maintain a client relationship in each transaction and also earn two commissions. The advantage to the consumer being represented is true representation with undivided loyalty in both the sale and the purchase.

■ Counseling Sessions Prior to Engagement

Usually, the single-agency practitioner does not agree to represent a client without first conducting a counseling session. Modern real estate practice is much more than just listing and selling. Buying property differs from buying an expensive car, for which the title, specifications and warranties are relatively consistent and clear. The real estate client's objectives, criteria and limitations must be clearly understood. The agent's job is to help develop this information before attempting to market or locate a property for a client. Then the property must be diligently investigated and the interests of others in the property ascertained. Most important, both agent and client must be comfortable in working together to meet the client's objectives.

Single-agency brokers represent clients, not just buyers or sellers. Some brokers specialize in representing buyers; however, they realize that in certain cases, their satisfied buyer clients may someday want to employ them to sell their property. In such a case, when a seller lists property with a single-agency broker, the broker will make full disclosure at the outset to buyer prospects that the broker represents the seller only. If a buyer makes an informed decision to continue a transaction without representation, the broker may commence working with the buyer to provide customer service, but not client representation.

Conflicts of Interest

Because the broker practicing single agency never acts as an intermediary, the broker may have to withdraw from representing one or both clients if a buyer-client becomes interested in a property listed by that broker. Typically, the broker will inform the buyer of the need to terminate the agency relationship for that particular transaction. If the buyer decides to continue with the transaction without representation, the broker will work with the buyer as a customer in this purchase from the seller-client.

Caution is advised if the seller asks the agent to disclose information about the buyer that was obtained in the earlier confidential agency relationship. Confidential information remains confidential even after the agency relationship is terminated. The agent should disclose to the seller-client that the buyer was, until recently, a client of the brokerage firm, and that confidential information about the buyer that was learned in the previous relationship cannot be disclosed. Should the seller object to the disclosure limitations, the broker may need to refer the seller-client to another broker for representation. However, there is no prohibition against revealing information about the former client that has been learned *since* the termination of the previous agency (the former buyer-client, now a buyer-customer, should be fully informed about the implications of the changed relationship).

As discussed in a previous chapter, some single-agency brokers and their associates will show all of the firm's listings to a buyer-customer before agreeing to represent that buyer as a client. While this lessens the chances of a conflict of interest, it doesn't eliminate the possibility that a buyer-client may later, after confidential matters and motives have been disclosed, decide to buy an in-house listing that was shown when the buyer was a customer. Nor does it preclude the ideal home for the buyer from coming into the firm's listing inventory after the buyer-customer has been converted to a buyer-client.

Hybrid Approach

With the passage of S.B. 489, companies that had used the consensual dual-agency approach in the past have switched to a combination of single-agency and intermediary brokerage for the sale of the firm's listings to buyer clients. Again, with full disclosure and the consent of both parties, the company could change its agency relationships with the parties and function as an intermediary, perhaps assigning a separate licensee to work with each party. A traditional single-agency broker would not use either of these hybrid approaches.

■ Advantages and Disadvantages

Some advantages of single agency follow.

- For the broker:

  Allows the agent to represent sellers and buyers, but in different transactions; therefore, the agent has a wider potential client base and can participate in more transactions with any given client, reducing the time and money required to produce new clients

  Reduces agent liability for undisclosed or consensual dual agency or intermediary brokerage.

  Increases client loyalty for professionalism, resulting in more referrals.

  Allows the agent to have a long-term, continuing client-level relationship with an individual, regardless of whether the individual buys or sells.

- For buyers and sellers:

  Ensures that clients receive full representation and undivided loyalty.

  Allows an individual to have a long-term, continuing client-level agency relationship with a specific and trusted agent, regardless of whether the individual buys or sells or acts as a landlord or tenant.

There also are some disadvantages of single agency.

- For the broker and associates:

  Reduces the possibility of earning an undivided commission when both parties require representation in a transaction; however, when only one of the parties desires representation, a broker practicing single agency might receive an undivided commission that otherwise would have been split with a subagent or the broker representing the other party.

  May result in loss of a buyer-client interested in a listing of the firm.

  Produces difficulty with switching back and forth from client to customer.

- For buyers and sellers:

  May not allow licensees to show their company's listings to buyer-clients without creating dual representation, thereby reducing a seller-client's access to potential buyers, although, in the event of a conflict of this type, the prospect could be referred to another brokerage firm.

■ Summary

A single-agency practice enables a broker to represent buyers or sellers. Single-agency brokers and their associates must be careful to avoid conflicts of interest caused by selling properties listed by the firm to buyer-clients. With the growing number of buyers desiring representation, the broker must consider the impact of the inability to offer intermediary services and develop viable alternatives for the represented buyer who becomes interested in a property listed by the firm. The use of a clear agency disclosure statement is helpful.

■ Key Points

- The single-agency broker represents either buyer or seller, but never both in the same transaction.

- Clients receive full representation, but they may have to switch to customer status if a conflict arises, or the broker may have to withdraw from a transaction altogether.

■ Suggestions for Brokers

If you choose the single-agency type of practice, decide how to handle the situation in which a prospective buyer wants you to locate property but does not want to sign a buyer-representation agreement. Single-agency practitioners will be limited in helping a buyer investigate properties listed by other brokers in the MLS if the buyer intends a broker to act as a subagent of the seller.

■ Quiz

1. The single-agency broker represents all of the following *except*

   A. the tenant or landlord.
   B. the buyer or seller.
   C. the vendee or vendor.
   D. both parties to a transaction.

2. The single-agency broker is least likely to

   A. be a seller's agent.
   B. be a buyer's agent.
   C. be a subagent of the seller.
   D. have conflicts concerning representation issues.

3. Betty wants to make an offer on a property listed by Sally, a single-agency broker. Who can help Betty submit an offer to buy?

   A. Another broker
   B. Betty herself
   C. Sally
   D. All of the above

4. All of the following are advantages of single agency *except*

   A. it reduces dual-agency liability.
   B. the broker has a wider potential client base than exclusive single agency.
   C. it increases the possibility of undivided commissions.
   D. it allows the broker and client to have a long-term professional relationship.

5. Which of the following best describes the single-agency broker's initial meeting with a prospective buyer or seller?

   A. The buyer or seller signs the listing agreement.
   B. The broker counsels the buyer or seller.
   C. The buyer or seller consults the broker.
   D. The broker receives an advance retainer fee.

6. If a buyer wants to be represented on a property listed by a single-agency firm, the single-agency firm

   A. should refer the buyer to a buyer's agent.
   B. should persuade the buyer to negotiate through the firm as a customer.
   C. should cancel the listing with the seller and represent the buyer in order to receive the greater commissions earned in an in-house sale.
   D. cannot serve the buyer in any capacity and maintain the single agency status.

7. The single-agency firm works

   A. with the buyer and for the seller.
   B. for the buyer and with the seller.
   C. with either the buyer or the seller.
   D. All of the above

8. A hybrid approach to agency is

   A. a combination of single agency and intermediary brokerage.
   B. a combination of single agency and dual agency.
   C. representation of the buyer and seller.
   D. any of the above.

9. A firm offering exclusive buyer agency would not

   A. ensure that clients receive full representation.
   B. reduce agent liability for undisclosed dual agency.
   C. represent both the buyer and the seller in the same transaction.
   D. allow the agent to have a long-term relationship with the client.

10. A firm wishing to maintain single agency

   A. could have difficulty switching representation from buyer to seller.
   B. may lose a buyer interested in a listing of the firm.
   C. could work with a customer and for a client.
   D. could do all of the above.

■ Discussion Questions

1. How does the single-agency broker normally handle the situation when both the buyer and the seller want the broker to represent them?

2. Why does single-agency practice not result in two brokers being required for every transaction?

3. What relation does buyer brokerage have to single-agency practice?

4. What is the difference between working *with* a buyer and working *for* a buyer?

10

Clarifying Agency Relationships

Most real estate licensees operate on the basis of high ethical standards that require fairness and honesty to customers and clients. Disclosure of their agency relationship to the buyer or seller in a real estate transaction has been required for decades. No consensus exists among real estate professionals on the best way to discuss and document agency relationships. However, Texas agency disclosure laws apply to commercial licensees as well as to residential licensees and to leases as well as to sales.

In many transactions, at least one person has the wrong impression of who represents whom. While there are no easy solutions, licensees can—and must—take steps to eliminate any confusion. The purpose of this chapter is to help licensees develop workable strategies to reduce complaints and avoid possible lawsuits while at the same time enhancing their professional reputation.

This chapter addresses the following:

Disclosure Policy
  Decide
  Disclose
  Document
  Do as You Say
Developing a Company Policy

■ Disclosure Policy

Much of the present confusion would be eliminated if licensees would

- *decide* in each particular transaction whether to represent the buyer or the seller, and whether intermediary brokerage is anticipated;

- *disclose* to the buyer and the seller whom they represent as soon as there is an agreement on the representation;

- *document* the disclosure with an adequate and timely written confirmation and

- *do* as they had declared, acting consistently with the disclosed decision.

Decide

Each transaction is different. A licensee must be prepared to decide in each transaction whom to represent and what the licensee's relationship will be to other participants. However, the licensee must take care not to proceed without consulting the parties involved. Because agency is a consensual relationship, a licensee may decide whom to represent but he or she must get the party's informed (and preferably written) consent to that representation.

Identification of the principal-client is sometimes difficult for licensees; it probably is more so for the buyers and sellers. Depending on the circumstance, the licensee may be representing only the seller, only the buyer, both the seller and buyer or possibly neither. The key for licensees is to understand fully the implications and obligations of each of the wide variety of situations that may develop. Before deciding on the appropriate working relationship, the licensee must *define* what role to play in each transaction. For example, a licensee may handle new property sales differently from resales, commercial property differently from residential property and first-time buyers differently from sophisticated buyers.

In any single transaction or in any relationship with a particular individual in multiple transactions, the real estate licensee can choose from a number of basic working relationships:

- Agent for either seller (or landlord) or buyer (or tenant), but not both (single agency)

- Intermediary broker between both buyer and seller, with the possibility of appointed licensees to each party

- Subagent for either buyer or seller (an agent who is working through another broker)

- Agent only for buyers (exclusive buyer representation)

- Agent only for sellers (exclusive seller representation)

- Agent for neither buyer or seller (non-agency)

Some relevant questions from the listing broker's perspective include the following:

- Is the listing salesperson the only licensee from the firm that is involved in the transaction, or is this an in-house sale of another salesperson's listing or one from a branch office of the firm?

- If another licensee presents an offer, is that licensee a subagent of the seller or an agent of the buyer?

- Does the listing agent have any prior or current relationship with the buyer, such as having listed the buyer's home, having acted as the property manager on one of the buyer's rental properties or having agreed to act as the buyer's agent in future transactions?

- Is the licensee working with a buyer who is only a customer, not a client?

Following are some relevant questions from the perspective of a licensee from another firm:

- Is this a multiple-listing service (MLS) sale?

- Is subagency being offered to other licensees?

- Is there a prior or present business relationship with the buyer? (This would be the case if, for example, the other licensee had listed the buyer's two-bedroom home and helped the buyer submit an offer on a three-bedroom home that is contingent on the sale of the buyer's two-bedroom home.)

It is not always easy to decide whom the real estate broker and associated licensees represent. When in doubt, ask these questions:

- Who is our client, and what services must we perform?

- Who is our customer, and what services can we perform?

- If the transaction involves intermediary brokerage, are there appointed associates, and what services can and cannot be performed for each party?

Disclose

It is not enough for the broker to decide whom to represent. Real estate agents must discuss with sellers and buyers (or landlords and tenants) all proposed agency relationships so that the principals can make informed choices. Agency is a consensual relationship that requires a delegation of authority by the principal and consent by the agent.

It is equally important for buyer and seller to know who will *not* be their agent. Buyers and sellers alerted to the fact that an agent does not represent them will recognize that they must take greater responsibility throughout a transaction to protect their own interests. *Timing of disclosure is critical,* and disclosure should occur before anyone can claim that an agency relationship already has been formed. If disclosure is delayed until closing or even until an offer is prepared, it is too late. Expectations of agency probably already have been created, and actions have been taken and confidences made in reliance on those expectations.

Senate Bill 489 (S.B. 489) amended the Real Estate License Act (TRELA) §15C, which outlines the specific duties of licensees to disclose their agency relationships. (See Appendix A.) In addition to TRELA requirements, S.B. 489 requires that certain written information be given to prospective buyers, sellers, tenants and landlords regarding the roles that a broker may assume in a transaction. As amended, §15C(a)-(c) reads as follows:

§15C(a) A licensee under this Act who represents a party in a proposed real estate transaction shall disclose that representation at the time of the licensee's first contact with (see Appendix A):

(1) another party to the transaction; or

(2) another licensee who represents another party to the transaction.

(b) the disclosure required under Subsection (a) of this section may be made orally or in writing.

(c) A licensee who represents a party in a real estate transaction acts as that party's agent.

In addition to the specific requirements for agency disclosure in §15C(a)-(c), §15C(d) requires that the licensee furnish prospective parties to a transaction a written information statement regarding the roles that the broker might be taking in the transaction. This statement must be given at the first face-to-face meeting at which substantive discussion occurs regarding real property. The written statement may be produced in any format desired by the broker *so long as the language is unchanged* and the print is no smaller than 10-point type.

The Texas Real Estate Commission (TREC) has produced a form that may be used by licensees, "Information About Brokerage Services," which meets the statutory requirement and is shown as Figure 10.1. (*Note:* §15C(f) allows the words *tenant* and *landlord* to be substituted for *buyer* and *seller.*) Many licensees mistakenly think the information statement is a disclosure of their agency status. However, the statute requires both the written information statement *and* a disclosure of any agency relationships. The agency disclosure is a separate duty; it can be either *oral or written.* Clearly, the careful broker will make sure the agency disclosure is written and acknowledged by the parties involved, even though Texas does not require that agency disclosure be in writing.

Certain exceptions to providing the written information about brokerage services occur when

- the proposed transaction is for a residential lease for not more than one year and no sale is being considered;

- the licensee meets with a party who is represented by another licensee;

- there is no substantive discussion regarding a specific property;

- the meeting occurs at a open house; and

- the meeting occurs after the parties have entered into a contract to sell, buy or lease.

Although these are the guidelines provided by TRELA, licensees may be wise to disclose any representation to parties with whom they meet early in the meeting. It is sometimes difficult to determine just when a conversation turns to more substantive matters that require disclosure.

Disclosure of information about agency relationships in general and whom the licensee currently represents, if anyone, relative to the contemplated transaction must take place according to Texas law as described

FIGURE 10.1

TREC Information About Brokerage Services

Approved by the Texas Real Estate Commission for Voluntary Use

Texas law requires all real estate licensees to give the following information about brokerage services to prospective buyers, tenants, sellers and landlords.

Information About Brokerage Services

Before working with a real estate broker, you should know that the duties of a broker depend on whom the broker represents. If you are a prospective seller or landlord (owner) or a prospective buyer or tenant (buyer), you should know that the broker who lists the property for sale or lease is the owner's agent. A broker who acts as a subagent represents the owner in cooperation with the listing broker. A broker who acts as a buyer's agent represents the buyer. A broker may act as an intermediary between the parties if the parties consent in writing. A broker can assist you in locating a property, preparing a contract or lease, or obtaining financing without representing you. A broker is obligated by law to treat you honestly.

IF THE BROKER REPRESENTS THE OWNER:
The broker becomes the owner's agent by entering into an agreement with the owner, usually through a written listing agreement, or by agreeing to act as a subagent by accepting an offer of subagency from the listing broker. A subagent may work in a different real estate office. A listing broker or subagent can assist the buyer but does not represent the buyer and must place the interests of the owner first. The buyer should not tell the owner's agent anything the buyer would not want the owner to know because an owner's agent must disclose to the owner any material information known to the agent.

IF THE BROKER REPRESENTS THE BUYER:
The broker becomes the buyer's agent by entering into an agreement to represent the buyer, usually through a written buyer representation agreement. A buyer's agent can assist the owner but does not represent the owner and must place the interests of the buyer first. The owner should not tell a buyer's agent anything the owner would not want the buyer to know because a buyer's agent must disclose to the buyer any material information known to the agent.

IF THE BROKER ACTS AS AN INTERMEDIARY:
A broker may act as an intermediary between the parties if the broker complies with The Texas Real Estate License Act.

The broker must obtain the written consent of each party to the transaction to act as an intermediary. The written consent must state who will pay the broker and, in conspicuous bold or underlined print, set forth the broker's obligations as an intermediary. The broker is required to treat each party honestly and fairly and to comply with The Texas Real Estate License Act. A broker who acts as an intermediary in a transaction:

(1) shall treat all parties honestly;
(2) may not disclose that the owner will accept a price less than the asking price unless authorized in writing to do so by the owner;
(3) may not disclose that the buyer will pay a price greater than the price submitted in a written offer unless authorized in writing to do so by the buyer; and
(4) may not disclose any confidential information or any information that a party specifically instructs the broker in writing not to disclose unless authorized in writing to disclose the information or required to do so by The Texas Real Estate License Act or a court order or if the information materially relates to the condition of the property.

With the parties' consent, a broker acting as an intermediary between the parties may appoint a person who is licensed under The Texas Real Estate License Act and associated with the broker to communicate with and carry out instructions of one party and another person who is licensed under that Act and associated with the broker to communicate with and carry out instructions of the other party.

If you choose to have a broker represent you,
you should enter into a written agreement with the broker that clearly establishes the broker's obligations and your obligations. The agreement should state how and by whom the broker will be paid. You have the right to choose the type of representation, if any, you wish to receive. Your payment of a fee to a broker does not necessarily establish that the broker represents you. If you have any questions regarding the duties and responsibilities of the broker, you should resolve those questions before proceeding.

Real estate licensee asks that you acknowledge receipt of this information about brokerage services for the licensee's records.

_____

Buyer, Seller, Landlord or Tenant   Date above. In addition, when attempting to secure a listing, the seller and the listing, the licensee should discuss

- whether the property is to be listed in the MLS;
- whether the prospective listing broker intends to operate as an intermediary, with buyers produced from the broker's client pool;
- who will have access to listing information;
- whether other licensees will be authorized to cooperate in the search for buyers;
- whether other licensees will be subagents of the seller's or buyer's agents; and
- whether the listing broker intends to share fees with subagents or with buyer's agents.

These matters should be clearly stated in a written listing contract between the broker and the seller.

Timing of Agency Disclosure. When working with buyers or tenants, the timing of the disclosure is frequently a problem. Disclosure is especially difficult with respect to a first-time buyer, who may have walked into the broker's office in response to a general advertisement or who may have met the listing licensee at an open house. No one seriously contends that the listing licensee should stop buyers after a friendly handshake and present them with the written statutory information statement or make an agency disclosure. Texas law, however, is quite specific and requires that a licensee who represents a party in a proposed real estate transaction shall disclose that representation at the time of the licensee's first contact with (1) another party to the transaction or (2) another licensee who represents another party to the transaction.

> The commission may suspend or revoke a license . . . at any time when it has been determined that . . . the licensee . . . has been guilty of . . . failing to make clear, to all parties of a transaction, which party the licensee is acting for, or receiving compensation from more than one party except with the full knowledge and consent of all parties. [TRELA §15(a)(6)(D)]

The disclosures required above may be made orally or in writing. Licensees should be cautioned that they must comply with both provisions. While §15C requires only that a licensee who already represents a party in a proposed transaction disclose that fact, §15(a)(6)(D) requires a licensee "to make clear, to all parties of a transaction, which party the licensee is acting for." The clear implication that can be drawn from that wording is that a licensee who does not represent any party in a transaction should disclose that fact as well (e.g., when a licensee is buying or selling a property for his or her own account). Otherwise, it could easily be assumed by one of the parties that the licensee represents him or her or, conversely, represents the other party.

The licensee must be sensitive to the problems created if the buyer is led to reveal confidential bargaining and financial information to the licensee, who, it turns out, actually represents the seller. Because the licensee is then obligated to relay such information to the seller, this gives the seller an unfair advantage over the buyer.

In practice, the real estate licensee may not, at first meeting, know whether to work with the buyer on a client or a customer basis. The first meeting might cover only general business practices, commission structures and market area specialty and be designed to convince the buyer to work with the licensee. Nevertheless, proper disclosure must be made. If, in fact, the broker is going to represent the buyer, they should enter into a written agreement that specifies the details of the relationship.

Ambiguous situations. There will, of course, be situations that are somewhat ambiguous, in which licensees may be unsure whether to discuss representation. Take the case of a real estate licensee who views a number of new listings of other brokers while on a company caravan tour. The licensee may not yet know whether he or she later will revisit such properties on behalf of a client or a customer. However, if meeting the seller face to face, the licensee must disclose his or her agency status. If meeting only with the seller's agent, the licensee minimally must discuss his or her status and future possibilities if, for example, that licensee has prospective clients that might be interested in purchasing that property.

A licensee must be especially careful to address squarely such undecided status in any discussions with the buyer, seller, tenant or landlord and other licensees. Agency and other working relationships should be firmed up as soon as possible in dealing with the buyer, but definitely before preparation of the buyer's offer.

Open houses have also created situations in which licensees may be unsure of disclosure policies. TREC, in an effort to clarify this circumstance, has stated that there is no requirement to give an open-house visitor the "Information About Brokerage Services" notice unless the party begins to ask in-depth questions or indicates an interest in making an offer on the property. Nevertheless, this does not relieve licensees of the duty to disclose to prospective buyers that they represent the seller—this can be done either orally or in writing.

What some listing agents do at an open house, for example, is show the property and answer general questions of a factual nature on such topics as available financing, municipal services and estimated closing costs. Questions concerning the seller's marketing position are addressed by the seller's agent and subagents in ways designed to encourage prospective buyers to make their best offer. If the conversation begins to move into any substantive discussion regarding a transaction, the licensee should immediately provide the prospect with the "Information About Brokerage Services" notice and take time to discuss and identify what the working relationship will be. At this point an agency disclosure statement should be made before going further.

Another disclosure issue will arise if the transaction involves intermediary brokerage. Recall that before entering into an intermediary transaction, written consent must be obtained from both parties. Typically this consent will be given in the listing agreement with the seller and in the buyer-representation contract with the buyer. Once consent has been obtained, the statute does not require any further notification when an intermediary transaction begins *unless* the broker appoints associates to the seller and buyer.

Remember that if the broker makes appointments, the parties must be informed *in writing* that appointments have been made, and such written notice must give the names of the appointees and identify the parties to whom they have been appointed. Even if no appointments have been made, the prudent broker should ensure that the parties are clear that an intermediary transaction is occurring. The Texas Association of REALTORS® "Notification of Intermediary Relationship" is an example of a form that accomplishes both notification objectives,

Document

To establish that the required disclosures have been given, the licensee should make the disclosures in writing and keep a copy of the disclosure forms signed by the buyer or the seller. This documentation will be especially important if any legal action results from the transaction. In addition, the licensee should obtain written confirmation on the final contract that the licensee disclosed who he or she represented and that the status of that representation has not changed. It is important that the licensee obtain such written proof because the oral declaration of the licensee in a lawsuit is given little weight in proving whom the licensee represented. It is sometimes equally important for licensees to prove that they were *not* agents of the buyer or the seller.

Do As You Say

If the buyer and licensee decide that the broker will not represent the buyer but instead will show the buyer properties as a subagent of sellers who have their properties listed in the MLS, the licensee should act as a subagent. A subagent of the seller, for example, would not suggest that the buyer start off by testing the seller with a nothing-down offer and a requirement that the seller carry back a note with interest deferred until the final balloon payment. Nor would a subagent of the seller suggest any negotiating strategies contrary to the best interests of the seller. However, the buyer could initiate any or all of these terms in submitting an offer to purchase the seller's property.

■ Developing a Company Policy

With the variety of agency relationships available, it is essential that every brokerage firm develop its own policy. The most effective way to establish a company policy on agency practice is to follow a simple but organized approach. Here's a suggested method:

Phase 1. Review the various agency options. Some options include:

- exclusive seller agency;
- exclusive buyer agency;
- seller/buyer agency with consensual intermediary brokerage or dual agency for in-company transactions and
- single agency (nonexclusive).

Phase 2. Review the advantages and disadvantages of each option as outlined previously.

Phase 3. Consider the size and experience of the office staff, the type of specialization, local market opportunities and financial expectations of the brokerage. For example, if most of the brokerage income comes from the sale of other brokers' listings, exclusive seller agency is probably not the best option.

Phase 4. Write a company policy. Start with a preliminary plan (see Figure 10.2), but make sure to submit the plan to key members of the brokerage staff and business and legal advisers for additional input.

A comprehensive plan should include a basic statement of policy. The plan should describe the procedures for handling common situations from the perspectives of both the listing office and the selling office. The plan should discuss the use of agency disclosure forms, especially the timing of oral or written agency disclosures and the furnishing of a mandatory written statement regarding representation alternatives. Above all, the plan should comply with all state laws. Company plans that are developed using textbook models or borrowed from out-of-state brokers should be carefully modified to conform to the Texas environment. Policies and procedures are generally written to protect the broker and associated licensees; however, they should clearly focus on serving both clients and customers while maintaining the highest ethical standards.

For example, a policy manual may include the following section on dealing with buyers at an open house:

Open House. Meeting potential buyers at an open house offers arguably one of the most complex agency situations in real estate. When a prospect comes into your open house, our duty is to the seller and we must use our efforts to sell the house to the prospect. This means that you cannot suggest other competing properties or offer to represent buyers until they have communicated to you that they are not interested in the property. If the buyer shows interest in the property or indicates that he or she might like to purchase the property, you must treat him or her as a customer and make immediate disclosures concerning agency options and positions, as required by state law and this policy manual, as follows:

- Confirm in writing and orally that the buyer understands that you represent the seller, and answer any questions that he or she might have.

- Determine that the prospect is interested in the property.

- Before substantive discussions concerning the buyer's qualifications for buying or points of negotiation in any subsequent offer, provide the buyer with the company brochure, which contains the written statement required by TRELA §15C(d) and Our Valued Customer letter (or other company-specific material).

Document in your file that you have delivered and discussed the written statement required by TRELA §15C(d). Request that the buyer sign the written statement, give him or her the original and retain copies for the company file on this property and a separate file on this customer. Should

FIGURE 10.2   Ingredients of a Company's Policies and Procedures

Basic agency philosophy
Strict adherence to state disclosure laws
Company disclosure guidelines
Summary of company policy

Handling common situations
Listing presentations
Buyer representation presentations
Intermediary representation without appointments
Intermediary representation with appointments
In-house sales without intermediary status
Subagency representation
Buying property for own account
Open houses

Dealing with outside companies
Cooperation regarding fee splitting, showing, presenting offers
Offer of subagency
Interacting with buyer's agents

Guidelines for the use of company agency forms
When
Why
How
Benefits

Common agency questions

the buyer refuse to sign the notice, make a notation on the notice to that effect and retain copies as defined above.

Phase 5. The broker should commence in-company training sessions and monitor the effectiveness of the policy. By using role-play and sample dialogue in training sessions, the sales staff can become more comfortable and competent in discussing agency in a way that showcases their professionalism. Rather than isolate discussions of agency, salespersons should be taught to integrate agency into their regular presentations. Finally, once you are certain your sales staff understands the policy, make sure staff members follow it. Be prepared to make exceptions in justified cases and to make changes to existing policy if exceptions begin to be the rule. (See Figure 10.3.)

■ Summary

Much of the confusion that exists on the issue of agency relationships can be eliminated as brokers become more comfortable and competent in discussing their roles in real estate transactions. Brokers should develop a company disclosure policy so that they take control over agency relationships and avoid unintended and illegal agencies. A basic policy consists of these four steps: (1) decide, (2) disclose, (3) document and (4) do. Without a doubt, timely, proper disclosure is the key ingredient to a successful and effective agency program.

FIGURE 10.3   **Agency Office Policy**

Agency Office Policy—Points to Ponder

Probably the best defense a company has today regarding problems in the area of agency is a well reasoned, written policy regarding agency relationships authorized and practiced by the company. Although the specific policy will be tailored to individual companies, an agency policy might include the issues on the following list.

How does your company address the following agency issues?

- A definition and explanation of duties of a seller's representative
- A definition and explanation of duties of a buyer's representative
- A definition and explanation of duties of an intermediary
- Statement regarding written listing agreements
- Instructions regarding procedures and paperwork, (including brokerage services notices and disclosures)
- Listing fees or commissions
- Policy regarding intermediary authorization in the listing agreement
- Statement regarding cooperation and compensation with Other Brokers (subagents and buyer agents)
- Procedures with first meeting with prospective buyers
- Policy regarding buyer representation
- Requirements for written buyer representation agreements
- Policy regarding intermediary authorization in the buyer representation agreements
- Commission or fee statements in buyer representation
- Policy relating to working with non-represented (customer) buyers, including written Information About Brokerage Services, and agency disclosure statements
- Policy statement relating to selling other firms listings as subagents or buyer's agent
- Policy relating to the sale of a FSBO to a buyer client or customer
- Policy relating to the in-house sale to a customer
- Policy relating to the intermediary transaction
- Policy relating to appointed associates (who and when)
- Disclosure of previous agency relationships and working with close friends and relatives
- Working with seller clients in purchasing a subsequent property
- Policy regarding working with competing buyers as customers or clients
- Policy relating to associates purchasing of the company's listings, or listings of other companies
- Associates selling their own properties or the property owned by another associate of the company

From *2000 and Beyond: An MCE Update.* Used with permission

■ Key Points

- Because real estate transactions vary widely, a brokerage firm must decide what role the firm and its associates will play.

- Once agency roles have been decided, the licensee must give full disclosure to all participants in the transaction.

- Throughout the transaction the licensee should take great care to properly document all aspects of the transaction.

- Once committed to a course of action, licensees must follow through and do as they have agreed to do.

- The firm should develop a written company policy outlining the basic agency philosophy, how to handle common real estate situations, dealing with other firms and use of agency forms.

■ Suggestions for Brokers

Develop a personalized disclosure brochure that includes the written statement required by TRELA §15C(d) and outlines the types of working relationships your firm offers to buyers and to sellers.

Outline some of the customer-level services you can provide to one person while remaining the exclusive agent of the other person.

Be careful not to use confusing language that might weaken the impact of meaningful agency disclosure and duties.

A broker who attempts to cloud the issues may find such a brochure being used in a lawsuit. Use of the §15C(d) written statement should help set the stage for meaningful discussions of your professional relationship and the needs of the prospect.

Although it is not required by law, attempt to get the prospective buyer or seller to sign an acknowledgment of receipt of the company form or letter, which discloses whom your brokerage represented, if anyone, at the time of first contact. If your company represents no one relative to the particular consumer being interviewed, say so in the form or letter. Also get an acknowledgment of receipt of the written information statement required by §15C(d). Then, if a relationship with the party appears imminent, carefully discuss the anticipated type of client or customer or other relationship before reaching a written agreement or obtaining consents and beginning a working relationship.

■ Quiz

1. When should a licensee disclose to the buyer the agency status of the listing broker?

   A. On recordation of the deed
   B. At the first contact with the buyer
   C. When the purchase contract is signed
   D. When the buyer telephones the broker to arrange an introductory meeting

2. When is the best stage of the transaction to present the required TRELA §15C(d) written statement to the seller regarding agency options?

   A. Just prior to submission of a first offer to the seller
   B. Immediately after listing the seller's property
   C. Immediately prior to signing the listing agreement
   D. At the time of the first face-to-face meeting with the seller

3. The other broker working with a buyer might represent

   A. the buyer.   C. the listing broker.
   B. the seller.   D. all of the above.

4. The listing broker should discuss all of the following with the seller at the time of the listing *except* the

   A. offer of subagency.   C. listing in the MLS.
   B. sharing of the listing fee.   D. buyer's motivation.

5. If a buyer-customer tells the listing broker that the buyer will pay up to the listed price, but first wants to submit an offer 10 percent below that price, what should the broker tell the seller?

   A. The buyer is qualified.
   B. The buyer has made a good offer.
   C. Don't risk losing the buyer by making a counteroffer.
   D. The buyer said he or she will pay up to the listed price.

6. When buyers attending open houses are "merely lookers." There is

   A. no need for licensees to disclose their relationship with the seller.
   B. still a need for licensees to disclose their relationship with the seller in writing.
   C. still a need for licensees to disclose their relationship with the seller, at least orally.
   D. no need for licensees to disclose their relationship with the seller, unless a buyer asks.

7. The buyer is considered to have received the required agency disclosure when the licensee

   A. delivers the TREC "Information About Brokerage Services" notice to the buyer and has the buyer sign the form.
   B. delivers the TREC "Information About Brokerage Services" notice to the buyer.
   C. discloses the agency relationship, either verbally or in writing, to the buyer.
   D. completes a purchase contract for the buyer.

8. There is no requirement for a licensee to deliver information regarding brokerage services to a buyer who is

   A. seeking to be represented by the firm.
   B. represented by another agent.
   C. referred by a former client.
   D. a friend.

9. When buyers' agents show a property listed by another firm, those buyers' agents must

   A. deliver the "Information About Brokerage Services" notice and disclose their representation of the buyer to the seller.
   B. verbally disclose their representation of the buyer to the seller.
   C. deliver the "Information About Buyers Services" notice to the seller.
   D. assume that the seller has been informed of the representation.

10. A broker should develop company policies that outline

    A. how to handle common real estate situations.
    B. how to deal with other firms.
    C. use of agency forms.
    D. all of the above.

■ Discussion Questions

1. What are the four steps a broker should take to clarify agency relationships?

2. In deciding whether to act as an agent of a buyer, what are some relevant questions for a listing broker to ask?

3. In deciding whether to act as a subagent of a listing broker while working with a buyer, what are some relevant questions for another broker to ask?

4. What are some key areas of the prospective agency relationship that the listing broker should discuss with the seller during the listing appointment?

5. When is the best time to make the disclosure of seller agency to the buyer?

11

Employment Issues

The extent of legal responsibility of a person who hires someone else to act for him or her depends on the relationship between them. As a general rule, the more extensively the person who contracts for a service controls the manner in which the service is performed, the greater that person's responsibility. For example, an employer has appreciable control over how an employee works. If an employee acts within the scope of his or her employment, the employer is responsible for any harm the employee causes. In real estate brokerage, the licensee's classification either as an independent contractor or as an employee is important for several reasons, including the establishment of agency relationships through employment contracts and listing agreements. Chapter 5 discussed, in detail, the listing agreement as the primary employment agreement between brokers and sellers. Likewise Chapter 6 took an in-depth look at the buyer-representation agreement as the primary employment agreement between brokers and buyers. This chapter explores some general employment issues and agreements as they affect brokers and licensed associates in their roles as principals and agents.

This chapter addresses the following:

Employment Relationships between Brokers and Principals
Employment Relationships between Brokers and Associates
 Employee versus Independent Contractor
 Sales Associate and Broker Associate Compensation
Employment and Compensation of Personal Assistants
Employment Relationships Between Brokers and Subagents
 MLS Subagency Agreements
 Non-MLS Subagency Agreements
 Agreements between Brokers
Other Compensation Issues
 Non-Licensee Compensation
 Foreign Brokers

■ Employment Relationships between Brokers and Principals

Brokers generally enter into employment contracts with property owners through listing agreements and property management agreements. Likewise, brokers enter into employment agreements with buyers and tenants through buyer/tenant-representation agreements. As discussed in previous chapters, these agreements set out the terms of employment and address issues of compensation.

Under the terms of most employment contracts with principals, brokers are responsible for the payment of brokerage expenses associated with the agreement. In addition, the broker pays any income tax due as a result of any compensation received during the course of the employment.

■ Employment Relationships between Brokers and Associates

In Texas, approximately two-thirds of all brokers work for the remaining one-third. The broker is held responsible to the state and the public for the conduct of licensees who are either licensed under the broker or working as independent contractors or employees. The responsible broker is frequently referred to as a *sponsoring broker, principal broker* or *designated broker*. The employed, associated or sponsored licensee is licensed either as a salesperson or as a broker. An associate who is a broker generally is referred to as a *broker associate*. Texas offers no broker associate license. An individual licensed as a salesperson is required to work under the direction and supervision of a sponsoring broker. The broker may either be a corporation or an individual. A person licensed as a broker may work independently or may enter into an agency relationship with another broker to represent that broker in dealings with the public.

Based on the Texas Real Estate License Act (TRELA) and the doctrine of *respondeat superior* ("Let the master answer"), the broker is responsible for the acts and conduct of all salesperson associates and broker associates during the ordinary course of employment [22 TAC §535.2(c), 22 TAC §535.141(c)]. Under general agency concepts, each of these licensed associates is the agent of the broker. Listings are made in the name of the broker, not the salesperson or broker associate. The broker is the party responsible to the public and to clients, whether acting directly or indirectly through his or her agents. If a broker has a listing (open or exclusive), that broker and all the licensed associates of that firm represent the seller in a fiduciary capacity. This is true of all licensed associates working in each of the listing broker's offices. (This rule, however, does not apply to franchise organizations in which each franchised brokerage firm is independently owned.)

It is important to understand that licensed salespersons cannot lawfully sell their services directly to the public. Salespersons must perform all tasks under the direct supervision of a broker. This is true even if the salesperson is, for tax purposes, an independent contractor. Under agency and licensing law and for purposes of supervision, salespersons who are licensed with a broker are agents and employees of the broker and act for the broker. The terminology *acts for,* as used in the Texas Real Estate Commission (TREC) Rules cited here, is equivalent to the description of an agency relationship [TRELA §1(b),(c)].

Licensed salespersons cannot legally

- list property in their own names [22 TAC §535.154(f)];

- enter into buyer agency or intermediary agreements in their own names, either orally or in writing;

- sue directly sellers, buyers, landlords or tenants for unpaid commissions (generally);

- open their own offices without hiring a broker to be responsible for all those licensees in the offices;

- work independently without having a licensed sponsoring broker to shelter or hold each salesperson's license;

- hold a license under more than one broker at the same time;

- take listings or buyer/tenant-representation agreements when they move to a new brokerage office with or without the current broker's consent (although the broker may release represented owners or buyers from their agreements and allow a salesperson's new broker to attempt to contract with the owners, buyers or tenants);

- advertise in their own names unless the broker's name also appears and it is clear to the public which one is the broker [TRELA §15(a)(6)(P); 22 TAC §535.154(d), (e)];

- open their own client trust accounts for sales or rentals [22 TAC §535.159(f)];

- accept compensation directly from clients or other brokers for real estate sales and transactions without the broker's consent [TRELA §1(d); 22 TAC §535.3] or

- pay a commission to any person except through the broker under whom they are licensed or with that broker's knowledge and consent [TRELA §1(e); 22 TAC §535.3].

Broker associates, on the other hand, because they have the same state license as the principal broker, may be allowed to do virtually any of these things if the broker they work for does not prohibit the broker associate from running another brokerage operation. This practice is not the norm, however, and any broker associate attempting any of the above-listed actions without the principal broker's knowledge and consent would likely be at risk.

TREC does not regulate the broker's contractual arrangements with other brokers [22 TAC §535.2(a)]. The principal broker of a broker associate should keep in mind—and make the associate aware—that the License Act holds the principal broker responsible for the acts of associated broker licensees [TRELA §1(c)]. In addition, in any lawsuit against the associate broker, if the plaintiff (the person bringing the suit) believes the associate acted in the name of the principal broker, the broker will most likely be named in the lawsuit and may be held liable for the damages caused by an associated broker. It is important to understand that when an associate of the broker secures a listing or buyer-representation agreement, it is the principal broker who is employed by the buyer or the seller.

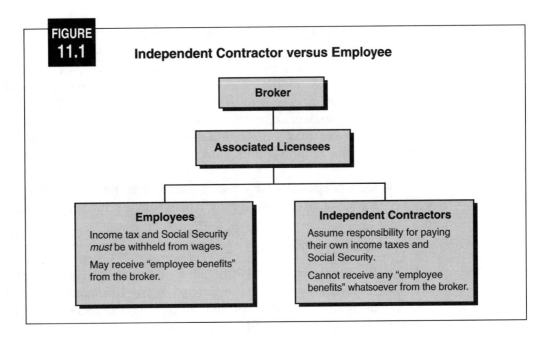

FIGURE 11.1   Independent Contractor versus Employee

Broker

Associated Licensees

Employees

Income tax and Social Security *must* be withheld from wages.

May receive "employee benefits" from the broker.

Independent Contractors

Assume responsibility for paying their own income taxes and Social Security.

Cannot receive any "employee benefits" whatsoever from the broker.

In Texas it is not legally possible to construct a figurative internal wall within a brokerage firm and argue that because different licensed associates act for the buyer and the seller, no dual agency exists. In Texas, such an attempt likely would not hold up in court or at a TREC disciplinary hearing. By analogy, a large law firm could not have one of its associates on the tenth floor represent the seller of a commercial warehouse and another associate on the eleventh floor represent the buyer without first obtaining from the buyer and the seller very complete and detailed consent to such dual representation and agreement to receive a very limited form of fiduciary representation.

Some brokerage firms advertise that they have salespersons who represent buyers and other salespersons who represent sellers. For example, Tom from Executive Realty, as the listing agent, innocently might tell an interested buyer who has expressed a desire to obtain her own agent, "I can't be your agent, but Dorothy in our other office is very knowledgeable, loves to represent buyers and can give you the type of representation you want."

Tom's firm must be careful to develop its company policies within the bounds of agency law. It is the firm, not the associates, that—by law—represents the buyer or seller. Listing brokers should set up internal management controls to ensure that their associates understand these basic agency principles.

Employee versus Independent Contractor

Brokers engage salespersons as either employees or independent contractors. Any agreements between brokers and their associates should be in the form of written contracts that define the obligations and responsibilities of the relationships. Whether an associate operates under the broker as an employee or as an independent contractor will affect the relationship between them. (See Figure 11.1.)

The nature of the employer-employee relationship allows a broker to exercise certain controls over associates who are employees. The broker may require that a employee adhere to regulations concerning such matters as working hours, office routine and dress or conduct. As an employer, a broker is required by the federal government to withhold Social Security and income taxes from wages paid to employees. The broker also is required to pay unemployment compensation taxes, as required by state and federal laws. In addition, a broker may be required to provide employees with such benefits as health insurance and profit-sharing plans.

An *independent contractor* operates more freely than an employee does, and the broker may not control his or her activities in the same way. Crucial elements of preserving independent contractor status are

- the independent contractor's services must be performed under the terms of a written contract between the broker and the associate;

- the broker may control *what* the independent contractor does, but not *how* it is done and

- the contract must state that the independent contractor assumes responsibility for paying any required income and Social Security taxes and receives nothing from the broker that could be construed as an employee benefit.

In Texas, brokers are not required to carry worker's compensation coverage for independent contractors.

To ensure that all licensed associates are treated by the Internal Revenue Service and the Texas Employment Commission as independent contractors, brokers are urged to maintain close contact with competent tax counsel and have their policies and procedures reviewed frequently for compliance. The broker should exercise great care to ensure that independent contractors understand their personal obligations under law.

Some people believe that the difference between an independent contractor and an employee is that the former works on a commission-only basis and the employee is salaried. That may be relevant, but it is not conclusive. Many salespersons are paid on commission but are considered employees because of other features of their employment situations.

Sales Associate and Broker Associate Compensation

An associate's compensation is set by mutual agreement between the broker and the associate. A broker may agree to pay a salary or share of the commissions from transactions originated by an associate. An associate may have a drawing account against his or her earned share of commissions. In such a case, the associate should sign a note for each draw to preserve the independent contractor status, if such status is desired.

A departure from traditional compensation plans is the 100 percent commission plan. Generally, in a brokerage firm that has adopted this system, associates pay a monthly service charge to the broker (to cover the costs of office space, telephone service, supervision and administration) and receive 100 percent of the commissions from the sales they negotiate.

■ Employment and Compensation of Personal Assistants

Many busy brokers and associates have found that employing personal assistants allows them to become more productive. Assistants are generally given responsibilities that do not require licensure, such as holding open houses, maintaining records, scheduling, and placing signs and lockboxes on properties. Some licensees employ assistants who are licensed so that more extensive duties can be assigned.

Employment agreements must be carefully considered. It may be difficult to employ a personal assistant as an independent contractor because the essence of the relationship is that the employer carefully directs and controls the actions of the assistant. Because an independent contractor must be able to perform his or her duties independent of employer control or direction, it may be difficult, if not impossible to convince the IRS that such a relationship exists with an assistant. Before entering into such an agreement it would be wise to consult an attorney or CPA who is familiar with all aspects of employment law.

■ Employment Relationships between Brokers and Subagents

Listing agreements and buyer representation agreements may, with the agreement of the principal, include a clause that allows the broker to appoint subagents. A buyer's broker, if given such permission, may appoint subagents as readily as a seller's broker.

MLS Subagency Agreements

Under most pre-1993 multiple-listing service (MLS) rules, all listings submitted to an MLS were required to contain mandatory offers of subagency to all other members. After discovering numerous potential legal problems with such a practice, most MLS systems now offer participants optional subagency; that is, the systems allow their participants to place listings that offer either subagency and compensation to other MLS members or cooperation and compensation but not subagency.

Non-MLS Subagency Agreements

Any brokers, even if they are not members of a multiple-listing service (MLS) system, can voluntarily contract with each other to create their own broker-to-broker subagency agreements, to cover either one property at a time or all properties in their respective inventories for any agreed period of time. Such subagency agreements generally do or should contain pre-agreed compensation amounts.

Agreements between Brokers

Not all agreements between cooperating brokers regarding compensation contain an offer of subagency. The special block titled "Broker Information and Ratification of Fees" that appears on the last page of the TREC residential sales contract, is such an agreement. It is merely a confirmation that the listing broker will compensate the other broker in a transaction by an amount specified in this abbreviated agreement, *when and if* the listing broker is compensated by the seller-principal.

If the buyer's broker is not protected by a buyer-representation agreement, and if at the closing the seller refuses to compensate the listing broker because of an alleged breach of fiduciary duty by the listing broker, the buyer's broker has no way to secure compensation from anyone in the transaction. Although buyer's brokers may not be fully protected by this TREC-developed compensation agreement, it can serve as a useful memorandum of the initial intent of the parties to the agreement.

Compensation to a broker operating under the terms of a buyer/tenant-representation agreement is dictated by the terms of the agreement. The Texas Association of REALTORS® agreement permits payment to be made directly by the client to the broker or permits the broker to be compensated through funds provided by the seller. In addition, the agreement may provide that the broker receive a flat fee, hourly compensation and/or for a retainer fee. Most often, the buyer's broker will be paid through funds paid by the seller in the same way that a subagent is usually compensated. Remember that, as in listing agreements, the compensation to a buyer's broker is fully negotiable between the buyer and the broker.

■ Other Compensation Issues

Nonlicensee Compensation

In Texas, it is illegal for a broker to share a commission with someone other than a principal in the transaction who is not licensed as a salesperson or broker or with someone who is exempt from licensure pursuant to Sections 3 and 14 of the TRELA. This has been construed to include the giving of certain items of personal property and other premiums, as well as finder's fees and portions of the commission that exceed $50 in value [22 TAC §535.20(a)]. Additionally, a 1990 Texas law prohibits a broker from sharing a sales commission with an attorney unless the attorney is also licensed as a broker [22 TAC §535.31 (a-g)]. However, an attorney may conduct real estate transactions for compensation as long as the attorney is paid directly by the principal.

Unlicensed brokerage owners. The issue of an unlicensed person who owns all or part of a real estate company sharing in the income earned by the company is clarified in 22 TAC §535.131(c) as follows: "An unlicensed person may share in the income earned by a real estate brokerage operation, provided that such unlicensed person performs none of the activities of a real estate broker and the public is not led to believe that such unlicensed person is in the real estate brokerage business."

Foreign Brokers

An exception to the prohibition for compensation to individuals licensed in Texas states that "a licensed broker may pay a commission to a licensed broker of another state. This exemption is valid only if the foreign broker [a broker who is licensed in another state] does not conduct in this state any of the negotiations for which the fee, compensation, or commission is paid" [TRELA §14(a)].

■ Summary

Although brokerage firms vary widely in size, few brokers perform their agency duties without the assistance of associated licensees. Consequently, much of a firm's success hinges on the broker-associate relationship. An agreement between a broker and an associate should be set in a written contract that establishes the obligations and responsibilities of each party. The salesperson may work on the broker's behalf as either an employee or an independent contractor.

A broker's compensation generally takes the form of a commission, paid either by the seller, under the terms of a listing agreement, or a buyer, under the terms of a buyer-representation agreement. Generally, the broker receiving compensation may share the commissions with other brokers who are acting as subagents or buyer brokers.

■ Key Points

- Brokers enter into employment agreements with property owners, buyers and tenants through listing and representation agreements.

- Sponsoring brokers and associated broker and salesperson licensees enter into employment agreements and conduct brokerage activities as employees of the firm or as independent contractors.

- Salesperson licensees cannot perform brokerage activities independently. All activities must be under the direction of the sponsoring broker.

- Independent contractors must (1) have a written contract with the broker, (2) be allowed to determine *how* they carry out brokerage functions and (3) pay their own income and Social Security taxes.

- Brokers may contract with other brokerage firms to represent their clients in a subagency capacity. Subagency can be achieved through an MLS or directly with selected brokers for a particular property or for an agreed-on period of time.

- Broker may *not* share compensations with unlicensed persons, other than the principals in a transaction, except as provided in TRELA.

Brokers licensed in other states may share in a broker's compensation if they "do not conduct in this state any of the negotiations . . ."

■ Suggestions for Brokers

Brokers should carefully document relationships with associates by entering into a written employment agreement with each associate. In addition, because most associates are not considered employees, the broker should understand and adhere to the strict guidelines regarding independent contract status, most importantly, the requirements relating to directing how their duties are to be performed.

■ Quiz

1. While employed by a real estate broker, a salesperson has the authority to

   A. act as an agent for the seller.
   B. assume responsibilities assigned by the broker.
   C. accept a commission from another broker.
   D. advertise the property on his or her own behalf.

2. Agreements that set the employment terms of an associated licensee include

   A. listing agreements.
   B. buyer-representation agreements.
   C. independent contractor agreements.
   D. property management agreements.

3. A broker has the right to dictate which of the following to an independent contractor?

   A. Number of hours worked   C. Acceptable dress code
   B. Work schedule   D. Duties

4. When a broker engages other brokers as associates of the company,

   A. the broker associate generally works under the guidance of the sponsoring broker.
   B. TREC will issue an "associate broker" license to the associated broker.
   C. the sponsoring broker will not incur any liability for the broker associate.
   D. broker associates will take listings in their own names.

5. Even though the broker and associate have a written independent contractor agreement,

   A. if the broker's conduct is that of an employer, the IRS will probably not consider that an employer-employee relationship exists.
   B. if the broker's conduct is that of an employer, the IRS will probably determine that an employer-employee relationship exists.
   C. the broker associate can conduct business activities free of any guidance.
   D. the broker will reimburse associates for all expenses.

6. An associate's compensation is set by

   A. mutual agreement between the broker and the associate.
   B. the local Board of REALTORS®.
   C. TRELA.
   D. TREC.

7. Unlicensed personal assistants hired by licensees

   A. can work for broker licensees only.
   B. must be taking real estate courses.
   C. are allowed to carry out all of the licensees' real estate duties.
   D. carry out limited functions that do not require a real estate license.

8. Multiple-listing service (MLS) listings

   A. require that compensation be paid by the seller.
   B. all carry a mandatory offer of subagency.
   C. do not cooperate with buyers' agents.
   D. offer optional subagency.

9. Brokers who do not belong to an MLS can

   A. elect to reject offers of subagency.
   B. have individual agreements with other brokers.
   C. have individual agreements with other brokers for limited periods of time.
   D. All of the above

10. The term *foreign broker* relates to a broker

    A. licensed in another state
    B. licensed in another country
    C. of foreign descent
    D. of a different firm

■ Discussion Questions

1. Explain why classifying a real estate salesperson as an independent contractor does not relieve the broker of responsibility for the salesperson's actions.

2. Discuss the differences between how a broker and a salesperson are compensated.

3. Discuss the exceptions to TRELA concerning payment of fees to individuals unlicensed in Texas.

CHAPTER 12

Deceptive Trade Practices and Consumer Protection Act

No evidence exists that misrepresentation and fraud are more prevalent in the real estate industry than in other sectors of the economy. If, however, deceptive acts occur in a real estate transaction, they may have a greater impact than in other areas for several reasons. First, most real estate transactions involve large sums of money; as a result, people who feel deceived are more apt to take action to assert their rights. A second reason is that licensing laws have placed substantial supervisory responsibility on brokers for the conduct of associated licensees. Deception by associated licensees, even if unintentional, can subject brokers to liability, including loss of license. Finally, in many transactions, little direct contact takes place between buyer and seller. Because information is often transmitted through a third party, misunderstanding and error can result in the buyer, the seller or both feeling that they have been deceived.

In Texas, a consumer's rights are protected by the Texas Deceptive Trade Practices and Consumer Protection Act (DTPA), Chapter 17, Subchapter E of the Business and Commerce Code. This act declares, among other things, that "false, misleading or deceptive acts or practices" in the advertising, offering for sale, selling or lease of any real or personal property are unlawful. How the DTPA affects real estate brokers and associated licensees is explored in this chapter. The DTPA applies to most businesses and is, therefore, potentially far reaching. This chapter will address the sections of DTPA that are most applicable to the practice of real estate; it is not intended to be an exhaustive study of the topic.

This chapter addresses the following:

Fraud versus Misrepresentation
Deceptive Trade Practices and Consumer Protection Act
Definitions of Terms
Deceptive Acts
Waivers of Rights under the DTPA
Notice and Inspection
Exemptions

Unconscionable Actions
Producing Cause
Damages
Defenses
Groundless Lawsuits

■ Fraud versus Misrepresentation

Fraud is a deceptive act practiced deliberately by one person in an attempt to gain an unfair advantage over another. There is always the *intention* to deceive. The elements of a cause of action for fraud are:

- an intentional false representation of material facts, either past or present;

- relience on the false representation by the person taking action;

- damage as a result of the action taken based on the false representation.

Because of the very strict requirements to prove fraud, it is not as frequently pursued in court actions involving real estate transactions.

Misrepresentation, on the other hand, is a false statement made negligently or innocently that is a material factor in another's decision to contract. There does not have to be an intention to deceive. Many real estate cases involve property owners and/or licensees *unintentionally* making false statements regarding material facts. Showing proof of misrepresentation is considerably easier than proving fraud, thus court actions involving real estate frequently pursue this course. See Figure 12.1 for a comparison of fraud and misrepresentation.

■ Deceptive Trade Practices and Consumer Protection Act

The Deceptive Trade Practices and Consumer Protection Act (DTPA) was passed by the Texas legislature in 1973. As the act was originally drafted, real estate transactions were excluded from coverage. In 1975, the act was amended to include transactions involving real property purchased or leased for use. The purpose of the law is to protect consumers against

- false, misleading and deceptive business practices;

- unconscionable actions and

- breaches of warranty.

This law creates a powerful weapon for consumers. It is effective for two reasons. First, proving that a deceptive act has occurred is easier under this law than under previous real estate statutes and even common law. Second, the law provides that consumers may recover more than their actual losses. Although an injured party can recover punitive (punishing) damages for fraud, the DTPA does not require proof that the defendant

---

FIGURE 12.1	Comparison of Actions for Fraud and Misrepresentation	
Cause of Action	**Factors To Be Proven**	**Remedies**
Common-Law Fraud (From decisions in court cases)	Was a false statement made? Was it made intentionally or negligently? Was the misstatement a material fact? Was the misstatement relied on? Was anyone injured?	Rescission Actual damages Actual damages and rescission Exemplary damages (to punish)
Statutory Fraud (From law enacted by the legislature)	Same factors as for common-law fraud Was a false promise made with intent not to perform? Did the person who benefited from the misrepresentation know that it had been made and fail to disclose the truth?	Same remedies as for common-law fraud Attorney fees, court costs and expert witness fees
Deceptive Trade Practices and Consumer Protection Act	Were any specifically listed acts committed? Were any deceptive acts committed? Were any misleading statements made? Were any false statements made, including innocent misstatements? Was an unconscionable act or course of action practiced against the victim? Were any of the acts listed above the producing cause of harm to the victim?	Economic damages Damages for mental anguish Up to 3× economic and mental anguish damages Attorney fees and court costs

---

intended to deceive or mislead. The mere occurrence of a deceptive act can result in damages in excess of the actual economic loss.

The first use of the DTPA in the real estate area involved cases concerning breach of warranty in the sale of new residential properties. The initial draft of the law allowed a consumer to recover three times the amount of actual damages suffered as a result of defective or unworkmanlike construction in a new home purchase. This generous remedy prompted consumers to bring all breach of warranty cases under the DTPA. In recent years, the law has been used by consumers against sellers of existing homes, brokers and lenders. The law no longer provides for the automatic trebling of damages (triple the amount of damages); however, it still allows for a recovery of damages in excess of actual economic loss.

Definitions of Terms

The DTPA includes specific definitions of thirteen words or phrases that are used in the act. As you read the following sections you should keep in mind that if a DTPA lawsuit goes to court the attorneys will be using these definitions in attempting to prove or disprove their cases, and the judge and/or jury will use these definitions in their conclusions. The following definitions are found in Section 17.45 of the act:

1. "Goods" means tangible chattels or real property purchased or leased for use.

2. "Services" means work, labor or service purchased or leased for use, including services furnished in connection with the sale or repair of goods.

3. "Person" means an individual, partnership, corporation, association or other group, however organized.

4. "Consumer" means an individual, partnership, corporation, this state or a subdivision or agency of this state who seeks or acquires by purchase or lease, any goods or services, except that the term does not include a business consumer that has assets of $25 million or more, or that is owned or controlled by a corporation or entity with assets of $25 million or more.

5. "Unconscionable action or course of action" means an act or practice which, to a consumer's detriment, takes advantage of the lack of knowledge, ability, experience or capacity of the consumer to a grossly unfair degree.

6. Trade" and "commerce" mean the advertising, offering for sale, sale, lease, or distribution of any good or service, of any property, tangible or intangible, real, personal, or mixed, and any other article, commodity or thing of value, wherever situated, and shall include any trade or commerce directly or indirectly affecting the people of this state.

7. "Documentary material" includes the original or a copy of any book, record, report, memorandum, paper, communication, tabulation, map, chart, photograph, mechanical transcription or other tangible document or recording, wherever situated.

8. "Consumer protection division" means the antitrust and consumer protection division of the attorney general's office.

9. "Knowingly" means actual awareness, at the time of the act or practice complained of, of the falsity, deception, or unfairness of the act or practice giving rise to the consumer's claim or, in an action brought under Subdivision (2) of Subsection (a) of Section 17.50, actual awareness of the act, practice, condition, defect, or failure constituting the breach of warranty, but actual awareness may be inferred where objective manifestations indicate that a person acted with actual awareness.

10. "Business consumer" means an individual, partnership, or corporation who seeks or acquires by purchase or lease any goods or services for commercial or business use. The term does not include this state or a subdivision or agency of this state.

11. "Economic damages" means compensatory damages for pecuniary loss, including costs of repair and replacement. The term does not include exemplary damages or damages for physical pain and mental anguish, loss of consortium, disfigurement, physical impairment or loss of companionship and society.

12. "Residence" means a building: (A) that is a single-family house, duplex, triplex or quadruplex or a unit in a multiunit residential structure in which title to the individual units is transferred to the owners

under a condominium or cooperative system; and (B) that is occupied or to be occupied as the consumer's residence.

13. "Intentionally" means actual awareness of the falsity, deception or unfairness of the act or practice, or the condition, defect or failure constituting a breach of warranty giving rise to the consumer's claim, coupled with the specific intent that the consumer act in detrimental reliance on the falsity or deception or in detrimental ignorance of the unfairness. Intention may be inferred from objective manifestations that indicate that the person acted intentionally or from facts showing that a defendant acted with flagrant disregard of prudent and fair business practices to the extent that the defendant should be treated as having acted intentionally.

Deceptive Acts

The act prohibits all false, misleading and deceptive acts in the conduct of business. The law lists a number of specific activities that violate the act. Although an awareness of the enumerated prohibited acts is important, a violation of the act is not limited to those listed and could include any type of deceptive act committed in a consumer transaction. The enumerated acts in Section 17.46—commonly called the *Laundry List*—include, among others, the following:

- Passing off goods or services as those of another.

- Causing confusion or misunderstanding as to the source, sponsorship, approval or certification of goods or services.

- Causing confusion or misunderstanding as to affiliation, connection or association with, or certification by another.

- Using deceptive representations or designations of geographic origin in connection with goods or services.

- Representing that goods or services have sponsorship, approval, characteristics, ingredients, uses, benefits, or quantities which they do not have or that a person has a sponsorship, approval, status, affiliation, or connection which he does not.

- Representing that goods are original or new if they are deteriorated, reconditioned, reclaimed, used, or secondhand.

- Representing that goods or services are of a particular standard, quality, or grade, or that goods are of a particular style or model, if they are of another.

- Disparaging the goods, services, or business of another by false or misleading representation of facts.

- Advertising goods or services with intent not to sell them as advertised.

- Making false or misleading statements of fact concerning the reasons for, existence of, or amount of price reductions.

- Representing that an agreement confers or involves rights, remedies, or obligations which it does not have or involve or which are prohibited by law.

- Knowingly making false or misleading statements of fact concerning the need for parts, replacement or repair service.

- Misrepresenting the authority of a salesman, representative or agent to negotiate the final terms of a consumer transaction.

- Representing that work or services have been performed on, or parts replaced in, goods when the work or services were not performed or the parts replaced.

- The failure to disclose information concerning goods or services which was known at the time of the transaction if such failure to disclose such information was intended to induce the consumer into a transaction into which the consumer would not have entered had the information been disclosed.

- Using the term "corporation," "incorporated," or an abbreviation of either of those terms in the name of a business entity that is not incorporated under the laws of this state or another jurisdiction.

- Taking advantage of a disaster declared by the governor under Chapter 418, Government Code, by:

  a. selling or leasing fuel, food, medicine, or another necessity at an exorbitant or excessive price; or

  b. demanding an exorbitant or excessive price in connection with the sale or lease of fuel, food, medicine, or another necessity.

Many of the prohibited acts listed above appear, at first glance, not applicable to real estate transactions; for instance, those sections pertaining to repairs. Real estate licensees often find that the parties require that repairs be completed prior to the closing of a sale or in conjunction with property management contracts. Licensees must exercise care when involved in these aspects of transactions.

Two aspects of the enumerated acts are important to remember. First, no law requires that the consumer prove the offending party intended to deceive or misrepresent the facts. In most cases, an *innocent misrepresentation* is as much a violation of the act as a fraudulent misrepresentation; it is not a defense to a lawsuit brought under this act that the defendant did not know that his or her action was illegal. Second, the act prohibits not only misrepresentations but also *misleading statements,* statements that lead the consumer in the wrong direction or create a misconception of the facts.

If a licensee has been found liable in a DTPA lawsuit, the court cannot suspend or revoke a real estate license; however, under the Real Estate License Act (TRELA) there are provisions for suspending or revoking a license for similar violations. Some of the provisions of TRELA §15(a)(6) that address actions corresponding with the DTPA are

A. making a material misrepresentation, or failing to disclose to a potential purchaser any latent structural defect or any other defect known to the broker or salesperson. Latent structural defects and other defects do not refer to trivial or insignificant defects but refer to those defects that would be a significant factor to a reasonable and prudent purchaser in making a decision to purchase;

* * *

B. pursuing a continued and flagrant course of misrepresentation or making of false promises through agents, salespersons, advertising, or otherwise;

* * *

D. failing to make clear, to all parties to a transaction, which party he is acting for, or receiving compensation from more than one party except with the full knowledge and consent of all parties;

* * *

H. accepting, receiving, or charging an undisclosed commission, rebate, or direct profit on expenditures made for a principal;

* * *

I. soliciting, selling, or offering for sale real property under a scheme or program that constitutes a lottery or deceptive practice;

* * *

K. guaranteeing, authorizing, or permitting a person to guarantee that future profits will result from a resale of real property;

* * *

M. inducing or attempting to induce a party to a contract of sale or lease to break the contract for the purpose of substituting in lieu thereof a new contract;

* * *

V. conduct which constitutes dishonest dealings, bad faith, or untrustworthiness . . .

Verbal And Nonverbal Communications. Licensees must be aware of both verbal and nonverbal communications with customers and clients. TRELA follows and expands on many of the prohibitions of the DTPA, and licensees can assume that a customer or client who files a DTPA suit also will file a complaint with the Texas Real Estate Commission. The following case demonstrates how liability can occur, even though no verbal representation had been made to the party that claimed there had been a violation of the DTPA.

 EXAMPLE: *Orkin Exterminating Co., Inc. v. LeSassier,* 688 S.W.2d 651 (Tex. Civ. App. 9 Dist. 1985). Ms. LeSassier contracted with Orkin Exterminating Co., Inc., for termite extermination services. On the date the serviceperson came to Ms. LeSassier's home, she let him in and then returned to her employment. Almost a year later, she noticed evidence of termite activity. An Orkin employee returned and treated her home. When she continued to have problems, she hired another firm of exterminators. She had the damage to her home repaired and sued Orkin, alleging violation of the DTPA in that Orkin had "represented that work or services had been performed when such work or services had not been performed." Orkin's defense was that the DTPA did not apply because Orkin made no verbal assertion that it had performed the termite treatment. The court held that the serviceperson's coming to Ms. LeSassier's home, beginning treatments and then leaving, never to return, was a representation that all the treatments called for in the contract had been performed.

While licensees are not responsible for performing repairs, they could be named in a DTPA suit as a result of recommending a particular serviceperson or company to a client or customer who subsequently believes that the DTPA has been violated.

Waivers of Rights under the DTPA

Under certain circumstances, consumers may wish to waive their rights under the DTPA. For example, a buyer may wish to purchase a property in obviously poor condition. The seller, however, fearful of a lawsuit related to the condition of the property after the sale, may refuse to sell the property to the buyer unless the buyer agrees to waive his or her right to sue the seller under the DTPA.

In this case, the buyer may be willing to waive the right in order to acquire the property. In general, however, a waiver of the right to bring action is considered to be "contrary to public policy and is unenforceable and void" [Sec. 17.42.(a)]. This prohibition of waiver of rights had been virtually absolute until 1995, when the act was amended to allow consumers to waive their rights under certain *very* strict guidelines. A written waiver is valid and enforceable if

- it is in writing and signed by the consumer;
- the consumer is represented by an attorney, in purchasing the goods or services, who is not directly or indirectly involved in or suggested by, or identified by the defendant or the defendant's agent and
- the consumer is not in a significantly disparate bargaining position.

The waiver is required to be in conspicuous, boldface type that is at least 10-point size, and to be titled "Waiver of Consumer Rights" or words of similar meaning. The body of the waiver must have wording similar to the following:

I waive my right under the Deceptive Trade Practice—Consumer Protection Act, Section 17.41 et seq., Business & Commerce Code, a law that gives consumers special rights and protections. After consultation with an attorney of my own selection, I voluntarily consent to this waiver [Sec. 17.42.(c)(3)].

One of the greatest concerns in real estate contracts has been whether a property that is purchased in "as is" condition is subject to DTPA. The following case is clear as to commercial buyers.

 EXAMPLE: *The Prudential Insurance Company v. Jefferson Associates, Ltd.,* 896 S.W.2d. 156 (Texas 1995). F. B. Goldman purchased a four-story office building from Prudential Insurance in 1984 on an "as is" basis. The purchaser was allowed full access to the property to conduct inspections, which he did. In fact, Mr. Goldman had an independent engineering firm, his maintenance supervisor and his property manager inspect the property. The inspections showed no evidence that the building contained asbestos. After the sale, Goldman conveyed the property to the limited partnership, Jefferson Associates, Ltd., of which he was a partner. Several years after the sale it was discovered that the building had a fireproofing material that contained asbestos. Goldman sued under DTPA.

The Supreme Court of Texas concluded that there was no evidence that Prudential had knowledge of the asbestos and therefore could not disclose its existence. They also noted that the purchase price reflected the "as is" terms, and that the purchaser was responsible for accepting the risk involved in such a transaction. The court ruling stated, "A buyer who agrees, freely and without fraudulent inducement, to purchase commercial real estate 'as is' cannot recover damages from the seller when the property is later discovered not to be in as good a condition as the buyer believed it was when he inspected it before the sale." The sales contract was clear regarding the buyer's duty to satisfy himself as to condition and that he was waiving his rights to action under the DTPA.

The courts are very careful to consider all of the facts in each case. It appears that courts place more responsibility on the buyer in a commercial transaction than in a residential transaction. This may be due to the assumption that commercial buyers are generally more knowledgeable, may be more likely to seek advice and opinions from experts and may be better able to assess their risks than average residential buyers. However, in *Prudential v. Jefferson,* the Texas Supreme Court noted that for an "as is" agreement to be effective, it must stand up to the following tests:

- All known defects must be disclosed by the seller.

- The seller must not obstruct the buyer's attempts to inspect the property.

- The "as is" clause must be an important element of the contract, not an incidental or boilerplate provision.

- The buyer and seller must not be in disparate (relatively unequal) bargaining positions.

Subsequently an appellate court used the *Prudential v. Jefferson* case in deciding the following "as is" residential property case, even though the purchaser was never required to sign a waiver of his rights under DTPA.

EXAMPLE: *Erwin v. Smiley,* 975 S.W.2d 335; (Tex. App. 1998). Archie and Maxine Erwin sold their property to David Smiley in "as is" condition. On several occasions prior to entering in the purchase agreement, Mr. Smiley inspected the property. On one occasion Mr. Smiley asked Mr. Erwin whether there had been termite problems. Mr. Erwin said that there had been termites and that they had remedied the problem. The purchase contract was drawn on a preprinted form showing that in the "Property Condition" section that the "Buyer accepts the Property in its present condition, subject only to any lender required repairs and as is." "As is" was typed into the blank supplied on the contract.

Approximately six months after Mr. Smiley bought the house he noticed termite trails. He had the house inspected by a termite contractor who found live termite infestation and said that he saw no evidence that the house had ever been treated for termites. The contractor also gave the opinion that the house had be infested for five to ten years. Mr. Smiley sued.

The jury in the lower court found that Archie Erwin committed false, misleading or deceptive acts or practices and awarded Smiley $15,000 to treat and/or repair the termite damage, and $30,000 in attorney's fees. The Erwins appealed.

The appellate court observed, "The validity of the 'as is' agreement is determined in light of the sophistication of the parties, the terms of the 'as is' agreement, whether the 'as is' clause was freely negotiated, whether it was an arm's length transaction, and whether there was a knowing misrepresentation or concealment of a known fact." They went on to say, "The evidence shows that the Erwins and Smiley were similarly situated parties and that the sale was an arm's length transaction. This transaction involved the sale of a residence. . . . Further, both parties were represented by counsel, and there was no evidence of a special relationship between the parties which would keep it from being an arm's length transaction. The evidence also shows that the 'as is' provision was freely negotiated, not merely 'boilerplate' language in the preprinted earnest money contract form; it was specifically added. There was evidence that, during the negotiations, Archie made Smiley aware that the sale was on an 'as is' basis. Smiley consulted his attorney before signing the earnest money contract. Furthermore, Smiley testified that he did not rely on any statement that Archie Erwin made regarding the meaning of the 'as is' term." The appellate court reversed the decision of the lower court in favor of the Erwins.

This case shows that the courts are beginning to use the same standard for residential transactions as for commercial transactions. This could be due to the greater sophistication of many sellers and purchasers in today's real estate market, and the greater number of principals who are seeking legal advice during the negotiating process.

Notice and Inspection

Before filing a lawsuit under DTPA, a consumer must give the would-be defendant a 60-day notice of intent to bring suit and must provide "reasonable detail of the consumer's specific complaint and the amount of economic damages, damages for mental anguish, and expenses, including attorneys' fees" [Sec. 17.505.(a)]. The defendant then may inspect the goods that are the basis of the intended action and attempt to settle the matter with the consumer.

The defendant can make an offer to settle the matter with the consumer. The law states that an offer to settle is not admission of guilt or wrongdoing. Often a defendant wants to settle just to avoid the cost and aggravation of a lawsuit.

If the defendant makes an offer to settle the matter and the consumer rejects the settlement, the defendant may file the offer with the court. If the court finds that the offer was "the same as, substantially the same as, or more than the damage found by the trier of fact [judge or jury], the consumer may not recover as damages any amount in excess of the *lesser* of:

1. the amount of damages tendered in the settlement offer; or

2. the amount of damages found by the trier of fact" [Sec. 17.5052.(g)].

If the court finds that the settlement offer was fair, it will determine what reasonable attorneys' fees would have been *before* the offer was rejected and use that amount in calculating the total settlement. The consumer could not recover the attorneys' fees incurred for representation in court.

Exemptions

In the past, most transactions could fall under the guidelines of the DTPA. The 1995 amendment provided for some exemptions important to real estate. The following exemption from prohibition against waiver under Section 17.49 (f) may apply if the transaction is the result of a written contract and meets the following criteria:

- The contract relates to a transaction, a project, or a set of transactions related to the same project involving total consideration by the consumer of more than $100,000.

- In negotiating the contract the consumer is represented by legal counsel who is not directly or indirectly identified, suggested or selected by the defendant or an agent of the defendant.

- The contract does not involve the consumer's residence.

Another exemption enacted in the new legislation exempts all transactions, whether written or not, that have consideration that exceeds

$500,000. This exemption does not include a consumer's residence [Section 17.49(g)].

Unconscionable Action

The DTPA also provides that a consumer can sue if the consumer has suffered economic damages produced by unconscionable action by another. *Unconscionable action* is a form of deception. Equitable relief can be afforded to a person who has been tricked or swindled to such an extent that it would be unfair to allow the transaction to stand. Unconscionability is a difficult legal concept to grasp because it is intentionally vague. In the case that follows, the Texas Supreme Court provides some guidance in understanding the type of action prohibited.

 EXAMPLE: *Smith v. Levine*, 911 S.W.2d 427, (Tex. App. 1995). The Smiths decided to sell a property they had previously leased. The tenant was interested in purchasing the house and had a structural inspection performed. The written report stated that the foundation "has deflected to the extent that it has damaged the superstructure and therefore the foundation is defective." The tenant decided against purchasing the property; however, he offered to give the seller a copy of the report if he would reimburse him for one-half of the cost. The sellers declined, and subsequently marketed the property themselves. They prepared newspaper ads and brochures claiming the property was in "excellent condition."

The Levines became interested in the home. They noticed minor cracks and a slight slope to the floor in one area; however, Mr. Smith assured them that the cracks were only superficial. They had the structure inspected; their inspector reported minor and superficial cracks in the foundation. The Levines closed the transaction, giving the Smiths full price with $25,000 at closing and a promissory note for the balance. They lived in the home for three years, until they had financial difficulties, and they decided to sell. They listed the home with a real estate firm, disclosing their inspection reports and subsequently accepted an offer from David Holmes to buy the home. By coincidence, Holmes employed the same structural inspector as the former tenant; the findings were the same. Holmes demanded the return of his earnest money and termination of the contract; the Levines immediately complied.

The Levines sued under DTPA. The Smiths then decided to call the promissory due and started foreclosure proceedings. Only a restraining order, issued three days before the foreclosure sale date, halted the foreclosure.

In the lower court, the jury found that the Smiths "knowingly engaged in a false, misleading or deceptive act or practice, as well as an unconscionable action or course of action, and both were a producing cause of damages to the Levines." They also found that the Smiths had knowingly or intentionally committed fraud. The jury's award was the difference in value of the house of $33,800, $14,400 each for Levine's mental anguish, and punitive damages in the amount of $65,000 against Mr. Smith and $32,750 against Mrs. Smith. The Smiths appealed; the appellate court affirmed the lower court's decision.

Producing Cause

Under the DTPA, the consumer must prove that a misleading, deceptive or fraudulent act was a producing cause of loss. A *producing cause* is a contributing factor that, in the ordinary sequence, produces injury or damage. In common-law and statutory fraud causes of action, the injured party is required to prove that the misrepresentation was of a relevant (material) fact and that this misrepresentation directly caused economic loss. Under the DTPA, the consumer is not required to prove that the deceptive act related to material fact or that the consumer relied on that misrepresentation. Furthermore, the consumer is not required to prove that the misleading or deceptive act directly caused his or her injury, only that they were a contributing factor.

 EXAMPLE: *Cameron v. Terrell and Garrett, Inc.,* 618 S.W.2d 535 (Tex. 1981). Jerry and JoAnn Cameron purchased a house. The house had been listed for sale by the sellers with their real estate agent, Terrell and Garrett, Inc. Terrell and Garrett had listed the house in the multiple-listing service (MLS) and, in doing so, included a statement that the house contained 2,400 square feet. The Camerons were shown this information about the house by their real estate agent. Subsequently, the Camerons closed the sale and moved in. The Camerons then had the house measured and discovered that it contained 2,245 square feet of heated and air-conditioned space. However, if the garage, porch and wall space were included, there was a total of 2,400 square feet. The Camerons sued Terrell and Garrett, Inc., under the Texas Deceptive Trade Practices Act, alleging misrepresentation. They claimed that Terrell and Garrett, Inc., had falsely represented the number of square feet in the house. They sought actual damages of $3,419.30.

After a trial and two appeals, judgment was rendered for the Camerons. The court stated that Terrell and Garrett had misrepresented the number of square feet through the MLS and that the Camerons were consumers under the law, even though they had no contact with Terrell and Garrett. The Camerons were required to prove that they had been adversely affected by the misrepresentation.

 EXAMPLE: *Weitzel v. Barnes,* 691 S.W.2d 598 (Tex. 1985). Barnes/ Segraves Development Company, seller, and the Weitzels, buyers, signed a contract to purchase a remodeled home. The written contract gave the Weitzels the right to inspect, among other things, the plumbing and air-conditioning systems in the house. The contract provided that if the Weitzels were dissatisfied with the systems, they could reject the contract. A contract addendum further provided that failure of the buyers to inspect and give written notice of repairs to the seller constituted a waiver of the buyers' inspection rights and amounted to the buyers' consent to purchase the property as-is. The Weitzels did not inspect the house. Prior to and after signing the contract, the seller had told the Weitzels that the plumbing and air-conditioning systems complied with the Fort Worth building code specifications.

After moving into the house, the Weitzels found that the equipment did not function properly and was not in compliance with the city code. The Weitzels claimed that the oral representations were deceptive acts under the DTPA. Barnes/Segraves asserted as its defense the written contract provision regarding inspections, repairs and waiver. The seller also argued that the buyers did not rely on the representations and, in fact, had notice prior to consummation of the sale that the city had posted a condemned notice on the house.

The court held for the Weitzels, reasoning that the buyers were not seeking to contradict the terms of the written agreement, nor were they claiming a breach of contract. Therefore, the verbal misrepresentations were admissible to prove a violation of the DTPA. Next, the court stated that the act does not require proof that the Weitzels relied on the oral misrepresentations. Reliance is not an element of producing cause. The court did point out that had the seller remained silent and not spoken to the quality or characteristics of the plumbing and air-conditioning systems, the seller would not have been liable. The contract provision regarding inspection, repairs and waiver would have been controlling.

■ Damages

The DTPA provides that a prevailing consumer can recover his or her economic damages, attorney fees and court costs. In addition, the judge or jury can award the consumer a sum of money in excess of his or her economic losses for mental anguish if the conduct has been committed knowingly or intentionally.

The consumer may receive *no more than* three times the economic damages for mental anguish if the act is committed *knowingly.* If the act is committed *intentionally,* the consumer may receive no more than three times the amount for economic damages *and* mental anguish.

■ Defenses

How can a person limit his or her liability for a deceptive or misleading act or practice? The DTPA specifically limits the enforceability of any waiver (written or oral) by the consumer to sue under the act. The act, however, does establish a procedure for limiting liability and for recovering damages from a consumer if the suit is filed in bad faith and if notice and settlement provisions have been satisfied. As mentioned earlier, some defense can be mounted during the required 60-day notice period if the defendant makes a reasonable offer of settlement. In addition, a second defense is the giving of timely written notice to the consumer of the broker's reliance on some other written information. This can greatly assist brokers and salespersons because they frequently rely on information provided by others, such as sellers, property inspectors, appraisers, engineers and perhaps even government agents. The key to the success of this defense depends on the following:

- The licensee must have received the information in writing.

- The licensee must have given written notice to the consumer prior to consummation of the sale that the licensee was relying on this written information.

- The licensee must establish that he or she did not know and could not have known that the information was false or inaccurate.

It is important for a licensee to remember that reliance on the written information must be reasonable considering his or her expertise in the area. However, a licensee who can prove that he or she has met this defense will not be liable for the consumer's damages.

In addition to protection for licensees, the following case illustrates how giving full and complete disclosure, unlimited access for the purpose of inspections, and clearly wording the terms of a purchase contract can be a defense for sellers against an unwarranted DTPA suit.

 EXAMPLE: *Zak v. Parks,* 729 S.W. 2d. 875 (Tex. App. 1987). The Zaks purchased a home with known and disclosed foundation problems from the Parks. Mr. Zak was an engineer and a licensed real estate agent and received a real estate commission from the Parks when he and his wife purchased the home. The Zaks were allowed to inspect the home, and in fact, did so four times before contracting to buy. In addition the Zaks hired a structural expert who discovered a fracture in the foundation of the master bedroom and estimated necessary repairs to be approximately $2000. After the inspection, an earnest money contract was drafted by Mr. Zak and signed by both Mr. & Mrs. Zak and Mr. & Mrs. Parks. It provided that the Parks would escrow funds in the amount of $2,300 "to correct structural defect of slab fracture." Any funds remaining in the escrow account after payment for repairs were to be returned to the Parks. Subsequently, the Parks placed $2,300 in an escrow account. Six weeks after closing Mr. Zak claimed that the slab problems were greater than he had anticipated and demanded that the Parks pay $17,300 for foundation repair, $15,000 to level the house with fifty piers and pay for numerous other unrelated repairs.

At trial, brought under the DTPA, Mr. Zak admitted that he had not used the escrowed funds to repair the foundation nor had he refunded the unused funds to the Parks. Mr. Barron, a foundation repair expert, testified that the foundation could have been repaired for less than $2,000.

The appellate court found, "The written agreement limiting the Parks' liability for foundation repair, coupled with Mr. Barron's testimony, is sufficient factual evidence for the jury to decide that the lawsuit demanding that the Parks assume additional liability for foundation repair was brought in bad faith or to harass the Parks.". . . "From the terms of the earnest money contract, it is clearly evident that the Zaks expressly agreed to a limit of $2,300 on the liability of the Parks for all expenses involved in repairing the slab. A lawsuit brought to recover an additional amount for repair of the slab defect is groundless as a matter of law." The court considered the case frivolous and unwarranted and entered a take nothing judgment against Zak. In addition, Zak was ordered to pay the Park's attorneys' fees in the amount of $42,500.

Unsuccessful Defenses. The previous case illustrated a successful defense against a DTPA claim. The following cases illustrate the powerful protection the DTPA offers to consumers and that many defenses that might have been possible under common law or statutory fraud are not available in DTPA cases.

 EXAMPLE: *Kennemore v. Bennett,* 755 S.W.2d 89 (Tex. 1988). Thomas and Charles Kennemore contracted with builder Bill Bennett for the construction of a home. When the Kennemores refused to pay Bennett the balance due on the contract and $4,542.55 for extras, he placed a mechanic's and a materialman's lien against the property. Bennett then sued to foreclose his liens. The Kennemores defended against Bennett's suit and counterclaimed that Bennett had failed to construct the house in a good and workmanlike manner. The Kennemores asserted this breach of warranty action under the Texas Deceptive Trade Practices Act. Prior to trial, the Kennemores paid Bennett in full, but proceeded to trial on their DTPA claim against Bennett. Bennett argued that the Kennemores had waived their DTPA action by moving into the house and paying Bennett the money demanded in Bennett's lawsuit. The Texas Supreme Court held that the DTPA claim was not waived by the consumers simply because they accepted the allegedly defective home.

 EXAMPLE: *Ojeda de Toca v. Wise,* 748 S.W.2d 449 (Tex. 1988). Rocio Ojeda de Toca purchased a house from Wise Developments, Inc. Approximately 11 months prior to the purchase, the city of Houston had recorded a document ordering that the house be demolished and placed a lien against the property for the demolition costs. Although Wise was aware of the demolition order, it did not notify Toca. While Toca was out of the country, the city demolished the house pursuant to the demolition order. Toca sued Wise for misrepresentation, fraud and violation of the Texas Deceptive Trade

Practices Act. Wise asserted in its defense that Toca had constructive notice of the demolition order under the recording statute. The court held that the legislature, in passing the DTPA, did not intend to bar a consumer's DTPA or fraud claim because an examination of the county records could have disclosed the seller's deception. The court also held that the recording statute is not to protect perpetrators of fraud. Therefore, Toca was allowed to recover from Wise for its failure to disclose the existence of the demolition order.

 EXAMPLE: *Alvarado v. Bolton,* 749 S.W.2d 47 (Tex. 1988). The Alvarados purchased 50 acres of land in Fort Bend County, Texas, from Bolton. The sales contract did not reserve any mineral rights for the seller (Bolton), but at the closing the deed specifically reserved for Bolton one-half of the mineral rights. After oil was discovered on the land, the Alvarados learned of Bolton's mineral reservations and sued to reform the deed and to receive damages under the DTPA. Bolton asserted that under the doctrine of merger, once a deed is delivered and accepted, the sales contract becomes merged into the deed and only those terms in the deed can be used to resolve disputes. Therefore, because the deed specifically reserved the mineral rights and the Alvarados accepted the deed, the Alvarados were not entitled to the mineral rights.

The court held that the doctrine of merger cannot be used to defeat a DTPA claim for breach of an express warranty made in a sales contract. Therefore, the Alvarados can prevail against Bolton if they can prove that Bolton had breached the sales contract.

Groundless Lawsuits

Brokers may be faced with groundless lawsuits that rob them of time, energy and productive activities. The law provides that if a suit is groundless, brought in bad faith or brought for the purpose of harassment, the defendant will be compensated for reasonable attorneys' fees and court costs. While this doesn't give compensation for lost time and energy it can have the effect of discouraging frivolous lawsuits.

■ Summary

Fraud is a deceptive act practiced deliberately by one person in an attempt to gain an unfair advantage over another. *Misrepresentation* is a false statement made negligently or innocently that is a material factor in another's decision to contract. In Texas, one of the methods for holding a person liable for fraud or misrepresentation is the DTPA, which prohibits not only false statements but also misleading statements or acts. A consumer who can prove that a misleading act was the producing cause of an injury can recover his or her economic damages, attorney fees, court costs and additional compensation up to three times the amount of the actual losses. One defense that can be particularly useful to brokers is giving timely written notice to a buyer or seller that the broker is relying on written information supplied by someone else. If this notice is given in a timely and proper manner, the broker is relieved from liability for false or misleading statements contained in such written reports.

■ Key Points

- The purpose of the DTPA is to protect consumers against false, misleading and deceptive business practices, unconscionable action and breaches of warranty.

- Under the DTPA a consumer may not have to provide proof that there was an intention to deceive or mislead, only that the result of the of the action or inaction did deceive or mislead. Before filing a lawsuit, the consumer must give a 60-day notice, following which the would-be defendant may inspect the "goods" that are the subject of the complaint and attempt to settle the matter with the consumer.

- The consumer may recover economic damages, attorney fees and court costs. If the act was done *knowingly or intentionally,* the consumer could receive up to three times the amount.

- The best defense is to encourage the use of information from reliable sources other than the broker, such as appraisers, engineers, property inspectors and government sources.

■ Suggestions for Brokers

Brokers should be particularly careful to instruct all associated licensees adequately about the proper means of obtaining information and subsequently relaying that information to clients and customers. A written policy of documenting all contacts and all sources of information could be helpful in the event of a lawsuit by a client or customer.

■ QUIZ

1. The DTPA prohibits as unlawful all of the following *except*

   A. false acts.   C. deceptive acts.
   B. misleading acts.   D. moral acts.

2. Which of the following statements is *not* true with respect to the Texas DTPA?

   A. A licensee can safely rely on a written and signed waiver.
   B. There is no requirement that the offending party intended to deceive.
   C. To prevail, the injured party must be a consumer as defined in the act.
   D. A written offer of settlement is some defense.

3. Which of the following is *not* an example of damages available under the Texas DTPA?

   A. Economic damages
   B. Mandatory four times the actual damages
   C. Court costs and attorney fees
   D. Three times the economic damages

4. In defending against a DTPA case, a licensee using the timely written notice defense must include all of the following *except*

   A. the licensee must have given written notice to the consumer prior to consummation of the sale that the broker was relying on this written notice.
   B. the licensee must have received the information in writing.
   C. the licensee must establish that he or she did not and could not know that the information was false or inaccurate.
   D. the licensee must produce evidence that three independent sources were consulted before the written notice was submitted to the consumer.

5. Which of the following is provided by the Texas Deceptive Trade Practices–Consumer Protection Act?

   A. A reasonable offer of settlement made within specified time limits is some defense.
   B. Transmittal of written information prepared by others along with a written statement of reliance on such information is a defense.
   C. Recovery of court costs and attorney fees is possible if the lawsuit is frivolous or harassing.
   D. All of the above

6. All of the following are included in the DTPA definition of *consumer except*

   A. individuals.
   B. partnerships and corporations.
   C. business consumers with assets of $25 million or more.
   D. the state of Texas.

7. To be considered a violation of the DTPA,

   A. it is not necessary for a consumer to prove that the licensee intended to deceive or misrepresent the facts.
   B. it is necessary for a consumer to prove that the licensee intended to deceive or misrepresent the facts.
   C. it is not necessary for the court to prove that the licensee intended to deceive or misrepresent the facts.
   D. it is necessary for the court to prove that the licensee intended to deceive or misrepresent the facts.

8. When a real estate salesperson licensee has been found guilty of a DTPA violation, the court

   A. can suspend or revoke the license of the salesperson.
   B. cannot suspend or revoke the license of the salesperson.
   C. can suspend or revoke the license of the sponsoring broker.
   D. can suspend or revoke the licenses of both the salesperson and the sponsoring broker.

9. *Unconscionable actions* in the DTPA is a vague term that allows the courts to

   A. use their discretion in deciding cases where persons have been tricked or swindled.
   B. use whatever measure they deem appropriate when deciding all DTPA cases.
   C. ignore other DTPA cases in their decisions.
   D. apply strict guidelines to DTPA cases.

10. All waivers of rights under the DTPA are

   A. automatically unenforceable by the court.
   B. automatically enforceable by the court.
   C. legal and cannot be interpreted by the court.
   D. subject to the consideration of the court.

■ Discussion Question

1. What types of statements might a broker make that would lead to possible innocent misrepresentation under the DTPA (e.g., saying "this is a well maintained home" when it would be better to say "this home appears to be well maintained")?

CHAPTER 13

Putting It All Together

In earlier chapters, we saw licensees facing situations involving possible lawsuits in which agency status was the main issue. If the licensees had practiced preventive brokerage, they might have lessened their risk.

This chapter addresses the following:

Preventive Brokerage
Subjects to Discuss at the Listing Presentation
Listing Broker Working with Seller
Listing Broker Working with Buyer-Customer
Listing Broker and Buyer's Broker
Other Broker as Subagent of Seller
Other Broker as Buyer's Broker
Buyer's Broker
Intermediary
Dual Agent (Common Law)
Other Considerations
Presentation of Offers by Listing Broker
Retained Earnest Money in the Event of a Default
Commissions
Written Agreements
Using Rehearsed Dialogue
Dialogues for Brokerage Situations

■ Preventive Brokerage

Regardless of whether a broker represents the seller or the buyer, the broker should do three things:

1. Use written disclosures

2. Clarify his or her role in the transaction

3. Use the help of others when needed

Brokers should recognize that the most frequent basis for complaints against real estate licensees is their failure to disclose material facts. As the listing agent, a brokerage must be prepared to prove in a legal dispute with a buyer customer that important information was, in fact, provided or, on the other hand, that such disclosure was prohibited by law.

Brokers also can help protect themselves by clarifying their roles in the transaction to the buyer and the seller. When licensees represent sellers, they should discuss openly what they can and cannot do. For example, if the licensee has never handled a tax-deferred exchange or the sale of a business opportunity, the client (or customer) should be aware of that fact and suggest the possible use of other experts. To present oneself as an expert not only is grounds for loss of license but also could form the basis of a lawsuit under the Deceptive Trade Practices and Consumer Act (DTPA). [TRELA §15(a)(6)(W); 22 TAC §535.157]. The licensee should discuss his or her duties and responsibilities and those of other licensees, as well as the use of subagents and the multiple-listing service (MLS).

Licensees who work with the buyer should clarify whether the buyer is a client or a customer. If properties are shown to a buyer-client, the licensee should make sure that the buyer understands that the licensee does not warrant the condition of the property.

The following list describes some of the distinctions between duties that a broker, acting as an agent for only one party in a transaction, has to a client versus the broker's duties to a customer.

- To a customer, the seller's agent points out remedies available to the seller in the event of a buyer's default on the purchase contract. To a client, the buyer's agent might discuss the meaning of *liquidated damages* in this context, making sure the buyer knows the earnest money may be forfeited. (Naturally, an agent must be very careful to avoid giving legal advice. If buyers or sellers have any questions about the standard default provisions, they should be advised to consult an attorney.) However, if it is evident that non-judicial alternatives would save them both money and reduce both their risks, it would be appropriate, in fact, *mandatory,* that the licensee make the parties aware of such alternatives.

- When the seller carries back financing, the seller's agent could negotiate or attempt to negotiate into the original offer many contract provisions that are different from those the buyer's agent might propose. Such provisions could include prepayment, due on sale, right to make improvements, nonrecourse (no personal liability), reinstatement prior to foreclosure sale, grace periods, late charges and so on.

- To a customer, the seller's agent discloses the existence of an underground water easement. To a client, the buyer's agent goes an extra step and reviews a copy of the grant of easement, just in case any restrictions affect the buyer's expected use of the property, such as a prohibition against constructing any improvement within a certain distance of the easement.

- To a customer, the agent emphasizes the attractive features of the seller's property. To a client, the agent points out the negative features.

■ Subjects to Discuss at the Listing Presentation

Listing Broker or Associate Working with Seller

The listing broker or associate, in working with the seller, should perform the following actions:

- At the beginning of the listing appointment, but before an agency relationship is established or the listing agreement is discussed, explain and discuss in detail the brokerage company's agency disclosure form and the broker's agency position at that time, as well as the Texas Real Estate Commission's (TREC) "Information About Brokerage Services" notice or the equivalent, required by the Real Estate License Act (TRELA) §15C(d), regarding the written statement concerning agency options.

- Explain what subagency means and the optional use of subagents in an MLS and obtain the seller's authorization to use subagents.

- Explain how commission fees may be split and obtain the sellers' approval or disapproval to split fees with sellers' subagents or buyers' brokers.

- If the listing broker or associate is a member of the MLS, verify that the listing agreement contains a provision granting the seller's permission to use the MLS and to release marketing and sales data to the MLS. If the seller elects not to have the listing broker offer subagency or elects to offer it on a selective basis, a decision must be made regarding the use of an MLS.

- On the subject of compensation, explain to the seller how commissions may be split with other brokers. Because there is a big difference between authorizing the listing broker to split commissions with a buyer's broker and authorizing the broker to split with a subagent of the seller, the seller's attention should be clearly directed to this provision before he or she signs the listing. If the listing broker decides to offer other brokers a less-than-attractive commission split, the seller should be notified because it may mean that other brokers will be less motivated to show the seller's property;

- Explain that many offers presented by buyers' brokers will contain a provision for the seller to pay the buyer's broker's fee and that the listing brokerage may be willing to compensate the seller by lowering its commission. The seller should be informed that compensation of the buyer's broker is another negotiable concession, like fixing the roof or paying the buyer's discount points, and that the seller is under no obligation to pay the buyer's broker.

- Explain how the seller may permit the listing broker to offer a commission split to other brokers but not to offer subagency (subagency optional).

- Explain the brokerage's policies on intermediary brokerage.

- Explain to the seller that it is customary to work with other real estate brokers or their associates to increase the likelihood of finding a suitable buyer for the seller's property.

Listing Broker or Associate Working with Buyer-Customer

At first contact concerning a specific property, the listing broker or associate should present and explain to a buyer-customer

- the TREC "Information About Brokerage Services" or equivalent;
- the difference between a client and a customer in terms of services, duties and appropriate expectations;
- that the broker is employed by the seller to sell the seller's property;
- that the buyer is free to seek and retain his or her own technical advisers;
- that if the buyer decides not to buy the listed property, the buyer may wish to use the services of the listing broker to search for another appropriate property; if so, the agency relationship and whether the buyer is a customer or a client must be clarified;
- the in-house sales practices of the listing broker; and
- that it is customary for a broker to show prospective buyers other listed properties.

In addition, listing brokers may

- provide ready access to inventory, including the MLS;
- collect pertinent data on property taxes, utility costs and general real estate values;
- provide information on municipal services and amenities;
- discuss financing alternatives;
- discuss loan qualification and processing;
- show properties;
- make appointments and schedule conferences;
- suggest ways to improve the suitability of the home;
- clarify the buyer's needs versus wants and affordability;
- evaluate the need for property management;
- arrange for and review fire or liability insurance;
- check inventory of personal property;
- check applicable zoning and building permits;
- estimate closing costs and monthly payments;
- explain standard forms;
- explain escrow or settlement procedures;
- transmit an offer and act as liaison between the buyer and seller (though negotiating at all times on behalf of the seller's interests);
- monitor closing and time deadlines; and
- recognize the buyer's need for expert advice and suggest possible advisers.

Properties the buyer should see. The seller's agent or subagent can make appointments, show properties meeting the buyer's stated criteria, describe general features and conditions, direct the buyer to needed sources of information, complete standard forms and transmit offers to the seller.

If the buyer decides that neither the seller's property nor any other properties listed with the broker are suitable, the listing agent then can discuss what further services could be provided to help the buyer locate the right property. When the licensee suggests that the buyer search through the MLS system for suitable properties, the broker must decide whether to act in a subagent capacity or as a buyer's broker. In either case, a written agreement should be prepared.

Listing Broker and Buyer's Broker

If the listing broker receives an offer through a buyer's broker, the listing broker should

- be cooperative, while respecting the agency relationships between the broker and the seller and between the buyer's broker and the buyer;

- agree on how best to handle payment of commissions consistent with the authorization of both the seller and the buyer;

- communicate to the seller the buyer's intention for payment of fees relative to the buyer's broker;

- be prepared for healthy and open negotiations; and

- evaluate all terms of the buyer's offer, recognizing that they were prepared with the buyer's best interests in mind.

Listing brokers should be prepared for the likelihood that they will receive offers from other brokers submitted on behalf of buyer-clients and should welcome these offers, working with the buyers' brokers in a spirit of cooperation and goodwill. At the same time, the listing broker should respect the fact that each broker owes undivided loyalty to his or her respective principal. Listing brokers generally recognize that it is in the best interests of the seller to cooperate with all brokers, one of whom may have the ultimate buyer for the seller's property. The key question regarding any offer, whether from a buyer or a buyer's broker, is What is the net effect to the seller?

Other Broker as Subagent of Seller

In those cases in which the other broker is a subagent of the seller, the other broker must

- disclose to the buyer, either orally or in writing, that the broker is an agent of the seller;

- provide the written statement required by TRELA §15C(d), unless the buyer or tenant is represented by an agent or the statement is not required for some other legitimate reason;

- discuss with the buyer or tenant what type of services the subagent can and cannot give;

- notify listing broker that the other broker is a subagent of the seller;

- verify each proposed commission split arrangement;

- inquire whether there are any special instructions or new information or whether the home is already under contract;

- inquire about the listing broker's policies regarding handling earnest money deposits, using a lockbox, drafting offers, choosing an escrow company and placing a loan; and

- act as a subagent of the seller, at all times in the best interests of the seller.

In deciding whether to represent the seller, the other broker should understand that as a subagent of the seller, the other broker may not be privy to the same information as the listing broker. Many sellers are reluctant to pass on confidential information to the other broker for fear the other broker will divulge this information to the buyer. Other brokers cooperating with the seller through the listing broker are normally viewed by sellers as conduits for the flow of facts and figures between buyers and sellers.

Other Broker as Buyer's Broker

If the other broker decides to act as a buyer's broker, then, at initial contact when discussing the property and the seller, the other broker should

- disclose to all listing brokers of properties shown or to all owners selling their own properties that he or she is a buyer's broker and

- disclaim any agency or subagency relationship with the seller or the listing agent.

Immediate disclosure will enable the listing broker to take appropriate action to represent the seller's best interests in any showing of the property to a prospective buyer.

As a practical matter, a broker may not have any particular customer or client in mind at the time of initial contact—for instance, on an MLS tour of homes. A broker who sometimes represents buyers should, however, inform the listing broker or seller that the other broker may later return either with a client or with a customer. Therefore, the listing broker should keep this in mind when discussing any information concerning the seller's marketing position.

■ Buyer's Broker or Associate

The buyer's broker or associate should

- explain to the buyer the services to be rendered by first presenting and discussing the TREC "Information About Brokerage Services" or equivalent written statement and then explaining that the broker is not the buyer's agent unless and until a consensual agreement has been reached;

- after consultation regarding the role of a buyer's broker and consent of the buyer or tenant, obtain from the buyer or tenant a written buyer-representation agreement;

- determine how fees are to be paid;

- disclose to all listing brokers and sellers of properties at the time of initial contact, before showing any properties, that the broker is a buyer's broker and rejects any offer of agency or subagency from the seller, builder or listing broker; and

- discuss with the listing broker either the possibility of a fee-splitting arrangement or how the buyer's broker's fee may affect the offering price.

Intermediary

Under TRELA §15C, an intermediary must

- obtain the written consent of all parties in a form that meets the specific requirements set forth in TRELA §15C;

- treat all parties fairly and honestly and avoid disclosure of any information that is confidential or that a party has requested not to be disclosed;

- determine if appointments will be made and, if so, disclose in writing to all parties that such has been done; and

- comply with the provisions of TRELA.

Dual Agent (Common Law)

Although not likely, if a broker wishes to act as a dual agent, the broker must

- notify all principals and brokers that might become involved in a particular transaction, at the earliest practical point, of the dual agency and, preferably, obtain a written dual agency agreement, using a dual agency contract that sets forth the source of any expected compensation, and

- discuss with buyer and seller the specifics of how the broker intends to act as a fiduciary to both parties at the same time and clarify state law, including limitations as to opinions of market value, negotiating strategies and advocacy.

■ Other Considerations

Presentation of Offers by Listing Broker

One of the important issues discussed in an earlier chapter was the duty of an agent to disclose information to his or her client. A key disclosure to sellers is any offer made to the seller by a potential buyer. Typically, the listing broker (or associate of the listing broker) will present all offers directly to the seller. It is not the prerogative of a listing broker to decide if an offer will or will not be presented to a seller, even if the broker knows (or believes) that the offer will be unacceptable to the seller. Only the seller has the right to accept, reject or counter an offer. If a seller insists on considering only those offers that meet or exceed a certain price and/or terms criteria, then the licensee must obtain *written instructions* from the seller stating his or her wishes (this should be done only after a lengthy discussion of why this is unadvisable).

It is the duty of the listing broker to explain the offer to the seller and to give the seller an accurate estimate of the costs and net proceeds. All offers should be presented as soon as possible—once the offer is available to the listing agent. The offer is privileged information and should be kept confidential, and the terms of the offer should not be made available to other licensees or potential buyers. Many ethics hearings have centered around the mishandling of offers of other brokers.

EXAMPLE: Martin listed Rowan's property for $125,000. Rowan stated that he would only accept a full price cash offer, and that he would not consider paying any closing costs. Several offers were submitted that did not met Rowan's terms and he immediately rejected them.

Cher viewed the property and thought it would be a nice investment. She asked her agent, Sonny, to prepare an offer for $115,000 with the seller paying all closing costs. After Cher signed the offer Sonny presented it to Martin. Martin refused to present the offer, saying that he was sure Rowan would not accept it, as he had turned down similar offers in the past.

1. Using only the facts in the example, was Martin right to refuse to present the offer?

2. Would it be advisable for Sonny to contact the local Board of REALTORS® and file an ethics complaint?

DISCUSSION

It is very tempting to refuse to present an offer when you are "sure" that a seller will reject the offer and send you on your merry way. What many licensees do not recognize, however, is that the seller's circumstances could change at any time, and those changes might make him or her more receptive to price and/or terms that were previously unacceptable.

From an ethical standpoint, it is unfair to the seller to refuse to present an offer. Every offer gives the seller an opportunity to try to negotiate. Many sales that began with outrageous prices and terms were negotiated to the satisfaction of both parties. We as licensees do not have the crystal ball that tells us which of these offers will result in acceptance and which will not.

Presentation of multiple offers. On occasion, a listing broker may have more than one offer to present to a seller. This can occur (1) when a second offer is given to the listing broker before the first offer has been presented or (2) when a seller has received an offer, but has not yet accepted it, and another offer is made by a second buyer.

In the first case, where the broker actually has two offers to present, the broker should prepare presentations of both offers with the appropriate net proceed statements for the seller. In addition, the broker should collect as much information about the prospective buyers as possible to enable the seller to make an informed decision. For example, while one offer may net a greater net dollar amount for the seller, the financial strength of the buyer, type of financing and other terms may make the offer less desirable than another offer that provides fewer dollars to the seller but under much more favorable terms. Remember that typical residential sellers are not very sophisticated about these issues and therefore have employed brokers to represent them in these negotiations. It is the agent's duty to give the client his or her best advice and opinions.

The agent should give no preference to one offer simply because it was received before another, although in some cases the seller may wish to know and consider the information in the decision-making process. The primary duty of the agent is to give the seller as much information as possible and help the seller make the best possible decision.

The second situation occurs when the agent receives a second offer while the seller is deliberating a first offer. In this instance the agent should immediately notify the seller of a second offer and advise the seller not to accept the first offer until the seller has an opportunity to consider the second. Consider the following situation:

EXAMPLE: Sue, a broker-associate of REI Realty, has secured a listing for the sale of the Edwards' condominium for a price of $200,000. At 10 AM on Tuesday, Bob, the owner of Maxheimer Realty, brings an offer for $185,000 to Sue. Sue knows that the seller will not be available until 8 PM that evening. At 2 PM the same day, Brenda, Sue's best friend, who is also an associate of REI Realty, rushes into the office, finds Sue and exclaims, "Guess what—I have an offer on the Edwards' condo—overpriced though it is!" Brenda's customers have offered $192,000. Late in the afternoon, while preparing the offer presentations for the Edwards, Sue receives a call from Mr. Koepke, a prospect to whom Sue had shown the Edwards' property during an open house the previous Sunday. Koepke wishes to come into the office and make a written offer on the property.

Presuming that the three offers are comparable in terms and that the buyers are equally qualified consider the questions that follow.

? QUESTIONS

1. Should Sue disclose to Brenda the existence of the offer from Maxheimer Realty?

2. If so, how much information should be given to Brenda regarding the offer?

3. Should Maxheimer be made aware of the second offer?

4. If so, how much information should be given to Maxheimer regarding the offer?

5. Should Sue's customer be made aware of the other offers?

6. If so, how much information should be given to Sue's customer regarding the offers?

7. How should Sue handle securing the offer from Koepke, considering the fact that she already knows the details of the previous offers?

DISCUSSION

In general, any information that is available to one party should be available to the other parties concerned. While the details of the other offer(s) should not be disclosed, the fact that other offers exist may be disclosed. In a sense of fairness to all participants, if one agent is made aware of an existing offer all agents involved should be made aware. In the example above, if Brenda, in Sue's office, was told of Maxheimer's offer, Maxheimer should have been contacted and made aware that Sue now has another offer.

From the seller's perspective, it is beneficial for all parties to know that multiple offers have arrived. Buyers who are truly interested in winning the bid will often want to increase the price offered or make the terms more favorable to the seller, thus giving the seller a more profitable sale.

From the buyer's perspective, if the property is one that has high personal value, this information gives the buyer the opportunity to assess the original offer, determine if it could be made more appealing to the seller, and determine whether his or her financial means will allow an adjustment that would have a better chance at a successful bid. This could be a win-win situation for all parties.

Sue is in a position of a potential conflict of interest if she writes a contract for Mr. Koepke. She knows too much about the offers that have already been submitted. It would be wise to bring the sponsoring broker (or a person of the broker's choice) into the transaction. This person could write the contract for Koepke and negotiate the details, if necessary. Sue would then be able to present all offers to the seller knowing that she did not have undue influence on the construction of Koepke's offer and unethically slant the outcome in her favor.

Presentation of subsequent or backup offers. On occasion, a buyer wishes to make an offer to a seller even though the seller is already under contract with another buyer. The second offer is usually called a backup offer and would become effective only if the first offer did not proceed to closing.

This can create difficult situations for both the parties and the broker, particularly if the backup offer is more desirable to the seller than the first accepted offer. The parties should proceed carefully because contract law provides that the first buyer may have legal recourse if a second contract interferes with his or her contract rights (called *tortious interference with a contract*). The seller should not entertain backup offers without the permission of the first buyer, because the buyer is said to have *equitable title* to the property. Equitable title is the buyer's right to have the property transferred to him or her once all conditions of the contract are fulfilled.

The first step in handling these issues is for the listing agent to determine if the seller wishes to consider backup offers. The Texas Association of REALTORS® listing agreement addresses this issue. If the seller chooses to consider backups, the listing provides that "If Broker is to submit subsequent or back-up offers, Seller shall specifically provide in any contract for the sale of the Property with a buyer that Seller may receive and negotiate subsequent or back-up offers." The TREC "one- to four-family" promulgated sales contracts provide that the seller may continue to offer the property for sale and negotiate and accept backup offers. If a buyer does not wish the seller to continue to solicit backup offers, special provisions must be added to the TREC contract offer that prohibit the seller from doing so.

Retained Earnest Money in the Event of a Default

TREC-promulgated "Residential Sales Contract" forms do not contain a standard provision that permits the listing broker to share in a portion of the earnest money deposit retained by the seller as liquidated damages in the event the buyer defaults. However, most listing agreements do contain such a protection for the listing broker.

Few agreements permit the other broker, as a subagent of the seller, to share in the portion allocated to the listing broker in the event of default. The "Broker Information and Ratification of Fee" section of the TREC form is silent as to a subagent broker's right to share in earnest money distributions in the event of default. If the listing broker has agreed to split commissions with the buyer's broker, however, the contract should clarify whether the listing broker is under any obligation to share the earnest money with the buyer's broker in the event of buyer default, and the buyer would have to consent to such an arrangement.

Commissions

One of the most important considerations is how to handle commissions. All commissions are negotiable. Who pays the commission does not determine who represents whom. The listing and the selling commissions normally are paid out of the sales proceeds at closing, but they do not have to be. Brokerage commissions are normally paid from the seller's proceeds, but they do not have to be; the buyer or tenant may pay the broker by agreement as well.

Many offers from buyers' brokers provide that the commission of the buyer's broker will be paid from the sales proceeds at closing. The offer may state that the broker represents the buyer and will participate in the commissions paid to the listing broker by the seller at closing. The listing broker and the seller have to decide whether such a commission arrangement is consistent with their mutual best interests. In most cases, the listing broker and the seller already have discussed this possibility, perhaps at the listing stage, and have decided to modify the listing commission distribution, just as they do when there is a subagency commission split to pay.

The listing broker should counsel the seller early in the transaction about working with various types of offers, including those prepared by buyers' brokers. Such preparedness helps the listing broker deal properly with a buyer's broker and represent the seller in a professional manner.

If the listing broker refuses to adjust the listing commission, the transaction may not work because too much money then may be directed to brokerage commissions. This may be unacceptable to the seller, the buyer and any lender. Note that the decision to adjust commissions belongs to the broker and not to the associate who obtained the listing and works with the seller.

The buyer's broker is hired to help the buyer prepare the best offer (sometimes in conjunction with the buyer's attorney or accountant) on the most suitable property. Open, honest and healthy negotiations usually precede a well-drawn offer. The listing broker can expect negotiations with a buyer's broker to be more active than they would be if the other broker were a subagent of the seller. The listing broker should inspect the offer carefully, ask the buyer's broker questions about it and then recommend appropriate action to the seller.

If the other broker is a subagent of the seller, the issue of compensation is usually much easier. The listing broker is obligated to pay the other broker the amount set forth in the offer of subagency, assuming the transaction closes.

Written Agreements

Prudent brokers should attempt to enter into written agency agreements with clients. While it is sometimes legal, it is nonetheless unwise to proceed on oral agreements. Brokers must recognize that some buyers are reluctant to sign a buyer-representation agreement, even though they will be loyal customers, because

- such an arrangement has not been customary in the past,
- they fear the closing costs will increase by an additional broker fee,
- they do not want to be tied to an exclusive contract or
- they do not understand the benefits of representation.

■ Using Rehearsed Dialogue

The broker's newly licensed real estate associates are usually uncomfortable making cold calls (calls to people they do not know) to obtain listings. Through sales and counseling training sessions that use role playing and sample dialogue, associates often overcome their initial uneasiness. In fact, many associates are able to use these acquired presentation and counseling skills to help distinguish themselves from their competitors.

Many of the top programs that deal with real estate counseling and buyer's brokerage stress learning the practical skills of how to ask more effective questions of prospects and client applicants and how to listen actively. The goal is to select from a group of prospects those who may be clients and those who may be customers.

The following section, containing possible questions to use and dialogue to develop in discussing the agency relationship issue, introduces the kinds of role-playing situations designed to reduce the anxiety level of real estate agents when discussing agency. Brokers should develop their own role-playing situations for use in training sessions and expand on the brief dialogue included here. Some licensees may prefer to write out these dialogues and practice them with a tape recorder. Often, it is not what is said, but *how* it is said, that makes the difference in explaining an important issue, such as what role a licensee will play in a transaction and whom he or she will represent.

Dialogues for Brokerage Situations

The best way to become comfortable and competent in discussing agency alternatives is to role-play common situations. The following short scenarios indicate how some brokers handle such discussions of agency in a way that actually enhances the professional image of the real estate licensee. Using them as guidelines, write the dialogues in your own language and style. After completing your own versions of possible dialogues for the situations below, develop dialogues for other common situations. Try them out, critique them and refine them, based on the concepts of agency you have learned in this text and developed through your own research.

Scene 1: Natalie is a customer; Andrea is an associate of a firm that practices exclusive seller agency. Natalie walks into an open house where Andrea of Henderson Realty is on duty for the broker. Andrea hands Natalie a fact sheet, shows her around and asks Natalie general questions concerning Natalie's wants and needs in housing, the general price range Natalie is considering and square footage requirements. Andrea notices that Natalie is not the typical looker but is serious about purchasing a property and seems very interested in this house. Andrea decides to turn the discussion to the subject of agency before the conversation gets too specific and Natalie begins to reveal confidences or begins to develop unwarranted expectations of services and information.

Andrea: Has anyone explained to you, Natalie, how real estate licensees work and the agency relationships licensees are allowed to develop with clients?

Natalie: No.

Andrea: Regarding this house you're looking at, I am the agent for the seller. The reason I'm holding this open house is to expose the seller's property to the market in the hope that a buyer such as you will decide to purchase the property. As the seller's agent, I can point out the many features of the property; answer many of your questions about financing, ownership and closing; help you prepare an offer the way you want it; and promptly present your offer to the seller. By law, I am obligated to treat you, as a customer for my seller's property, honestly and fairly in the transaction. There are, however, other services that I cannot perform for you as an agent of the seller. Before we proceed, I would like you to consider the information about brokerage services contained in our company's agency disclosure brochure. As a licensee, I am required to make clear whom I will represent in any given transaction.

After developing this dialogue as if Andrea were an exclusive seller's agent, assume that she and her broker practice single agency and see where the dialogue takes you. Critique your results in class. Then attempt the same process, assuming Andrea and her brokerage offer intermediary brokerage services. Have several classmates or family members play the part of the open house owner who accidentally overhears the entire series of dialogues, then ask what the owner would think about the agent's conduct.

Scene 2: A buyer's broker has an advantage over other brokers in contacting an FSBO. The buyer's broker does not look to the seller either for a listing or in an attempt to bargain a commission from the seller. The following dialogue could be used in a face-to-face meeting or in a telephone presentation.

Kim: Good morning, Mr. Owner, I am Kim of Gold Coast Realty. I am a real estate licensee, but I am not here [calling] to ask for a listing on your home. The reason for my visit [call] is to see if your property might fit the needs of my client. I saw your For Sale sign [ad]. Do you have a few minutes to see if you can be of help to my buyer and me?

Owner: Yes, but not a whole lot more than a few minutes. And I don't want to list my property.

Kim: I can see [understand] you're busy. I'll be very brief. My buyer, through his buyer-representation agreement with me, has agreed to include enough money in any offer he might make for your property to cover any concessions he might ask you to make, including such things as roof repairs, discount points and my fee for services to him. Therefore, I will not personally attempt to negotiate a fee for myself from you. I am the agent for the buyer, and I will not be your agent. You will not have to list your property or publicly advertise it for sale. My buyer is ready, willing and able to pay a fair price should you and he be able to come to a mutually acceptable agreement. If you are willing to sell for an acceptable price and terms, I would appreciate the opportunity to preview your house, with or without my client, and develop a report to my client regarding your property's suitability for his needs. Then we could prepare an offer for your consideration. Could I make an appointment with you to preview your property sometime today or early tomorrow?

Owner: I'm telling you right now, I'm not listing with you and I'm not paying any commissions for anybody.

Kim: I understand, Mr. Owner, and I hear your frustration. As far as the real estate fees are concerned, my agreement with my buyer-client is an enforceable written contract in which my client has agreed to pay my fee for services to him in one of two ways. He might include enough in the offer to the owner so that the owner can pay my fee and net just as much money. Or, should my client not be able to negotiate that point with the owner but still desires the property, he has agreed to compensate me in addition to whatever the final purchase price is. If that is acceptable to you, I'd like to come out and give you my company's agency disclosure form, which includes information about brokerage services. This form will confirm in writing what I've told you. I'll also bring a state-required seller's disclosure of property condition form, discuss both forms with you for 10 to 15 minutes and then preview your house for my client.

Kim, in the above scenario, practices exclusive buyer agency. If she practiced single agency, would her conversation with the owner be different? Could she start talking with the owner about becoming his agent for the purchase of his next home? What conflicts of interest could develop? What would happen if her brokerage practiced the hybrid form of agency, where the client is required to consent to intermediary brokerage, in advance, should the situation require it? Develop dialogue and disclosures for these scenarios.

■ Summary

When you become comfortable handling your relationship both with customers and with clients, you will experience enhanced professional stature and esteem. You will discover a sense of freedom in being able to more actively represent the best interests of your clients, whether buyers or sellers, when you negotiate against the other side, whether represented or unrepresented.

■ Key Points

- In practicing preventative brokerage, brokers should use written disclosures, clarify the roles of associated licensees and when needed, use the services of others in their real estate transactions.

- Licensees should carefully prepare their clients and customers for the real estate transaction by explaining the process and providing disclosures.

- Offers to purchase should be presented in a timely manner. Multiple offers should be presented together, thereby giving the seller opportunity to accept the offer that best meets the selling goals. The seller should have the choice of whether or not to accept backup offers.

- There should be an understanding of how retained earnest money will be divided in case of a buyer's default.

- Commissions are negotiable and may be paid by either a client or customer.

- Agency agreements should be in writing; however, oral agreements can create an agency relationship.

- Using rehearsed dialog will help licensees overcome uneasiness with situations that are difficult for them.

■ Suggestions for Brokers

Practice real-life situations in your training classes and learn the most effective ways to discuss agency relationships to prepare yourself for future discussions. Then put your practice sessions to work in the field.

■ Quiz

1. Brokers should do all of the following *except*

   A. use written disclosures.
   C. use the help of others when needed.
   B. clarify their roles in the transaction.
   D. warrant the condition of a property.

2. Listing brokers

   A. always offer subagency to other brokers.
   B. should explain brokerage policies regarding representation of clients.
   C. are not required to use disclosures other than those in the listing contract.
   D. may assume that sellers are aware of how commissions are split with other brokers.

3. When selecting properties to show a buyer-customer, the licensee

   A. should select those properties that best match the buyer's desires.
   B. should show only the company's listings because of fiduciary duties to their sellers.
   C. match available properties with the buyer's needs, desires and ability to pay.
   D. always should show properties somewhat above the buyer's desired price range, because buyers typically "buy up" from their initial requested price range.

4. Which of the following terms best describes a real estate licensee, working through a listing broker, who is paid a fee for working with a buyer but is not an agent of the buyer?

   A. Listing broker   C. Finder
   B. Subagent   D. Buyer's broker

5. A broker wishing to act as an intermediary in a transaction may do so only if

   A. all parties give written approval.
   B. the buyers give written approval.
   C. the sellers give written approval.
   D. the parties give written or verbal approval.

6. If a second offer is received by the listing broker while a seller is deliberating an offer, the broker

   A. must not present the second offer until the seller has made a decision on the first offer.
   B. must present the offer but explain to the seller that the second offer can be considered only as a backup offer and cannot be acted on until the first offer is negotiated.
   C. must present the second offer and explain to the seller that the seller is free to consider the second offer without regard to the first offer.
   D. should advise the licensee bringing the second offer that the seller is deliberating a first offer and to delay bringing a second offer until negotiations on the first offer are completed.

7. If earnest money is used to liquidate damages in a transaction, the listing broker

A. is not entitled to share in the earnest money.
B. is automatically entitled to share in the earnest money.
C. is entitled to share in the earnest money only if the listing agreement or purchase agreement contains such a provision.
D. is not entitled to share in the earnest money because listing agreements and purchase agreements never contain such a provision.

8. Who can pay the buyer's broker's fee?

A. Seller
B. Buyer
C. Both seller and buyer
D. Neither seller nor buyer

9. If a listing broker receives an offer from a buyer's broker in which the buyer's broker's fee is to be paid by the seller, the listing broker should

A. reject the offer.
B. renegotiate the offering.
C. increase the listing fee.
D. present the offer to the seller.

10. Rehearsed dialogue should

A. never be used in presentations to buyers or sellers because it sounds like a "canned sales pitch."
B. be used in presentations because it helps licensees become more comfortable in handling common situations.
C. not be used in presentations because it makes licensees look insincere.
D. be used in presentations because it guarantees that licensees will avoid lawsuits.

■ Discussion Questions

1. You are the listing agent. A buyer wants to submit an offer to buy through you. The buyer hands you three envelopes with instructions to present a certain one first. Only if the seller rejects the offer found in the first envelope are you to present the others. What should you advise your seller? Would you do anything differently if you were the other broker acting as a subagent on an MLS listing? If you were a buyer's broker?

2. A buyer asks you how much her monthly payment will be for her mortgage loan. You explain that the monthly payment is $1,400, which will be used to pay principal, interest, taxes and insurance. The buyer neglects to obtain fire insurance because she thinks it is included in the monthly payment when, actually, the monthly payment includes only the mortgage insurance premium. The house burns down. Are you liable? Are you more likely to be liable if you are the buyer's agent than if you are the listing agent?

3. As the other broker acting in a subagency capacity with the seller, you find a buyer who purchases a home at $20,000 in excess of the true market value. Nine months later, the buyer comes to you and asks you to list the property for sale. What listing price do you suggest? How

do you explain helping the buyer acquire the property, which was clearly overpriced?

4. Sally of Bay Realty signs a listing with George on a penthouse apartment. George asks Sally to find him a bigger penthouse. Who does Sally represent on the current penthouse? Who does Sally represent if she shows George one of Bay Realty's listings that was obtained by another agent? Who does Sally represent if she shows George a property listed with another brokerage through the MLS? How does Sally explain to George the various working relationships open to them?

APPENDIX A

Selected Texas Statutes and TREC Rules

This appendix contains selected statutes and TREC Rules that relate to a real estate licensee's fiduciary duties when acting as an agent; a broker's duties as a TRELA §15c intermediary; and an appointed licensee's duties in a real estate transaction. The selection also includes:

- important statutes and rules governing the relationship of principal broker to licensed associate;

- what constitutes "acting as a broker";

- a licensee's legal and required duties relative to the use of certain contract forms when carrying out the licensee's agency and

- other aspects of the real estate licensee's duties when functioning as an agent in a real estate transaction.

It is important to know what the law says before trying to decide what the law means. Therefore, the following laws should be researched, read and reread by the instructor and by each student. It is the licensee's legal and ethical responsibility to be familiar with these laws that affect daily real estate business.

How to Read this Section

The selections from the Texas statutory law known as *The Real Estate License Act* are identified as "TRELA," together with the appropriate sections and paragraph indications; and begin at the far left margin of each page. Those sections and paragraphs of the Texas Administrative Code quoted are indented to the right of the far left margin and labeled "22 TAC," with the appropriate sections, subsections and paragraphs indicated. The real-estate-licensee related sections of the Texas Administrative Code are generally referred to as the *Rules of the Texas Real Estate Commission* or *TREC Rules*. The TREC Rules, which use a different numbering scheme than TRELA sections, follow immediately and are indented from the TRELA sections that the rules are intended to explain, modify or clarify.

Authors' Note: The reader should keep in mind that these are "selected" rules and statutes; therefore, many gaps occur in the numbering sequences. They do, however, follow a numerical order of progression. The rules are keyed to the statutes they modify regardless of their individual numbering.

TREC Rules have the *force and effect of law* and are considered by the courts of this state to be included in any contracts involving real estate licensees and their duties to and relationships with members of the public [*Kinnard v. Homann,* 750 S.W.2d 30 (Tex App. Austin 1988)]. These laws do not appear officially in the arrangement and order shown in this text. Here, the rules are listed immediately below the sections of the License Act they are intended to clarify to help the reader understand the statutory context, which gives rise to the rule and to better comprehension of how TREC views the meaning of the statutes.

The legislature will frequently change provisions of TRELA in response to the changing needs of the public and the real estate industry. TREC Rules are subsequently changed to accommodate the TRELA. Readers are encouraged to keep current with changes to TRELA and the TREC Rules. TRELA and the Rules of TREC can be found on the TREC internet web page; their address is www.trec.state.tx.us. The first three TREC Rules listed have no particular statute section to follow, reference or clarify. They are listed here first and as they appear in the official rules of the Texas Real Estate Commission. These three rules come from Chapter 531 of the Texas Administrative Code and are referred to collectively as the "Canons of Professional Ethics and Conduct for Real Estate Licensees." The ethical canons of TREC should not be confused with the NAR® Code of Ethics. The TREC canons set the tone for and spirit of the conduct expected of real estate licensees when acting as agents.

CANONS OF PROFESSIONAL ETHICS AND CONDUCT FOR REAL ESTATE LICENSEES

22 TAC §531.1 Fidelity

A real estate broker or salesperson, while acting as an agent for another, is a fiduciary. Special obligations are imposed when such fiduciary relationships are created. They demand

(1) that the primary duty of the real estate agent is to represent the interests of the agent's client, and the agent's position, in this respect, should be clear to all parties concerned in a real estate transaction; that, however, the agent in performing duties to the client, shall treat other parties to a transaction fairly;

(2) that the real estate agent be faithful and observant to trust placed in him, and be scrupulous and meticulous in performing the agent's functions;

(3) that the real estate agent place no personal interest above that of the agent's client.

22 TAC §531.2 Integrity

A real estate broker or salesperson has a special obligation to exercise integrity in the discharge of the licensee's responsibilities, including employment of prudence and caution so as to avoid misrepresentation, in any wise, by acts of commission or omission.

22 TAC §531.3 Competency

It is the obligation of a real estate agent to be knowledgeable as a real estate brokerage practitioner. The agent should

(1) be informed on market conditions affecting the real estate business and pledged to continuing education in the intricacies involved in marketing real estate for others;

(2) be informed on national, state and local issues and developments in the real estate industry;

(3) exercise judgment and skill in the performance of the work.

TRELA § 1.

(a) This Act shall be known and may be cited as "The Real Estate License Act."

(b) It is unlawful for a person to act in the capacity of, engage in the business of, or advertise or hold that person out as engaging in or conducting the business of a real estate broker or a real estate salesperson within this state without first obtaining a real estate license from the Texas Real Estate Commission. It is unlawful for a person licensed as a real estate salesperson to act or attempt to act as a real estate broker or salesperson unless that person is, at such time, associated with a licensed Texas real estate broker and acting for the licensed real estate broker.

(c) Each real estate broker licensed pursuant to this Act is responsible to the commission, members of the public, and the broker's clients for all acts and conduct performed under this Act by the broker or by a real estate salesperson associated with or acting for the broker.

(d) No real estate salesperson shall accept compensation for real estate sales and transactions from any person other than the broker under whom the salesperson is at the time licensed or under whom the salesperson was licensed when the salesperson earned the right to compensation.

(e) No real estate salesperson shall pay a commission to any person except through the broker under whom the salesperson is at the time licensed.

22 TAC §535.1(c) and (d) License Required

(c) Unless otherwise exempted by the Act, a person must be licensed as a real estate broker or salesperson to show a broker's listings, solicit listings of real property, perform any act defined as that of a real estate broker by the Act. An unlicensed person may be hired by a broker to act as a host or hostess at a property being offered for sale by the broker, provided the unlicensed person engages in no activity for which a license is required.

(d) The employees, agents or associates of a licensed broker, including a corporation or limited liability company, licensed as a broker, must be licensed as real estate brokers or salespersons if they direct or supervise other persons in the performance of acts for which a license is required. A license is not required for the performance of secretarial, clerical, or administrative tasks, such as training personnel, performing duties generally associated with office administration and personnel matters. Unlicensed employees, agents, or associates may not solicit business for the broker or hold themselves out as authorized to act as real estate brokers or salespersons.

TRELA §1(c)

Each real estate broker licensed pursuant to this act is responsible to the commission, members of the public, and the broker's clients for all acts and conduct performed under this act by the broker or by a real estate salesperson associated with or acting for the broker.

22 TAC §535.2(a), (b), (c) Broker's Responsibility

(a) A broker is responsible for the authorized acts of the broker's salespersons, but the broker is not required to supervise the salespersons directly.

(b) A real estate broker acting as an agent owes the very highest fiduciary obligation to the agent's principal and is obliged to convey to the principal all information of which the agent has knowledge and which may affect the principal's decision. A broker is obligated under a listing contract to negotiate the best possible transaction for the principal, the person the broker has agreed to represent.

(c) A broker is responsible for the proper handling of escrow monies placed with the broker, although the broker may authorize other persons to sign checks for the broker.

TRELA §1(d) and (e)

(d) No real estate salesperson shall accept compensation for real estate sales and transactions from any person other than the broker under whom the salesperson is at the time licensed or under whom the salesperson was licensed when the salesperson earned the right to the compensation.

(e) No real estate salesperson shall pay a commission to any person except through the broker under whom the salesperson is at the time licensed.

TRELA §2(1)

"Real estate" means a leasehold, as well as any other interest in land, whether corporeal, incorporeal, freehold, or nonfreehold, and whether the real estate is situated in this state or elsewhere. The term does not include an interest given as security for the performance of an obligation.

TRELA §2(2)

"Real estate broker" means a person who, for another person and for a fee, commission, or other valuable consideration, or with the intention or in the expectation or on the promise of receiving or collecting a fee, commission, or other valuable consideration from another person

(A) sells, exchanges, purchases, rents, or leases real estate;

(B) offers to sell, exchange, purchase, rent, or lease real estate;

(C) negotiates or attempts to negotiate the listing, sale, exchange, purchase, rental, or leasing of real estate;

(D) lists or offers or attempts or agrees to list real estate for sale, rental, lease, exchange, or trade;

(E) appraises or offers or attempts or agrees to appraise, real estate;

(F) auctions, or offers or attempts or agrees to auction, real estate;

(G) buys or sells or offers to buy or sell, or otherwise deals in options on real estate;

(H) aids, attempts, or offers to aid in locating or obtaining for purchase, rent, or lease any real estate;

(I) procures or assists in the procuring of prospects for the purpose of effecting the sale, exchange, lease, or rental of real estate; or

(J) procures or assists in the procuring of properties for the purpose of effecting the sale, exchange, lease, or rental of real estate.

22 TAC §535.12 (a) and (b)

(a) A person may invest in real estate or contract to purchase real estate and then sell it or offer to sell it without having a real estate license. Texas real estate licensure is not required of one who buys and sells real property only for his own accord.

(b) A person who owns property jointly may sell and convey title to his or her interest in the property, but the person must be licensed to act for compensation as an agent for the other owner unless otherwise exempted by Texas Civil Statutes, Article 6573a, (the Act).

22 TAC §535.16(b) and (c)

(b) A "net listing" is a listing agreement in which the broker's commission is the difference ("net") between the sales proceeds and an amount desired by the owner of the real property. A broker may not take net listings unless the principal requires a net listing and the principal appears to be familiar with current market values of real property. When a broker accepts a listing, the broker enters into a fiduciary relationship with the principal, whereby the broker is obligated to make diligent efforts to obtain the best price possible for the principal. The use of a net listing places an upper limit on the principal's expectancy and places the broker's interest above the principal's interest with reference to obtaining the best possible price. If a net listing is used, a broker should modify the listing agreement so as to assure the principal of not less than the principal's desired price and to limit the broker to a specified maximum commission.

(c) A real estate licensee is obligated to advise a property owner as to the licensee's opinion of the market value of a property when negotiating a listing or offering to purchase the property for the licensee's own account as a result of contact made while acting as a real estate agent.

TRELA §14(a)

It is unlawful for a licensed broker to employ or compensate directly or indirectly a person for performing an act enumerated in the definition of real estate broker in Section 2 of this Act if the person is not a licensed broker or licensed salesperson in this state. However, a licensed broker may pay a commission to a licensed broker of another state if the foreign broker does not conduct in this state any of the negotiations for which the fee, compensation, or commission is paid.

Authors' Note: A real estate licensee may no longer compensate an attorney "for performing an act enumerated in the definition of real estate broker in Section 2." However, a real estate licensee is *not prohibited* by the License Act from compensating one of the principals to the transaction so long as there is full disclosure to and consent of all parties, including third party lenders, if any. The reasoning is that a principal to the transaction does not perform an act of a broker because the act is for himself or herself and not for another. If a principal to a real estate transaction also happens to be an attorney, that principal is *not* divested of the right to compensation merely because he or she possesses an attorney's license.

22 TAC §535.131(a), (c), and (d)

(a) The Real Estate License Act permits Texas-licensed brokers to cooperate with and share earned commission with persons licensed as brokers in other states, but all negotiations within Texas must by handled by Texas licensees.

(c) An unlicensed person may share in the income earned by a real estate brokerage operation, provided that such unlicensed person performs none of the activities of a real estate agent and the public is not led to believe that such unlicensed person is in the real estate brokerage business.

(d) If a member of a partnership or an officer of a corporation does not engage in the activity of a real estate agent, he is not required to be licensed and may share in the income earned by the partnership or corporation.

TRELA §15(a)

The commission may, on its own motion, and shall, on the signed complaint in writing of a consumer or service recipient, provided the complaint, or the complaint together with evidence, documentary, or otherwise, presented in connection with the complaint, provides reasonable cause, investigate the actions and records of a real estate broker or real estate salesperson. The commission may suspend or revoke a license issued under the provisions of this Act at any time when it has been determined that: . . .

22 TAC §535.141(c)

A real estate broker is responsible for all acts and conduct performed by a real estate salesperson associated with or acting for the broker. A complaint which names a licensed real estate salesperson as the subject of the complaint but does not specifically name the salesperson's sponsoring broker, is a complaint against the broker sponsoring the salesperson at the time of any alleged violation for the limited purposes of determining the broker's involvement in any alleged violation and whether the broker fulfilled his or her professional responsibilities to the commission, members of the public, and his or her clients, provided the complaint concerns the conduct of the salesperson as an agent for the broker.

TRELA §15(a) [continued]

(2) the licensee has procured, or attempted to procure, a real estate license, for himself or a salesperson, by fraud, misrepresentation, or deceit, or by making a material misstatement of fact in an application for a real estate license;

(3) the licensee, when selling, buying, trading, or renting real property in his own name, engaged in misrepresentation or dishonest or fraudulent action;

> **22 TAC §535.144**
>
> A licensee, when engaging in a real estate transaction on his or her own behalf, is obligated to inform any person with whom the licensee deals that he or she is a licensed real estate broker or salesperson acting on his or her own behalf either by disclosure in any contract of sale or rental agreement, or by disclosure in any other writing given prior to entering into any contract of sale or rental agreement. A licensee shall not use the licensee's expertise to the disadvantage of a person with whom the licensee deals.

TRELA §15(a) [continued]

(6) the licensee, while performing an act constituting an act of a broker or a salesperson, as defined by this Act, has been guilty of . . .

(A) making a material misrepresentation or failing to disclose to a potential purchaser any latent structural defect or any other defect known to the broker or salesperson. Latent structural defects and other defects do not refer to trivial or insignificant defects but refer to those defects that would be a significant factor to a reasonable and prudent purchaser in making a decision to purchase;

(B) making a false promise of a character likely to influence, persuade, or induce any person to enter into a contract or an agreement when the licensee could not or did not intend to keep such promise;

> **22 TAC §535.145**
>
> "False promise" includes both oral and written promises. The fact that a written contract between the parties to a real estate transaction does not recite a promise made by a real estate licensee to one of the parties will not prevent the commission from determining that a false promise was made. When the commission decides whether this section has been violated, neither a written contractual provision disclaiming oral representations nor the parole evidence rule shall prevent the commission from considering oral promises made by a licensee.

TRELA §15(a)(6) [continued]

(C) pursuing a continued and flagrant course of misrepresentation or making of false promises through agents, salespersons, advertising, or otherwise;

(D) failing to make clear, to all parties of a transaction, which party the licensee is acting for, or receiving compensation from more than one party except with the full knowledge and consent of all parties;

(F) paying a commission or fees to or dividing a commission or fees with anyone not licensed as a real estate broker or salesperson in this state or any other state for compensation for services as a real estate agent;

22 TAC §535.147

(b) "Commission or fees" includes any form of compensation received for services as a real estate agent.

(c) "Services as a real estate agent" refers to the acts of a "real estate broker" as enumerated in Section 2(2)(A-J) and Section 2(3), when those acts are performed for another and for compensation.

Authors' Note: The principals to a transaction may compensate a lawyer for conducting a real estate transaction; however, the real estate licensee is *prohibited* from doing so unless the lawyer is also a licensed real estate broker in Texas.

TRELA §15(a)(6) [continued]

(G) failing to specify in a listing contract a definite termination date which is not subject to prior notice in a contract, other than a contract to perform property management services, in which the licensee agrees to perform services for which a license is required under this Act;

(J) acting in the dual capacity of broker and undisclosed principal in a transaction;

22 TAC §535.150

A licensee may not covertly or through a third party purchase his principal's property and recover a commission from the principal. A licensee must disclose to the other party to a transaction that the licensee is acting in the dual capacity of both agent and principal in that transaction.

TRELA §15(a)(6) [continued]

(L) placing a sign on real property offering it for sale, lease, or rent without the written consent of the owner or the owner's authorized agent;

22 TAC §535.152

"Written consent" as required by this section of the Act may be obtained in a listing agreement or any other appropriate agreement that has been reduced to writing.

TRELA §15(a)(6) [continued]

(M) inducing or attempting to induce a party to a contract of sale or lease to break the contract for the purpose of substituting in lieu thereof a new contract;

(N) negotiating or attempting to negotiate the sale, exchange, lease, or rental of real property with an owner or lessor, knowing that the owner or lessor had a written outstanding contract granting exclusive agency in connection with the property to another real estate broker;

22 TAC §535.153

Although a licensee, including one acting as agent for a prospective buyer or prospective tenant, may not attempt to negotiate a sale, exchange, lease, or rental of the property under exclusive listing with another broker, the Real Estate License Act (Act) §15(a)(6)(N) does not prohibit a licensee from soliciting a listing from the owner while the owner's property is subject to exclusive listing with another broker.

TRELA §15(a)(6) [continued]

(O) offering real property for sale or for lease without the knowledge or consent of the owner or the owner's authorized agent, or on terms other than those authorized by the owner or the owner's authorized agent;

(P) publishing, or causing to be published, an advertisement including, but not limited to, advertising by newspaper, radio, television, or display which is misleading, or which is likely to deceive the public, or which in any manner tends to create a misleading impression, or which fails to identify the person causing the advertisement to be published as a licensed real estate broker or agent;

> **22 TAC §535.154(d)**
>
> If a broker advertises under an assumed name, and that assumed name does not readily identify the broker as a real estate agent, the broker's advertisement must include an additional designation such as "agent," "broker" or a trade association name which serves clearly to identify the advertiser as a real estate agent.

TRELA §15(a)(6) [continued]

(T) failing or failing on demand to furnish copies of a document pertaining to a transaction dealing with real estate to a person whose signature is affixed to the document;

(V) conduct which constitutes dishonest dealings, bad faith, or untrustworthiness;

> **22 TAC §535.156(a), (b), (c) and (d)**
>
> (a) A licensee's relationship with the licensee's principal is that of a fiduciary. A licensee shall convey to his principal all known information which would affect the principal's decision on whether or not to accept or reject offers; however, the licensee shall have no duty to submit offers to the principal after the principal has accepted an offer.
>
> (b) The licensee must put the interest of the licensee's principal above the licensee's own interest. A licensee must deal honestly and fairly with all parties; however, the licensee represents only the principal and owes a duty of fidelity to such principal.
>
> (c) A licensee has an affirmative duty to keep the principal informed at all times of significant information applicable to the transaction or transactions in which the licensee is acting as agent for the principal.
>
> (d) A licensee has a duty to convey accurate information to members of the public with whom the licensee deals.

TRELA §15(a)(6) [continued]

(W) acting negligently or incompetently in performing an act for which a person i: required to hold a real estate license;

> **22 TAC §535.157**
>
> A licensee should not undertake to perform a service or handle a transaction for which the licensee lacks the requisite knowledge or expertise.

TRELA §15(a)

(9) the licensee has failed without cause to surrender to the rightful owner, on demand. document or instrument coming into the licensee's possession.

TRELA §15(b)

The provisions of this section do not relieve a person from civil liability or from crimi prosecution under this Act or under the laws of this state.

TRELA §15C

(a) A licensee under this Act who represents a party in a proposed real estate transaction shall disclose that representation at the time of the licensee's first contact with

(1) another party to the transaction; or

(2) another licensee who represents another party to the transaction.

(b) The disclosure required under Subsection (a) of this section may be made orally or in writing.

(c) A licensee who represents a party in a real estate transaction acts as that party's agent.

(d) Except as provided by Subsection (e) of this section, a licensee shall furnish to a party in a real estate transaction at the time of the first face-to-face meeting with the party the following written statement:

"Before working with a real estate broker, you should know that the duties of a broker depend on whom the broker represents. If you are a prospective seller or landlord (owner) or a prospective buyer or tenant (buyer), you should know that the broker who lists the property for sale or lease is the owner's agent. A broker who acts as a subagent represents the owner in cooperation with the listing broker. A broker who acts as a buyer's agent represents the buyer. A broker may act as an intermediary between the parties if the parties consent in writing. A broker can assist you in locating a property, preparing a contract or lease, or obtaining financing without representing you. A broker is obligated by law to treat you honestly.

"IF THE BROKER REPRESENTS THE OWNER: The broker becomes the owner's agent by entering into an agreement with the owner, usually through a written listing agreement, or by agreeing to act as a subagent by accepting an offer of subagency from the listing broker. A subagent may work in a different real estate office. A listing broker or subagent can assist the buyer but does not represent the buyer and must place the interests of the owner first. The buyer should not tell the owner's agent anything the buyer would not want the owner to know because an owner's agent must disclose to the owner any material information known to the agent.

"IF THE BROKER REPRESENTS THE BUYER: The broker becomes the buyer's agent by entering into an agreement to represent the buyer, usually through a written buyer representation agreement. A buyer's agent can assist the owner but does not represent the owner and must place the interests of the buyer first. The owner should not tell a buyer's agent anything the owner would not want the buyer to know because a buyer's agent must disclose to the buyer any material information known to the agent.

"IF THE BROKER ACTS AS AN INTERMEDIARY: A broker may act as an intermediary between the parties if the broker complies with The Texas Real Estate License Act. The broker must obtain the written consent of each party to the transaction to act as an intermediary. The written consent must state who will pay the broker and, in conspicuous bold or underlined print, set forth the broker's obligations as an intermediary. The broker is required to treat each party honestly and fairly and to comply with The Texas Real Estate License Act. A broker who acts as an intermediary in a transaction: (1) shall treat all parties honestly; (2) may not disclose that the owner will accept a price less than the asking price unless authorized in writing to do so by the owner; (3) may not disclose that the buyer will pay a price greater than the price submitted in a written offer unless authorized in writing to do so by the buyer; and (4) may not disclose any confidential information or any information that a party specifically instructs the broker in writing not to disclose unless authorized in writing to disclose the information or required to do so by The Texas Real Estate License Act or a court order or if the information materially relates to the condition of the property. With the parties' consent, a broker acting as an intermediary between the parties may appoint a person who is licensed under The Texas Real Estate License Act and associated with the broker to communicate with and carry out instructions of the other party.

"If you choose to have a broker represent you, you should enter into a written agreement with the broker that clearly establishes the broker's obligations and your obligations. The agreement should state how and by whom the broker will be paid. You have the right to choose the type of representation, if any, you wish to receive. Your payment of a fee to a broker does not necessarily establish that the broker represents you. If you have any questions regarding the duties and responsibilities of the broker, you should resolve those questions before proceeding."

(e) A licensee is not required to provide the written information under Subsection (d) of this section if:

(1) the proposed transaction is for a residential lease for not more than one year and no sale is being considered; or

(2) the licensee meets with a party who is represented by another licensee.

(f) In the written information required to be provided under Subsection (d) of this section, the licensee may substitute the word "buyer" with "tenant," and "seller" with "landlord," as appropriate.

(g) The written information required to be provided under Subsection (d) of this section may be printed in any format that uses at least ten-point type.

(h) A real estate broker may act as an intermediary between the parties if:

(1) the real estate broker obtains written consent from each party to the transaction for the real estate broker to act as an intermediary in the transaction; and

(2) the written consent of the parties under Subdivision (1) of this subsection states the source of any expected compensation to the real estate broker.

(i) A written listing agreement to represent a seller or landlord or a written agreement to represent a buyer or tenant which also authorizes a real estate broker to act as an intermediary in a transaction is sufficient to establish written consent of the party to the transaction if the written agreement sets forth, in conspicuous bold or underlined print, the real estate broker's obligations under Subsection (j) of this section.

(j) A real estate broker who acts as an intermediary between parties in a transaction:

(1) may not disclose to the buyer or tenant that the seller or landlord will accept a price less than the asking price unless otherwise instructed in a separate writing by the seller or landlord;

(2) may not disclose to the seller or landlord that the buyer or tenant will pay a price greater than the price submitted in a written offer to the seller or landlord unless otherwise instructed in a separate writing by the buyer or tenant;

(3) may not disclose any confidential information or any information a party specifically instructs the real estate broker in writing not to disclose unless otherwise instructed in a separate writing by the respective party or required to disclose such information by this Act or a court order or if the information materially relates to the condition of the property;

(4) shall treat all parties to the transaction honestly; and

(5) shall comply with this Act.

(k) If a real estate broker obtains the consent of the parties to act as an intermediary in a transaction in compliance with this section, the real estate broker may appoint, by providing written notice to the parties, one or more licensees associated with the broker to communicate with and carry out instructions of one party and one or more other licensees associated with the broker to communicate with and carry out instructions of the other party or parties. A real estate broker may appoint a licensee to communicate with and carry out instructions of a party under this subsection only if the written consent of the parties under Subsection (h) or (I) of this section authorizes the broker to make the appointment. The real estate broker and the appointed licensees shall comply with Subsection (j) of this section. However, during negotiations, an appointed licensee may provide opinions and advice to the party to whom the licensee is appointed.

(l) The duties of a licensee acting as an intermediary provided by this section supersede and are in lieu of a licensee's duties under common law or any other law.

(m) In this section:

(1) "Face-to-face meeting" means a meeting at which a substantive discussion occurs with respect to specific real property. The term does not include a meeting that occurs at a property being held open for prospective purchasers or tenants or a meeting that occurs after the parties to the transaction have signed a contract to sell, buy, rent or lease the real property concerned.

(2) "Intermediary" means a broker who is employed to negotiate a transaction between the parties subject to the obligations in Subsection (j) of this section and for that purpose may be an agent of the parties to the transaction. The intermediary shall act fairly so as not to favor one party over the other. Appointment by the intermediary of associated licensees under Subsection (k) of this section to communicate with, carry out instructions of, and provide opinions and advice to the parties to whom the licensees are appointed impartial act.

(3) "Licensee" means a real estate broker or real estate salesperson and includes a licensed associate of a licensee.

(4) "Party" means a prospective buyer, seller, landlord, or tenant or an authorized representative of a party, including a trustee, guardian, executor, administrator, receiver, or attorney-in-fact. The term does not include a licensee who represents a party.

(5) "Subagent" means a licensee who represents a principal through cooperation with and consent of a broker representing the principal and who is not sponsored by or associated with the principal's broker.

TRELA §15D

No licensed real estate broker, licensed real estate salesperson, or not for profit real estate board which provides information about real property sales prices or terms of sale for the purpose of facilitating the listing, selling, leasing, financing, or appraisal of real property shall be liable to any other person as a result of so providing such information unless the disclosure of same is otherwise specifically prohibited by statute.

TRELA §15F

(a) A party is not liable for a misrepresentation or a concealment of a material fact made by a licensee in a real estate transaction unless the concealment party knew of the falsity of the misrepresentation or/and failed to disclose the party's knowledge of the misrepresentation or concealment.

(b) A licensee is not liable for a misrepresentation or a concealment of a material fact made by a party in a real estate transaction unless the licensee knew of the falsity of the misrepresentation or concealment and failed to disclose the licensee's knowledge of the falsity of the misrepresentation or concealment.

(c) A party or a licensee is not liable for a misrepresentation or a concealment of a material fact made by a subagent in a real estate transaction unless the party or licensee knew of the falsity of the misrepresentation or concealment and failed to disclose the party's or licensee's knowledge of the falsity of the misrepresentation or concealment.

(d) The provisions of this section shall prevail over common law and any other law. This section does not diminish a real estate broker's responsibility for the acts or omissions of the broker's salespersons associated with or acting for the real estate broker, as provided by Section 1 of this Act.

(e) In this section, "licensee," "subagent," and "party" have the meaning assigned to those terms by Section 15C of this Act.

TRELA §16(a), (b), (c), (d) and (e)

(a) A license granted under the provisions of this Act shall be suspended or revoked by the commission on proof that the licensee, not being licensed and authorized to practice law in this state, for a consideration, reward, pecuniary benefit, present or anticipated, direct or indirect, or in connection with or as part of the licensee's employment, agency, or fiduciary relationship as a licensee, drew a deed, note, deed of trust, will, or another written instrument that may transfer or anywise affect the title to or an interest in land, except as provided in the subsections below, or advised or counseled a person as to the validity or legal sufficiency of an instrument or as to the validity of title to real estate.

(b) Notwithstanding the provisions of this Act or any other law, the completion of contract forms which bind the sale, exchange, option, lease, or rental of any interest in real property by a real estate broker or a real estate salesperson incident to the performance of the acts of a broker as defined by this article does not constitute the unauthorized or illegal practice of law in this state, provided the forms have been promulgated for use by the commission for the particular kind of transaction involved, or the forms have been prepared by an attorney at law licensed by this state and approved by said attorney for the particular kind of transaction involved, or the forms have been prepared by the property owner or prepared by an attorney and required by the property owner.

(c) A Texas Real Estate Broker-Lawyer Committee is hereby created which, in addition to other powers and duties delegated to it, shall draft and revise contract forms capable of standardization for use by real estate licensees and which will expedite real estate transactions and reduce controversies to a minimum while containing safeguards adequate to protect the interests of the principals to the transaction.

(d) The Texas Real Estate Broker-Lawyer Committee shall have 12 members including 6 members appointed by the commission and 6 members of the State Bar of Texas appointed by the President of the State Bar of Texas. The members of the committee shall hold office for staggered terms of six years with the terms of two commission appointees and two State Bar appointees expiring every two years. Each member shall hold office until the member's successor is appointed. A vacancy for any cause shall be filed for the expired term by the agency making the original appointment. Appointments to the committee shall be made without regard to race, creed, sex, religion, or national origin.

(e) In the best interest of the public the commission may adopt rules and regulations requiring real estate brokers and salespersons to use contract forms which have been prepared by the Texas Real Estate Broker-Lawyer Committee and promulgated by the commission; provided, however, that the commission shall not prohibit a real estate broker or salesperson from using a contract form or forms binding the sale, exchange, option, lease or rental of any interest in real property which have been prepared by the property owner or prepared by an attorney and required by the property owner. For the purpose of this section, contract forms prepared by the Texas Real Estate Broker-Lawyer Committee appointed by the commission and the State Bar of Texas and promulgated by the commission prior to the effective date of this Act shall be deemed to have been prepared by the Texas Real Estate Broker-Lawyer Committee. The commission may suspend or revoke a license issued under the provisions of this article when it has been determined that the licensee failed to use a contract form as required by the commission pursuant to this section.

22 TAC §537.11(c), (d), (e), (f) and (g)

(c) A licensee shall not practice law, offer, give, nor attempt to give advice, directly or indirectly; he shall not act as a public conveyance nor give advice or opinions as to the legal effect of any contracts or other such instruments which may affect the title to real estate; he shall not give opinions concerning the status or validity of title to real estate; and he shall not attempt to prevent nor in any manner whatsoever discourage any principal to a real estate transaction from employing a lawyer. However, nothing herein shall be deemed to limit the licensee's fiduciary obligation to disclose to his principals all pertinent facts which are within the knowledge of the licensee, including such facts which might affect the status of or title to real estate.

(d) A licensee shall not undertake to draw or prepare documents fixing and defining the legal rights of principals to a transaction. In negotiating real estate transactions, the licensee may fill in forms for such transactions, using exclusively forms which have been approved and promulgated by the Texas Real Estate Commission or such forms as are otherwise permitted by these rules. When filling in such a form, the licensee may only fill in the blanks provided and may not add to or strike matter from such form, except that licensees shall add factual statements and business details desired by the principals and shall strike only such matter as is desired by the principals and as is necessary to conform the instrument to the intent of the parties. A licensee shall not add to a promulgated earnest money contract form factual statements or business details for which a contract addendum, lease or other form has been promulgated by the commission for mandatory use. Nothing herein shall be deemed to prevent the licensee from explaining to the principals the meaning of the factual statements and business details contained in the said instrument so long as the licensee does not offer or give legal advice. It is not the practice of law as defined in this Act for a real estate licensee to complete a contract form which is either promulgated by the Texas Real Estate Commission or prepared by the Texas Real Estate Broker-Lawyer Committee and made available for trial use by licensees with the consent of the Texas Real Estate Commission. Contract forms prepared by the Texas Real Estate Broker-Lawyer Committee for trial use by licensees with the consent of the Texas Real Estate Commission. Contract forms prepared by the Texas Real Estate Broker-Lawyer Committee for trial use may be used on a voluntary basis after being approved by the commission.

(e) Where it appears that, prior to the execution of any such instrument, there are unusual matters involved in the transaction which should be resolved by legal counsel before the instrument is executed or that the instrument is to be acknowledged and filed for record, the licensee shall advise the principals that each should consult a lawyer of his choice before executing same.

(f) A licensee shall not employ, directly or indirectly, a lawyer nor pay for the services of a lawyer to represent any principal to a real estate transaction in which he, the licensee, is acting as an agent. The licensee may also employ and pay for the services of a lawyer to represent only the licensee in a real estate transaction, including preparation of the contract, agreement, or other legal instruments to be executed by the principals to the transactions.

(g) A broker shall advise the principals that the instrument they are about to execute is binding on them.

Authors' Note: This Rule does not contain the phrase *intended to be.* However, this additional phrase is included in the TREC-promulgated contract forms. If a broker were to follow Subparagraph (g) as written, without including the phrase *intended to be,* it appears that the broker may automatically violate Subparagraph (c) of this same section by giving "advice or opinions as to the legal effect of any contracts."

TRELA §20(a)

A person may not bring or maintain an action for the collection of compensation for the performance in this state of an act set forth in Section 2 of this Act without alleging and proving that the person performing the brokerage services was a duly-licensed real estate broker or salesperson at the time the alleged services were commenced, or was a duly licensed attorney at law in this state or in any other state.

22 TAC §535.191

A real estate licensee's commission is not set by statute, but is a matter to be agreed upon by the parties to a transaction.

TRELA §20(b)

An action may not be brought in a court in this state for the recovery of a commission for the sale or purchase of real estate unless the promise or agreement on which the action is brought, or some memorandum thereof, is in writing and signed by the party to be charged or signed by a party lawfully authorized by him to sign it.

> **22 TAC §535.192**
>
> Section 20(b) of the Act is not applicable to an agreement between real estate licensees to share a commission received by one of them for selling real estate.

TRELA §20(c)

When an offer to purchase real estate in this state is signed, the real estate broker or salesperson shall advise the purchaser or purchasers, in writing, that the purchaser or purchasers should have the abstract covering the real estate which is the subject of the contract examined by an attorney of the purchaser's own selection, or that the purchaser or purchasers should be furnished with or obtain a policy of title insurance. Failure to advise the purchaser as provided in this subsection precludes the payment of or recovery of any commission agreed to be paid on the sale.

Authors' Note: TREC-promulgated contract forms contain this written notice. For transactions where of the TREC forms are not required, licensees are cautioned to use some form or letter that puts the wording of this statute in writing, furnish it to the purchaser and obtain a written receipt acknowledging that the notice has been furnished. Failure to furnish written notice by the time of contract may result in loss of commission; failure to do so by closing could result in loss of license under TRELA §15(a)(6)(U).

APPENDIX B

Questions and Answers Regarding Disclosure of Agency and Intermediary Practice

QUESTIONS AND ANSWERS REGARDING DISCLOSURE OF AGENCY AND INTERMEDIARY PRACTICE

The following 49 questions and answers have been developed to assist licensees in complying with Section 15C of The Real Estate License Act. These answers are intended to address general situations only and are not intended as legal opinions addressing the duties and obligations of licensees in specific transactions. What licensees say and do in a specific transaction may cause these general answers to be inapplicable or inaccurate. Licensees should consult their own attorneys for legal advice concerning the law's effect on their brokerage practices.

Q: **Explain how a typical intermediary relationship is created and how it would operate.**

A: At their first face to face meeting with a seller or a prospective buyer, the salespersons or brokers associated with a firm would provide the parties with a copy of the statutory information about agency required by The Real Estate License Act (TRELA). The statutory information includes an explanation of the intermediary relationship. The brokerage firm would negotiate a written listing contract with a seller and a written buyer representation agreement with a buyer. In those documents, the respective parties would authorize the broker to act as an intermediary and to appoint associated licensees to work with the parties in the event that the buyer wishes to purchase a property listed with the firm. At this point, the broker and associated licensees would be still functioning as exclusive agents of the individual parties. The listing contract and buyer representation agreement would contain in conspicuous bold or underlined print the broker's obligations set forth in Section 15C(j) of TRELA. When it becomes evident that the buyer represented by the firm wishes to purchase property listed with the firm, the intermediary status would come into play, and the intermediary may appoint different associates to work with the parties. The intermediary would notify both parties in writing of the appointments of licensees to work with the parties. The associates would provide advice and opinions to their respective parties during negotiations, and the intermediary broker would be careful not to favor one party over the other in any action taken by the intermediary.

Q. **What is the difference between a dual agent and an intermediary?**

A: A dual agent is a broker who represents two parties at the same time in accordance with common law obligations and duties. An intermediary is a broker who negotiates the transaction between the parties subject to the provisions of Section 15C of The Real Estate License Act. The

---

1

intermediary may, with the written consent of the parties, appoint licensees associated with the intermediary to work with and advise the party to whom they have been appointed. In a dual agency situation in which two salespersons are sponsored by the same broker but are working with different parties, the broker and the salespersons are considered to be agents of both parties, unable to act contrary to the interests of either party.

Q: In what way does Section 15C prohibit or permit disclosed dual agency?

A: Disclosed dual agency is not specifically addressed in Section 15C. Since disclosed dual agency is not prohibited, licensees may, with appropriate disclosure and consent of the parties, act as dual agents.

Q: What is the advantage for the broker in acting as an intermediary?

A: If the broker and associates are going to continue to work with parties they have been representing under listing contracts or buyer representation agreements, the intermediary role is the only statutorily addressed vehicle for handling "in-house" transactions, providing both parties the same level of service.

Q: If a salesperson or associated broker lists a property and has also been working with a prospective buyer under a representation agreement, how can the salesperson or associated broker sell this listing under Section 15C?

A: There are three alternatives for the brokerage firm and the parties to consider:
(1)   the firm, acting through the salesperson or associated broker, could represent one of the parties and work with the other party as a customer rather than as a client (realistically, this probably means working with the buyer as a customer and terminating the buyer representation agreement).
(2)   if the firm has obtained permission in writing from both parties to be an intermediary and to appoint licensees to work with the parties, the salesperson or associated broker could be appointed by the intermediary to work with one of the parties. Note: **Another licensee would have to be appointed to work with the other party under this alternative. The law does not permit an intermediary to appoint the same licensee to work with both parties.**
(3)   if the firm has obtained permission in writing from both parties to be an intermediary, but does not appoint different associates to work

with the parties, the salesperson or broker associate could function as a representative of the firm. Since the firm is an intermediary, the salesperson and associated broker also would be subject to the requirement not to act so as to favor one party over the other.

Q: If a salesperson may provide services to a party under Section 15C without being appointed, why would a broker want to appoint a salesperson to work with a party?

A: Appointment following the procedures set out in Section 15C would permit the salesperson to provide a higher level of service.   The appointed salesperson may provide advice and opinions to the party to whom the salesperson is assigned and is not subject to the intermediary's statutory duty of not acting so as to favor one party over the other.

Q: Is an intermediary an agent?

A: Yes, but the duties and obligations of an intermediary are different than for exclusive, or single, agents.

Q: What are the duties and obligations of an intermediary?

A: Section 15C requires the intermediary to obtain written consent from both parties to act as an intermediary.   A written listing agreement to represent a seller/landlord or a written buyer/tenant representation agreement which contains authorization for the broker to act as an intermediary between the parties is sufficient for the purposes of Section 15C if the agreement sets forth, in conspicuous bold or underlined print, the broker's obligations under Section 15C(j) and the agreement states who will pay the broker.
   If the intermediary is to appoint associated licensees to work with the parties, the intermediary must obtain written permission from both parties and give written notice of the appointments to each party.   The intermediary is also required to treat the parties fairly and honestly and to comply with TRELA.   The intermediary is prohibited from acting so as to favor one party over the other, and may not reveal confidential information obtained from one party without the written instructions of that party, unless disclosure of that information is required by TRELA, court order, or the information materially relates to the condition of the property.   The intermediary and any associated licensees appointed by the intermediary are prohibited from disclosing without written authorization that the seller will accept a price less than the asking price or that the buyer will pay a price greater than the price submitted in a written offer.

Q: Can salespersons act as intermediaries?

A: Only a broker can contract with the parties to act as an intermediary between them. In that sense, only a broker can be an intermediary. If, however, the broker intermediary does not appoint associated licensees to work with the parties in a transaction, any salesperson or broker associates of the intermediary who function in that transaction would be required to act just as the intermediary does, not favoring one party over the other.

Q: Can there be two intermediaries in the same transaction?

A: No.

Q: Can a broker representing only the buyer be an intermediary?

A: Ordinarily, no; the listing broker will be the intermediary. In the case of a FSBO or other seller who is not already represented by a broker, the broker representing the buyer could secure the consent of both parties to act as an intermediary.

Q: May an intermediary appoint a subagent in another firm to work with one of the parties?

A: Subagency is still permitted under the law, but a subagent in another firm cannot be appointed as one of the intermediary's associated licensees under the provisions of Section 15C.

Q: May the same salesperson be appointed by the intermediary to work with both parties in the same transaction?

A: No; the law requires the intermediary to appoint different associated licensees to work with each party.

Q: May more than one associated licensee be appointed by the intermediary to work with the same party?

A: Yes.

Q: How should an intermediary complete Paragraph 8 of the TREC contract forms?

A: Brokers who are acting as intermediaries after January 1, 1996 should use the TREC addendum approved for that purpose in lieu of completing Paragraph 8.

Q: May a broker act as an intermediary prior to January 1, 1996, the effective date of the TRELA amendment?

A: No.

Q: What is the difference between an appointed licensee working with a party and a licensee associated with the intermediary who has not been appointed to work with one party?

A: During negotiations the appointed licensee may advise the person to whom the licensee has been appointed.   An associated licensee who has not been appointed must act in the same manner as the intermediary, that is, not giving opinions and advice and not favoring one party over the other.

Q: Who decides whether a broker will act as intermediary, the broker or the parties?

A: Initially, the broker, in determining the policy of the firm.   If the broker does not wish to act as an intermediary, nothing requires the broker to do so.   If the broker's policy is to offer services as an intermediary, both parties must authorize the broker in writing before the broker may act as in intermediary or appoint licensees to work with each of the parties.

Q: When must the intermediary appoint the licensees associated with the intermediary to work with the parties?

A: This is a judgment call for the intermediary.   If appointments are going to be made, they should be made before the buyer begins to receive advice and opinions from an associated licensee in connection with the property listed with the broker.   If the broker appoints the associates at the time the listing contract and buyer representation agreements are signed, it should be clear that the appointments are effective only when the intermediary relationship arises.   **The intermediary relationship does not exist until the parties who have authorized it are beginning to deal with each other in a proposed   real estate transaction; for example, the buyer begins to negotiate to purchase the seller's property.**   Prior to the creation of the intermediary relationship, the broker will typically be acting as an exclusive agent of each party.   It is important to remember that **both** parties must be notified in writing of **both** appointments. If, for example, the listing agent is "appointed" at the time the listing is taken, care must be taken to ensure that the buyer is ultimately also given written notice of the appointment.   When a buyer client begins to show interest in a property listed with the firm and both parties have authorized the intermediary relationship, the seller must be notified in writing as to which associate has been appointed to work with the buyer.

Q: Can the intermediary delegate to another person the authority to appoint licensees associated with the intermediary?

A: The intermediary may delegate to another licensee the authority to appoint associated licensees. **If the intermediary authorizes another licensee to appoint associated licensees to work with the parties, however, that person must not appoint himself or herself as one of the associated licensees, as this would be an improper combination of the different functions of intermediary and associated licensee. It is also important to remember that there will be a single intermediary even if another licensee has been authorized to make appointments.**

Q: May a broker act as a dual agent after January 1, 1996?

A: Dual agency is not prohibited, but the broker who attempts to represent both parties may be subject to common law rules if the broker does not act as an intermediary. Brokers who do not wish to act as exclusive agents of one party should act as a statutory intermediary as provided by §15C and call themselves "intermediaries" rather than "dual agents."

Q: What are the agency disclosure requirements for real estate licensees after January 1, 1996?

A: To disclose their representation of a party upon the first contact with a party or a licensee representing another party.

Q: Is disclosure of agency required to be in writing?

A: After January 1, 1996, the disclosure may be oral or in writing.

Q: Will use of TREC 3 be required after January 1, 1996?

A: No, TREC has repealed the rule requiring use of TREC 3.

Q: Will licensees be required to provide parties with written information relating to agency?

A: Yes. Section 15C will require licensees to provide the parties with a copy of a written statement, the content of which is specified in the statute. The form of the statement may be varied, so long as the text of the statement is in at least 10 point type.

Q: Are there exceptions when the statutory statement is not required?

A: Yes; the statement is required to be provided at the first face to face meeting between a party and the licensee at which substantive discussion occurs with respect to specific real property. The statement is **not** required for either of the following:
(1) a transaction which is a residential lease no longer than one year and no sale is being considered; or
(2) a meeting with a party represented by another licensee.

Q: Are the disclosure and statutory information requirements applicable to commercial transactions, new home sales, farm and ranch sales or transactions other than residential sales?

A: Except as noted above, the requirements are applicable to all real estate transactions. Licensees dealing with landlords and tenants are permitted by the law to modify their versions of the statutory statement to use the terms "landlord" and "tenant" in place of the terms "seller" and "buyer."

Q: What are the penalties for licensees who fail to comply with Section 15C?

A: Failure to comply is a violation of TRELA, punishable by reprimand, by suspension or revocation of a license, or by an administrative penalty (fine).

Q: In what way does Section 15C prohibit or permit disclosed dual agency?

A: Section 15C does not prohibit disclosed dual agency, so licensees may act as dual agents with appropriate disclosure and consent.

Q: Is the licensee required under any circumstance, to provide the "written statement" to buyer prospects at properties held open for prospective buyers?

A: An encounter at an open house is not a meeting for the purposes of Section 15C. A licensee would not be required to provide the statutory statement at the open house. However, at the first face to face meeting thereafter with the buyer regarding a specific property and during which substantive discussions occur, the licensee will be required to provide the statement.

Q: When acting as an appointed licensee what "agency" limitations does the licensee have when communicating with a buyer/tenant or seller/ landlord that an agent representing one party only doesn't have?

A: The appointed licensee may not, except as permitted by Section 15C(j) of TRELA, disclose to either party confidential information received from the other party. A licensee representing one party would not be prohibited from revealing confidential information to the licensee's principal, and if the information were material to the principal's decision, would be required to reveal the information to the principal.

Q: If a buyer's agent is required to disclose that licensee's agency status to a listing broker when setting up an appointment showing, must the listing broker also disclose to the buyer's agent that the listing broker represents the seller?

A: Yes, on the first contact with the licensee representing the buyer.

Q: Does the TREC encourage brokerage companies to act for more than one party in the same transaction?

A: No.

Q: Must the intermediary broker furnish written notice to each party to a transaction when the broker designates the appointed licensees?

A: Yes.

Q: How is a property "showing" different from a proposed transaction?

A: The question appears to be "may an associate show property listed with the associate's broker while representing the buyer without first being appointed by the intermediary, and if so, why?"   Yes.   Only showing property does not require the associate to be appointed, because it does not require the licensee to give advice or opinions (only an appointed associate may offer opinions or advice to a party).   If no appointments will be made, of course, the associate will be working with the party and will not be authorized to provide opinions or advice.

Q: Does TREC recommend that licensees provide a written disclosure of agency?

A: It is the licensee's choice as to whether disclosure is in writing or oral, just as it is the licensee's choice as to whether proof of disclosure will be easy or difficult.

Q: Our company policy requires all buyers and sellers to agree to the intermediary practice before commencing to work with them. Does the law permit a broker employment agreement to specify this practice only?

A: If by "broker employment agreement" you mean a listing contract or buyer representation agreement, yes.

Q: What are the differences between the duties provided to the seller or landlord by the intermediary broker and the duties provided to the buyer or tenant by the appointed licensee?

A: The intermediary and the appointed licensees do not provide duties; they perform services under certain duties imposed by the law. The intermediary is authorized to negotiate a transaction between the parties, but not to give advice or opinions to them in negotiations. The appointed licensee may provide advice or opinions to the party to which the licensee has been appointed. Both intermediary and appointed licensee are obligated to treat the parties honestly and are prohibited from revealing confidential information or other information addressed in Section 15C(j) of TRELA.

Q: Must each party's identity be revealed to the other party before an intermediary transaction can occur?

A: Yes. If associates are going to be appointed by the intermediary, the law provides that the appointments are made by giving written notice to both parties. To give notice, the intermediary must identify the party and the associate(s) appointed to that party. The law does not require notice if no appointments are going to be made. The law provides that the listing contract and buyer representation agreement are sufficient to establish the written consent of the party if the obligations of the broker under Section 15C(j) are set forth in conspicuous bold or underlined print.

Q: **As a listing agent I hold open houses. If a buyer prospect enters who desires to purchase the property at that time, can I represent that buyer and, if so, must my broker designate me as an appointed licensee and provide the parties with written notice before I prepare the purchase offer?**

A: As a representative of the seller, you would be obligated to disclose your representation to the buyer at the first contact. The disclosure may be in writing or oral. As an associate of the listing broker, you can enter into a buyer representation agreement for your broker to act as an intermediary in a transaction involving this buyer and the owner of the property. If the owner has similarly authorized the broker to act as an intermediary, it will depend on the firm's policy whether appointments are to be made. If appointments are not going to be made, you may proceed in the transaction as an unappointed licensee with a duty of not favoring one party over the other. If appointments are going to be made, the parties must both be notified in writing before you may provide opinions or advice to the buyer in negotiations.

Q: **I have a salesperson's license through a broker and I also have a licensed assistant. Can that assistant be an appointed licensee under me as an intermediary?**

A: Your broker, not you, will be the intermediary. The intermediary may appoint a licensed associate to work with a party. If the licensed assistant is an associate of the broker, the licensed assistant could be appointed by the intermediary to work with one of the parties. If the licensed assistant is not an associate of the broker, the licensed assistant cannot be appointed. NOTE: IF THE LICENSED ASSISTANT IS LICENSED AS A SALESPERSON, THE LICENSED ASSISTANT MUST BE SPONSORED BY, AND ACTING FOR, A BROKER TO BE AUTHORIZED TO PERFORM ANY ACT FOR WHICH A REAL ESTATE LICENSE IS REQUIRED. IF THE LICENSED ASSISTANT IS SPONSORED BY A BROKER WHO IS NOT ASSOCIATED WITH THE INTERMEDIARY, THE LICENSED ASSISTANT WOULD NOT BE CONSIDERED AN ASSOCIATE OF THE INTERMEDIARY EITHER.

Q: **I am a listing agent and a buyer prospect wants to buy the property I have listed. How can I sell my own listing?**

A: See the three alternatives discussed in the related question on page 2. You could alter the agency relationships and only represent one party, you could be appointed to work with one party and another associate could be appointed to work with the other party, or no appointments would be made, or you could work with the parties being careful not to favor one over the other or provide advice or opinions to them.

Q: **Must the respective appointed licensees each provide an opinion of value to the respective buyer prospect and seller prospect?**

A: At the time a property is listed, the licensee is obligated to advise the owner as to the licensee's opinion of the market value of the property. Once appointments have been made, the appointed associates are permitted, but not required, to provide the party to whom they have been appointed with opinions and advice during negotiations.

Q: **How can the intermediary broker advise the seller or buyer on value, escrow deposit amount, repair expenses, or interest rates?**

A: When the listing contract or buyer representation agreement has come into existence, and no intermediary status yet exists, the broker may advise the parties generally on such matters. Offers from or to parties not represented by the intermediary's firm may have made the parties knowledgeable on these matters. Once the intermediary status has been created, however, the intermediary broker may not express opinions or give advise during negotiations. Information about such matters which does not constitute an opinion or advice may be supplied in response to question. For example, the intermediary could tell the buyer what the prevailing interest rate is without expressing an opinion or giving advice. The seller's question about the amount of earnest money could be answered with the factual answer that in the broker's experience, the amount of the earnest money is usually $1,500 to $2,000, depending on the amount of the sales price. If the buyer asks what amount of money should be in the offer, the intermediary could respond with the factual statement that in the intermediary's experience, those offers closest to the listing price tend to be accepted by the seller. The intermediary also could refer the party to an attorney, accountant, loan officer or other professional for advice.

Q: **I was the listing agent for a property that didn't sell but was listed by another broker after the expiration of my agreement. I now have a buyer client who wants to see that same property. Must the new broker, or my broker, designate me as an appointed licensee or how may I otherwise act?**

A: Assuming an agreement with the listing broker as regards cooperation and compensation, you may represent the buyer as an exclusive agent. You cannot be appointed by the intermediary because you are not an associate of the listing broker, and from the facts as you describe them, no intermediary status is going to arise. Confidential information obtained from the seller when you were acting as the seller's agent, of course, could not be disclosed to your new client, the buyer.

Q: How is the intermediary broker responsible for the actions of appointed licensees when a difference of opinion of property value estimates is provided?

A: Brokers are responsible for the actions of their salespersons under TRELA. Opinions of property values may be different and yet not indicative of error or mistake by the salespersons. If a salesperson makes an error or mistake, the sponsoring broker is responsible to the public and to TREC under Section 1(c) of TRELA..

Q: Although both the buyer and the seller initially consented to the intermediary broker practice at the time each signed a broker employment agreement, must each party consent again to a specific transaction to ensure there are not potential conflicts?

A: TRELA does not require a second written consent. TRELA does require written notice of any appointments, and the written notice would probably cause any objection to be resolved at that point. A broker would not be prohibited from obtaining a second consent as a business practice, so that potential conflicts are identified and resolved. The sales contract, of course, would typically identify the parties and show the intermediary relationship if the broker completes the "Broker Identification and Ratification of Fee" at the end of the TREC contract form.

Q: In the absence of the appointed licensees, can the intermediary broker actually negotiate a purchase offer between the parties?

A: Yes. See the answer to the question relating to the duties of an intermediary.

Q: May a licensee include the statutory statement in a listing agreement or buyer representation agreement, either in the text of the agreement, or as an exhibit?

A: Yes, but the licensee should provide the prospective party with a separate copy of the statutory statement as soon as is practicable at their first face-to-face meeting.

Approved by the Texas Real Estate Commission for Voluntary Use

Texas law requires all real estate licensees to give the following information about brokerage services to prospective buyers, tenants, sellers and landlords.

Information About Brokerage Services

Before working with a real estate broker, you should know that the duties of a broker depend on whom the broker represents. If you are a prospective seller or landlord (owner) or a prospective buyer or tenant (buyer), you should know that the broker who lists the property for sale or lease is the owner's agent. A broker who acts as a subagent represents the owner in cooperation with the listing broker. A broker who acts as a buyer's agent represents the buyer. A broker may act as an intermediary between the parties if the parties consent in writing. A broker can assist you in locating a property, preparing a contract or lease, or obtaining financing without representing you. A broker is obligated by law to treat you honestly.

IF THE BROKER REPRESENTS THE OWNER:
The broker becomes the owner's agent by entering into an agreement with the owner, usually through a written listing agreement, or by agreeing to act as a subagent by accepting an offer of subagency from the listing broker. A subagent may work in a different real estate office. A listing broker or subagent can assist the buyer but does not represent the buyer and must place the interests of the owner first. The buyer should not tell the owner's agent anything the buyer would not want the owner to know because an owner's agent must disclose to the owner any material information known to the agent.

IF THE BROKER REPRESENTS THE BUYER:
The broker becomes the buyer's agent by entering into an agreement to represent the buyer, usually through a written buyer representation agreement. A buyer's agent can assist the owner but does not represent the owner and must place the interests of the buyer first. The owner should not tell a buyer's agent anything the owner would not want the buyer to know because a buyer's agent must disclose to the buyer any material information known to the agent.

IF THE BROKER ACTS AS AN INTERMEDIARY:
A broker may act as an intermediary between the parties if the broker complies with The Texas Real Estate License Act.

The broker must obtain the written consent of each party to the transaction to act as an intermediary. The written consent must state who will pay the broker and, in conspicuous bold or underlined print, set forth the broker's obligations as an intermediary. The broker is required to treat each party honestly and fairly and to comply with The Texas Real Estate License Act. A broker who acts as an intermediary in a transaction:

(1) shall treat all parties honestly;

(2) may not disclose that the owner will accept a price less than the asking price unless authorized in writing to do so by the owner;

(3) may not disclose that the buyer will pay a price greater than the price submitted in a written offer unless authorized in writing to do so by the buyer; and

(4) may not disclose any confidential information or any information that a party specifically instructs the broker in writing not to disclose unless authorized in writing to disclose the information or required to do so by The Texas Real Estate License Act or a court order or if the information materially relates to the condition of the property.

With the parties' consent, a broker acting as an intermediary between the parties may appoint a person who is licensed under The Texas Real Estate License Act and associated with the broker to communicate with and carry out instructions of one party and another person who is licensed under that Act and associated with the broker to communicate with and carry out instructions of the other party.

If you choose to have a broker represent you,
you should enter into a written agreement with the broker that clearly establishes the broker's obligations and your obligations. The agreement should state how and by whom the broker will be paid. You have the right to choose the type of representation, if any, you wish to receive. Your payment of a fee to a broker does not necessarily establish that the broker represents you. If you have any questions regarding the duties and responsibilities of the broker, you should resolve those questions before proceeding.

Real estate licensee asks that you acknowledge receipt of this information about brokerage services for the licensee's records.

_____   _____
Buyer, Seller, Landlord or Tenant   Date

Agency Cases from 50 States

This appendix contains an annotation of 600 cases from all 50 states illustrating a number of the agency issues raised in the text.

CHAPTER 2. BASIC AGENCY RELATIONSHIPS AND DUTIES OF THE AGENT

The Fiduciary Relationship

Fiduciary Duties—Persons dealing with a real estate licensee may naturally assume that the broker possesses the requisites of an honest and ethical person. *Ellis v. Flink,* 301 So.2d 493 (FL 1974); *Department of Employment v. Bake Young Realty,* 560 P.2d 504 (ID 1977); *Easton v. Strassburger,* 199 Cal.Rptr. 383 (CA App. 1984); *Zichlin v. Dill,* 25 So.2d 4 (FL 1946). Brokers hold themselves out to the public as having particular skills and knowledge in the real estate field. In essence, the law creates a public duty.

In any lawsuit alleging that the broker breached a fiduciary duty, the broker must prove no breach of duty occurred. *Vogt v. Town & Country Realty of Lincoln,* 231 N.W.2d 496 (NE 1975).

In a suit for negligence against a real estate broker, the Nebraska Supreme Court held that a special two-year statute of limitations for "professional negligence" was inapplicable because "real estate brokers are not professionals." *Tylle v. Zouche,* 412 N.W.2d 438 (NE 1987).

Duty of Loyalty—Of all the obligations imposed by the fiduciary duty, loyalty is the essential virtue required of a broker. *Rose v. Showalter,* 701 P.2d 251 (ID 1985); *Wegg v. Henry Broderick, Inc.,* 557 P.2d 861 (WA 1976); *Cogan v. Kidder, Mathews & Segner, Inc.,* 648 P.2d 875 (WA 1982).

Disclosure

1. Relationship—*Mersky v. Multiple Listing Bureau of Olympia, Inc.,* 437 P.2d 897 (WA 1968); *Kimmell v. Clark,* 520 P.2d 851 (AZ 1974); *Ross v. Perelli,* 538 P.2d 834 (WA 1975) (relationship between subagent and buyer); *Wilkinson v. Smith,* 639 P.2d 768 (WA 1982); *John J. Reynolds v. Snow,* 174 N.E.2d 753 (NY 1961); *Velten v. Robertson,* 671 P.2d 1011 (CO 1983); *Smith v. Zak,* 98 Cal.Rptr. 242 (CA 1971); *Jenkins v. Wise,* 574 P.2d 1337 (HI 1978); *Silva v. Bisbie,* 628 P.2d 214 (HI 1981); *Ramsey v. Sedlar,* 454 P.2d 416 (WA 1969); *Abell v. Watson,* 317 P.2d 159 (CA 1957) (buyer was broker's wife). See also *Handy v. Garmarker,* 324 N.W.2d 168 (MN 1982); *Christman v. Seymour,* 700 P.2d 898 (AZ 1985); *Drake v. Hasley,* 713 P.2d 1203 (AK 1986).

The broker must disclose any interest in a corporation offering to buy a listed property, even if the broker is a minority shareholder or is a director or an officer and has no stock ownership. *Bell v. Routh Robbins Real Estate Corp.,* 147 S.E.2d 277 (VA 1966); *McKinney v. Christmas,*

353 P.2d 373 (CO 1960); *Treat v. Schmidt,* 193 P.666 (CO 1920); *Newell-Murdoch Realty Co. v. Wickham,* 190 P. 359 (CA 1920); *Batson v. Strehlow,* 441 P.2d 101 (CA 1968); *Wendt v. Fischer,* 154 N.E. 303 (NY 1926); *Travagliante v. J. W. Wood Realty Company,* 425 S.W.2d 208 (MO 1968). Brokerage breached fiduciary duty owed seller by not disclosing that one of its general partners was part purchaser of listed property. *Designer Showrooms v. Kelley,* 405 S.E.2d 417 (SC 1991).

The fact that the broker is licensed or has an interest in the buyer does not preclude the broker from participating in the transaction and earning a commission, provided the seller receives full disclosure of the conflicting interests. *In re Estate of Baldwin,* 110 Cal.Rptr. 189 (CA App 1973); *Rosenfeld v. Glick Real Estate Co.,* 291 S.W.2d 863 (MO 1956); *Stevens v. Hutton,* 163 P.2d 479 (CA 1946). Failure to disclose broker's romance with divorce attorney of client's ex-spouse might influence complete loyalty to client. *Silverman v. Pitterman,* 574 So.2d 275 (FL 1991).

Note that a licensee acting as a principal in the sale or purchase of real estate should disclose to the other party the fact of licensure. An inactive licensee may have no duty of disclosure, although it would be preferable to disclose. *Gregory v. Selle,* 206 N.W.2d 147 (WI 1973). Upheld ruling that use of phrase by broker "for sale by owner" was misleading. *HelpSell v. Maine REC,* 611 A.2d 981 (ME 1992). Broker not liable for making repairs as personal guarantor when he signed agreement on line marked "witness." *McGinney v. Jackson,* 575 So.2d 1070 (ALA 1991).

2. Other Offers—The broker must present all offers as a matter of top priority. It is also advisable to inform the seller of facts that indicate another offer may be presented shortly and to present offers even after the seller has accepted an offer, in the event the seller wishes to have back-up offers. The broker should tell the buyer that making a full-price offer does not mean the seller must accept such offer. The broker should avoid giving to the buyer "rights of first refusal" or assuring the buyer that the seller will accept a certain amount.

The broker must submit an offer even if the broker believes it is too low to warrant consideration. *E. A. Strout Realty Agency, Inc. v. Wooster,* 99 A.2d 689 (VT 1955).

The listing broker is under an affirmative duty to disclose a second offer to purchase and, by failing to disclose such offer, has made a representation that no other offer exists. Failure to disclose could result in loss of commission, loss of license or even punitive damages. The buyer may sue the broker for money damages resulting from the broker's failure to present the buyer's offer. Such cases usually involve situations in which the broker purchases the property. *Simone v. McKee,* 298 P.2d 667 (CA 1956); *Cisco v. Van Lew,* 141 P.2d 433 (CA 1943); *Southern Cross Industries, Inc. v. Martin,* 604 S.W.2d 290 (TX 1980); *Hickman v. Colorado Real Estate Commission,* 534 P.2d 1220 (CO 1975); *Virginia Real Estate Commission v. Bias,* 308 S.E.2d 123 (VA 1983); *Githens v. Johnson,* 192 N.W. 270 (IA 1923); *Brown v. Carpenter,* 134 S.W. 1150 (KY 1911); *Barbat v. M.E. Arden Co.,* 254 N.W.2d 779 (MI 1977); *Harper v. Adametz,* 113 A.2d 136 (CT 1955); *Arnato v. Latter & Blum, Inc.,* 79 So.2d 873 (LA 1955); *Phillips v. Lynch,* 704 P.2d 1083 (NV 1985).

Brokers must respect the confidentiality of offers. The listing broker should not disclose to other salespersons in the broker's office the amount of a cooperating broker's offer. Nor should the listing broker reveal the amount of a previous counteroffer made by the seller. Likewise, the listing broker should not disclose the amounts of previously rejected offers unless the seller agrees to this strategy. Buyers should be encouraged to submit their best offers. Knowledge of other offers may result in a buyer submitting a lower offer than originally planned.

Brokers must also disclose any information that a prospective buyer may be willing to offer better terms or a higher price than the offer presented. *Carter v. Owens,* 50 So. 641 (FL 1909); *Gillespie v. Rosenbaum,* 173 N.Y.S.429 (NY 1918); *Raleigh Real Estate & Trust Co. v. Adarns,* 58 S.E. 1008 (NC 1907); *Mason v. Bulleri,* 543 P.2d 478 (AZ 1975). Broker not liable to buyer for failure to convey purchase offer accurately to seller. *Andrie v. Crystal-Anderson,* 466 N.W.2d 393 (MI 1991).

3. Status of Deposit Money—*De St.Germain v. Watson,* 214 P.2d 99 (CA 1950) (failed to disclose payment in form of promissory note); *Nugent v. Scharff,* 476 S.W.2d 414 (TX 1971); *Roy H. Long Realty Company v. Vanderkolk,* 547 P.2d 497 (AZ 1976); *Merkeley v. MacPherson's Inc.,* 420 P.2d 205 (WA 1966); *Hughey v. Rainwater Partners,* 661 S.W.2d 690 (TN 1983) (seller awarded 100 percent of deposit); *Reich v. Christopulos,* 256 P.2d 238 (UT 1953); holding no violation of licensing law to fail to disclose postdated check is Lowe v. State Dept. of Commerce, Real Estate Division, 515 P.2d 388 (NV 1973); *Huizenga v. Withey Sheppard Associates,* 167 N.W.2d 120 (MI 1969); see *Wilson v. Lewis,* 165 Cal.Rptr. 396 (CA 1980).

A broker is liable for failure to disclose to the property owner that the broker did not collect the security deposits as indicated in the rental agreements. In *Murphy & Fritz's Place, Inc. v. Loretta,* 447 N.Y.S.2d 205 (NY 1982), the broker was held liable for failure to disclose that he had not received the initial or additional deposit the contract required the buyer to make. Broker liable for advising buyer to make a $50,000 down payment to person claiming falsely to be the owner of the property (rather than place money in escrow). *Keystone Realty v. Osterhus,* 807 P.2d 1385 (NV 1991).

4. Buyer's Financial Condition—*Miller v. Berkoski,* 297 N.W.2d 334 (IA 1980) (broker loaned buyer money for down payment); *McGarry v. McCrone,* 118 N.E.2d 195 (OH 1954); *Farrell v. Score,* 411 P.2d 146 (WA 1966); *Mason v. Bulleri,* 543 P.2d 178 (AZ 1975); *Alhino v. Starr,* 169 Cal.Rptr. 136 (CA 1980); *Banville v. Schmidt,* 112 Cal.Rptr. 126 (CA 1974); *R.A. Poff & Co. v. Ottaway,* 62 S.E.2d 865 (VA 1951). *In Fulsom v. Egner,* 79 N.W.2d 25 (MN 1956), the broker failed to disclose that the buyer's ability to pay was contingent on the outcome of a pending lawsuit.

When the broker makes a credit check of the buyer and discovers many negative features, the broker must disclose this information to the seller. Even though a failure to disclose may not amount to misrepresentation, it is still a breach of fiduciary duty sufficient to justify nonpayment of commission, as held in *White v. Boucher,* 322 N.W.2d 560 (MN 1982).

The seller is justified in relying on the broker's representation that the buyer is financially sound, without having to make an independent investigation of the buyer's finances. *Phillips v. JCM Development Corporation,* 666 P.2d 876 (UT 1983). But if the broker makes reasonable inquiry into the buyer's financial condition and discloses this to the seller, the broker is not liable if the buyer later defaults. *Zwick v. United Farm Agency, Inc.,* 556 P.2d 508 (WY 1976).

Disclosure of financial condition is especially important when the buyer is a salesperson of the cooperating broker. *L.A. Grant Realty v. Cuomo,* 396 N.Y.S.2d 524 (NY 1977); *Hercules v. Robedeaux Inc.,* 329 N.W.2d 240 (WI App. 1982).

In *Prall v. Corum,* 403 So.2d 991 (FL 1981), the broker was held liable for failure to disclose the buyer's financial inability to purchase the property and the fact that the broker loaned the buyer money to close.

5. Property Value—The broker is liable for rendering a false opinion of value. *Eastburn v. Joseph Esphalla Jr. & Co.,* 112 So. 232 (AK 1927); *Moore v. Turner,* 71 S.E.2d 342 (WV 1952); *Iriart v. Johnson,* 411 P.2d 226 (NM 1966). In *Duhl v. Nash Realty, Inc.,* 429 N.E.2d 1267 (IL 1982), the seller bought another property relying on the broker's assurance that the property would sell quickly. A mere mistake in judgment of value is not a breach. *Smith v. Fidelity & Columbia Trust Co.,* 12 S.W.2d 276 (KY 1928). No commission is owed a broker who withholds information that a property being taken by the broker's client in an exchange is overvalued due to faulty construction. The client may be justified in relying on the professional opinion of the broker without making an independent investigation. *Smith v. Carroll Realty Co.,* 335 P.2d 67 (UT 1959); *Frederick v. Sguillante,* 144 So.2d 848 (FL 1962). In some cases, the broker is liable for deliberately undervaluing the property and then attempting to buy it and resell it at a quick profit. *Barnard v. Gardner Inv. Corporation,* 106 S.E. 346 (VA 1921). Broker not liable for negligent misrepresentation of value of land. *1488, Inc. v. Philsec Inc.,* 939 F.2d 1281 (5th Cir. 1991).

When the broker learns of factors affecting the value of the property after the listing is signed, the broker must disclose such factors so the price can be adjusted in accordance with actual conditions. It is sometimes difficult, however, to pinpoint when a market is surging upward. *Holmes v. Cathcart,* 92 N.W. 956 (MN 1903). In *Ramsey v. Gordon,* 567 S.W.2d 868 (TX 1978), the broker-buyer was to be paid a commission by the seller. The seller was allowed to void the contract because the broker breached a fiduciary duty by not disclosing the increasing value of the property during the listing period. In *Ridgeway v. McGuire,* 158 P.2d 893 (OR 1945), the broker-buyer was held liable for failure to advise the seller that the property would be valued higher if it were subdivided. In *Schoenberg v. Benner,* 59 Cal.Rptr. 359 (CA 1967), the listing broker was held negligent for failing to verify the appraised value of property that secured the buyer's purchase money note carried back by the seller.

6. Commission Split—Failure to disclose a secret fee-splitting arrangement with the buyer's broker (as opposed to a subagent) can result in loss of commission by the listing broker. *Tracey v. Blake,* 118 N.E. 271 (MA 1918); *Devine v. Hudgins,* 163 A.83 (ME 1932); *Peaden v. Marler,* 189 P.741 (OK 1920). There is generally no prohibition against the listing broker dividing the commission with the buyer, as such a reduction in commission is a personal sacrifice on the broker's part to further the interests of the seller. *Banner v. Elm,* 248 A.2d 452 (MD 1968); *McCall v. Johns,* 294 S.W.2d 869 (TX 1956); *Douell v. Rosenstein,* 208 N.W. 651 (MN 1926); but see *Greenberg v. Meyer,* 363 N.E.2d 779 (OH 1977), in which broker was held to have breached duty of loyalty.

7. Contract Provisions—The broker must disclose important provisions of contracts that the client is expected to sign. Brokers have been held liable for not discussing with sellers the effect of accepting unsecured promissory notes or the fact that the sellers would receive minimal cash. *Morley v. J. Pagel Realty & Ins.,* 550 P.2d 1104 (AZ 1976); *Buffington v. Haas,* 601 P.2d 1320 (AZ 1979); *Wesco Realty, Inc. v. Drewry,* 515 P.2d 513 (WA 1973); *Reese v. Harper,* 329 P.2d 410 (UT 1958). While a listing broker clearly has a duty to advise the seller concerning tying up the seller's VA eligibility on an assumption by a nonveteran buyer, it has been held that a buyer's broker has no such duty. *Hurney v. Locke,* 308 N.W.2d 764 (SD 1981). The broker may be liable for failure to disclose that a listing agreement is an exclusive right to sell, *Lyle v. Moore,* 599 P.2d 336 (MT 1979), or the effect of an extender or a carryover clause, *Baird v. Madsen,* 134 P.2d 885 (CA 1943).

Some courts extend the duty of the broker to discuss with the buyer certain contract provisions, such as the seller's remedies upon default of the buyer. *Wegg v. Henry Broderick, Inc.,* 557 P.2d 861 (WA 1976); *Swift v. White,* 129 N.W.2d 748 (IA 1964); for a contrary result, see *Crawford v. Powers,* 419 F.Supp. 723 (D.S.C.), applying South Carolina law, *Kidd v. Maldonado,* 688 P.2d 461 (UT 1984). In an exchange, the broker was liable for failing to disclose that a second mortgage contained a due-on-sale clause, and the plaintiff lost the property through foreclosure, *Pepitone v. Russo,* 134 Cal.Rptr. 709 (CA 1976). In *Alhino v. Starr,* 169 Cal.Rptr.136 (CA 1980), the salesperson failed to disclose to the seller that the purchase money note was unsecured and did not contain the customary attorney fees and acceleration provisions. Broker acting as buyer owes duty of fair disclosure to seller (explain consequence of taking "subject to" as compared to "assumption of" loan). *Sigmen v. Arizona Dept. Real Estate,* 819 P.2d 969 (AZ 1991).

Sellers not required to pay commission when broker failed to comply with state disclosure law. *Huijers v. DeMarrais,* 12 Cal.App.4th 676 (CA December 1992).

Faithfulness

A broker who induces a buyer to believe that a property can be bought for less than the asking price may fail to discharge the duty of loyalty and, therefore, forfeit the commission. See *Beckwith v. Clevenger Realty Co.,* 360 P.2d 596 (AZ 1961), in which the broker told the buyer the seller was anxious to sell due to poor health; *Haymes v. Rogers,* 222 P.2d 789 (AZ 1950), in which the court held the broker liable only if done in bad faith. Likewise, the broker should not make an unauthorized statement that the property is listed at $195,000, but the seller yesterday countered another buyer's offer at $187,000.

Preparing two ascending offers for the buyer and presenting only the lower one without informing the seller that the buyer will go higher violates the broker's duty of loyalty. It is unfaithful for the broker to attempt to sell property well above the listing price to pocket the difference. *Mason v. Bulleri,* 543 P.2d 478 (AZ 1975); *Gillespie v. Rosenbaum,* 173 N.Y.S.429 (NY 1918); *Rattray v. Scudder,* 169 P.2d 371 (CA 1946); *Sankey v. Cramer,* 131 P. 288 (CO 1913). A broker who persuaded the buyer to buy elsewhere breached the fiduciary duty of good faith in *Lyon v. Giannoni,* 335 P.2d 690 (CA 1959). Broker breached duty of honesty to buyer of second home (former seller-client of broker). *Youngblood v. Wall,* 815 S.W.2d 512 (TN 1991).

Any collusion by the broker with the buyer will forfeit the broker's right to a commission, even though the seller obtains the full asking price. *Carter v. Owens,* 50 So. 641 (FL 1909); *Sternberger v. Young,* 75 A. 807 (NJ 1908). In *Greenfield v. Bausch,* 263 N.Y.S. 19 (NY 1933), the buyer agreed to pay the broker half of any amount by which the seller's listing price was reduced through the broker's efforts. The broker cannot suggest that the buyer offer terms less advantageous to the seller than the buyer had indicated the buyer would make. *Investment Exchange Realty, Inc. v. Hillcrest Bowl, Inc.,* 513 P.2d 282 (WA 1973); *Mitchell v. Gould,* 266 P. 565 (CA 1928).

Brokers cannot make false promises to induce their principals to enter into contracts, as in *Brown v. Coates,* 253 F.2d 36 (DC 1958). In *Jory v. Bennight,* 542 P.2d 1400 (NV 1975), the broker was held liable for the misconduct of its two salespersons, who falsely promised that the seller would receive additional monies outside of escrow.

Denial of commission due to conflict of interest when listing broker failed to disclose that salesperson in office was selling similar property to same buyer. *Reinhold v. Mallery,* 599 A.2d 126 (NH 1991).

Broker not liable to seller for damages caused as a result of buyer receiving inaccurate income financial information supplied by seller. *Burton v. Mackey,* 102 Or.App. 361 (OR 1990).

In *Moser v. Bertram,* No. 20692 (August 10, 1993), the New Mexico Supreme Court faced the issue of whether the listing salesperson was liable to a buyer client of the firm for breach of fiduciary duty. The buyer failed to close on an earlier contract with the listing salesperson's seller. The buyer subsequently arranged financing, expecting to consummate the sale, but was told the seller had accepted another offer. The buyer sued for loss of investment opportunity. The listing salesperson was the only one left with money. The court held that "although agency fiduciary obligations and liabilities may extend from a salesperson to the qualifying broker, the fiduciary duties of one real estate salesperson are not attributable to another salesperson operating under the same qualifying broker unless one salesperson is at fault in appointing, supervising, or cooperating with the other." See *Restatement (Second) of Agency 358(1)* (1957).

The broker should not return deposit money to the buyer without first checking with the seller, as in *Kruger v. Soreide,* 246 N.W.2d 764 (ND 1976).

Many of the reported cases involve buyers' brokers who find the ideal properties for their clients, but first buy the properties themselves, then sell them to the buyers at a secret profit. *Des Fosses v. Notis,* 333 A.2d 822 (ME 1975); *Green v. Jones-Murphy Properties, Inc.,* 335 S.W. 2d 822 (AR 1960); *Hyman v. Burmeister,* 216 Ill.App. 98 (IL 1919); *Kurtz v. Farrington,* 132 A. 540 (CT 1926).

If the broker is not the agent of the buyer, however, the broker may owe no duty to disclose to the buyer the broker's interest in purchasing the property. *Fish v. Teninga,* 161 N.E. 515 (IL 1928); *Warren v. Mangels Realty,* 533 P.2d 78 (AZ 1975). Buyer's brokers cannot profit by their own unfaithfulness. *Hilbolt v. Wisconsin Real Estate Brokers' Board,* 137 N.W.2d 482 (WI 1965); *Neff v. Bud Lewis Company,* 548 P.2d 107 (NM 1976); *Pouppirt v. Greenwood,* 110 P. 195 (CO 1910); *Roquemore v. Ford Motor Company,* 290 F.Supp. 130 (TX 1967); *United Homes, Inc. v. Moss,* 154 So.2d 351 (FL 1963); *Kroeker v. Hurlbert,* 101 P.2d 101 (CA 1940); *Degner v. Moncel,* 93 N.W.2d 857 (WI 1959); *Smith v. Howard,* 322 P.2d 1034 (CA 1958).

In *Sawyer Realty Group, Inc. v. Jarvis Corp.,* 432 N.E.2d 849 (IL 1982), the seller's brokers breached a duty of good faith to the buyer by not disclosing the fact that after the buyer submitted an offer, the seller sold the property to the brokers. In *Funk v. Tiff,* 515 F.2d 23 (9th Cir. FL 1975), the buyer made an offer through the listing broker, who, in turn, submitted a similar offer for himself and his partner. The court held that the listing broker had a duty to deal fairly and honestly with the buyer and that outbidding the prospective buyer without adequate disclosure to the buyer was a breach. The listing broker held the property as a constructive trustee for the benefit of the buyer.

Self-Dealing

> The real estate broker is brought by his calling into a relation of trust and confidence. Constant are the opportunities by concealment and collusion to extract illicit gains. We know from our judicial records that the opportunities have been not lost. *Roman v. Lobe,* 152 N.E. 461 (NY 1926) (Cardoza, J.)

Unfortunately, the casebooks are filled with lawsuits in which the real estate broker purchased property and was sued because either (1) the broker did not disclose to the seller that the broker or a relative was the real buyer or (2) the buyer's broker secretly purchased a property and then resold it to the buyer client at a profit in a double escrow or "flip" transaction. Some of the self-deal cases in which the broker is an undisclosed buyer are *Batson v. Strehlow,* 441 P.2d 101 (CA 1968); *Riley v. Powell,* 665 S.W. 2d 578 (TX 1984); *Rodes v. Shannon,* 35 Cal.Rptr. 339 (CA 1963); *Rosenfeld v. Glick Real Estate Co.,* 291 S.W.2d 863 (MO 1956); *Buckley v. Savage,* 7 Cal.Rptr. 328 (CA 1960). When the broker fully discloses the facts and takes no unfair advantage, no breach of fiduciary duty occurs, as in *Fisher v. Losey,* 177 P.2d 334 (CA 1947).

In some cases, the broker uses a dummy purchaser to buy and then sell at a secret profit. *Loughlin v. Idora Realty Company,* 66 Cal.Rptr. 747 (CA 1968); *Schepers v. Lautenschlager,* 112 N.W.2d 767 (NE 1962); *Alley v. Nevada Real Estate Division,* 575 P.2d 1334 (NV 1978) (double escrow); *Carluccio v. 607 Hudson Street Holding Co.,* 57 A.2d 452 (NJ 1948); *M.S.R., Inc. v. Lish,* 527 P.2d 912 (CO 1974); *Wendt v. Fischer,* 154 N.E. 303 (NY 1926); *Simone v. McKee,* 298 P.2d 667 (CA 1956).

Listing agent found out about seller's bid on a replacement home. Agent used the information to outbid seller. Court found no breach of fiduciary duty. *Walter v. Murphy,* 573 N.E.2d 677 (OH 1988). *Note:* In today's environment the result may have been considerably different.

Punitive damages awarded to buyer, whose offer was never presented by listing agent, who bought the property at a lower price from desperate seller. *Forbus v. City Realty,* Case No. 90-131 (AL 1992).

In *Thompson v. Searl,* 301 P.2d 804 (WY 1956), the seller broker breached its fiduciary obligation by accepting a commission from the buyer for selling the buyer's home that was used as part payment of the sales price, without first obtaining the seller's consent.

In some cases, the self-dealing broker is sued by the buyer who hired the broker to locate a property. *Henderson v. Hassur,* 594 P.2d 650 (KS 1979); *Quinn v. Phipps,* 113 So. 419 (FL 1927); *Rogers v. Genung,* 74 A.473 (NJ 1909); *Kurtz v. Farrington,* 132 A.540 (CT 1926); *Zichlin v. Dill,* 25 So.2d 4 (FL 1946); *Volz v. Burkeheimer, Inc.,* 21 P.2d 285 (WA 1933); *Barber's Super Markets, Inc. v. Stryker,* 500 P.2d 1304 (NM 1972); *Baskin v. Dam,* 239 A.2d 549 (CT 1967); *Spindler v. Krieger,* 147 N.E.2d 457 (IL 1958); *Jarvis v. O'Brien,* 305 P.2d 961 (CA 1957). Often, the buyer sues to impose a constructive trust in favor of the buyer. *Mitchell v. Allison,* 213 P.2d 231 (NM 1949); *Ward v. Taggart,* 336 P.2d 534 (CA 1959); *Antle v. Haas,* 251 S.W.2d 290 (KY 1952), *Green v. Jones-Murphy Properties, Inc.,* 335 S.W.2d 822 (AR 1960); *Burton v. Pet, Inc.,* 509 S.W.2d 95 (MO 1974); *Sierra Pacific Industries v. Carter,* 163 Cal.Rptr. 764 (CA 1980); *Hughes v. Miracle Ford, Inc.,* 676 S.W.2d 642 (TX 1984).

In cases where brokers act on their own behalf in a sale or purchase of property, they are generally held to a higher standard than non-licensees. In *Mississippi Real Estate Commission v. Ruby Henessee,* Supreme Court 92 CC 1230 (April 1996) the broker maintained that she was not subject to the Mississippi license law since she was acting on her own behalf. The real estate commission suspended her license for 90 days for making misrepresentations in the sale of her property. She took her case to the circuit court who ruled in her favor, thus against the Commission. The Commission appealed to the Supreme Court who ruled for the Commission saying, . . . "To allow Ruby, or any other licensed broker, not to be held responsible for misrepresentations made during the course of the sale of property wholly owned by the broker, while simultaneously holding that a broker will be held responsible for making misrepresentations during the sale of another's property, would create logically inconsistent results."

Duty of Obedience

When the seller instructed the broker not to return the buyer's deposit money without first obtaining a written appraisal (confirming the buyer's contingency that the sales price be at or below fair market value), and the broker failed to obtain such appraisal, the broker could not recover the commission. The seller's instructions were reasonable and material and, if carried out, could have prevented litigation. *Jackson v. Williams,* 510 S.W.2d 645 (TX 1974). When the listing agreement stated that the broker was to lease a warehouse subject to the owner's approval of the tenant, and the broker allowed the tenant to move in without prior owner approval, the broker was not entitled to receive a commission. *Latter & Blum v. Richmond,* 388 So.2d 368 (LA 1980); *Owen v. Shelton,* 277 S.E.2d 189 (VA 1981).

The broker was held to have breached its fiduciary duty of obedience by failing to obey the seller's instruction to revoke a counteroffer prior to the buyer's acceptance. *Abboud v. State Real Estate Commission,* 316 N.W.2d 608 (NE 1982).

Duty to Use Reasonable Skill and Care

The broker's duties of care and disclosure are greater when the client is unsophisticated and unknowledgeable in real estate transactions. *Prall v. Gooden,* 360 P.2d 759 (OR 1961); *Bjornstad v. Perry,* 443 P.2d 999 (ID 1968); *Fairfield S&L v. Kroll,* 246 N.E.2d 327 (IL 1969).

The duties of reasonable skill and care are imposed not only by the common law of agency, but frequently also by the terms of the listing contract, and thus support a breach of contract action or defense. In most professional liability lawsuits, it is necessary to produce expert testimony regarding the standard of care required of the professional. This is not required in malpractice actions against a real estate broker. *Jorgensen v. Beach 'N' Bay Realty, Inc.,* 177 Cal.Rptr.882 (CA 1981); *Easton v. Strassburger,* 199 Cal.Rptr.383 (CA 1984). The complaining party's testimony may be sufficient to prove broker malpractice. Buyer's broker held to have fiduciary duties to discover and disclose material facts, such as existence of declaration of restriction against property prohibiting business use. *Lewis v. Long & Foster Real Estate,* 584 A.2d 1325 (MD 1991).

The broker should make a reasonable inquiry into the creditworthiness of a proposed buyer seeking to have the seller's carryback financing. The broker must exercise care in evaluating or preparing contract provisions and must use correct information, facts and figures. Important facts, such as sewer connections and zoning, must be carefully researched and verified. The real estate broker is held to a standard of care that requires that the broker possess ordinary professional knowledge concerning the title and natural characteristics of the property being sold. *Brady v. Carmanl,* 3 Cal.Rptr. 612 (CA 1960). Broker not liable when buyer defaulted on seller carryback mortgage. *Garcia v. Unique Realty,* 92 FCDR 2162 (GA 1993).

The case of *Perkins v. Thorpe,* 676 P.2d 52 (ID 1984), involved the question of whether the broker breached a fiduciary duty owed to the seller by negligently misadvising the seller on the value of the listed property and failing to disclose that the broker represented the buyer in a separate but related transaction. The court stated:

> The law imposes upon a real estate broker a fiduciary obligation of utmost good faith, integrity, honesty, and loyalty as well as a duty of due care and diligence. Breach of the fiduciary duty may result in the broker's loss of commission and in liability in damages. A broker ultimately is responsible to the public for the actions of real estate salespersons whom he employs.

> A broker is obligated to employ that degree of skill in his calling usually possessed by others in the same business. The broker's conduct is required to meet a standard of competence because he is issued a license and permitted to hold himself out to the public as qualified by training and experience to render a specialized service in the field of real estate transactions. The law requires that the broker perform [at] a certain level of skill; for if he failed to do so, instead of being the badge of competence and integrity it is supposed to be, the broker's license would serve only as a foil to lure the unsuspecting public in.

The broker is liable to the seller whenever the broker's carelessness results in a buyer's successfully suing the seller for money damages or rescission. This is true even when the broker acts gratuitously, as in *Green v. Jones-Murphy Properties, Inc.,* 335 S.W.2d 822 (AR 1960). A gratuitous buyer's broker was held liable for failure to transfer the seller's insurance policy to the buyer as agreed in *Estes v. Lloyd Hammerstad, Inc.,* 503 P.2d 1149 (WA 1972). Consider the following:

- Broker innocently misstated the net operating income to indicate a positive cash flow.

- Broker failed to reveal that seller had only oral permission for a driveway access.

- Broker failed to ascertain that the property being sold was owned jointly, only one owner signed the acceptance and the transaction failed; likewise, when the unsophisticated seller owned only a life estate.

- Broker failed to verify the issuance of a valid septic tank permit, a critical contingency to the sales contract. The broker is required to employ a reasonable degree of effort and professional expertise to confirm or refute important information obtained from the seller. *Tennant v. Lawton,* 615 P.2d 1305 (WA 1980).

- Broker assisted seller in preparing a financial statement based on a check register. Buyer canceled due to erroneous financial information supplied to buyer. Although brokers are not usually held to the standard of care of accountants, a broker must exercise extreme care when acting like an accountant in voluntarily assisting in the preparation of financial information for the broker's principal. *Lunden v. Smith,* 632 P.2d 1344 (OR 1981).

In some cases, the broker is liable to the seller for failing to properly advise and protect the seller's best interests. *Nolan v. Wisconsin Real Estate Brokers' Board,* 89 N.W.2d 317 (WI 1958). Suppose the broker allows the seller to carry back a $50,000 note not secured by a mortgage or deed of trust without first making sure that the seller understands the consequences of taking an unsecured note. See *Morley v. J. Pagel Realty & Insurance,* 550 P.2d 1104 (AZ 1976), in which the court said the broker must use all of his professional ability and knowledge to make sure the client understands the facts. Or suppose, in a contemplated transaction, that (1) the broker promises the seller that a sale will occur by a date sufficient to have funds to purchase another property, (2) the broker fails to recommend protective contingency language in both contracts and (3) the broker represents both ends of the transaction. Or suppose the broker advises the seller that the seller is entitled to keep the earnest money deposit on default, yet fails to mention that escrow usually requires mutual releases and deducts cancellation charges prior to paying out the deposit.

What if the broker fails to tell the seller about restrictions on VA and FHA financing, such as substitution of VA eligibility and the need to make repairs under minimum property requirements? See *Monty v. Peterson,* 540 P.2d 1377 (WA 1975); *Reese v. Harper,* 329 P.2d 410 (UT 1958). In *Jones v. Maestas,* 696 P.2d 920 (ID 1985), the court held that the broker was not required to communicate the meaning of an exclusive listing agreement that was unequivocally expressed by the instrument itself.

The broker was held liable when the broker wrote the purchase contract incorrectly and not according to specifications in *Mattieligh v. Poe,* 356 P.2d.328 (WA 1960). The broker is required to act with due diligence to inquire about an apparent discrepancy in property size. The broker must point out the desirable features of the seller's property. *Schackai v. Lagreco,* 350 So.2d 1244 (LA 1977); *Mallallieu-Golder, Inc. v. O'Neal,* 16 Pa. D & C 2d 594 (PA 1959).

The real estate broker is expected to do more than find a buyer for a seller's property. The broker must diligently exercise skill and care on behalf of the client. To illustrate the extent of the broker's obligation beyond matchmaking, refer to the checklist of listing broker responsibilities in the typical residential transaction.

Duty to Account

The broker must not commingle client funds with the broker's own funds. Brokers usually maintain separate client trust fund accounts. The broker should use one account for sales transactions and another for rental property management transactions.

State licensing law usually contains strict rules on trust fund accounting. The Texas Real Estate Commission can suspend or revoke a broker's license for not properly accounting for client funds. *Kilgore v. Texas Real Estate Commission,* 565 S.W.2d 114 (TX 1978). Brokers must deposit checks by the next business day after receipt unless special permission is obtained to hold the checks in uncashed form. Rather than use a client trust fund account, some brokers suggest the buyer's deposit check be payable directly to the escrow company or settlement agent.

Misrepresentation

Regarding the element of reliance, courts have held that the buyer is entitled to relief if the representations were a material inducement to the contract, even though the buyer may have made efforts to discover the truth thereof and did not rely wholly on the veracity of the representations. *Foxley Cattle Co. v. Bank of Mead,* 241 N.W.2d 495 (NE 1976); *Erickson v. Midgarden,* 31 N.W.2d 918 (MN 1948); *Schechter v. Brewer,* 344 S.W.2d 784 (MO 1961).

It is sometimes difficult to distinguish between fact and opinion. "Real property taxes are low" is different from "real property taxes are $1,000 per year." In *Foreman & Clark Corporation v. Fallon,* 479 P.2d 362 (CA 1961), the court found no breach because the statements as to the tenant's future sales in a percentage lease case were mere expressions of opinion, were not material and were not relied on by the landlord. *Coleman v. Goran,* 168 N.E.2d 56 (IL 1960); *Lone Star Machinery Corporation v. Frankel,* 564 S.W.2d 135 (TX 1978). In *Peterson v. Auvel,* 552 P.2d 538 (OR 1976), the buyer relied on the broker's opinion that the earnest money contract was not enforceable. *Eyers v. Burbank Co.,* 166 P.656 (WA 1917). See *Gross v. Sussex, Inc.,* 630 A2d 1156 (MD 1993).

Examples of Misrepresentation

Even if a broker acts in good faith, he may still be liable for failure to exercise reasonable care or competence in obtaining or communicating information that the broker knew or should have known. The broker may be liable for (1) negligently failing to discover and disclose building defects that were discoverable upon exercising reasonable care, *Easton v. Strassburger,* 199 Cal.Rptr. 383 (CA 1984); *Gouveia v. Citicorp.,* 686 P.2d 262 (NM 1984); *Amato v. Rathbun Realty, Inc.,* 647 P.2d 433 (NM 1982); (2) making representations regarding title that the agent does not know to be true, *Hall v. Wright,* 156 N.W.2d 661 (IA 1968); or (3) representing the property as a "buildable site," *Tennant v. Lawton,* 615 P.2d 1305 (WA 1980).

It normally is no defense that the broker was simply passing on information received from the seller. *Dugan v. Jones,* 615 P.2d 1239 (UT 1980) (total acreage conveyed was 7 acres, not 23 acres, as represented); *Nordstrom v. Miller,* 605 P.2d 545 (KS 1980); *Gaurrky v. Rozga,* 332 N.W.2d 804 (WI 1983); *Hoffman v. Connall,* 718 P.2d 814 (WA 1986). For the broker to recover from the seller based on indemnity, the broker must show that the broker used due care and was justified in relying on the seller's representations. *Barnes v. Lopez,* 544 P.2d 694 (AZ 1976). Seller told broker the water well was "good" in *Bevins v. Ballard,* 655 P.2d 757 (AK 1982). See *Rach v. Kleiber,* 367 N.W.2d 824 (WI 1985).

The broker has been held liable for misrepresentation in the following types of cases:

1. *Water leakage.* Broker should have known basement had a seepage problem. Broker knew of serious problems with leaking sewage from neighbor's yard and with drainage of water from property. *Sawyer v. Tildahl,* 148 N.W.2d 131 (MN 1967); *McGerr v. Beals,* 145 N.W.2d 579 (NE 1966); *McRae v. Bolstad,* 646 P.2d 771 (WA 1982); *Berryman v. Reigert,* 175 N.W.2d 438 (MN 1970); *Richmond v. Blair,* 488 N.E.2d 563 (IL 1985). Broker liable for misrepresentation regarding leaks and dampness. *Silva v. Stevens,* 589 A.2d 852 (VT 1991). Broker not liable when broker pointed out water stains and recommended buyer hire home inspector. *Connor v. Merrill Lynch Realty,* 581 N.E.2d 196 (IL 1991).

2. *Operating expenses and income.* Broker showed that buyer falsified operating statements and promised to help run the restaurant. *Jennings v. Lee,* 461 P.2d 161 (AZ 1969). Broker incorrectly assured buyer that the property would generate monthly income of $900 without having checked available income records. *Ford v. Cournale,* 111 Cal.Rptr. 334 (CA 1974). Broker carelessly assured buyer that the property could be rented. *Emily v. Bayne,* 371 S.W.2d 663 (MO 1963).

3. *Free of termites.* Seller's broker, who assured buyer that the property was free of termites, dry rot and fungi, was held liable in *Johnson v. Sergeants,* 313 P.2d 41 (CA 1957), and *Saporta v. Barbagelata,* 33 Cal.Rptr. 661 (CA 1963). *Maples v. Porath,* 638 S.W.2d 337 (MO 1982); *Neveroski v. Blair,* 358 A.2d 473 (NJ 1976); *Miles v. McSwegin,* 388 N.E.2d 1367 (OH 1979); *Obde v. Schlemeyer,* 353 P.2d 672 (WA 1960). Broker with two termite reports intentionally concealed termite condition and was liable for punitive damages for intentionally inflicting emotional distress on buyer by concealing negative termite report and showing only the positive report in *Godfrey v. Steinpress,* 180 Cal.Rptr. 95 (CA 1982); *Lynn v. Taylor,* 642 P.2d 131 (KS 1982); and *Dicker v. Smith,* 523 P.2d 371 (KS 1974). Failure to disclose termites. *Wire v. Jackson,* 576 So.2d 1198 (LA 1991). Real estate broker acting as seller had plastered over the termite damage. In a subsequent sale, buyer not able to recover against original broker-seller. *Katz v. Schacter,* 251 N.J.Super. 467 (NJ 1991).

The mere use of an "as is" clause without a more specific explanation of the defect may not eliminate a customary requirement of the seller to provide a termite clearance report or protect against claims for concealed termite damage. Seller liable for not disclosing known latent termite damage despite "as is" clause. *Stemple v. Dobson,* 400 S.E.2d 561 (WV 1990). Buyer denied recovery in *Van Gessel v. Fold,* 569 N.E.2d 141 (IL 1991). Fraudulent concealment of termite report despite "as is" clause. *Rayner v. Wise Realty,* 504 So.2d 1361 (FL 1987).

4. *Free of liens and encumbrances.* Broker erroneously represented that seller owned the property free and clear of all encumbrances. *Floyd v. Myers,* 333 P.2d 654 (WA 1959); *Carl Needham, Inc. v. Camilleri,* 533 P.2d 765 (NV 1975); *Wilson v. Hisey,* 305 P.2d 686 (CA 1957); *Mayflower Mortgage Company v. Brown,* 530 P.2d 1298 (CO 1975); *Grandchamp v. Patzer,* 197 N.W.2d 537 (MI 1972). Minor encroachments sometimes do not render title unmarketable (free and clear of encumbrances) if the encroachment would not cause a prudent person to hesitate before buying.

5. *Filled land.* Broker told buyer that the property listed was not a "filled lot." Buyer's house sank, and buyer successfully recovered against seller, who then sued broker for the loss caused by broker's unauthorized false representation. *Kruse v. Miller,* 300 P.2d 855 (CA 1956); *Sorrell v. Young,* 491 P.2d 1312 (WA 1971) (constructive fraud); *Thacker v. Tyree,* 297 S.E.2d 885 (WV 1982); *Ashburn v. Miller,* 326 P.2d 229 (CA 1958).

6. *Property condition.* Salesperson stated the heater was in good working condition. Actually, seller had concealed the fact that the heater was broken. "Fraud includes the pretense of knowledge when there is none." *Spargnapani v. Wright,* 1 10 A.2d 82 (DC 1954). In *Fowler v. Benton,* 185 A.2d 344 (MD 1962), the broker failed to disclose that the house was built in a slide area. Silence is not golden when the broker has a duty to speak. Silence breaches an implied duty to warn of defects. *Henderson v. Johnson,* 403 P.2d 669 (WA 1965); *Easton v. Strassburger,* 199 Cal.Rptr. 383 (CA 1984); *Hunter v. Wilson,* 355 So.2d 39 (CA App. 1978) (leaking roof); *Berman v. Watergate West, Inc.,* 391 A.2d 1351 (DC 1978) (defective air-conditioning system); *Brown v. Pritchett,* 633 S.W.2d 294 (MO 1982); *Milliken v. Green,* 583 P.2d 548 (OR 1978); *Robert v. Estate of Barbagallo,* 531 A.2d 1125 (PA 1987). Faulty heating system was known to broker, who had managed the property for former owner. *Ne Bud v. Lewis Company,* 548 P.2d 107 (NM 1976); *Byrn v. Walker,* 267 S.E.2d 601 (SC 1980); *Sorensen v. Gardner,* 334 P.2d 471 (OR 1959) (misrepresented that plumbing complied with building code). Building in state of disrepair and had been placed for condemnation by city officials. *Lingsch v. Savage,* 29 Cal.Rptr. 201 (CA 1963); *Cooper v. Jevne,* 128 Cal.Rptr. 724 (CA 1976); *Merrill v. Buck,* 375 P.2d 304 (CA 1962). Cracked foundation. *Pinger v. Guaranty Investment Co.,* 307 S.W.2d 53 (MO 1957); *Josephs v. Austin,* 420 So.2d 1181 (LA 1982). Sewer not connected or backs up. *Kraft v. Lowe,* 77 A.2d 554 (DC 1950); *Shane v. Hoffman,* 324 A.2d 532 (PA 1974); *Crum v. McCoy,* 322 N.E.2d 161 (OH 1974). Broker misrepresented condition of foundation and past repairs. *Schechter v. Brewer,* 344 S.W.2d 784 (MO 1961). Relied on broker's advice to purchase a new house with substantial defects. *Menzel v. Morse,* 362 N.W.2d 465 (IA 1985).

No duty to warn buyer of readily observable condition (stepped on insulation and fell through attic). *Zaffiris v. O'Loughlin,* 585 NYS 2d 94 (NY 1992). Seller's agreement to repair faulty septic system not terminated by doctrine of merger. *Andreychak v. Lint,* 607 A.2d 1346 (NJ 1992). Seller liable for innocent misrepresentation regarding repairs to septic system. *Zimmerman v. Kent,* 575 N.E.2d 70 (MA 1991). Broker not liable for failure to disclose latent defect; seller normally has no duty to disclose defect in used property unless asked by buyer. *Commercial Credit Corp. v. Lisenby,* 579 So.2d 1291 (AL 1991). Broker held to have no duty to buyer to inspect property for defects beyond asking sellers if such defects existed. *Kubinsky v. Van Zandt Realtors,* 811 S.W.2d 711 (TX 1991). Former seller not liable to buyer for concealment of defects even though seller is now mortgagee and buyer defaulted under mortgage. *Kovach v. McLellan,* 564 So.2d 274 (FL 1990). Agent failed to disclose that "independent" property inspector had previously inspected home; house later found to be not structurally sound. *Johnson v. Beverly-Hanks,* 400 S.E.2d 38 (NC 1991). Seller-broker represented that house needed no repair. Both seller and appraiser held liable because house needed $23,000 of repairs to make it eligible for FHA financing. *Rene Lenoir v. Judy Hill Realty,* Case No. 5200 (2d District, MS 1990). Lead paint, see *Richwind v. Brunson,* 625 A2d 326 (MD 1993).

7. *Easements.* When the buyer questioned the broker about an easement, the broker said not to worry. Three months after closing, the city used the easement to lay water pipes. The broker was held liable. *Brady v. Carman,* 3 Cal.Rptr. 612 (CA 1960); *Gilby v. Cooper,* 310 N.E.2d 268 (OH 1973); *Norgren v. Harwell,* 172 So.2d 723 (LA 1965); *Stone v. Lawyers Title Insurance Corp.,* 554 S.W.2d 183 (TX 1977).

8. *Zoning.* Broker disclosed zoning restrictions, but negligently failed to disclose private recorded restrictions that diminished the value of the lot, in *Monty v. Peterson,* 540 P.2d 1377 (WA 1975). Broker negligently misrepresented actual zoning. *Barnes v. Lopez,* 544 P.2d 694 (AZ 1976), in which broker merely affirmed the erroneous information given by seller. *Brandt v. Koepnick,* 469 P.2d 189 (WA 1970); *Asleson v. West Branch Land Co.,* 311 N.W.2d 533 (ND 1981); *Burien Motors, Inc. v. Balch,* 513 P.2d 582 (WA 1973); *Granberg v. Turnham,* 333 P.2d 423 (CA 1958). Broker represented that it would be easy to change the zoning. *Nantell v. Lim-Wick Construction Company,* 228 So.2d 634 (FL 1969). See *Blaine v. Jones Construction,* 841 SW2d 703 (MO 1992).

Holding seller had no duty to disclose zoning problem in *City of Aurora v. Green,* 467 N.E.2d 1069 (IL 1984); *Denton v. Hood,* 461 N.E.2d 1069 (IL 1984); *O'Brien v. Noble,* 435 N.E.2d 554 (IL 1982); *Goldfarb v. Dietz,* 506 P.2d 1322 (WA 1973) (nonconforming use). Some courts distinguish statements of law from statements of fact and hold the seller liable only for misstatements of fact. Whether a statement was one of law or fact is not relevant in an equitable action for rescission based on mutual mistake. *Gartner v. Eikell,* 319 N.W.2d 397 (MN 1982); *Gardner Homes, Inc. v. Gaither,* 228 S.E.2d 525 (NC 1976). But see *Steinberg v. Bay Terrace Apt. Hotel Inc.,* 375 So.2d 1089 (FL 1979).

9. *Size of property.* Brokers frequently get into trouble because they say "Here is the boundary line" when they're not sure, rather than, "I don't know; let's order a survey and find out." This is especially true with unintentional misrepresentations of square footage or acreage. *Alexander Myers & Company v. Hopke,* 565 P.2d 80 (WA 1977); *Nathanson v. Murphy,* 282 P.2d 174 (CA 1955); *Mikkelson v. Quail Valley Realty,* 641 P.2d 124 (UT 1982); *Carrel v. Lux,* 420 P.2d 564 (AZ 1966); *Dixon v. MacGillivray,* 185 P.2d 109 (WA 1947); *Cameron v. Terrell & Garrett, Inc.,* 618 S.W.2d 535 (TX 1981); *Shaffer v. Earl Thacker Co., Ltd.,* 716 P.2d 163 (HI 1986). Broker liable for misrepresentation of home's square footage even though buyer toured home. *John v. Robbins,* 764 F.Supp. 379 (NC 1991).

Broker not liable for statement that boundary line "probably went to that stake." *Bischoff Realty v. Ledford,* 562 N.E.2d 1321 (IN 1990).

10. *"As is" clause.* Use of a general "disclaimer" clause does not protect against fraud. *Smith v. Rickards,* 308 P.2d 758 (CA 1957); *Wittenberg v. Robinov,* 173 N.E.2d 868 (NY 1961). An "as is" clause generally is sufficient to indicate that the seller will not make any repairs. *Lenawee County Bd. of Health v. Messerly,* 331 N.W.2d 203 (MI 1982). Selling a property "as is" does not relieve the broker from revealing known defects that are not readily observable to the buyer. *Lingsch v. Savage,* 29 Cal.Rptr. 201 (CA 1963); *Crawford v. Nastos,* 6 Cal.Rptr. 425 (CA 1960); *Katz v. Dept. of Real Estate,* 158 Cal.Rptr. 766 (CA 1979); *Weitzel v. Barnes,* 691 S.W.2d 598 (TX 1985); *Prichard v. Reitz,* 223 Cal. Rptr. 734 (CA 1986); *Davies v. Bradley,* 676 P.2d 1242 (CO 1983); *Prudential v. Jefferson Associates,* 839 S.W.2d 866 (TX 1992); *George v. Lumbrazo,* 584 NYS 2d 704 (1992); *Grube v. Thieol,* Wisconsin Ct.App. 91-2322 (WI 1992).

Buyer could not recover for injuries to child from falling tree because buyer purchased property in "as is" condition. *Stonecipher v. Kornhaus & Moorman,* Miss. S.Ct. (MI June 17, 1993).

11. *Lawful use.* The doctrine of caveat emptor continues to govern the disclosure of unlawful land usages. In many jurisdictions, the buyer is responsible for determining whether existing land uses are unlawful by checking zoning ordinances, building codes, occupancy rules and restrictive covenants. These courts view the risk of illegal use as foreseeable and place that risk on the buyer. *Cousinea v. Walker,* 613 P.2d 608 (AK 1980) (caveat emptor in general); *Oates v. Jag, Inc.,* 311 S.E.2d 369 (NC 1984). Holding that the seller has no duty to disclose to the buyer a large increase in the assessed value of the property is *Lenzi v. Morkin,* 469 N.E.2d 178 (IL 1984). Once buyer asked broker why other homes were built on stilts, broker obligated to disclose

material facts about building code violation and flood insurance. *Revitz v. Terrell,* 572 So.2d 996. See *Randels v. Best Real Estate,* 243 ILL App. 3d 801 (IL 1993).

The recent trend is to interpret certain seller conduct as an implied representation of lawful use, which would support a buyer's claim for misrepresentation. *Iverson v. Solsbery,* 641 P.2d 314 (CO 1982); *Strickland v. Vescovi,* 484 A.2d 460 (CT 1984); *Kannavos v. Annino,* 247 N.E.2d 708 (MA 1969); *Dettler v. Santa Cruz,* 403 S.W.2d 651 (MO 1966).

12. *Miscellaneous.* Concealed fact of prior grisly murder on the property, *Reed v. King,* 193 Cal.Rptr.130 (CA 1983); misrepresented location of lots, *Blanke v. Miller,* 268 S.W.2d 809 (MO 1954); misrepresented that property bounded on a river, *Carrington v. Graves,* 89 A. 237 (MD 1913). Broker intentionally inflated price of comparable sales in the area, *Miller v. Boeger,* 405 P.2d 573 (AZ 1965). Broker misrepresented the value of a property to be exchanged, *Quistgard v. Derby,* 250 P.2d 2 (CA 1952). Broker sent to jail for misrepresenting to lender existence of second mortgage on property purchased by broker in violation of 18 U.S.C.A. 1015, *U.S. v. Gregoria,* 956 F.2d 341 (1st CIR 1992).

Broker misrepresented the duration of the lease because broker failed to read the lease completely; court also held that buyer had no independent duty to investigate because buyer had no reason to believe that the representations were false. *Hagar v. Mobley,* 638 P.2d 127 (WY 1981). Broker liable for failing to disclose to buyer that property was undergoing a foreclosure procedure. *Gray v. Boyle,* 803 S.W.2d 678 (TN 1990).

Positive misrepresentations as to the asking price were held to go beyond the scope of "clever salesmanship." *Collins v. Philadelphia Oil Co.,* 125 S.E. 223 (WV 1924); *Booker v. Pelkey,* 180 N.W. 132 (WI 1920); *Huttig v. Nessy,* 130 So. 605 (FL 1930); *Stevens v. Reilly,* 156 P. 157 (OK 1916).

In *Jerger v. Rubin,* 471 P.2d 726 (AZ 1970), the salesperson misrepresented that he was negotiating with a potential resale client, which would enable the plaintiff-buyer to sell off a portion of the property being purchased and thus afford the payoff of the additional financing. In *Foster v. Cross,* 650 P.2d 406 (AK 1982), the buyer's broker misrepresented the buyer's development experience and financial condition.

Question of fact whether broker breached duty to homeowner to disclose recent "lock box burglaries" in area. *Moore v. Harry Norman Realtors,* 404 S.E.2d 793 (GA 1991). Suspicion of the presence of ghosts in residential property deemed a latent defect that must be disclosed to buyer. *Stambovsky v. Ackley,* 572 NYS 2d 672 (NY 1991). Broker held not liable for alleged negligent misrepresentation concerning railroad service to site. *Chicago Export Packing v. Teledyne,* 566 N.E.2d 326 (IL 1990). Adequate circumstantial evidence to prove fraud and justify million-dollar punitive damage award. *Kuhnert v. Allison,* No. 14956 (HI Supreme Court 1993). Duty to disclose known pollution problem limited to residential properties; the rule is caveat emptor with commercial properties. *Futura Realty v. Lone Star,* 578 So.2d 363 (FL 1991). Tenant in shopping center sued broker for misrepresentation allegedly based on written material supplied by seller. *Henry S. Miller v. Bynum,* 797 S.W.2d 51 (TX 1990).

CHAPTER 3 CREATION AND TERMINATION OF AGENCY

Termination of Agency Relationship

Like marriage, an agency relationship is easy to create, but can be hard to terminate. The two main ways to terminate an agency are by acts of the parties and by operation of law.

An agency may end at the time stated in the listing agreement or, if no time is specified, within a reasonable period of time. A principal is justified in revoking the agency if the agent has breached any fiduciary duty. Also, the principal has the unilateral power to revoke the agency at any time, except in the rare case in which an agency is coupled with some interest of the broker in the property. Thus, the principal could revoke the agency and forbid the agent to show the property. Or a rental agent may be fired and asked to turn over keys and security deposits. The principal may have the power to terminate an agency, but not the legal right. If the principal wrongfully terminates the agency, the principal may be liable for the damages caused the agent in revoking the agency prior to the termination date. *Roth v. Moeller,* 197 P.62 (CA 1921); *Sun-*

shine v. Manos, 496 S.W.2d 195 (TX 1973); *Chain v. Pye,* 429 S.W.2d 630 (TX 1968). Likewise, the agent can renounce the agency relationship, but only after adequate notice is given the principal. Fiduciary duty did not end when seller rejected a full-price offer. *Quechee Lakes v. Boggers,* No. 89-87 (Vermont S.C. 1992).

Courts are sometimes asked to determine when the agency relationship is ended, especially when the broker decides to become a principal in the transaction or decides to represent an adverse party. In cases in which the commission is earned only if the transaction closes, the broker's fiduciary duties continue throughout the entire closing and do not cease when the buyer is found and the purchase contract is signed. The broker's duty of disclosure as well as the other fiduciary duties continue until the transaction closes and the purpose of the agency comes to an end. *Cooke v. Iverson,* 500 P.2d 830 (ID 1972); *Zikratch v. Stillwell,* 16 Cal.Rptr. 660 (CA 1961); *Bate v. Marsteller,* 346 P.2d 903 (CA 1959); *Menzel v. Salka,* 4 Cal.Rptr. 78 (CA 1960); *Ramsey v. Sedlar,* 454 P.2d 416 (WA 1969); *Wesco Realty Inc. v. Drewry,* 515 P.2d 513 (WA 1973); *One Twenty Realty Co. v. Baer,* 272 A.2d 377 (MD 1971); *Pilling v. Eastern & Pacific Enterprises,* 702 P.2d 1232 (WA 1985), which held that a subagent has no duty to attend closing or perform services to the seller during closing.

In *Hardy v. Davis,* 164 A.2d 281 (MD 1960), the broker secretly loaned the buyer money to complete the purchase. The court held the agency terminated when the sale was made. Thus, the agent could properly deal with the other party if such dealing was not inconsistent with the broker's duty to the principal. *Sears v. Polans,* 243 A.2d 602 (MD 1968); *Olson v. Brickles,* 124 S.E.2d 895 (VA 1962).

The fiduciary relationship between a real estate broker and principal may, under certain circumstances, exist even in the absence or after the expiration of a listing agreement. *Swallows v. Laney,* 691 P.2d 874 (NM 1984); *Wheeler v. Carl Rabe Inc.,* 599 P.2d 902 (CO 1979); *West v. Touchstone,* 620 S.W.2d 687 (TX 1981); *Cogan v. Kidder, Mathews & Segner, Inc.,* 600 P.2d 655 (WA 1979); *Harvey v. Tucker,* 12 P.2d 847 (ECS 1932). The burden of proving a termination of agency is on the party asserting it. In canceling an agency for an indefinite term, notice to the other party is generally required. *George v. Bolen,* 580 P.2d 1357 (KS 1978). Usually a broker can collect a commission after an exclusive listing agreement expires if an agreement between the seller and a buyer was reached before the listing expired. *Nicholson v. Myers,* 931 S.W. 2d 188 (MO App. 1996).

If state law requires that the agent's authority be express and in writing, the sales contract is unenforceable when one seller signs both sellers' names to a contract and that seller was not authorized in writing to act as the other's agent and when the nonsigning seller did not ratify the contract in writing. *Fejta v. GAF Companies, Inc.,* 800 F.2d 1395 (LA 1986).

The agency relationship may also be terminated through operation of law. Death of the agent or principal prior to the broker finding a ready, willing and able buyer will terminate the listing, as will insanity, destruction of the listed premises (or a taking by eminent domain) and bankruptcy of the principal, who loses all control of the property to the court. If the broker is decreed a bankrupt, the broker may be required to surrender the license to the Texas Real Estate Commission.

Payment of Fee

A review of the legal cases reveals that the mere fact that the buyer undertakes to pay the commission does not itself create an agency relationship between the buyer and broker. The courts have held that the establishment of an agency relationship does not stand or fall on the determination of whether a commission was to be paid. *Business Properties, Inc. v. Thomas,* 46 S.E.2d 337 (VA 1948); *Richardson v. DuPree,* 122 S.E. 707 (GA 1924); *Velten v. Robertson,* 671 P.2d 1011 (CO 1983). Broker is entitled to commission if licensed at time brokerage services were rendered, even if not licensed at closing. *Bersani v. Basset,* 585 NYS 2d 245 (NY 1992).

Even though the seller pays the fee, the broker may still be deemed to be the agent of the buyer. In *Brean v. North Campbell Professional Building,* 548 P.2d 1193 (AZ 1976), the broker first contacted the potential buyer with the idea of finding a desirable property and then searched for land and obtained a listing. *Mead v. Hummel,* 121 P.2d 423 (AZ 1942); *Wright v. Dutch,* 296 P.2d 34 (CA 1956); *Stephens v. Ahrens,* 178 P. 863 (CA 1919), holding that an agency is a consensual relationship and the broker is the agent of the person who first employs the broker. *Sands v.*

Eagle Oil & Refining Co., 188 P.2d 782 (CA 1948); *Norville v. Palant,* 545 P.2d 454 (AZ 1976); *Duffy v. Setchell,* 347 N.E.2d 218 (IL 1976); *Tanner Associates v. Ciralddo,* 161 A.2d 725 (NJ 1960); *Downing v. Buck,* 98 N.W.388 (MI 1904); *Walters v. Marler,* 147 Cal.Rptr.655 (CA 1978), *Pepper v. Underwood,* 122 Cal.Rptr. 343 (CA 1975).

As stated in *Wise v. Dawson,* 353 A.2d 267 (DE 1975), the splitting of fees between two brokers is not an indication of agency, but only a recognition of the mutual effort and cooperation used to effect the sale of the property. The splitting of fees frequently occurs in independent contractor situations. As held in *Banner v. Elm,* 248 A.2d 452 (MD 1968), it is not uncommon to provide in the purchase contract that the seller will pay the buyer's broker. *Dunatoo v. Home of the Good Shepherd of Omaha,* 228 N.W.2d 287 (NE 1975); *Antle v. Haas,* 251 S.W.2d 290 (KY 1952); *Price v. Martin,* 147 S.E.2d 716 (VA 1966).

Other cases hold that no compensation is necessary to create an agency relationship. A gratuitous agent may become an agent without compensation. *Kurtz v. Farrington,* 132 A. 540 (CT 1926). In *Walter v. Moore,* 700 P.2d 1219 (WY 1985), the court found that no agency was created with the buyer when the broker was doing a favor and not receiving any compensation. In *Canada v. Kearns,* 624 S.W.2d 755 (TX 1981), the broker unsuccessfully argued that the broker should not be responsible for the misrepresentation of one of the broker's salespersons selling the salesperson's own home through the broker for no fee.

Because agency is a consensual relationship, there is no legal barrier to having the seller authorize the listing broker to share fees with a buyer's broker. But consent is essential. Any secret agreement by a broker to split fees with the broker of the other principal is void as against public policy. *Sweeney & Moore Inc. v. Chapman,* 294 N.W. 711 (MI 1940); *Devine v. Hudgins,* 163 A. 83 (ME 1932); *Quinn v. Burton,* 81 N.E. 257 (MA 1907); *Corder v. O'Neill,* 106 S.W. 10 (MO 1907); *Ornamental and Structural Steel, Inc. v. BBG Inc.,* 509 P.2d 1053 (AZ 1973); *Greater Bloomfield Real Estate Co. v. Braun,* 235 N.W.2d 168 (MI 1975). Broker may compensate unlicensed finder who simply finds and introduces parties, but not someone who acts as a broker and is unlicensed. *Preach v. Monter Rainbow,* 12 Cal.App.4th 1441 (CA 1993).

Despite the fact that payment of the commission does not necessarily determine agency, the prudent broker will nevertheless document whom the broker represents. If no agency documentation exists, courts will likely use the commission payment as strong evidence of an agency relationship. *Price v. Eisan,* 15 Cal.Rptr. 202 (CA 1961); *St. James American Church of Los Angeles v. Kurkjian,* 121 Cal.Rptr. 214 (CA 1975); *Hickam v. Colorado Real Estate Commission,* 534 P.2d 1220 (CO 1975); *Standard Realty & Development Co. v. Ferrara,* 151 Cal.App.2d 514 (CA 1957); *Wilkie v. Abbott's Executrix,* 178 S.W.2d 210 (KY 1944); *Prichard v. Reitz,* 223 Cal.Rptr. 734 (CA 1986).

A finder is subject to licensing law and cannot qualify for a commission. *Cooney v. Ritter,* 939 F.2d 81 (3rd Cir. 1991). For special rules related to lawyers acting as brokers, see *Matter of Roth,* 577 A.2d 490 (NY 1990); *Lovett v. Estate of Lovett,* 593 A.2d 382 (NJ 1991).

Buyer's broker entitled to commission from buyer if the procuring cause of sale. *Douros Realty v. Kelley Properties,* 799 S.W.2D 179 (MO 1990). Buyer claimed that sales agent concealed facts about roof condition and about agent representing seller. Court held for agent because agency disclosure was made in sales contract prior to alleged concealment. *Magliaro v. Lewis,* Case No. A91A1912 (GA 1992). Broker entitled to commission from buyer based on oral agreement. *Weichert Co. Realtors v. Ryan,* 128 N.J. 427 (NJ 1992). Buyer's broker held not to have an enforceable agency agreement in commercial lease situation. *White & Associates v. Decker & Hallman,* Case No. A91A1595 (GA Ct. of Appeals Feb. 1992). Brokers successfully sued for commission on a contract not consummated. *Callaway v. Overholt,* 796 S.W.2d 828 (TX 1990).

CHAPTER 6. SUBAGENCY

The rules of the multiple-listing service (MLS) usually create a system whereby members offer subagency to other members on behalf of the seller. People ex rel. *Woodard v. Colorado Springs Board of REALTORS®,* 692 P.2d 1055 (CO 1984); *United States v. Realty Multi-Lists,* 629 F.2d 1351 (5th Cir. 1980); *Iowa v. Cedar Rapids Board of REALTORS® 300 N.W.2d 127 (IA 1981); Derish v. San Mateo-Burlingame Board of REALTORS®, et al.,* 186 Cal.Rptr. 390 (CA 1982). See *also 1983-2 Trade Cas (CCH) Section 65,718; 1978-2 Trade Cas (CCH) Section 62,388; and*

1977-1 Trade Cas (CCH) Section 61,435. In State v. Black, 676 P.2d 963 (WA 1984), the court found no antitrust violation against certain brokers after they lowered their commission splits with alternative brokers who provided limited service to sellers at reduced fees. The MLS may be guilty of unlawful tie-in when it requires that participants belong to the Board of REALTORS®. *Fletcher Thomson v. Metropolitan Multi-List, Inc.,* 934 F.2d 1566 (11th Cir. 1991).

In *Wolfson v. Beris,* 295 N.W.2d 562 (MN 1980), the court held that the cooperating broker was the subagent of the seller. It was immaterial that the seller did not know the cooperating broker or authorize his actions. The cooperating broker did not become an agent of the buyer by merely preparing a purchase agreement with terms provided by the buyer. *First Church v. Dunton Realty, Inc.,* 574 P.2d 1211 (WA 1978); *Hale v. Wolfson,* 81 Cal.Rptr. 23 (CA 1969); *White v. Lobdell,* 638 P.2d 1057 (MT 1982); *Fred Tuke and Son v. Burkhardt,* 160 N.E.2d 283 (OH 1959); *Elliot v. Barnes,* 645 P.2d 1136 (WA 1982); *Granberg v. Turnham,* 333 P.2d 423 (CA 1958); *White v. Boucher,* 322 N.W.2d 560 (MN 1982); *Coons v. Gunn,* 69 Cal.Rptr. 876 (CA 1968); *Price v. Eisan,* 15 Cal.Rptr. 202 (CA 1961); *Timmerman v. Ankrom,* 487 S.W.2d 567 (MO 1972); *Hicks v. Wilson,* 240 P.289 (CA 1925); *Van Denberg v. Northside Realty Associates, Inc.,* 323 S.E.2d 839 (GA 1984); *Award Realty, Inc. v. Copeland,* 698 S.W.2d 337 (TN 1985); *Buzzard v. Bolger,* 453 N.E.2d 1129 (IL 1983).

In *Reich v. Christopulous,* 256 P.2d 238 (UT 1953), the agency relationship was created with the subagent by the MLS agreement and express language in the listing. In *Pilling v. Eastern & Pacific Enterprises,* 702 P.2d 1232 (WA 1985), the court held that the selling broker, in a multiple-listing situation, is an authorized subagent of the listing broker and, therefore, owes the seller the same duties owed by the listing broker. In *Fennell v. Ross,* 711 S.W.2d 793 (AR 1986), the court was concerned with the issue of reliance on a misrepresentation when the cooperating broker knew the falsity of the statements about commercial use and a floodplain zone. The court concluded that the selling broker in an MLS listing is the subagent of the seller, even though the broker had worked with these buyers for a year before locating the property in question. Therefore, the knowledge of the cooperating broker was not imputed to the buyer.

Subagencies may be created even though the property is not listed in an MLS, as is frequently the case in commercial real estate transactions. *Marra v. Katz,* 347 N.Y.S.2d 143 (NY 1973).

Not all courts agree that the cooperating broker is the subagent of the seller. *Cashion v. Ahmadi,* 345 So.2d 268 (AL 1977); *Lester v. Marshall,* 352 P.2d 786 (CO 1960); *Lageschulte v. Steinbrecher,* 344 N.E.2d 750 (IL App. 1976). A participating member of an MLS was found to be the buyer's broker in *Gillen v. Stevens,* 330 S.W.2d 253 (TX 1959). Finding neither seller nor listing broker liable for the misrepresentation of the cooperating broker, the court in *Wise v. Dawson,* 353 A.2d 207 (DE 1975), found that no agency relationship existed between listing brokers and cooperating brokers in an MLS-type system. See *Pumphrey v. Quillen,* 141 N.E.2d 675 (OH 1955). The Supreme Court of Arizona ruled that the selling broker was not the agent of the seller in *Buffington v. Haas,* 601 P.2d 1320 (AZ 1979); *Brean v. North Campbell Professional Building,* 548 P.2d 1193 (AZ 1976); *Norville v. Palant,* 545 P.2d 454 (AZ 1976). The fact that the selling broker may share in the listing broker's fee does not necessarily create a subagency, *Hiller v. Real Estate Commission,* 627 P.2d 769 (CO 1981). In *Sullivan v. Jefferson,* 400 A.2d 836 (NJ 1979), the listing broker was held not liable for the wrongful act of an MLS cooperating broker who stole the buyer's earnest money deposit in a situation in which it was customary for the cooperating broker to hold the deposit check.

Imputed Notice

Notifying an agent is the same thing as notifying a principal. *Haislmaier v. Zache,* 130 N.W.2d 801 (WI 1964); *3 Am.Jur.2d Agency* Section 152, page 543: "Notice to a subagent appointed by authority is imputable to, and is the equivalent of, notice to the principal." This imputed notice rule may make it critical in a lawsuit whether the cooperating broker is held to be a subagent of the seller or an agent of the buyer. Consider these situations:

- Purchase contract required buyer to give seller written notice of loan approval by May 8. Buyer notified cooperating broker on May 8, but broker did not tell seller, who then attempted to cancel on May 10. Court in *Grant v. Purdy,* 73 D & C 2d 42 (PA 1974), held that cooperating broker was, in reality, a subagent of the seller and, therefore, notice was imputed to seller by the May 8 deadline. Thus, seller could not cancel.

- Buyer notified cooperating broker with whom buyer was working that buyer accepted seller's counteroffer on a property listed in the MLS. Meanwhile, seller had received a higher offer, so seller attempted to revoke the counteroffer. If the cooperating broker is held to be a subagent of the seller, the revocation, coming after notice of acceptance to the seller's subagent, is too late and the contract is binding. If the cooperating broker is held to be the buyer's broker, no binding contract exists because the seller's revocation was effective before the seller was notified of the acceptance. *Stortroen v. Beneficial Finance Co.,* No.85CA0548 (CO 1985); *Shriver v. Carter,* 6S I P.2d 436 (CO 1982); *Darling v. Nineteen-Eighty Corporation,* 176 N.W.2d 765 (IA 1970).

- Buyer Betty was working with salesperson Alice of South Side Realty, a large brokerage firm. Alice helped Betty prepare an offer on a property listed by South Side Realty salesperson Tom. The offer was contingent on Betty receiving a title report by July 10. Tom received the title report by July 10, but failed to tell Betty, who later attempted to cancel the contract. The trial court held that timely receipt of the report by South Side Realty, as agent of Betty, was imputed to Betty, and thus, the contract was binding. *Little v. Rohauer,* 707 P.2d 1015 (CO 1985).

- Note, to avoid the effect of the imputed notice rules, the seller could require that notice is not effective until delivered directly to the seller.

Good Faith

The subagent is under the same duty as the listing broker to exercise utmost good faith toward the principal and the listing broker. It is bad faith for the subagent to lead the buyer to believe the property could be bought for less than the listed price because this could "either force from the seller a lower price than that fixed or delay the sale, even if he finally buys at the price fixed, both detrimental to the interest of the seller." The subagent has a similar duty to disclose all material facts. In *re Sivert's Estate,* 135 N.W.2d 205 (MN 1965); *Kruse v. Miller,* 300 P.2d 855 (CA 1956); *Alford v. Creagh,* 62 So.254 (AL 1913); *Hughey v. Rainwater Partners,* 661 S.W.2d 690 (TN 1983); *Skopp v. Weaver,* 546 P.2d 307 (CA 1976).

The subagent may also be liable for the misrepresentations of the listing broker. In *First Church, etc. v. Cline J. Dunton Realty, Inc.,* 574 P.2d 1211 (WA 1978), the subagent was liable for not confirming the boundary description, even though the subagent relied on the information provided by the listing broker. Also, *Gauerke v. Rozga,* 332 N.W.2d 804 (WI 1983).

The listing broker must disclose any relationship between the proposed buyer and the subagent. This is true even if the MLS regulations do not create a seller subagency. *Frisell v. Newman,* 429 P.2d 864 (WA 1967). Even if the listing broker was unaware of the kinship ties between one of its subagents and the buyer, the seller may still have the right to rescind the sale and recover any profit gained by the broker or recoup the commission paid. *Mersky v. Multiple Listing Bureau of Olympia, Inc.,* 437 P.2d 897 (WA 1968). Also, *Kline v. Pyms Suchman Real Estate Company,* 303 So.2d 401 (FL 1974); *Ross v. Perelli,* 538 P.2d 834 (WA 1975).

Does a buyer who is a broker and also a member of the MLS have a fiduciary duty to the seller as a subagent? The cases holding no fiduciary duty of disclosure are *Case v. Business Centers, Inc.,* 357 N.E.2d 47 (OH 1976); *Cook v. Westersund,* 179 Cal.Rptr. 396 (CA App. 1981); *Blocklinger v. Schlegel,* 374 N.E.2d 491 (IL 1978); *Stout v. Edmonds,* 225 Cal.Rptr. 345 (CA 1986). When the prospective buyer was an MLS member, the listing broker owed a duty as agent to the seller only and not to the broker-buyer in *Carroll v. Action Enterprises, Inc.,* 292 N.W.2d 34 (NE 1980). Nor does the broker-buyer have a duty to discover listing mistakes made by the listing broker, even if the broker-buyer receives a commission split. *Asleson v. West Branch Land Co.,* 311 N.W.2d 533 (ND 1981); *Lageschute v. Steinbrecher,* 344 N.E.2d 750 (IL 1976).

Compensation

Many of the subagency cases are concerned with the cooperating broker seeking a commission. The majority of the cases hold that the cooperating broker and the listing broker are joint venturers who owe certain fiduciary duties between themselves, including the payment of fees, even under oral arrangements. *Nutter v. Bechtel,* 433 P.2d 993 (AZ 1967); *Moore v. Sussdorf,* 421 S.W.2d 460 (TX 1967) (even if the listing between seller and broker is not in writing, as required by law); *J.A. Cantor & Associates, Inc. v. Devore,* 281 So.2d 245 (FL 1973); *Sorenson v. Brice Realty Company,* 282 P.2d 1057 (OR 1955); *Hapsas Realty, Inc. v. McCoun,* 579 P.2d 785 (NM

1978); *Dean Vincent, Inc. v. Russell's Realty, Inc.,* 521 P.2d 334 (OR 1974). But in *Gray v. Fox,* 198 Cal.Rpts 720 (CA 1984), the buyer identified himself as a licensed real estate broker and received a share of the listing broker's commission. Unknown to anyone, the buyer immediately resold the property at a profit in a double escrow. The court found that the buyer was an agent for the seller and breached fiduciary duties owed to the seller by failing to disclose the resale and the secret profit.

While a fiduciary relationship exists between the cooperating broker and the seller, no contractual relationship does; therefore, the cooperating broker usually has no cause of action against the seller for payment of commission. *Gibson v. W.D. Parker Trust,* 527 P.2d 301 (AZ 1974); *Panorama of Homes v. Catholic Foreign Mission,* 404 N.E.2d 1104 (IL 1980); *Goodwin v. Glick,* 294 P.2d 192 (CA 1956); *Smith v. Wright,* 10 Cal.Rptr. 675 (CA 1961); *Philbrick v. Chase,* 58 A.2d 317 (NH 1948). In *Ju v. Jacoby,* 177 Cal.App.3rd 239 (CA 1986), the court held that the mere designation of a cooperating broker in a contract between buyer and seller did not give such a broker a right to enforce the contract in the absence of an intention on the part of the seller to personally secure for the cooperating broker the benefit of the contract. For a contrary result, see *Vanderschuct v. Christiana,* 198 N.Y.S.2d 768 (NY 1960); *Steve Schmidt & Co. v. Berry,* 228 Cal.Rptr. 689 (CA 1986), permitting recovery by the cooperating broker subagent on a third-party beneficiary theory.

A salesperson could sue the client for a commission, but could sue a creditor of the broker who had put a hold on all commission monies owed the broker. *Best-Morrison Properties v. Dennison,* 468 So.2d 483 (FL 1985).

In *Walters v. Marler,* 147 Cal.Rptr. 655 (CA 1978), the court held that a broker retained by the buyer is the agent of the buyer and owes the buyer a fiduciary duty, even though, as cooperating broker, his fee is paid by the seller.

In *Richard H. Huff Realty, Inc. v. Andrews,* 564 P.2d 93 (AZ 1977), the listing salesperson unsuccessfully sought to collect the selling agent's portion of the listing fee when the buyer was another salesperson in the listing broker's office. The court upheld the salesperson-buyer's claim to the selling commission. See *Fitzgerald v. Shannon & Luchs Co.,* 600 F. Supp.106 (DC 1984).

CHAPTER 7. REPRESENTING MORE THAN ONE PARTY IN A TRANSACTION: DUAL AGENCY AND INTERMEDIARY BROKERAGE

A real estate broker cannot act as the agent for buyer and seller in the same transaction without the informed consents of both. When the broker assumes to act in a dual capacity without the intelligent consents of both parties, the transaction is voidable as a matter of law. *Taborsky v. Mathews,* 121 So.2d 61 (FL 1960); *Brockman v. Delta Mfg. Co.,* 87 P.2d 968 (OK 1939); *Darling v. Nineteen Eighty Corporation,* 176 N.W.2d 765 (IA 1970); *Shepley v. Green,* 243 S.W.2d 772 (MO 1951) (consent implied by failure to object); *Gordon v. Beck,* 239 P.309 (CA 1925); *Quest v. Barge,* 41 So.2d 158 (FL 1949); *Price v. Martin,* 147 S.E.2d 716 (VA 1966). Undisclosed dual agency has been held "a species of fraud." *Peyton v. Cly,* 7 Cal.Rptr. 504 (CA 1960); *Moore v. Mead,* 182 N.W. 29 (MI 1921); *Greater Bloomfield Realty Co. v. Brown,* 235 N.W.2d 168 (MI 1975). Listing broker breached duty to seller by actively participating in assisting buyer without informing seller of the dual capacity. *Gillmore v. Morelli,* 472 N.W.2d 738 (ND 1991).

In addition, the undisclosed dual agent cannot recover any commission. *Leno v. Stewart,* 95 A. 539 (VT 1915); *Spratlin et al. v. Hawn,* 156 S.E.2d 402 (GA 1967); *Investment Exchange Realty, Inc. v. Hillcrest Bowl, Inc.,* 513 P.2d 282 (WA 1973); *Panorama of Homes, Inc. v. Catholic Foreign Mission Society, Inc.,* 404 N.E. 2d 1104 (IL 1980); *Phillips v. Campbell,* 480 S.W.2d 250 (TX 1972); *Meerdink v. Kreiger,* 550 P.2d 42 (WA 1976); *Miller v. Berkoski,* 297 N.W.2d 334 (IA 1980). Even if the seller is not injured by the failure to disclose, the broker forfeits any right to a commission. A broker may act for both parties only if there is full disclosure to both principals, so that the principals may deal at arm's length. *Silverman v. Bresnahan,* 114 A.2d 307 (NJ 1955); *Lawton v. McHale Realty Co.,* 131 A.2d 679 (RI 1957). For want of proof that the parties consented to a dual commission arrangement, payments by one precluded recovery from the other. *Porter v. Striegler,* 533 S.W.2d 478 (TX 1976). No rule of law is better settled than the one that an agent cannot serve two masters. *McMichael v. Burnett,* 17 P.2d 932 (KS 1933); *Mortgage Bankers Assn. of New Jersey v. New Jersey Real Estate Commission,* 491 A.2d 1317 (NJ 1985).

Dual agency situations can also arise in real estate exchanges in which one broker represents both sides of the transaction. *Hays v. Ryker,* 118 So. 199 (MS 1928); *Rodenkirch v. Layton,* 176 N.W. 897 (IA 1920); *Hageman v. Colombet,* 198 P. 842 (CA 1921); *Hughes v. Robbins,* 164 N.E.2d 469 (OH 1959); *Homefinders v. Lawrence,* 335 P.2d 893 (ID 1959); *Galyen v. Voyager Inn, Inc.,* 328 F.Supp. 1299 (MO 1971).

Sometimes, the dual agency arises because of a prior long-standing relationship between the listing broker and the buyer. *Koller v. Belote,* 528 P.2d J 000 (WA 1974); *Adarns v. Kerr,* 655 S.W.2d 49 (MO 1983) (listing broker also managed properties for buyer). Other times, the broker "adopts" the buyer prior to or during the closing process. The broker might reach an agreement with the buyer prior to presenting the offer that the broker will manage the property or sell it at a profit for the buyer, as in *Dickinson v. Tysen,* 103 N.E. 703 (NY 1913); or receive a percentage commission upon resale of the property at a profit, as in *Wilson v. Southern Pacific Land Company,* 215 P. 396 (CA 1923).

It may not be a breach of duty to reach an agency agreement with the buyer after the contract is signed, although the broker still should disclose this fact to the seller. *Currier v. Letourneau,* 373 A.2d 521 (VT 1977). It may not be a dual agency for the listing broker also to become the listing broker of the buyer's existing home, although the professional broker will disclose this fact to all parties. *Hall v. Williams,* 50 S.W.2d 138 (MO 1932); *Fred Tuke & Son v. Burkhardt,* 156 N.E.2d 490 (OH 1958). In *Harvey v. Tucker,* 12 P.2d 847 (KS 1932), the court held that fraud would not be presumed and dual agency would not apply when an agent immediately resells a property for the buyer, even if the transaction is near the "danger zone." In *Urban Investments, Inc. v. Branham,* 464 A.2d 93 (DC App. 1983), the court recognized that a broker can act as a dual agent when the buyer first engages the broker to sell the buyer's home and the broker subsequently represents the buyer in the purchase of a new home.

A broker may be the agent of two contracting parties in certain instances, but only on the fullest disclosure by the broker of the fact that the broker represents both parties, and the fullest comprehension of that fact by those contracting. *Quest v. Barge,* 41 Sa.2d 158 (FL 1949); *Barbat v. M.E. Arden Co.,* 254 N.W.2d 779 (MI 1977); *Napier v. Adams,* 158 S.E.18 (GA 1931); *Holley v. Jackson,* 158 A.2d 803 (DE 1954). The duty of care owed to each party by a dual agent is to exercise the same full and truthful disclosure of all known facts, or facts reasonably discoverable, in the exercise of due diligence, that are likely to affect either principal's interests and actions. *Brandt v. Koepnick,* 469 P.2d 189 (WA 1970); *Martin v. Hieken,* 340 S.W.2d 161 (MO 1960). For example, when a dual agent broker discovers an encumbrance and fails to further inquire whether the seller has marketable title, the broker has breached a fiduciary duty to the buyer and is liable for the loss of the buyer's down payment. *Garl v. Mihuta,* 361 N.E.2d 1065 (OH 1975). In *Wilson v. Lewis,* 165 Cal.Rptr. 396 (CA 1980), a cooperating broker retained by the buyer was held to also be the agent of the seller because the broker was receiving a 3 percent commission from the seller. The broker breached a duty by failing to disclose to the seller that the buyer's deposit check was postdated and could not be negotiated until after inspection of the property.

Dual agency was disclosed in an in-house sale, but the disclosure was inadequate because the broker intentionally misled the seller into thinking the buyer was an owner-occupant, whereas the buyer was an investor, and the broker had a substantial personal stake in retaining the buyer's continued business. *Jorgensen v. Beach 'N' Bay Realty,* 177 Cal.Rptr. 882 (CA 1981).

When several principals employ the same broker, misconduct of the broker cannot be imputed to any one of the principals who is not actually at fault, each of the principals being under an equal duty to supervise the broker and protect the principal's interests. *Whittlesey v. Spence,* 439 S.W.2d 195 (MO 1969).

In *Smith v. Sullivan,* 419 So.2d 184 (MS 1982), the broker breached its fiduciary duty to the seller by representing the buyer in a purchase from the seller after the listing had expired. The broker failed to disclose the identity and financial responsibility of the buyer. Buyer's agent obtained a one-time showing listing from seller. Held to be a dual agent. *Culver & Associates v. Jaoudi Industries,* 1 Cal.Rptr.2d 680 (CA 1991).

The dual agent has a duty to act with fairness to each party and to disclose to each all facts that the agent knows or should know would reasonably affect the judgment of each in permitting such dual agency. According to the *Restatement (Second) of Agency,* Section 392:

The agent's disclosure must include not only the fact that he is acting on behalf of the other party, but also all facts which are relevant in enabling the principal to make an intelligent determination. . . . The agent, however, is under no duty to disclose, and has a duty not to disclose to one principal, confidential information given to him by the other, such as the price he is willing to pay. If the information is of such a nature that he cannot fairly give advice to one without disclosing it, he cannot properly continue to act as advisor.

In *Foster v. Blake Heights Corporation,* 530 P.2d 815 (UT 1974), the court held that a broker negotiating a transaction does not have to be exclusively the agent for either the buyer or seller, but may be a go-between acting for both.

Consent must be knowing, intelligent and obtained in such a way as to ensure that the client has had adequate time to reflect on the choice. Consent must not be forced on the client by the pressures of closing. *Matter of Dolan,* 384 A.2d 1076 (NJ 1978). In a complex commercial real estate transaction, an attorney may not represent both buyer and seller, even if both give their informed consents. *Baldasarre v. Butler,* A 49-50 N.J. S.C. 1993. *Bokusky v. Edina Realty,* Civ. 3-92-223 (D. Minn. 1993). Issue is the adequacy of informed consent to a dual agency. The only disclosure was a statement in the sales contract that the individual sales agent represented the buyer and the listing brokerage represented the seller. Certified as a class action suit with remedy sought being the disgorgement of all commissions earned on in-house sales.

Even though the broker acts as a dual agent, there will be no rescission and no forfeiture of commission if both parties intelligently consent to the common representation. *Nahn-Heberer Realty Co. v. Schrader,* 89 S.W.2d 142 (MO 1936), although the court still inquired whether the broker was disloyal to either party; *Panebianco v. Berger,* 199 N.W. 545 (NE 1924); *Lamb v. Milliken,* 243 P. 624 (CO 1926); *Cole v. Brundage,* 344 N.E.2d 583 (IL 1976); *Bonaccorso v. Kaplan,* 32 Cal.Rptr. 69 (CA 1963); *Lemons v. Barton,* 186 N.E.2d 426 (IN 1962); *Zimmerman v. Garvey,* 71 A. 780 (CT 1909); *Phillips v. Campbell,* 480 S.W.2d 250 (TX 1972); *Hladik v. Allen,* 147 P.474 (CA 1915); *Olson v. Brickles,* 124 S.E.2d 895 (VA 1962). As a general rule, dual agency does not apply to insurance agents, a rule some real estate agents may refer to. *Wright v. Providence Washington Ins. Co.,* 286 P.237 (KS 1930).

Broker breached fiduciary duty resulting in forfeiture of commission. *Wallace v. Odham,* 579 So.2d 171 (FL 1991). A buyer's broker who shows property listed in an MLS which offers subagency risks being a dual agent. *Stefani v. Baird & Warner,* 510 N.E.2D 65 (IL).

APPENDIX D

Ethical and Legal Responsibilities

This appendix contains

- a comprehensive list of common state licensing law violations;
- examples of what constitutes unlawful conduct and unethical practices;
- interpretations of the code of ethics involving subagency cases;
- nine practical steps to lessen the risk of misrepresentation claims;
- procuring-cause guidelines;
- considerations of the entire course of events; and
- a checklist of a listing broker's obligations.

COMMON STATE LICENSING LAW VIOLATIONS

In addition to the common-law agency responsibilities of a fiduciary, the real estate broker and salesperson also must abide by contract obligations and by ethical responsibilities found in the licensing law of the state in which they do business and in industry rules of conduct. Some of the more common rules of ethical conduct follow, many of which are grounds for the suspension or revocation of the real estate agent's license. In this section, the word licensee refers to the broker or the salesperson.

1. The licensee shall make no material misrepresentation or false promise of a character likely to influence, persuade or induce.

2. The licensee must not act for more than one party in a transaction without the knowledge or consent of all parties thereto.

3. The licensee cannot commingle the money or property of others that is received and held by the licensee with the licensee's own money or property.

Comment: It is commingling to keep commission monies in a client trust account after closing.

4. The licensee shall not demand a fee under an exclusive listing that fails to contain a definite, specified date of final and complete termination. This rule also applies to buyer's listings.

5. A licensee may not claim or take any secret or undisclosed amount of compensation, commission or profit.

6. The licensee may not use an option to purchase in a listing agreement, except when the licensee, prior to exercising such option, obtains the owner's consent approving the amount of the disclosed profit.

7. The licensee shall not willfully use the term REALTOR® or any tradename or insignia of membership in any real estate organization of which the licensee is not a member.

8. The licensee must not demonstrate negligence or incompetence.

9. As a broker, the licensee must exercise reasonable supervision over associated salespersons' activities.

10. The licensee shall not solicit or induce the sale, lease or listing for sale or lease of residential property on the grounds, wholly or in part, of loss of value, increase in crime or decline of the quality of the schools, due to the present or prospective entry into the neighborhood of a person or persons of another race, sex, color, religion, ancestry or national origin.

11. The licensee, as a salesperson, may not accept compensation from anyone other than the employing broker.

Comment: Even if the owner wants to give the salesperson a bonus for doing a great job, this money must first go through the salesperson's broker.

12. As a salesperson, the licensee cannot act as a broker.

Comment: Sometimes a salesperson handles the rental of a property purchased by a client. The salesperson cannot independently set up a rental management account. This is a brokerage activity and must go through the broker.

13. The licensee shall not be a party to the naming of a false consideration in any document, unless it is the naming of an obviously nominal consideration.

Comment: Brokers should avoid preparing dual contracts, especially if their purpose is to circumvent government financing regulations covering VA and FHA transactions.

14. For the protection of all parties with whom the licensee deals, the licensee shall see that financial obligations and commitments regarding real estate transactions are in writing, expressing the exact agreements of the parties, and that copies of those agreements, at the time they are executed, are placed in the hands of all parties involved.

Comment: Although brokers cannot engage in the unauthorized practice of law, they nevertheless are obligated to make sure that their clients understand the key points of the purchase contract and that the contract contains the necessary protective provisions. It is often advisable to assist the client in retaining an attorney to advise on the legal aspects of the contract and the transaction.

15. When acting as agent in the management of property, the broker shall not accept any commission, rebate or profit on expenditures for an owner without the owner's knowledge and consent.

16. The broker shall not submit or advertise property without written authorization, and in any offering, the price quoted shall not be other than that agreed on with the owner as the offering price.

17. Each written offer, on receipt by the listing broker, shall be transmitted to the seller as a matter of top priority. In the event that more than one formal written offer on a specific property is made before the owner has accepted an offer, any other formal written offer presented to the broker, whether by a prospective purchaser or another broker, shall be immediately transmitted to the owner for decision. If an offer or a counteroffer is rejected, the rejection shall be noted on the offer or counteroffer or, in the event of the seller's or buyer's neglect or refusal to do so, the broker for the rejecting party shall note the rejection on the offer or counteroffer and return a copy immediately to the originator of the offer or counteroffer.

18. The broker shall not compensate a licensee of another broker in connection with a real estate transaction without the knowledge of the other broker. This requirement does not apply in cases where the licensee receives compensation from a former broker for a commission earned while affiliated with that former broker.

19. A licensee shall not place any sign indicating that a property is for sale, rent, lease or exchange without the written authorization of the owner or seller.

20. The broker shall maintain a fixed office located in the state in which he or she is licensed at a business address registered with the commission, and it shall be an office from which the broker does, in fact, conduct business and where the broker's books and records are maintained.

21. The licensee shall ascertain and disclose all pertinent facts concerning every property for which the licensee accepts the agency so that the licensee may fulfill the obligation to avoid error, misrepresentation or concealment of pertinent facts.

Comment: The licensee should take care to discover and disclose such relevant information as sewer connections, known building code violations, terms of any lease, private restrictions and easements, zoning, boundary problems, condominium parking stalls, pending assessments, the owners of record and property condition, such disclosure should include any known roof or water infiltration problems.

22. The licensee shall not claim to be an expert in an area of specialization in real estate brokerage—for example, appraisal, property management, commercial leasing or business opportunities—if, in fact, the licensee has had no special training, preparation or experience in such area.

23. The licensee shall recommend that title be examined, survey be conducted and appraisal or legal counsel be obtained when the interests of either party require it. When accepting an exclusive listing, the licensee shall provide written comparable market data and/or shall advise that a professional appraisal be secured. The licensee shall adequately explain the meaning of a contingency clause or a unique provision, such as an "as is" clause, or shall recommend that the parties seek legal counsel.

24. An exclusive listing must state a definite termination date. No later than five calendar days after the termination of any exclusive listing, the licensee must register any prospective buyers with the owner and disclose the exercise of the extension period in the listing contract, if any.

25. The licensee shall not knowingly underestimate the probable closing costs, including loan fees, in a transaction to the prospective buyer or seller of real property to induce that person to make or to accept an offer to purchase the property.

26. Any listing agreement shall contain a statement like the following: "The amount or rate of a real estate commission is not fixed by law. It is set by each broker individually and may be negotiable between the seller and the broker."

27. The principal broker or designated representative of the listing broker should review each purchase contract prior to acceptance.

28. While the broker may discuss the different methods of holding title for the buyer, the broker may not determine the best form of ownership for the buyer. This should be determined by the buyer or the buyer's attorney or accountant.

EXAMPLES OF UNLAWFUL CONDUCT

1. Knowingly making a substantial misrepresentation of the likely market value of real property to its owner, either for the purpose of securing a listing or for the purpose of acquiring an interest in the property for the licensee's own account.

2. The statement or implication by a licensee to an owner of real property during the listing negotiations that the licensee is precluded by law, regulation or the rules of an organization, other than the brokerage firm seeking the listing, from charging less than the commission or fee quoted to the owner by the licensee.

3. The failure by a licensee acting in the capacity of an agent in a transaction for the sale, lease or exchange of real property to disclose to a prospective purchaser or lessee facts known to the licensee that materially affect the value or desirability of the property when the licensee has reason to believe that such facts are not known to or are not readily observable by a prospective purchaser or lessee.

4. When seeking a listing, representation to the owner of the real property that the soliciting licensee has obtained a bona fide written offer to purchase the property, unless, at the time of the representation, the licensee has possession of a bona fide written offer to purchase.

5. The willful failure by a listing broker to present or cause to be presented to the owner of the property any offer to purchase received prior to the closing of a sale, unless expressly instructed by the owner not to present such an offer.

Comment: In many states, offers must be presented only up to the time the seller first accepts an offer. The better practice is one of full disclosure of all offers throughout the closing process. The seller may want to accept a back-up offer in the event the buyer defaults under the first contract; however, the buyer must agree to this at the time of contract.

6. Presenting competing offers to purchase real property to the owner by the listing broker in such a manner as to induce the owner to accept the offer that will provide the greatest compensation to the listing broker, without regard to the benefits, advantages or disadvantages to the owner.

7. Knowingly underestimating the probable closing costs in a transaction in a communication to the prospective buyer or seller of real property to induce that person to make or accept an offer to purchase the property.

8. Failing to explain to the parties or prospective parties to a real estate transaction the meaning and probable significance of a contingency in an offer or a contract that the licensee knows or reasonably believes may affect the closing date of the transaction or the time the property is vacated by the seller or occupied by the buyer.

9. Knowingly making a false or misleading representation to the seller of real property as to the form, amount or treatment of a deposit toward purchase of the property made by an offeror.

Comment: Sometimes the broker tells the seller that the seller will receive the entire earnest money deposit if the buyer defaults. The seller should know that the escrow agent will be reluctant to transfer the deposit to the seller unless both buyer and seller sign a cancellation letter authorizing such transfer. Also, costs and expenses may be deducted before transferring the deposit money.

10. The refunding by a licensee, when acting as an agent or a subagent for seller, of all or part of a buyer's purchase money deposit in a real estate sales transaction after the seller has accepted the offer to purchase, unless the licensee has the express permission of the seller to make the refund.

11. Failing to disclose to the seller of real property in a transaction in which the licensee is acting in the capacity of an agent the nature and extent of any direct or indirect interest that the licensee expects to acquire as a result of the sale. The prospective purchase of the property by a person related to the licensee by blood or marriage, purchase by an entity in which the licensee has an ownership interest and purchase by any other person with whom the licensee has a special relationship—all situations in which a reasonable probability exists that the licensee could indirectly acquire an interest in the property—shall be disclosed.

12. A representation made as principal or agent to a prospective purchaser of a promissory note secured by real property with respect to the fair market value of the securing property without a reasonable basis for believing the truth and accuracy of the estimate of fair market value.

13. Making an addition to or a modification of the terms of an instrument previously signed or initialed by a party to a transaction without the knowledge and consent of the party.

EXAMPLES OF UNETHICAL PRACTICES

1. Representing, without a reasonable basis, the nature or condition of the interior or exterior features of a property when soliciting an offer.

2. Failing to respond to reasonable inquiries of a principal as to the status or extent of efforts to market property listed exclusively with the licensee.

3. Representing as an agent that any specific service is free when, in fact, it is covered by a fee to be charged as part of the transaction.

4. Failing to disclose to a person, when first discussing the purchase of real property, the existence of any direct or indirect ownership interest of the licensee in the property.

5. Recommending that a particular lender or escrow service be used when the salesperson believes the sponsoring broker has a significant beneficial interest in such entity without disclosing this information at the time the recommendation is made.

6. Using the term *appraisal* in any advertising or offering for promoting real estate brokerage business to describe a real property evaluation service to be provided by the licensee, unless the evaluation process will involve a written estimate of value based on the assembly, analysis and reconciliation of facts and value indicators for the real property in question.

7. Representing to a customer or prospective customer that because the licensee or broker is a member of, or is affiliated with, a franchised real estate brokerage entity, such entity shares substantial responsibility with the licensee or broker for the proper handling of transactions, if such is not the case.

8. Demand for a commission or discount by a licensee purchasing real property for his or her own account after an agreement in principle has been reached with the owner as to the terms and conditions of purchase without any reference to price reduction because of the agent's licensed status.

HOW TO AVOID MISREPRESENTATION CLAIMS

1. Question the seller thoroughly regarding the property. Use a property condition disclosure form; and cover the following questions:

   - Owners and interests?
   - Condition of improvements, utility systems?
   - History of repairs? Warranties?
   - Easements? Where? Purpose? Restrictions on use?
   - Boundaries and encroachments? Stakes visible?
   - Nonconforming or illegal uses?
   - Lease restrictions, permitted uses?
   - Current and future zoning?
   - Special ordinances concerning height limits, design standards?
   - State and municipal improvements, assessments?
   - Outstanding building permits and violations? Citations?
   - Financing restrictions?
   - Is land filled?
   - Any declaration of covenants, conditions and restrictions (CC&R's)?
   - On income properties, are expense and income projections accurate?
   - Any significant neighborhood trends? School busing?
   - Termite or rodent problems?
   - Any other matters that might affect the value of the property?

2. Make an independent investigation of the property.

   Remember that the real estate agent's job is not simply to pass on information from sellers, but to keep the agent and the sellers out of trouble by stressing completeness and accuracy of information. As the agent, you owe a duty of due care to the seller and the buyer. Satisfy yourself because you may be the one left holding the bag after the seller leaves the state. A disgruntled buyer may prefer to sue a stationary broker rather than a moving seller.

- Check out the items under Section 1, above, especially those you find to be sensitive or suspicious.

- Pay attention to decorative improvements that might conceal defects, such as new plaster over a cracked wall.

- If a matter is technical and important, suggest to the seller that it might be wise to bring in expert assistance, such as a soil engineer or a swimming pool contractor.

3. On condominium sales, check into the following common problem areas:

- House rules regarding children, pets, waterbeds and barbecuing

- Location of lockers, parking stalls

- Any special assessments? For what and how much?

- What is included in the maintenance fee? Any proposed increases?

4. Check into factors external to the property that might influence its value and affect a person's decision to buy. For example:

- Abutting and nearby uses (present and proposed—a rock band next door, for example)

- Highway expansion, rerouting of a bus line

5. Do not make statements concerning matters about which you do not have first-hand knowledge or that are not based on expert opinion or advice.

- Avoid beginning your statements with words like "A neighbor told me that . . . ." It would be better to say, "According to Mr. Jones at the Building Department, who handles these matters . . . ."

- If you do not know the answer to a buyer's question, it is better to say: "I don't know, but I'll find out for you or find someone who will."

6. Have a list of government agencies you can call to get further information.

- Use the list to investigate the seller's information and find out things for the buyer. Urge the buyer to check things out, too, by giving the buyer the proper departments and numbers to call.

- Offer to assist the buyer, but don't volunteer highly technical information. That should come directly to the buyer from the government agency.

7. Do not participate with the seller in nondisclosure of information. If the seller refuses to disclose such things as citations for building code violations, decline the listing. No listing is worth damages, loss of reputation and loss of license.

8. Avoid exaggeration, and be circumspect with opinions.

- Exaggeration is unethical and could even be considered misrepresentation, depending on the statement's context and the listener's background.

- If you wish to venture a quick opinion, make sure the buyer understands that it is only a guess, that it is not necessarily an educated one and that the buyer should not rely on it in making a decision. While it is permissible to give factual sales data, try to avoid giving an opinion of value increases. If you feel compelled to give such an opinion, it is best to do so in writing and with proper caveats and disclaimers.

9. Obtain and disclose certain pertinent information in writing.

- Obtain a property condition disclosure form from the seller.

- Give a fact sheet, memo or tactful letter to the buyer whenever disclosures are appropriate. For example, such a letter would confirm earlier discussions in which you pointed out, perhaps, a leaky roof or the need to consult with a soil engineer and would affirm that neither you nor the seller makes any warranty as to the condition of the roof or the foundation.

- Keep copies of these in the client's file; maintain a paper trail in the event you later have to testify about the transaction.

PROCURING CAUSE

The following guidelines are excerpts from the NAR Code of Ethics and Arbitration Manual:

Communication and Contact—Abandonment and Estrangement

Many arbitrable disputes will turn on the relationship (or lack thereof) between a broker (often a cooperating broker) and a prospective purchaser. Panels will consider whether, under the circumstances and in accord with local custom and practice, the broker made reasonable efforts to develop and maintain an ongoing relationship with the purchaser.

Panels will want to determine, in cases in which two cooperating brokers have competing claims against the listing broker, whether the first cooperating broker actively maintained ongoing contact with the purchaser or whether the broker's inactivity, or perceived inactivity, may have caused the purchaser to reasonably conclude that the broker had lost interest or disengaged from the transaction (abandonment).

In other instances, a purchaser, despite reasonable efforts by the broker to maintain ongoing contact, may seek assistance from another broker. Panels will want to consider why the purchaser abandoned the first broker.

In still other instances, there may be no question that there was an ongoing relationship between the broker and purchaser; the issue then becomes whether the broker engaged in conduct that caused the purchaser to terminate the relationship (estrangement). This can be caused, among other factors, by words or actions. Panels will want to consider whether such conduct caused a break in the series of events leading to the transaction and whether the successful transaction was actually brought about through the initiation of a separate, subsequent series of events by the second cooperating broker.

CONSIDERATION OF THE ENTIRE COURSE OF EVENTS

The standard of proof in board-conducted arbitration is a preponderance of the evidence, and the initial burden of proof rests with the party requesting arbitration (see Professional Standards Policy Statement 26). This does not, however, preclude panel members from asking questions of the parties or witnesses to ensure their understanding of testimony concerning the events that led to the transaction and to the request for arbitration. Because each transaction is unique, it is impossible to develop a comprehensive list of all issues or questions that panel members may want to consider in a particular hearing. Panel members are advised to consider the following, which are representative of the issues and questions frequently involved in arbitration hearings:

- What was the nature of the transaction giving rise to the arbitration request?
- Was the property listed or subject to a management agreement?
- Who was the listing agent?
- What was the nature of the listing or other agreement: exclusive right to sell, exclusive agency, open or some other form of agreement?
- Was the agreement in writing?
- Was it in effect at the time the dispute arose?
- Who was the cooperating broker or brokers?
- Are all appropriate parties to the matter joined?
- Is or was the matter the subject of litigation?
- Were any of the parties acting as subagents? As buyer's brokers? As intermediaries? In some other capacity?

- Did any of the cooperating brokers have an agreement, written or otherwise, to act as agent or in some other capacity on behalf of any of the parties?

- Were any of the brokers (including the listing broker) acting as a principal in the transaction?

- Did all brokers comply with all disclosures mandated by law or the Code of Ethics?

- Who introduced the ultimate purchaser or tenant to the property?

- When and how was the introduction made?

- Did the introduction of the purchaser or tenant to the property start an uninterrupted series of events leading to the sale (or to any other intended objective of the transaction), or was the series of events hindered or interrupted in any way?

- If an interruption or a break in the original series of events occurred, how was it caused and by whom?

- Did the broker making the introduction to the property maintain contact with the purchaser or tenant, or could the broker's inaction have reasonably been viewed by the buyer or tenant as the broker's withdrawal from the transaction?

- Did the broker making the introduction to the property engage in conduct (or fail to take some action) that caused the purchaser or tenant to use the services of another broker?

- Was there interference in the series of events from any outside or intervening cause or party?

- What were the brokers' relationships with respect to the seller, the purchaser, the listing broker and any other cooperating brokers involved in the transaction?

- What offers (if any) of cooperation and compensation were extended to cooperating brokers acting as subagents or buyer's brokers or to brokers acting in any other capacity?

- If an offer of cooperation and compensation was made, how was it communicated?

- If the cooperating brokers were subagents, was there a faithful exercise of agency on their part or was there any breach or failure to meet the duties owed to a principal?

- If the cooperating brokers were buyer-agents or were acting in an intermediary capacity, were their actions in accordance with the terms and conditions of the listing broker's offer of cooperation and compensation (if any)?

- If more than one cooperating broker was involved, was either (or both) aware of the other's role in the transaction?

- If more than one cooperating broker was involved, how and when did the second cooperating broker enter the transaction?

- If more than one cooperating broker was involved, was the second cooperating broker aware of any prior introduction of the purchaser to the property by the listing broker or by any other cooperating broker?

- Was the entry of any cooperating broker into the transaction an intrusion into an existing relationship between the purchaser and another, or was it the result of abandonment or estrangement of the purchaser or at the request of the purchaser?

- Did the cooperating broker (or second cooperating broker) initiate a separate series of events, unrelated to and not dependent on any other broker's efforts, which led to the successful transaction?

- Is there any other information that would assist the hearing panel in having a full, clear understanding of the transaction giving rise to the arbitration request or in reaching a fair and equitable resolution to the matter?

These questions are typical, but not all-inclusive, of the questions that may help hearing panels understand the issues before them. The objective of a panel is to carefully and impartially weigh and analyze the whole course of conduct of the parties and render a reasonable peer judgment with respect to the issues and questions presented and to the request for an award.

Glossary of Key Terms

accidental agency. An unintended agency relationship that is created by actions or words.

agency relationship. The fiduciary relationship that exists when one person (agent) represents the interests of another (principal) in dealings with others, with their consent and under their control.

agent. (1) A broker who represents a seller, landlord, buyer or tenant. (2) A salesperson or broker licensee who represents the broker with whom he or she is associated.

associate. A salesperson or broker licensee who is associated with a broker.

blanket offer of subagency. The offer made by the listing broker on behalf of the seller to all other participants in the multiple listing service to act as a subagent for the seller. The seller has the option of making a blanket unilateral offer of subagency or making no offer of subagency; in either case, under MLS rules, an offer to cooperate must include an offer to compensate.

broker associate. A broker associated with and conducting all or part of his or her business as an agent of another broker.

broker licensee. An individual holding a broker's license issued by the Texas Real Estate Commission (TREC). Brokers may act independently in conducting real estate transactions or may engage other broker licensees or salesperson licensees to represent them in the conduct of their real estate business.

buyer's agent. A broker who is representing the buyer in a real estate transaction. Also referred to as a *buyer's broker, selling broker* or *selling agent.*"

buyer's broker. A real estate broker who is employed by and represents only the buyer in the transaction, regardless of whether the commission is paid by the buyer directly or by the seller through a commission split with the listing broker. To be distinguished from brokers who represent the seller but nevertheless "work with" the buyer; these brokers are not referred to as "buyers' brokers." They are subagents of the seller. Also, brokers acting as dual agents for buyers and sellers are not referred to as buyers' brokers. Buyer brokerage is one part of a single-agency real estate practice.

client. A person, sometimes called a *principal,* who engages the professional advice or services of another, called an *agent,* and whose interests are protected by the specific duties and loyalties of an agency relationship.

commission split. The sharing of the seller-paid commission between the listing broker and the selling broker. An MLS listing generally indicates the compensation being offered by the listing broker to the other MLS participants, either as a percentage of the gross selling price or as a definite dollar amount. Thus, MLS members know what they will earn on finding a suitable buyer.

company policy. A set of rules and principles that establishes how a brokerage company is to operate. Every firm should have a clear company policy on agency and take steps to ensure that the sales staff follows it.

consensual dual agency. The practice of representing both the buyer and the seller provided both have given their informed consents.

cooperating broker. The real estate broker working with the prospective buyer on a property listed with another broker. The cooperating broker traditionally is compensated through a commission split with the listing broker. The cooperating broker, also called the *selling broker, participating broker, outside broker* or *other broker,* may be either a subagent acting on behalf of the seller or a buyer's broker, both of whom "cooperate" to make a sale. In some states, the cooperating broker may act as a transaction broker or transaction coordinator.

customer. A buyer or seller in a real estate transaction being assisted by a broker, but without the benefits of an agency relationship.

dual agency. The practice by which the same broker works as an agent for both the buyer and the seller in the same real estate transaction. The dual agency may be either intended or unintended. As a rule of agency law, dual agency is not legally prohibited provided both parties give their informed consents to this limited representation. In actual practice, it may be difficult to achieve this "knowing consent" of the buyer and the seller. It is also difficult to balance the needs of the buyer and the seller without inadvertently favoring one over the other.

exclusive listing.   A written listing of real property in which the seller agrees to appoint only one broker to handle the transaction. Two types apply to the seller:

1. The exclusive-right-to-sell listing obligates the seller to pay a commission if anyone, including the seller, procures a ready, willing and able buyer.

2. The exclusive agency listing reserves for the owner the right to sell the property directly without owing a commission. The exclusive agent is entitled to a commission if the buyer is procured by anyone other than the seller.

A third type applies to the buyer:

3. The exclusive-right-to-represent listing obligates the buyer to pay a commission if the buyer agrees to buy a described type of property located by the broker, the buyer or anyone else during the listing period.

facilitator.   A person who assists the parties to a potential real estate transaction in communication and negotiation without being an advocate for any interest except the mutual interest of all parties to reach agreement. Also called a *middleman, mediator, nonagent* or *transaction broker.*

fiduciary.   1. A relationship of trust and confidence between principal and agent. The law imposes on the agent duties of loyalty, confidentiality, accounting, obedience and full disclosure, as well as the duty to use skill, care and diligence. A real estate agent owes complete fiduciary duties to the principal and must act in the best interests of the principal (the client) while also being competent with and honest to the other side (the customer, whether the seller or the buyer). 2. The agent is referred to as the *fiduciary*—one who holds the faith, confidence and trust of the client.

finder.   One who produces a buyer or locates a property—nothing more. The finder is not an agent and owes no fiduciary duties.

FSBO.   For sale by owner." A property that is being offered for sale by the owner without the benefit of a real estate broker.

general agency.   The agent who is authorized to conduct an ongoing series of transactions for the principal and can obligate the principal to certain types of contractual agreements.

implied agency.   An agency relationship created by the words or conduct of the agent or principal rather than by written agreement. A listing agent who acts like a buyer's agent in negotiating for the buyer can become involved in an accidental dual agency (express agent of seller and implied agent of buyer).

informed consent.   A person's approval based on full disclosure of all the facts needed to make the decision intelligently. To consent to a dual agency, the buyer and seller need to understand the liability involved, the alternatives and the roles that they and the real estate licensees will play.

in-house sale.   A sale involving only one brokerage firm acting as both the listing and the selling agent; the listing agent is also the selling agent. Frequently, one real estate agent in the firm secures the listing and works with the seller, and a different member of the same firm finds and works with the buyer. Unless the broker clearly discloses to the buyer that the broker and all the salespersons represent the seller, a potential dual agency conflict exists. Even though different salespersons from the firm work with the buyer and seller, the firm itself may become the agent of both the buyer and the seller (a dual agent). Assuming careful disclosure and conduct by the listing broker, however, there is nothing improper about selling a listing in-house; in fact, the seller lists the property so that the broker will find a qualified buyer.

intermediary.   A broker who is employed to negotiate a transaction between the parties subject to the obligations in Subsection (j) of this section [of TRELA §15C] and for that purpose may be an agent of the parties to the transaction. The intermediary shall act fairly so as not to favor one party over the other [TRELA §15C(l)(2)].

landlord's agent.   A broker who is representing the landlord in a real estate transaction.

licensee.   A person licensed by TREC to act as a broker or salesperson in a real estate transaction.

limited agency.   A form of agency relationship permitted under some state statutes in which the buyer and seller, with the agreement of the broker, designate one salesperson from the brokerage firm to act as agent and knowingly waive the right to individual loyalty from the firm and any of its other agents and employees. In some cases the buyer designates one salesperson and the seller designates a different salesperson; none of the other salespersons represents buyer or seller.

listing.   An agreement that establishes the rights and obligations between the seller and the broker or between the buyer and the broker. A salesperson usually obtains the listing of a seller's property in the name of the broker. The broker is called the *listing broker;* the salesperson is sometimes called the *listing agent.*

listing broker.   In this textbook, refers to the seller's agent. A buyer's agent can also list the buyer.

middleman.   A person who facilitates a real estate transaction by introducing a buyer to a seller, both of whom negotiate their own transaction; a finder. Provided the middleman exercises no discretion in facilitating the transaction, the middleman, in some states, may be exempted from the traditional fiduciary duties owed by an agent to a principal. Very seldom does a real estate broker conform to this middleman concept. Middleman status could occur when a buyer works with a broker, but specifically refuses to authorize the broker to act as the buyer's agent; likewise, the seller does not authorize the broker to act as a subagent. See *facilitator.*

MLS (multiple-listing service).   An information service, generally owned and operated by a local association of brokers, in which members pool their listings (primarily residential) and agree to share commissions with other member brokers who find purchasers. Most MLSs are affiliated with the National Association of Realtors®, which considers the MLS to be a formal system of presenting listings in which blanket offers of cooperation and compensation are made to other MLS members.

open listing.   A listing in which the broker has the nonexclusive right to sell the property and receive a commission. If the sale results through the efforts of the seller or another broker, the open listing broker receives no commission. Controversies may arise over which broker actually was the procuring cause of the sale.

optional offer of subagency.   The MLS policy that affords a seller represented by a participating member the option of whether to offer subagency. The seller can choose to make a blanket offer of subagency or to offer cooperation and compensation to buyer agents, subagents and other licensed participants in the MLS. No mandatory offer of subagency exists.

principal.   1. A person who employs an agent to represent him or her as a client, especially if referred to with the use of a pronoun: his or her principal. 2. One of the primary parties to a transaction, whether or not an agency relationship is involved (i.e., the buyer or seller, especially if referred to as the principal).

rescission.   A mutual cancellation of a contract by all parties.

representation.   To act on another's behalf (the principal) as an agent owing fiduciary duties to such principal. There is a definite distinction between "working with" a buyer (who is then a customer or prospect) and "representing" a buyer (who is then a client). Buyers often believe they are being represented when, in fact, they either are not represented or are "represented" by seller's agents in undisclosed dual agencies.

While a listing broker frequently works with buyers to encourage them to buy listed properties, the listing broker should be careful that the broker's words and actions do not lead the buyers to expect that the broker represents them. It is the conduct of the broker that usually forms the basis for the reasonable expectations of a buyer or seller. If, in fact, the broker represents both buyer and seller, appropriate dual agency disclosures must be given and the informed consents of the buyer and the seller must be obtained to this form of limited representation.

sales associate.   Salesperson licensee associated with and conducting business as an agent of his or her sponsoring broker.

salesperson.   A person who meets the state's requirements for a salesperson's or broker's license and who works for and is licensed under a broker or a brokerage firm. Salespersons are commonly referred to as *real estate agents,* even though they are not the primary agents of sellers or buyers; in essence, they are agents of agents (brokers). This is an important concept to keep in mind when discussing the in-house sale dual agency situation in which, for example, salesperson Alice from Bay Realty is thought to represent the seller, and salesperson Sally, also from Bay Realty, is thought to represent the buyer. In this situation, both the buyer and the seller have the same agent (Bay Realty). Separate agents do not represent the buyer and the seller. Salesperson Alice is not the seller's agent, and salesperson Sally is not the buyer's agent; rather, Bay Realty is the only agent—in this case, a dual agent. Bay Realty is the primary fiduciary that owns the listing. Bay Realty is obligated by the licensing law to supervise its salespersons and is responsible for and bound by their actions.

salesperson licensee.   An individual holding a salesperson's license issued by TREC—an agent of the sponsoring broker. Salesperson licensees may conduct business only through their sponsoring brokers.

seller's agent.   A broker who is representing the seller in a real estate transaction. Also referred to as a *seller's broker, listing broker* or *listing agent.*

selling broker.   The broker working with or representing the buyer in the purchase of a listed property. Also called the *cooperating broker, participating broker* or *other broker* when the selling broker is a member of a firm other than the listing firm. The selling broker may be the listing broker, a cooperating broker (subagent) or a buyer's broker, depending on the facts of each case.

single agency.   The practice of representing either the buyer or the seller, but never both in the same transaction. The single-agency broker may be compensated indirectly through an authorized commission split or directly by the principal who employs the agent to represent him or her.

subagency. A theory of agency law applicable to the agent of a person who already acts as an agent for a principal. In real estate, the client (usually the seller) lists with an agent, who, in turn, retains the services of subagents to find a buyer. A seller may limit the authority of the broker to appoint subagents. Cooperating broker members of the MLS may reject any blanket offer of subagency. Nevertheless, listing brokers customarily use subagents to market real estate, especially if the property is listed in the MLS.

subagent. A licensee *not associated with the broker who is representing a client,* but who is representing the client through a cooperative agreement with the client's broker. Also called the *other broker.*

tenant's agent. A broker who is representing a tenant in a real estate transaction.

unintended dual representation. Accidental representation of both the buyer and the seller by the same broker. This is especially prevalent when the broker does not declare, and the principal does not affirm, the agency status of the broker.

universal agency. A type of agency in which the agent is empowered to conduct every type of transaction that may be legally delegated by a principal to an agent.

Index

Real Estate Products for a New Century

Pass Your Exam the First Time

Real Estate Exam Guide, ASI
by William H. Pivar

$27.95 Paper *254 pages*

A precisely guided tour for prospective real estate prelicensees. Chances for testing dramatically increase because of numerous practice opportunities for all real estate topics covered on the ASI exam.

Guide to Passing the PSI Real Estate Exam
by Lawrence Sagar

$24.95 Paper *264 pages*

The original national PSI exam manual, repeatedly acclaimed by real estate salesperson and broker candidates sitting for their state license exams.

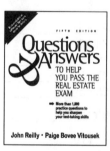

Q&A to Help You Pass the Real Estate Appraisal Exams
by Jeffrey D. Fisher and Dennis Tosh

$39.95 Paper *258 pages*

Hands-on practice gets you ready to pass the new exams. Over 1000 practice exam questions that follow the exam style and content outline for ASI and independent testing services.

Your Guide to Passing the AMP Real Estate Exam, 2nd Ed.
by Joyce Bea Sterling

$27.95 Paper *280 pages*

Close to 600 questions test students' mastery of essential concepts, as well as their ability to master the AMP question style and format.

Real Estate Education Company®
A Kaplan Professional Company

See the order form on back for a complete listing of materials.

The Language of Real Estate
by John W. Reilly

$32.95 Paper *528 pages*

More than 2,800 terms are clearly defined in detail and extensively cross-referenced, allowing users to grasp even complicated concepts easily.

Jump Start Your Career

Up & Running in 30 Days
by Carla Cross

$25.95 Paper *161 pages*

For any agent who wants to improve and make more money. Includes dozens of worksheets, exercises, and self-assessments to help improve your practice.

For Top Producers

Click & Close
by John Tuccillo and James F. Sherry

$24.95 Paper *258 pages*

John Tuccillo & Jim Sherry explain **how** to utilize technology and stay competitive in an Internet-oriented market place. This includes how to make a technology plan, how to create a more efficient and cost-effective back office operation, how to engage the consumer, how to train a staff and much more.

Eight New Rules of Real Estate
by John Tuccillo

$24.95 Paper *208 pages*

John Tuccillo's eagerly awaited book delivers the kind of thoughtful, witty, on-target industry analysis that thousands of professionals have come to depend on over the last decade.

Real Estate Products for a New Century

To order, fax this form to (312) 836-9958 or call (800) 437-9002

Order Number		Product Format	Qty.	Price Each	Total Amount
	Pass Your Exam the First Time				
1970-0405	Questions & Answers To Help You Pass the Real Estate Exam, 5th Ed.	Print	_____	$27.95	_____
1516-035A	Exam Guide Interactive Software to Help you Pass the Real Estate Exam, 5.1	Software	_____	$42.95	_____
1516-0114	Key Point Review Audio Tapes for Modern Real Estate Practice, 15th Ed.	Audio	_____	$26.95	_____
1511-0415	CD-ROM Study Guide for Modern Real Estate Practice	Software	_____	$39.95	_____
1512-1006	Mastering Real Estate Math, 6th Ed.	Print	_____	$26.95	_____
1961-0104	Language of Real Estate, 4th Ed.	Print	_____	$32.95	_____
1518-0201	Language of Real Estate Audio Tapes	Audio	_____	$27.95	_____
1556-1202	Q & A To Help You Pass the Real Estate Appraisal Exams, 2nd Ed.	Print	_____	$39.95	_____
197011-02	Your Guide to Passing the AMP Real Estate Exam, 2nd Ed.	Print	_____	$27.95	_____
197006-05	Real Estate Exam Guide (ASI), 5th Ed.	Print	_____	$27.95	_____
1516-2401	Real Estate Exam Guide Software (ASI)	Software	_____	$41.95	_____
197009-03	Guide to Passing the PSI Real Estate Exams, 3rd Ed.	Print	_____	$24.95	_____
151708-01	Guide to Passing the PSI Real Estate Exams, Software	Software	_____	$42.95	_____
151708-01	SuccessMaster Math Tutor Software	Software	_____	$42.95	_____
	Jump Start Your Career				
1965-0932	Realty Bluebook and Financial Tables Set, 32nd Ed.	Print	_____	$37.46	_____
1907-1301	Up and Running in 30 Days	Print	_____	$25.95	_____
1907-1601	Terri Murphy's Listing and Selling Secrets	Print	_____	$24.95	_____
	Professional Reference				
5608-7103	Real Estate Investor's Tax Guide, 3rd Ed.	Print	_____	$27.95	_____
1557-1009	Essentials of Real Estate Finance, 9th Ed.	Print	_____	$45.95	_____
1551-1006	Property Management, 6th Ed.	Print	_____	$40.95	_____
1965-0105	Real Estate Brokerage: A Management Guide, 5th Ed.	Print	_____	$44.95	_____
1560-0104	Real Estate Law, 4th Ed.	Print	_____	$69.95	_____
	For Top Producers				
1907-2501	Click & Close: E-Nabling the Real Estate Transaction	Print	_____	$24.95	_____
1907-2401	The Eight New Rules of Real Estate	Print	_____	$24.95	_____
1913-3202	Targeting the Over-55 Client, 2nd Edition	Print	_____	$19.95	_____
1907-1101	Real Estate Agent's Business Planning Guide	Print	_____	$25.95	_____
5608-8801	Multiply Your Success with Real Estate Assistants	Print	_____	$25.95	_____

Subtotal _____

Please indicate form of payment:

(Please add applicable sales tax for the following states: CA, FL, IL, NY) Tax _____

❏ Check

❏ Credit Card

Shipping/Handling $7.00

❏ Visa   ❏ Master Card   ❏ American Express

Total _____

Card #: _____

Exp. Date: _____ / _____   Signature _____

Ship to:

Name _____

Company _____

Street Address _____

City _____ State _____ Zip _____

Daytime Phone (_____) _____

Fax _____ E-mail _____

Risk-Free, 100% Money-Back Guarantee

If you are not satisfied for any reason, simply return any of the products you have ordered within 30 days in good condition for a full refund. Software products cannot be returned if opened.

Real Estate Education Company®
A Kaplan Professional Company
155 North Wacker Drive
Chicago, Illinois 60606-1719

Order by Fax: (312) 836-9958   Order by Phone: (800) 437-9002